MARTIN LUTHER

Martin Luther's radical actions in sixteenth-century Germany sparked off the dramatic process of the European Reformation. Following the publication of the 95 Theses in 1517, he began deeply to question the practices of the Catholic Church. He set in place a chain of events, which divided the Church and brought about the Protestant Reformation. Famously appearing before the secular authorities at the Diet of Worms in 1521 to defend his dissident beliefs, Luther worked throughout his life to further the Reformation movement.

But were Luther's motivations as clear-cut as they might seem? Was he merely self-obsessed and egotistical rather than a guiding prophet of God? This important new biography portrays Luther, his concerns and his achievements with clarity and verve, and provides a comprehensive introduction for students, general readers and those seeking to understand the roots of the continuing discords in modern Christianity. Self-aware yet violently prejudiced, bigoted yet inspiring, Luther is presented here with unflinching candour and honesty.

Michael A. Mullett is Professor of Cultural and Religious History at the University of Lancaster, where he has taught since 1968. He is the author of *Luther* (1986) and *The Catholic Reformation* (1999).

ROUTLEDGE HISTORICAL BIOGRAPHIES

SERIES EDITOR: ROBERT PEARCE

Routledge Historical Biographies provide engaging, readable and academically credible biographies written from an explicitly historical perspective. These concise and accessible accounts will bring important historical figures to life for students and general readers alike.

In the same series:

Bismarck by Edgar Feuchtwanger
Churchill by Robert Pearce
Gandhi by Crispin Bates
Gladstone by Michael Partridge
Henry VII by Sean Cunningham
Henry VIII by Lucy Wooding
Hitler by Martyn Housden
Jinnah by Sikander Hayat
Martin Luther King Jr. by Peter J. Ling
Mary Queen of Scots by Retha Warnicke
Lenin by Christopher Read
Mao by Michael Lynch
Mussolini by Peter Neville
Nehru by Ben Zachariah
Emmeline Pankhurst by Paula Bartley
Franklin D. Roosevelt by Stuart Kidd
Stalin by Geoffrey Roberts
Trotsky by Ian Thatcher
Mary Tudor by Judith Richards

MARTIN LUTHER

Michael A. Mullett

Routledge
Taylor & Francis Group

LONDON AND NEW YORK

First published 2004
by Routledge
11 New Fetter Lane, London EC4P 4EE

Simultaneously published in the USA and Canada
by Routledge
29 West 35th Street, New York, NY 10001

Routledge is an imprint of the Taylor & Francis Group

Typeset in Garamond and Scala Sans
by Keystroke, Jacaranda Lodge, Wolverhampton
Printed and bound in Great Britain
by MPG Books Ltd, Bodmin

British Library Cataloguing in Publication Data
A catalogue record for this book is available from the British Library

Library of Congress Cataloging in Publication Data
Mullett, Michael A.
    Martin Luther/Michael A. Mullett.
       p. cm. — (Routledge historical biographies)
    1. Luther, Martin, 1483–1546. 2. Reformation—Germany—Biography.
    3. Lutheran Church—Germany—Clergy—Biography. I. Title.
    II. Series.
    BR325.M936 2004
    284.1′092—dc22   2003023382

ISBN 0–415–26167–8 (hbk)
ISBN 0–415–26168–6 (pbk)

For my 'Special Subject' students at the University of Lancaster, past, present and future

CONTENTS

PLATES

(between pages 128 and 129)

1   Portrait of Martin Luther. Lucas Cranach, the Elder (1472–1553) © The
    Bridgeman Art Library.
2   Martin Luther, later in life. Lucas Cranach, the Elder (1472–1553) © The
    Bridgeman Art Library.
3   Hans Luther (1459–1530), father of Martin Luther. Lucas Cranach, the
    Elder (1472–1553) Sammlungen auf der Wartburg, Eisenach, Germany
    © The Bridgeman Art Library.
4   Margarethe Luther (c. 1463–1531), mother of Martin Luther. Lucas
    Cranach, the Elder (1472–1553) Sammlungen auf der Wartburg,
    Eisenach, Germany © The Bridgeman Art Library.
5   Katharina von Bora, wife of Martin Luther. Lucas Cranach, the Elder
    (1472–1553) Sammlungen auf der Wartburg, Eisenach, Germany © The
    Bridgeman Art Library.
6   Philip Melanchthon. Albrecht Dürer © The Bridgeman Art Library.
7   Erasmus of Rotterdam. Albrecht Dürer. Hood Museum of Art,
    Dartmouth College, Hanover, New Hampshire; bequest of Hugh
    Mason Wade in Memory of Alfred Byers Wade. Copyright © 2000
    Trustees of Dartmouth College, Hanover, New Hampshire.

Preface and
Acknowledgements

This life of Luther is dedicated to my History 'Special Subject' students at the University of Lancaster with whom I have been able to share my enthusiasm for this subject over the course of the years. Teachers, it is well known, teach students, but what is sometimes less evident is that students teach their teachers. In my case in particular, class after class of fine and dedicated students over the years have shown me how to explain and to clarify material that is not always readily amenable to minds formed in a 'post-Christian' culture, and they have rightly required me to show why what mattered to Martin Luther *mattered* – and may even matter. I have learned also from those student colleagues, from their eager seminar presentations, their carefully prepared essays, their scholarly dissertations and, yes, even from their examination scripts.

As always, I have received constant encouragement from my beloved University of Lancaster and from the friendship of colleagues in a leading History Department where research and teaching are a passion . . . and administration an efficiently discharged necessity. My editor for this book, Robert Pearce, has been an untiring source of support, encouragement and judicious and positive criticism.

Gerard, Kathryn, Nicklaus, and Lorenz, James, Marie and Hayley have been there with love and happiness, and Natasha's clear love of books has spurred me on to finish this one. My family in South Wales have always given loving support, though my brother's kind claim that I know more about Luther than Luther did may not necessarily stand up to rigorous scrutiny. Untiring help in everything, including discussions of the ideas in this book as it has proceeded, have come from my adored wife, Lorna.

Lancaster, on the Feast of St Cajetan, 2003

CHRONOLOGY

Personal		Political		General	
1483	Luther born	1485	Henry VII king of England	1484	Birth of Huldrych Zwingli
				1492	Columbus lands in America
1497	Luther at school in Magdeburg			1497	Birth of Melanchthon
1498	Luther at school in Eisenach				
1501	Luther enters Erfurt University	1500	Birth of Charles V		
1502	(September) Luther BA				
1505	(January) Luther MA (July) Thunderstorm at Stotternheim				
1505	Luther enters monastery in Erfurt				
1507	(April) Luther ordained				
1507	(May) Luther's first Mass				
1508	Luther teaches at Wittenberg				
1509	(October) Luther returns to Erfurt	1509	Accession of Henry VIII of England	1509	Birth of John Calvin

Personal	Political	General
1510 Luther visits Rome		
1511 Transfer to Wittenberg		
1512 (October) Luther Doctor of Theology		
1513 Luther begins lectures on Psalms		1513 Leo X Pope
1515 Luther begins lectures on Romans		
1516 (September) Luther closes the Romans lectures		1516 Erasmus's Greek New Testament
1517 (September) Luther attacks Scholastic theology (October) Luther posts the 95 Theses		
1518 (April) Heidelberg disputation (July) Prierias condemns Luther (August) Luther responds to Prierias (October) Luther's interviews with Cajetan	1518 Diet of Augsburg	
1519 Luther's second lectures on the Psalms (July) the Leipzig debates	1519 Death of Maximilian Accession of Charles V	

Personal	Political	General
1520 (June) Papal bull of excommunication (August) The 'Address to the Christian Nobility' (October) 'The Babylonian Captivity of the Church' Luther receives the Pope's bull (November) 'The Freedom of a Christian' (December) Burning of the papal bull		
1521 (January) Luther's excommunication finalised (March) Luther summoned to the Diet of Worms (April) Luther's appearance at Worms (May) Luther taken into the Wartburg and Edict of Worms issued (December) Luther visits Wittenberg and returns to the Wartburg	1521 Opening of the Diet in Worms	
1522 Translation of the New Testament		1522 Accession of Pope Hadrian VI

Personal		Political		General	
	(March) Luther returns to Wittenberg (September) Luther's German New Testament				
1523	Luther publishes 'That Jesus Christ was Born a Jew' and 'Temporal Authority: To What Extent it Should be Obeyed'			1523	Accession of Pope Clement VII
		1524	(August) Peasant Revolt begins	1524	(September) Erasmus publishes the 'Freedom of the Will'
1525	Luther publishes 'Against the Robbing and Murdering Hordes of Peasants' (June) Luther's marriage (December) Luther publishes 'On the Bondage of the Will'	1525	(March)The Twelve Articles of Memmingen (May) Death of Frederick the Wise, accession of John the Steadfast		
		1526	First Diet of Speyer Turkish victory at Mohács		
		1527	The Sack of Rome		
1529	Luther publishes the Small and Large Catechisms (October) The colloquy at Marburg	1529	Second Diet of Speyer Siege of Vienna		

Personal		Political		General	
1530	(April) Luther at Feste Coburg (May) Death of Luther's father Luther publishes 'Exhortation to All Clergy Assembled at Augsburg'	1530	Diet of Augsburg and Augsburg Confession		
1531	Death of Luther's mother. Luther publishes 'Dr Martin Luther's Warning to His Dear German People'			1531	Death of Zwingli
		1532	Death of John the Steadfast Accession of John Frederick I		
1534	Luther's whole Bible in German	1534	England's Breach with Rome begins	1534	Accession of Pope Paul III
1539	Luther publishes 'On the Councils and the Church'				
		1540	The bigamy of Philip of Hesse		
1541	Luther publishes 'Against Hans Worst'				
1542	Death of Luther's daughter Magdalene				
1543	Luther publishes 'On the Jews and Their Lies'				

Personal	Political	General
1545 Luther publishes 'Against the Roman Papacy, an Institution of the Devil'		1545 Convening of the Council of Trent
1546 Death of Luther at Eisleben		

1

INTRODUCTION

In this book we shall be considering the Protestant Reformation launched by Martin Luther from 1517 onwards as a major event in world history, and especially within the great saga of the history of human freedom. In this Introduction we shall be considering in particular the way that the religious changes he instigated have been discussed and debated in English and other European historical writing since the sixteenth century: our concluding chapter will also return to some of those themes.

Our subject, Luther, saw himself as a liberator and has been represented in the tradition of historical writing about him – the 'historiography' – as one who struck some of the heaviest blows ever delivered for human freedom by his work as a theologian in freeing Christians of his own and subsequent ages from a burdensome Catholic religious system. As it gained its own historiography between the sixteenth and the eighteenth centuries, Protestant ideology justified the Reformation as a liberating movement setting masses of people free from an essentially corrupt and unfree medieval Catholic system which had seized the once pure Christian Church of New Testament antiquity and created a tyranny of oppression and lies.

'CHRISTIAN LIBERTY' AND THE REFORMATION

The notion of the Protestant Reformation as a milestone in the history of human freedom goes back in fact to the Reformation itself, when the first Protestant reformers acclaimed their own acts of liberation from the medieval Church's alleged tyranny. Here, for example, is the early Swiss Protestant leader Huldrych Zwingli (1484–1531) announcing his abandonment of the Catholic Church's strict fasting laws as a major contribution to human freedom of choice and action:

> if you want to fast, do so; if you do not want to eat meat, don't eat it; but allow Christians a free choice. . . . if the spirit of your belief teaches you thus, then fast, but grant also your neighbour the privilege of Christian liberty . . . [and do not] make what man has invented greater before God than what God himself has commanded. . . . Further, we should not let ourselves be concerned about such 'works', but be saved by the grace of God only.

Zwingli's understanding of freedom with regard to fasting in fact represented a kind of theological libertarianism according to which we are free of such imposed restrictions because we are 'saved by the grace of God only' and not by the legal coercion of any established religious system. Luther himself confirmed that insight:

> the papal dominion . . . makes rules about fasting, praying and butter eating, so that whoever keeps the commandments of the pope will be saved and whoever does not keep them belongs to the devil. It thus seduces the people with the delusion that goodness and salvation lies in their own works. But I say that none of the saints, no matter how holy they were, attained salvation by their works.[1]

Early reformers, then, saw themselves as proclaiming a libertarian jubilee of freedom from centuries of Catholic enslavement. Luther himself made a major contribution to the unfolding of a historiography that portrayed his reforms as the antidote to the decadence that had crept over the course of time into the Roman Church. He represented Catholicism's moral, institutional and, above all, doctrinal abuses as time's evil legacy to the Church. The centuries had, he believed, left a thick dust of moral decay, when, for example, over the course of time, 'Avarice grew impatient at the long time it took [for Rome] to get hold of all the bishoprics, and my Lord Avarice devised the fiction that the bishoprics should be nominally abroad but that their origin and foundation is at Rome.' In terms of his own view of his role in restoring for the messianic future the purity of the distant past of the Christian Church lost in more recent recorded time, Luther came to see the papacy as the Antichrist coming between God and His people and he showed how the papal office had over the course of time introduced into the Church the institutions of the non-Christian world: 'the pope's teaching is taken from the Imperial, pagan law'.

As we shall see in Chapter 3, as a consequence of his attack on the papal system of indulgences in 1517, in 1519 Luther was involved in debates in Leipzig with the Catholic controversialist Johannes Maier von Eck (1486–1543). The Leipzig debates turned into a protracted historical and theological review of the proceedings of the Council of Constance (1414–17) of a century before. The debates raised the specific issue of whether the Council's denunciations and eventual execution of the Czech dissident John Hus (c.1369–1415) made a heretic of Luther himself, as a critic of the Church. In the intervals of the Leipzig debate Luther carried out historical study, closely examining Hus's doctrines, and began to draw lessons against papal claims from out of Church history. In the following year, Luther published an essay with an historical theme, 'The Babylonian Captivity of the Church', showing that the papal bondage was the malign legacy of time. In particular, baptism, the eucharist and penance, the three ancient core sacraments – channels of divine grace to Christians – had 'been bound by the Roman Curia [papal court] in a miserable captivity . . . and the Church has been deprived of all her freedom'. His own historical importance, he was convinced, was not that of innovator – innovation was the sin committed against the true Church by the papal tyranny – but of restorer. Over indulgences, for example – that long tail of abuse that had grown on to the sacrament of the forgiveness of sins, penance – Luther claimed, 'I alone rolled this rock away.'[2]

THE CONTINENTAL HISTORIOGRAPHICAL TRADITION

Within the sixteenth century Luther's historic overview of a Church held prisoner by the toils of time was given scholarly form by the Lutheran historian Matthias Flacius Illyricus (1520–75), along with a team of ecclesiastical historians working in the German Lutheran city of Magdeburg. Published in Basel in Switzerland between 1559 and 1574, the resultant ecclesiastical history, known as the 'Magdeburg Centuries', provided fuller narrative underpinning for Luther's claim, not to be an innovator but rather a restorer of the pristine purity of the Church that had been lost in the long and dark ages of papal power. The authors – known as the 'Centuriators' – would point, for example, to the story of the medieval monk Malchus to illustrate vividly how the Catholic Church's gross doctrinal misunderstandings created a world of error, credulity and breach of God's law from which Luther, the liberating and loving restorer, came to free the Church. Malchus as a monk had broken three of the ten commandments: the fourth (like young Luther) by entering the monastery in defiance of parental commands; the fifth by attempting suicide in order to keep chaste; and the seventh by cheating his employer in returning to the monastery after having abandoned it. In cycling such stories, the Centuriators made Church history a key part of the justifying libertarian propaganda of the Lutheran Reformation.[3]

Luther as a great historical force became a subject of popular mythology in Germany, and the historian Robert Scribner traced the fascinating process by which the Luther-myth became enmeshed in German popular culture between the sixteenth and twentieth centuries. He arose as a surrogate saint, with a festival dedicated to him, and he was readily incorporated into the extant German tradition of folk tales as a wonder-worker, a healer, superman and benevolent magician, particularly kind and helpful to peasants (in ways that in life he had not always been). When a collection of these accumulated folk tales concerning Luther was published in Germany in 1917, it was designed to coincide with the fourth centenary of the inception of the Reformation in 1517 and to confirm the identity of Luther and the Reformation. Typical of the tales that set out the historical importance of Luther was one published in 1617, the first centenary of the Reformation year. It was of a vision purveyed to Luther's overlord and patron Frederick the Wise (1463–1525), Elector of Saxony. In this fable Frederick falls into a sleep, to dream that God sends a handsome and noble monk, a 'son' of St Paul, whose teachings, as we shall see, were the strongest influence on Luther as a theologian. With Frederick's assistance, this monk, Luther, proceeds to bring down the tyrant's papal throne in Rome. The story further affirmed Luther's cosmic importance by linking him with the historical figure of John Hus, as an earlier demolisher of papal claims. But the allusion to Luther's connection with St Paul and, in other representations, with the four evangelists or with St John and with key figures of prophecy, were all designed to attest Luther's exceptional historical role as, in Scribner's words, the 'bearer of salvation', the restorer of Christianity's chronically dilapidated edifice. That his role was to be seen as a salvation from the delusions and oppressions of the medieval Catholic Church was underlined by an illustration dated 1524 showing Luther as Moses – and leading Israel out of the slavery and darkness of Egypt into the light of Christ. Light again surrounded the image of Luther the enlightener in a first-centenary medallion representing him as nothing less than the 'light of the world'. The systematic creation of images of Luther – whether, as seems more likely, those responsible were intellectuals or whether the rise of the Luther legend was a spontaneous eruption from popular culture – confirms the reformer's acclaimed standing as the destroyer of an ancient oppression, history's most important spiritual liberator since Christ. It was, according to this projection, the gross corruption, the spiritual and practical despotism of Rome, built up over centuries of accumulated enslavement, that gave Luther his epic historical importance as a herald of freedom.

Even so, around the time of the centenary of his 1517 protest, it began to appear that his liberating achievement was in fact endangered by a Catholic recovery set in motion by a rejuvenated papacy and Catholic episcopate, by the Catholic Church's Council of Trent (1545–63) and by new religious orders, above all the Jesuits. The crusade of recovery on the part of a reinvigorated papal Church was soon, in the Thirty Years War (1618–48), to be championed by Habsburg Catholic aggression that threatened the very survival of the Reformation in its German birth-place and throughout central and northern Europe. Thus, because the Reformation had already come to be sealed as the great moment of Christian liberation from ancient Roman Catholic tyranny, it was vital to have it protected by courageous heroes in Luther's own mould. Thus, for example, Denmark's Lutheran Thirty Years War champion, King Christian IV (1577–1648), was projected as a 'brave warrior', 'a lord and hero who is true to the Word of God' and who 'struggles with great danger for the pure teaching of God's word': 'he intends to struggle and fight a Christian battle against the enemies of [Protestant] Christendom'. The Reformation had become projected as a liberation and a salvation, and a century and more after its outbreak, insofar as the Thirty Years War was fought as a Protestant crusade, it was waged on the basis of conviction that Luther's salvation of Christianity had to be saved, his redemption of the Church redeemed and his liberation liberated from re-enslavement.[4]

ENGLISH HISTORICAL WRITING

The conviction that the Protestant Reformation launched by Luther had freed a people in bondage to 'popery' became a fixed point of Protestant historical thought in Reformation Europe. In Reformation England, it is true, there was recognition of the value of much of the pre-Reformation ecclesiastical tradition, and in *De Antiquitate Ecclesiae et Privilegiis Ecclesiae*

Cantuariensis cum Archiepiscopis ejusdem 70 ('Concerning the Antiquity and Privileges of the Church of Canterbury [i.e. the Church of England] with an account of its 70 Archbishops') Elizabeth I's first archbishop of Canterbury, Matthew Parker (1504–75), drew inspiration from the historicity of the ancient institution known as *Ecclesia Anglicana*, 'the English Church'. However, better known as an Elizabethan ecclesiastical historian, and more fully open to Continental Protestant intellectual influences, was the great chronicler of religion and the Reformation in England, John Foxe (1516–87), the author of the *Actes and Monuments of the Church*, popularly known as the 'Book of Martyrs' and first published in 1563. To Foxe the medieval Catholic system was a huge deceit, tyranny and burden in which:

> The world, leaving and forsaking the lively power of God's spiritual word and doctrine, was altogether led and blinded with outward ceremonies and human traditions, wherein the whole scope . . . of all christian perfection, did consist and depend. . . .
>
> The people were taught to worship no other thing but that which they did see; and did see almost nothing which they did not worship.
>
> The church, being degenerated from the true apostolic
>
> institution above all measure, . . . did fall into a kind of extreme tyranny . . . . With how many bonds and snares of daily new-fangled ceremonies were the silly [simple] consciences of men, redeemed by Christ to liberty, ensnared and snarled. . . . All the whole world was filled and overwhelmed with error and darkness. . . .

And it was Luther's mission to undertake the destruction of 'that wretched thraldom in which Christians were detained', to speak out fearlessly with 'stoutness of stomach and Christian constancy'. Foxe indeed incorporated in his account the projection we observed above of Luther as a saint, and, playing with one of the Catholic criteria of sainthood, reviewed 'miracles' associated with him. However, Luther's real miracle was that of heroic, liberating courage, a seemingly puny David standing up to an apparently invincible Goliath:

> What a miracle might this seem to be, for one man, and a poor friar, creeping out of a blind cloister, to be set up against the Pope, the universal bishop, and God's mighty vicar on earth; to withstand all his cardinals, yea, and to sustain the malice and hatred of almost the whole world being set against him; and to work that against the said

Pope, cardinals, and Church of Rome, which no king or emperor could
ever do. . . .

On account of such bravery, Luther was in Foxe's view the undisputed
'master' of the Reformation. At the same time, though, Foxe was an
intensely patriotic English Protestant historian, who drew particular
attention to the vital part played by his home-grown English hero of
religious freedom, the dissident John Wyclif (*c*.1329–84), whom Foxe's
Protestant patriotism pronounced to be 'the valiant champion of the
truth'. Wyclif's calling was also for Foxe that of initiating a liberation
from deception and servitude: 'through him the Lord would first waken
and raise up in the world, which was overmuch drowned and whelmed in
the deep stream of human tradition . . . to revoke and call back the church
from her idolatry, to some better amendment . . .'.[5]

Foxe's interpretation – learned, exhaustive, consummately eloquent as
it was – became the cornerstone of the Anglo-Protestant interpretation of
ecclesiastical history in terms of a sequence of pristine purity lost and
recovered, the story of the Church's rescue from the clutches of the papal
Antichrist being a reflection of the drama of human redemption itself.
Luther taught, and Zwingli echoed him, that one of the chief marks of the
papal Antichrist's tyranny was the imposition of rules and regulations
impeding the freedom won for Christians by Christ crucified. For Foxe's
fellow Elizabethan Protestant writer John Bale (1495–1563), one of the
impresses of despotic Antichrist's regime was the needless imposition of
the rules of celibacy on the clergy of the Church. Around AD 1000, Bale
thought, the imposing of enforced formal chastity on the clergy under
pressure from Rome in order 'utterly to dyssolve prestes marage' was a key
strategic victory for the Antichrist as a usurping moral dictator.

In such ways the Tudor school of English Protestant historiography
passed on a tradition that depicted 'medieval' ecclesiastical and clerical
overlordship dominating the life of the Church in England and elsewhere,
certainly in the first half of the second millennium, as a tyranny evident
in daily enslavements and in the deliberate promotion of superstition
and error, but to be vanquished by the light of the gospel restored, Luther
being the primary restorer. The Reformation was to be seen, then, as a
restitution of doctrine and elimination of abuse, but, even before those
things, it was to be considered as a release from a most grievous subjection,
a 'Babylonian captivity', to use Luther's term of 1520, in thrall to
Antichrist. By the later seventeenth century, when the Protestant bishop
of the Church of England Gilbert Burnet (1643–1715) produced the first

two volumes of his *History of the Reformation* in 1679–81, a Protestant historiography had become firmly established according to which medieval 'popish' ecclesiasticism represented a fusion of delusion and servitude. The Protestant Reformation, with Luther as its captain, meant Luther's doctrine of the priesthood of all believers, the consequent loosening of the ties of 'priestcraft' and the simultaneous delivery, of which Luther was the trail-blazer, of the Scriptures to the people in their own language. Burnet asked:

> What is to be said of implicit Obedience, the priestly dominion over consciences, the keeping the Scripture out of the people's hands, and the Worship of God in a strange tongue, but that these are so many arts to deceive the world, and to deliver it up into the hands of an ambitious clergy?[6]

It was no coincidence that when Burnet issued the overture to his great history, the Reformation seemed to many in the British Isles to be, once more, in peril of re-enslavement, for the mighty power of Louis XIV's France, combining military, political and religious grandeur and servitude, was abroad to reverse the Reformation, while in England itself the revelations of Titus Oates (1649–1705) in and following 1678 seemed to reveal a 'popish' campaign to destroy freedom – both religious and political – and restore the slavery and deceits of the ages before Luther.

THE REFORMATION AS A POLITICAL REVOLUTION

The English case also seemed to show the equation between religious liberty and political freedom, more narrowly construed. Other nations of the Reformation apart from the English were able to trace in their histories the dramatic liberating effects of the Protestant restoration of the Church. For the Dutch in the seventeenth century, the Protestant Reformation was the concomitant of their national struggle for freedom, the Eighty Years War, 1567–1648 – part of the set of providential processes that ensured national and republican freedom from colonialist, autocratically monarchical, papistical Spain. With that political emancipation came the luminescence of the light of the gospel, along with the marvellous commercial, rural and urban wealth that came to that new and free Israel, Holland. Thus the seemingly unwearied scriptural themes of Israel set loose from the houses of bondage in Egypt and Babylon could be once more recited, to celebrate the birth of freedom and prosperity blest by the shining of the gospel released by the demise of tyranny.

In that largely Calvinist republic, though, the credit for breaking with the toils of political servitude to Spanish state tyranny and religious bondage to Antichrist had to recognise the vital role of the Calvinist, rather than the Lutheran, Reformation legacy. The sixteenth-century Dutch Church historian Adriaan van Haemstede had already traced a Calvinist martyrology which embraced the heroes of the early and post-Apostolic Church, as well as those slain by the papacy in the Middle Ages, and went on to give to the emergent godly rulers of the Netherlands patterns to emulate of the saviours of Israel in the Old Testament, Moses, Joshua and the rest, protectors of a chosen people. One further freedom was thought to have been gained from the Reformation that Luther spearheaded, the precious freedom of the mind, to question, to speculate and to challenge. Thus the Netherlands freedom-fighter against both Spanish and Romish tyranny, Philip Marnix van Sint Aldegonde (1538–98), in his 'The Roman Beehive' (1569), pictured the tyranny of Catholicism as an intellectual trap – an imprisoning hive, close woven out of cunning theological sophistries from such medieval theologians as Thomas Aquinas and John Duns Scotus.[7]

THE ENGLISH HISTORIOGRAPHICAL TRADITION

Before the end of the Reformation century a Protestant view of the movement Luther launched as the great hiatus of post-scriptural history seemed firmly in the ascendant and historians writing in the period to come, such as Burnet, continued to accept a view of the religious renewal Luther had initiated as the great Red Sea of Christian history: for Marnix, it cleared away 'olde rubbish or chalkie dust' 'digged out of the decayed welles of mens superstitions'. It is true that in the 1630s the line of thought that stretched from Foxe to Burnet was disturbed, as some ecclesiastical opinion in Protestant England itself was becoming less convinced of the beneficial effects of the Reformation stemming from Martin Luther. Thus, whereas Foxe's historical symphony explained and justified the Reformation, William Laud (1573–1645), archbishop of Canterbury from 1633 to his death in 1645, was more firmly in the line of his predecessor Parker, looking, as Damian Nussbaum says, 'to [the] medieval Catholic Church as the forerunner of the reformed Church of England'. Though Protestants, Laud and his party, in the ascendant in the Church of England in the 1630s and early 1640s, upheld attitudes to the sacraments and to worship that were in many ways close to those of mainstream Catholicism and they claimed the legacy of the medieval

Church. In historical terms, they sought inspiration, not in rejecting the Catholic past, but in laying claim to its inheritance. For that reason, the Foxeian view of the Reformation as a restorative revolution was sidelined in Laudian ecclesiastical historiography.[8]

Yet, despite Laudian-inspired historical revisionism, for much of the seventeenth and eighteenth centuries the prevailing historiographical orthodoxy within the Church of England concerning its historical roots, along with the whole issue of the historical necessity of the Protestant Reformation initiated by Luther, remained broadly Foxeian. Indeed, it came to be accepted not only that the Reformation was launched by Luther but that its survival was constantly under renewed threat from its tyrannical foe, Rome. Therefore, the narrative of post-Reformation English history was systematically recast as a series of narrow escapes for Protestant liberty from Catholic despotism. The first assault nearly killed English Protestantism shortly after its birth, though the danger was headed off, as *The Protestant Almanac* of 1700 recalled, through 'Our first Deliverance from Popery by K. *Edward* VI' – the Protestant-inspired government of the boy-king Edward VI (1547–53). Post-Reformation English history was, then, increasingly reorganised conceptually as a cycle of near-mortal threats, each narrowly averted, to the legacy that came from Luther. Within that cycle, a particularly high level of menace came, following Edward VI's Protestant reign, from the Catholic reaction inspired by Queen Mary Tudor between 1553 and 1558. Then, 'The Ruin'd Abbey; or, The Effects of Superstition' by William Shenstone (1714–63) reminded its readers, England witnessed the restitution of an ancient and cruel popish despotism,

> whose revengeful stroke
> Ting'd the red annals of Maria's reign.
> When from the tenderest breast each wayward priest
> Could banish mercy and implant a fiend!
> When Cruelty the funeral pyre uprear'd,
> And bound [Protestant] Religion there, and fir'd the base!

Once again the Reformation legacy derived from Luther was to be rescued, as *The Protestant Almanac* recalled, with 'Our second Deliverance from Popery by Q. *Elizabeth*'. The threat, though, was far from over even then. In the collective national historical imagination, wave after wave of new popish dangers to the traditions of Luther and liberty were depicted. Included amongst these were: the attempt by Catholic terrorists to assassinate the godly King James I and his parliament in the Gunpowder Conspiracy of 1605; the massacre of Irish Protestants by Catholic insurgents in 1641; the firing of London in 1666 in an attempt by papists to wipe from the earth its greatest Protestant city; next, the alleged popish plot against Protestantism and freedom in favour of absolutism and Catholicism disclosed by the informer Titus Oates; followed by King James II's use of arbitrary measures allegedly to annul the Reformation, between 1687 and 1688. The last, *The Protestant Almanac* recounted, was followed by 'Our third Deliverance from Popery, by K. *Will*. & Q. *Mary*', in the Glorious Revolution of 1688–9.[9]

REVISIONIST HISTORIOGRAPHY

That Revolution was an international event, concerned as much with curbing the power of Catholic-absolutist France in Europe at large as with ensuring the survival of Luther's heritage within the British Isles. Within the decade when the Revolution took place, the revocation by Louis XIV in 1685 of the 1598 Edict of Nantes, which had guaranteed religious and civil freedom to French Protestants, was a further reminder from the wider European theatre that the price of Protestant survival in the face of popery was eternal vigilance against its constantly renewed assaults, while Catholic persecutions of Luther's spiritual descendants on the Continent in the course of the eighteenth century acted as further memoranda in that direction. Even so, a new ambivalence began to appear in Protestant thinking about the reality of the danger to the great tradition of the Protestant Reformation that Luther had set in motion. Scepticism, even, over the continuing scale of the popish menace begins to be apparent, for example, in John Bunyan's *The Pilgrim's Progress*, part I, published in 1678 when the power of popish Louis XIV was at a high point. In this work the ultra-Protestant Bunyan, a passionate admirer of Luther's work and theology, imagined the emblematic figure of 'giant pope', a farcical, superannuated and harmless relic of the past, once formidable but 'grown so crazy and stiff in his joints, that he can now do little more than sit in his Caves mouth, grinning at Pilgrims as they go by, and biting his nails, because he cannot come at them'.[10]

So a new ambiguity began to arise in Protestant thinking about the Luther tradition of Protestantism: was it in fact a vulnerable holy grail that had constantly to be guarded from its popish would-be thieves? On the one hand, Hanoverian Protestant Britain's growing wealth had constantly to be protected from the beggary that popery brought with it: 'Pontific fury! English wealth exhaust[ed] . . . the beggar'd shore . . . what Rome might pillage uncontroll'd', as it was imagined. On the other hand, the very wealth of the great Protestant realm provided its own securities against dangers to its economy, its global trade protected by the Royal Navy, its currency and investments guarded by prudent Whig government and the Bank of England. On the political front, too, the last Catholic Jacobite military threat to Protestant Britain in 1745 both signalled that there was once more a danger to the Reformation – but also revealed that it was largely illusory. Increasingly, then, thinking Protestants could afford to become less fevered, more relaxed about Catholicism as a primordial foe and about its place in a schematic construction of the past. This is even evident in Shenstone's poem 'The Ruin'd Abbey', in which the surviving, ruined physical remnants of medieval popery – a monastic 'mouldering wall, with ivy crown'd;/ or Gothic turret, pride of ancient days!' – while safe in the Protestant hands of English estate-owners, could sufficiently quieten the still necessary fear of popery in the breasts of 'the sons/ of George's reign, reserv'd for fairer times'. Thus the very antiquity – specifically the medievality – of popery partly inoculated it as far as progressive-minded Protestant Hanoverian Britons were concerned.

Its historic menace largely assuaged, 'Popery' was no longer necessarily or continuously seen as an unmitigated evil, nor was the Reformation legacy of Luther and his followers necessarily viewed as an unalloyed good. The lexicographer and, probably, Jacobite supporter of the Catholic Stuarts' dynastic claims Dr Samuel Johnson (1709–84) typified a new willingness to see things of value in what the recorder of Johnson's observations, James Boswell (1740–95), himself briefly a convert to Catholicism, termed '*the old religion*'. Thus the Catholic doctrine of purgatory was to Johnson's way of thinking 'very harmless', with 'nothing unreasonable' to it; there was 'no idolatry in the mass' – as close as he could approach to a direct repudiation of his own Church of England's description in the Thirty-Nine Articles of Religion (1563) of the rite as 'blasphemous fables and dangerous deceits'. Catholics, Johnson pointed out, did 'not worship saints; they invoke them; they only ask their prayers'. The Catholic sacrament of penance seemed to him 'a good thing'. As for the Catholic issue in the affairs of his own day, Johnson sympathised with the London Catholics attacked in what he called the 'miserable sedition' of the anti-popish Gordon Riots of 1780 and, perhaps even more remarkably, was on the side of the Catholic Irish 'in a most unnatural state, for we see there the minority prevailing over the majority. There is no instance . . . of such severity as that which the Protestants of Ireland have exercised against the Catholicks'. 'I would be a papist if I could', he exclaimed in the year of his death, when he 'argued in defence of some of the peculiar tenets of the Church of Rome'.

Johnson was by no means an uncritical admirer of Catholicism: he decried, for example, its concealment of the Scriptures from the people and the Catholic Church's practice of withholding the chalice from the laity in the eucharist. He also largely shared the inherited view of Romanism as an ancient corruption:

> In the barbarous ages . . . priests and people were equally deceived; but afterwards there were gross corruptions introduced by the clergy, such as indulgencies or priests to have concubines, and the worship of images, not indeed, inculcated, but knowingly permitted.

For all that, Johnson, one of the most influential British public voices of his day, typified in the second half of the eighteenth century a revolution in British Protestant views of Catholicism prevalent at least amongst educated elites, and issuing in moderate pro-Catholic legislation in 1778 and 1791. Whether this reversal of attitudes to the Catholic faith would be reflected in an altered view of the Catholic Church's moral and spiritual quality in the Middle Ages would depend in part upon the momentum of a revolution in aesthetics and sensibility – the Romantic movement, especially in literature and the arts and already in part traceable within Johnson's lifetime.[11]

Shenstone's cult of the 'mouldering wall with ivy crown'd' was certainly part of a love of the medieval, and therefore Catholic-linked, picturesque fostered by the Romantic poet Richard Payne Knight (1750–1824) in his celebration

> Bless'd is the man in whose sequester'd glade,
> Some ancient abbey's walls diffuse their shade.

William Wordsworth (1770–1850) was a literary disciple of the man he called 'the Roman Catholic clergyman', the Jesuit Thomas West (1720–79) whose *Guide to the Lakes* largely pioneered Lakeland tourism. But Wordsworth was able to find more than merely picturesque significance in the extant ruins of the medieval monastic architecture of worship. Wordsworth's discovery of the spiritual value of the Catholic past recalls something of Parker's and Laud's ability to see merit in the pre-Reformation Church. His particular interest as a poet lay in the beautiful architectural legacy of Catholicism within the landscape of England and Wales (Furness Abbey, Tintern Abbey) and on the Continent (Catholic Bruges and Cologne) and was expressed in a string of poems that unmistakably create a sense of empathy for medieval Catholic Christianity. He further developed the affection for ivy-clad monastic ruins that was characteristic of the earlier literary picturesque school into an appreciation for monastic meditation typical of the instinctual, a-rational leanings of the Romantics,

> And meditate upon everlasting things
> In utter solitude.

While Wordsworth had no patience with what he termed the 'Revival of Popery' in his own day, and was perfectly capable of delivering routine anti-popish copy, our own interest is held by his cultivation of a highly enthusiastic sense of Catholic history: of the heroised Catholic figures of Mary Queen of Scots (1542–87); of the Polish Catholic king Jan Sobieski (1624–96) whom Wordsworth acclaimed as the 'Deliverer' for his rescue of Vienna from the Turks in 1683; of the Catholic martyrs under Henry VIII, 'saintly Fisher' (Bishop St John Fisher, 1469–1535) and the 'gay genius' of St Thomas More (1478–1535). He deeply appreciated the wisdom of medieval Scholasticism, the valour of the Crusades and the beauty of the medieval cult of Mary, while strongly deploring the Dissolution of the Monasteries (1536–40) by Henry VIII – 'choirs un-roofed by selfish rage'. Wordsworth's preparedness to see in medieval catholicity, not unmixed merit – that might have been rather too much for him or his readers to take on – but the lineaments of 'Justice and peace; – bold faith' opened up, under the inspiration of Romanticism and medievalism, the strong possibility, in Europe's most important Protestant state, of a receptivity to the medieval Catholic Church, its aspirations and achievements, and a gradual retreat from an historical interpretation that had justified Luther's Reformation itself as a necessary liberation from enslaving superstition.[12]

If Wordsworth was able to see medieval Catholicism in a relatively favourable light, as part of that new appreciation of the Middle Ages and their mystique that was at the centre of Romanticism from the late eighteenth century onwards, his English contemporary William Cobbett (1763–1835) was savagely iconoclastic about Catholicism's replacement, Luther's invention, Reformation Protestantism, and its effects in and on

England. He considered these to have been acutely injurious to the poor – not an emancipation of the masses but their economic and social enslavement. In his *History of the Reformation in England and Ireland* (1824–7) Cobbett claimed to 'show not only that the people were better off, better fed and clad, before the "Reformation" than they have ever been since, but that the nation was more populous, wealthy, powerful and free before than it has ever been since that event'. Indeed, pre-Reformation England was a social utopia in which 'Usury among Christians was unknown until the wife-killing tyrant [Henry VIII] laid his hands on the property of the Church and of the poor'. What was for Wordsworth a cultural and aesthetic loss, the Dissolution of the Monasteries, was to Cobbett a social catastrophe because it suppressed the charity and welfare dispensed by the monks: 'When the Protestant religion came . . . the poorer classes were plundered of their birthright and thrown out to prowl about for what they could beg or steal.' Subsequently, 'When Elizabeth had put the finishing hand to the plundering of the Church and poor, once happy and free and hospitable England became a den of famishing robbers and slaves' and in Elizabeth's reign 'we have the great, the prominent, the staring, the horrible and ever [en]during consequences of the "Reformation", that is to say, pauperism established by law'. It hardly needs adding that Cobbett's strictures are not history: they made up propaganda for his radical Tory critique of a commercial and industrialising country that he condemned as driven by a hard-nosed and selfish money-making ethos.[13]

Some years previous to Cobbett's production, in 1802 Wordsworth's almost exact French contemporary, the Catholic aristocratic royalist François René, Vicomte de Chateaubriand (1768–1848), had turned his own attention to defending the values of traditional and medieval Catholicism against the rationalist, secularist, modernising codes that the French Revolution had championed, and he was able intellectually to go a great deal further than Wordsworth in saluting the immense positive contribution to human progress and welfare made by the medieval Catholic Church. The sacrament of penance, for instance, often regarded as the linchpin of clerical dictatorship over the laity, was to Chateaubriand 'one of the strongest barriers against vice and a masterpiece of wisdom'. Chateaubriand even had the ingenuity to cite the twin icons of the eighteenth-century anti-Catholic rationalist Enlightenment, Jean-Jacques Rousseau (1712–78) and François-Marie Arouet de Voltaire (1694–1778), in defence of penance. Indeed, for Chateaubriand – and intrinsic spiritual considerations apart – the whole Catholic sacramental system conduced vastly to natural human morality and benefit. The Church's sacrament of matrimony he believed did so pre-eminently, and it was in discussing this rite that Chateaubriand embarked on a hymn to the medieval Church's entire civilising achievement:

> Europe still owes to the Church the scanty number of good laws that it possesses. There is, surely, no social situation that has not been provided for by [the Church's] canon law, the fruit of the wise experience of fifteen hundred years, and of the genius of those [medieval] popes of the name of Innocent and Gregory.[14]

Chateaubriand, indeed, should be regarded as the founder of a Catholic school of historical writing that came, confidently, almost defiantly, to rejoice in the grandeur and the achievements of the medieval 'ages of faith', and to deplore Luther's Protestant Reformation as an historical catastrophe. As history rather than rhetoric, Chateaubriand's work should no doubt have admitted more of the faults of the medieval ecclesiastical set-up, and *The History of England to 1688* published between 1819 and 1830 by the Lancashire-based Catholic priest John Lingard (1771–1851) was candid in admitting those defects that had led to the outbreak of the Protestant Reformation in Germany: that country's high-born prince bishops

> neglected the episcopal function; the clergy, almost free from restraint, became illiterate and immoral; and the people, ceasing to respect those whom they could not esteem, inveighed against the riches of the church, complained of the severity with which the clerical dues were exacted in the spiritual courts, and loudly called for the removal of many real or imaginary grievances. . . .

However, although Lingard acknowledged that there were genuine sources of more or less secular-based dissatisfaction with the medieval Church, in his eyes Luther, an opportunistic coward, with 'liberty . . . constantly in his mouth' and writing '"Christian Freedom"' and '"Bondage of the Church"', 'converted the general feeling to his own purpose', which was 'to subvert the foundations of the existing church, that he might raise another on its foundations'. The Reformation was born, then, of no high historical necessity but out of Martin Luther's ability to exploit social grievances for his own ends.[15]

Increasing confidence was henceforward to mark new generations of Catholic historians in defending the record of their Church and in calling into question the historical justification for Luther's Protestantism. By the beginning of the twentieth century the English Benedictine monk, cardinal and historian Francis Aidan Gasquet (1846–1929), fostered a species of Catholic historical writing that boosted the claims of the medieval Church to social benevolence and pastoral and spiritual care. Gasquet's 1906 *Parish Life in Mediæval England* in particular forms a vivid evocation of a devout, medieval English Catholic population of willing daily Mass-attenders receiving the sacraments with joy and frequency. Of these, penance was no burden or enslavement of the conscience, for the disciplinary canons of what Gasquet called the 'English Church' instructed confessors 'to hear what anyone may want to say, bearing with them in the spirit of mildness, and not exasperating them by word or look' . The administration of this sacrament also opened up the egalitarianism of the medieval Church, for in it, wrote Gasquet, on the basis of a fifteenth-century book of confessional *Instructions*, all, 'rich and poor, noble and simple, . . . were treated alike'. Indeed, Gasquet's understanding of the institutions of the medieval Church was that they made up a progressive and sociable entity, one whose guilds and confraternities resembled the emergent trade unions of his own day as well as those other bodies representative of self-help and sociability, benefit societies and provident associations. Indeed, the cooperative spirit sponsored by the medieval Church made village life under the care of one pre-Reformation County Durham monastery resemble 'some Utopia of dreamland'. There were plentiful holidays based on holy days, provision of entertaining and instructive religious plays, and conviviality upheld in village 'ales' put on by the Church – though, lest any reader come away with the wrong idea, Gasquet's version of the potation provided at those treats seems to have resembled nothing so much as a kind of sarsparilla, 'a sweet beverage . . . hardly an intoxicant'. Finally, this whole *tableau vivant* of innocent, cooperative and soberly merry Catholic English life was led by a dedicated and educated parish clergy, ably assisted by a full range of conscientious parish officers. The Protestant Reformation engineered by Luther could be seen only as the most deplorable explosion of that serene world, like a wild boar invading a vineyard.[16]

Further into the twentieth century, a Catholic philosopher of history, Christopher Dawson (1889–1970), echoed Gasquet's encomium of medieval Christian confraternal life and developed it into a hymn of praise for what he saw as its realisation of some of the highest ideals of human society, brought to near perfection in the city of the Catholic Middle Ages:

> it was the medieval city which first provided the favourable conditions for a thorough-going christianization of social life . . . the medieval city succeeded in reconciling the interest of the consumer with the corporate freedom and responsibility of the producer . . . it was this integration of corporate organization, economic function and civic freedom which makes the medieval city the most complete embodiment of the social ideas of the Middle Ages, as we see them in their most highly developed form in the writings of St Thomas Aquinas.

It is particularly noteworthy from our point of view that Dawson linked medieval Catholic society so closely and repeatedly with *freedom*. Thereby, the notion inherited from the reformers that the Catholic system had meant bondage, and the Reformation liberty, had been turned on its head. Meanwhile, more popular Catholic writers such as G.K. Chesterton (1874–1936) spread the romantic medieval vision, while his co-religionist Hilaire Belloc (1870–1953) called for the restoration of the medieval guilds.[17]

Alongside the influence of Christian socialism, or of an anti-capitalist ideological reaction, in romanticising a vision of a cooperatist and corporatist Catholic Middle Ages, the Christian ecumenical movement gaining ground after the Second World War sidelined the older kind of confident Protestant historiography, deriving in England ultimately from Foxe, which had so sweepingly discredited the Catholic Middle Ages and Church. For instance, the Anglican historian A.G. Dickens in his masterly 1964 *The English Reformation* was notably cautious in his attitudes to assumptions about late medieval Catholic clerical corruption in England, and in his introductory survey 'Scenes from Clerical Life' put his readers on their guard against, for example, the bias of Tudor governmental reportage of scandals in the monasteries and convents, data produced so as to justify politically motivated suppression. When J.J Scarisbrick published *The Reformation and the English People* in 1984 and Christopher Haigh issued *The English Reformation Revised* three years later, the intellectual foundations were already in place for the building of Eamon Duffy's magnificent scholarly defence of the viability and popularity of the late medieval Catholic religious and social system in which, Duffy wrote, 'Corporate Christians' occupied a zone of 'holy neighbourliness': *The Stripping of the Altars: Traditional Religion in England c.1400–c.1580*. In one of the most emphatic reversals of historiographical consensus ever achieved, by the 1990s, in the most influential English-language studies of the Reformation and pre-Reformation, the medieval Catholic system had come to be represented as workable, beautiful and popular, with, to say the least, a strong suspicion that the Reformation, at least in the British Isles, represented a victory of absolute and ruthlessly enforced state power to uproot people, as painfully as a mandrake torn up, from ancient and beloved rites and social customs.

Could there be any dissent from this new apparent orthodoxy? Available in German since 1939 Joseph Lortz's *Die Reformation in Deutschland* appeared in English translation in 1968 and delivered to English-speaking readers a sustained and angry condemnation of the late medieval Church – the 'disintegration of the Christian priesthood', 'an un-Christian way of life . . . regarded as normal', 'scandals of the Renaissance papacy', 'the terrible extent of corruption', 'the general decline of the religious orders', the supposedly austere Cistercian monks living for 'the enjoyment of pleasure', 'widespread decay amongst the higher and lower clergy', cynical mechanisation of piety. The entire system was, indeed, a kind of Babylonian captivity, and Lortz cited a view of Luther's Reformation as a deliverance: 'The Reformation came like the fulfilment of a long-overdue self-liberation'. So concluded the Catholic scholar Lortz, returning to the concept with which we began this chapter, that the Reformation was a major human emancipation. So, until we have made further progress with this book the jury of my readers may not yet be able to deliver any verdict on whether or not the Luther-movement was in the end the striking-off of fetters tying down the Christian soul.[18]

2

MARTIN LUTHER'S BACKGROUND, UPBRINGING AND EDUCATION, 1483–1513

LUTHER'S SOCIAL BACKGROUND

> John Luther was an upright, straightforward, hard-working man, with a firmness of character bordering on obstinacy. Of a more cultivated mind than usual with persons of his class, he was a great reader. . . . [His wife] Margaret possessed the virtues, which adorn honest and pious women. She was remarked, in particular, for her modesty, her fear of God, and her spirit of prayer.

This excerpt is taken from one of the several Victorian or Edwardian popular lives of Luther designed to project him in heroic light for a British Protestant readership: 'What a splendid narrative does Luther's battle for the truth comprise,' the author added. The habit then current in British historical writing of anglicising non-English names – 'Lewis XIV' and so on – seemed almost to domesticate Luther's parents as a respectable British Christian couple, 'John' and 'Margaret', industrious, religious, plebeian, 'labouring', though keen on education and self-improvement. The couple's and their growing family's steady rise in prosperity – Luther senior gradually became 'somewhat more easy in his circumstances' – provided an object lesson in the rewards of hard work: 'Promises are given to the just man's labour, and John Luther experienced the reality of them.' First, though, difficulties had to be overcome – those of a peasant background. Luther's father was 'of the peasantry of Thuringia' and encountered poverty in an industrious early married life, 'attended with painful privations to honest John and his wife; for they lived some time in great poverty'. In such ways, the family background of the founder of Protestantism, born to the Luther couple in Eisleben in Electoral Saxony in November 1483, might show pointers to the prizes in the currency of worldly success held out to reward the virtues of industry which Protestant Christianity was, by the time that Thomas Sefton Rivington wrote *The Story of Luther's Life*, widely thought to offer.[1]

Later in life, in dinner-table conversational reminiscences, Martin Luther himself made a substantial contribution to the delineation of his background in terms of peasant poverty. He would dwell on the deprivation of his background and boyhood with skilled narrative detail: 'In his youth my father was a poor miner. My mother carried all her wood home on her back. It was in this way that they brought me up.' Luther would also strenuously insist on his peasant antecedents: 'I am the son of a peasant.'[2]

This picture, though, is, literally, one-sided, for Luther undoubtedly exaggerated the lowliness and deprivation of his background, by focusing only on his paternal descent from a father born a peasant. However, the patrilineal family of Luther (otherwise Luder or Lüder) were themselves substantial farmers in the Thuringian village of Möhra within Electoral Saxony and had successfully pursued a policy of using marriage to consolidate farms and rise up the social scale. The whole patient, if not grasping, process of farm consolidation, in a region characterised by considerable agricultural prosperity and by political freedom and participation and light dues for the much-envied 'quit-rent' peasant farmers, would have been thwarted if Luther's father, Hans, had had to share a holding with brothers. Thus, the wise, if harsh, laws or customs of primogeniture which ensured farmer affluence through the retention in the Luther family's homeland of undivided farms, inherited, in fact, by the youngest son, dictated that Hans Luther would have to leave the sizeable family holding and seek his fortune elsewhere. However, his migration is far from meaning that Hans Luther's was a destitute background. In part, such an impression may have been conveyed to generations of English-language readers by the connotations of disadvantage contained in the word that Luther is rendered as having used for his father's status – 'peasant', a word in the English language with associations of serfdom. However, if we go back to what Luther actually said, in German, that his father had been a *'Bauer'*, a better English translation would be 'farmer', a word in modern British usage with, on the whole, stronger resonances of affluence than of poverty. As in twenty-first-century Britain, so in late medieval Germany the category embraced in fact a wide range of economic strata, and in the late medieval German Lands certainly included families well placed, in terms of type of tenure, quality of soil and extent of acreage, to take advantage of the demands placed on food supply by population recovery from about 1470 onwards. A category of substantial 'peasant' farmers of the kind that in late-nineteenth and early-twentieth-century Russia would be classified as '*kulaks*' emerged, and to that kind of group Martin Luther's recent paternal ancestors belonged. As Luther's principal assistant in the Reformation, Philip Melanchthon (1497–1560), was to recall in a biographical memoir, the Luthers were not noble, but of some substance and presence: 'There is an old and widely distributed family of ordinary people surnamed Luther, within the jurisdiction of the renowned counts of Mansfeld.'[3]

Enough has already been said, then, to correct any impression that on his father's side Luther came from the lowest ranks of the German social ladder. Next we should develop our picture of the reformer's class background in the knowledge that the family of his mother Margarethe (known as 'Hannah'), the Lindemanns, were well-established, well-educated, deeply pious, affluent, urban bourgeois professionals, in Melanchthon's words 'an old and respected family' of Eisenach in Saxony, one of whose members was serving as burgomeister of the town when Luther arrived there for schooling in 1497: as Ian D. Kingston Siggins writes, 'Martin Luther liked to claim that he was a real peasant, but on his mother Hannah's side, Luther sprang from a highly educated urban professional family. The Lindemanns of Eisenach, Luther's maternal cousins, supplied Saxony with an impressive number of professional people – doctors, lawyers, mayors, magistrates and teachers.' When Luther was entered into the University of Erfurt in 1501 with the intention of studying law, he was very much following in the expected grooves of what he was to call 'my whole family . . . in Eisenach', and when that first plan was skewed and he eventually became a professor at the University of Wittenberg (where a Lindemann relative was to be a colleague, as professor of medicine), he was doing exactly the kinds of things that were expected of a member of a rich, high-achieving, confidently bourgeois-professional urban family in Renaissance Germany. It may be true that it was a somewhat unexpected, though not unheard-of, outcome in late medieval or early modern Europe for, as Luther put it, 'the son of a peasant' to become 'a doctor of the Holy Scriptures'. However, that career trajectory was a much more probable one for an Eisenach Lindemann. Luther's maternal family was also in a position to assist the fortunes of their member by marriage, Hans Luther. Hans himself moved into his wife's burgher social class, became a mining industrialist and town councillor, brought his formidable power of personality to try to insist that his son Martin follow the kind of career curve into the learned professions followed by the successful Lindemanns, had his portrait painted late in life as an opulently fur-clad citizen and left a large sum of money in his will. His success story in becoming a respected and utterly respectable urban bourgeois, a mirror image of the family into which he married, was captured by Melanchthon: he 'became a magistrate and won the utmost respect of all good men for his integrity'.[4]

Our knowledge that Luther was 'the son of a peasant' only at a distance and our awareness that he had a stronger claim to urban-bourgeois than to peasant antecedents will help us to understand key features of his later attitude to the German peasantry. It is clear that he came to regard this class as both an alien and privileged species, living easily, 'wicked', a godless 'them' to be distinguished from a godly 'us':

> I don't believe our Lord God will ever give more than he has given to the peasants. He gives them such good wine, grain, eggs, chickens etc. Indeed, he gives them all created things. One thing he doesn't give them, however, and that is himself. From the fact that he bestows such great gifts on the wicked and those who blaspheme him, we can conclude what he will give us.

At other times, his heavy humour expressed deep prejudice against his own supposed ancestral social class: for example, on one occasion, enjoying play with his baby son, he exclaimed, 'Oh, this is the best of God's blessings. The peasants don't deserve it. They ought to have sows.' Stereotypes of his prejudiced humour included the stupid, drunken peasant who misheard a medical prescription of coriander for a diet of calendars, which he dutifully consumed, and the peasant who prayed to the 'four evangelists', 'Matthew, Mark, Pilate and Herod'. On another occasion, his was the voice of a townsman's complaint about peasants cutting off food supplies to the city of Wittenberg during plague – though bringing food in, along with infection, when there was epidemic in the countryside. He also complained of the peasants' exercising a stranglehold on produce. Nor should it surprise us that the mature Luther did speak with a townsman's voice, denouncing the farmers of the countryside, since for most of his career, as a university professor settled in Wittenberg from 1522 onwards, he was in essence an urban professional, of strongly burgher background, bourgeois by education and eventual career choice. As we have seen, when it suited him, and perhaps out of vanity, to highlight his own success as a self-made man, Luther liked to claim peasant antecedents. Even so, and as we shall see in Chapter 8 of this book, when in the mid-1520s the German peasants rose in revolt against harsh social conditions, Luther savagely condemned their actions, calmly accepting his role in crushing the rebels − 'I, Martin Luther, slew all the peasants in the uprising, for I ordered that they be put to death; all their blood is on my neck.' That position was entirely consistent with his overall attitude of scorn and hostility towards a social class to which emphatically he did not belong.[5]

LUTHER AND HIS PARENTS

Rivington's characterisation of Martin Luther's father as a man of 'firmness of character bordering on obstinacy' helps lead us into a discussion of possible collision between his will and his son's. Few autobiographical fragments can have been picked over as sedulously as the following excerpt from Luther's autobiographical reminiscences has been in Luther scholarship: 'My father once whipped me so severely that I ran away from him, and he was worried that he might not win me back again.' On the basis of what could, clearly, be a tense and complex relationship between Martin Luther and his father, the pioneer psychoanalytical historian Erik Erikson constructed, in *Young Man Luther*, a controversial hypothesis to the effect that what emerged as young Luther's difficulties with a harsh and judgemental God were anchored in his clash with a violent and censorious father. Whatever confidence we place today in a psychoanalytical approach to history in general or in a psychoanalytical investigation of the roots of Luther's theology − especially when the data for such an enquiry may be teasingly scanty − it does seem clear that there was friction in the relationship between Luther and his father. It is true that in Luther's day beating was widely accepted as a mainstay of child-rearing. However, the considerable authority of the father in the early modern family was intended to be exercised constitutionally rather than despotically and limits were set to the severity of beatings. So Luther's objection may not have been that his father beat him, but that he beat him on one occasion too heavily and thereby threatened their relationship by making it a one-sided one of fear and power, so that his 'worried' father had to go out of his way to win back his son's endangered love. A balance had been lost: as Luther commented on another occasion, his ineptly over-disciplinarian parents 'weren't able to keep a right balance between temperament and punishment'. However, the boy Luther exercised his own power in these relationships and could both judge his parents and, in a sense, punish his father by temporarily exercising his own right of withholding a cherished love. Evidently, the emotional play-off between Martin Luther and his parents, and especially between him and his father, was no simple or purely physical one but one of extensive negotiation and continuing adjustment measured out in words and argument as much as in actions. Even so, Luther's words about his father's being 'worried' following chastisement of his son may have over-dramatised the situation.[6]

Alongside and following child-rearing in the home came Luther's education in a series of schools, from primary schooling in the town of Mansfeld, some miles south of Eisleben, to 1496 or 1497, higher schooling in Magdeburg, north of Eisleben (1497–8) and grammar school in Eisenach (1498–1501). The ultimate intended outcome of this schooling may be summed up in the words that Luther recalled from his Eisenach schoolmaster to the effect that God had marked out some of his pupils for public office. Capped by higher education in law at the highly esteemed University of Erfurt in his native Saxony, the course of studies was intended to lead to a life of honourable and lucrative public service, as outlined by the Eisenach schoolmaster. Martin Luther's education would in fact lead him into a career typical of the Lindemann urban dynasty into which Hans Luther had married. In 1505, three years after graduating from Erfurt, and about to embark on legal studies, Luther rejected that route and, motivated by a vow to a major saint, made in a moment of danger, chose entry into a monastery, in order to save his soul. His father did not block that choice, though he was to criticise it severely. Now, if for a moment we leap beyond the further details of Luther's education to consider his decision in 1505, it is with a view to using that crisis of choice further to explore the nature of Luther's relations with his parents, the possibility that they presented opposing outlooks to him and the conclusion that his mother's was the most decisive influence on his formation, above all his religious evolution.

Hans Luther was not irreligious. In criticising his son's rebellious decision in 1505 to enter the monastery, he knew enough doctrine to be able to turn Scripture against Martin and to quote the commandment against disobeying one's parents. However, he was emphatically opposed to Martin's course of action. Indeed, from his peasant background Hans was likely to have inherited the accumulated anti-clericalism of that class, perhaps exacerbated by the resentment of the diligent self-made man against easy-living clerics: Luther later recalled that his father 'saw through the knavery of the monks very well'. When his son claimed visionary inspiration to validate his entry into the monastery, his reaction, uttered at the time of Martin's ordination as a priest in 1507 – 'Just so it wasn't a phantom you saw!' – suggests, if not an ingrained sceptic, then a man with his feet firmly on the ground of reality. Yet if Hans Luther's piety was not overt, we still have the problem of discerning the influences that made his son such a devout boy and young man as to become a monk in his early twenties. Whatever the nature and extent of his father's piety, there are in fact strong clues of a dominant religious aura in the Luther home. These included his very prompt baptism within a day of his birth: as Melanchthon was to minute from a conversation with Luther's mother, the very next day after his birth, 'he was grafted into the Church of God by baptism'. Further evidence of that aura of piety comes from the fact of his Christening, not with one of the family Christian names – Hans (his father), Heine (his paternal grandfather), or Heinrich, a Lindemann favourite – but with the saint's name of his baptismal day, Martin. True, the custom of naming children after saints was becoming increasingly common in late medieval Germany, but it was undoubtedly a pious usage and may not have been an impulse on Hans Luther's part.

This leaves us seeking for an alternative – a maternal, rather than paternal, influence in shaping young Luther's pronounced religious devotion – so that the steps of piety leading to Martin Luther's entry into the monastery in 1505 may well have been laid by his mother. In fact, he was later actually to blame his parents for his decision of 1505. He singled out his mother's brutal discipline – 'For the sake of [stealing] a mere nut my mother beat me until the blood flowed' – and he added 'By such strict discipline they finally forced me into the monastery'. However, he said that in 1537, long after he had renounced the cloister. It seems more likely to have been the case, though, that Margarethe Luther was responsible, not for 'forcing' her son into monasticism, but for creating the kind of domestic religious ambience that was to direct her son towards the monastery door as his own choice in 1505. In short, his resolution to become a monk was formed by 'the diligent instruction at home' to which those who knew Luther well alluded and by what Kingston Siggins terms the 'God-fearing, prayerful, saintly and wise' religious ambience fostered by Margarethe in the Luther home, in which, as we shall see, a copy of the Bible may have been at hand. That atmosphere was undoubtedly generated by Margarethe Luther, who, Melanchthon recalled, 'possessed all the . . . virtues which are fitting in an honourable woman, . . . shone especially in modesty, fear of God and prayer, and other upright women used to take her as an example of virtue'. When her son adopted the option of the cloister in the teeth of his formidable father's opposition, Martin felt it necessary to validate his choice by citing a kind of visionary mandate in its support: 'he excused himself by stating that he was so frightened by a storm that he was compelled to become a monk' (his father, as we saw, was not impressed). However, it seems significant that the holy interventionists in his life at that crux were not male avatars – Christ, or his own patron St Martin.

What, then, were young Luther's visionary encounters which, he claimed, directed him towards the monastery? In the first place, in a serious accident with a sword in 1503 when he was a student at Erfurt, he cried out, 'Mary help'. Perhaps there is nothing particularly remarkable in that appeal: the cult of the Virgin had reached dizzy heights in late medieval Catholic piety and Mary was particularly acclaimed as protectress in Germany. However, in a second trauma, on 2 July 1505, threatened by a terrifying thunderstorm near the village of Stotternheim, when he was returning to university after a visit home, probably to discuss his future, he called out for help, this time, to Mary's own mother, St Anne, 'Anna', a variant of Luther's mother's alternative name: 'Help me, St Anne: I will become a monk.' It is true that the cult of St Anne (and of her husband Joachim) was a favourite among German miners – though the student Luther was not a miner, only the son of one. However, devotion to St Anne was strongly maintained in Hannah Luther's home town, Eisenach. Martin Luther's spontaneous appeals, in situations of grave emergency, to these two female saints, Mary and Anne, daughter and mother, may well, then, indicate the impact upon him, via his own mother, of a strongly feminised Catholic piety. As with other great Christian religious leaders, including John and Charles Wesley, the founders of Methodism, the critical influence on Luther's religious development seems likely to have been his mother's. What seems most probable, then, and what can be reconstructed from his 1505 decision, is that, even before his formal education got fully under way, Luther was exposed, through his mother, to some of the main currents of late medieval German piety, centring, above all, on a sense of the individual's own responsibility for his or her spiritual welfare in the sight of God.[7]

LUTHER'S EDUCATION

Luther's account of his schooling linked its contents to discipline and control. A particularly marked feature was the enforced replacement of the child's natural leanings – especially, in his case, his inclination to speak his mother tongue, German – with the requirements of training for adulthood and the linguistic discipline of Latin, the language of rules and reason, that would equip him for the professional career for which his entire schooling was intended to groom him. His later criticisms of his school teaching – a packaged rote-training system of Latin-learning that was 'nothing short of torture' – followed on quite naturally from his condemnations of his parents' excessive discipline. In his later conversational reminiscences, he was in fact finding fault with the whole educational system and philosophy to which he had been exposed – criticising what it was in fact intended to achieve, an outcome in which, as he said, 'children and pupils lose their spirit on account of their parents and teachers', and slamming its failure to take account of the 'difference in aptitudes' of children as individuals. However, the then-prevailing educational mode was not in fact a system intended to run with the grain of the particular child's individuality but was, rather, designed to put in place a standard human product, disciplined, re-modelled. The training programme was directed at the subordination of the child's intrinsic nature, a process to which young Luther seems to have been strongly resistant, so that he was beaten as often as fifteen times in a morning, as part of the deliberate process of suppressing his will. In that regime, the inculcation of Latin, proscribing and belittling the child's natural preference for his vernacular, was central to the whole pedagogic outcome sought. The learning of Latin, through rote repetition and by means of the acquisition of a formal grammar of language, was an end in itself, a training pole around which the resistant bent of the child's nature had to be forced to grow. Latin, schematised into a grammar, was regarded as the language of disciplined reason, held to be the mature male prerogative, as opposed to the feminine, vernacular 'mother tongue' of infancy and instinct.

In Luther's case, learning the language of Rome was also a means to the eventual end of equipping the intended lawyer of the future to handle the laws of Rome, contained within the covers of the Roman emperor Justinian's (482–565) *Corpus Juris*, the digest of a legal system celebrated for its spirit of authority, clarity and order, and of rationality – 'what commends itself to human reason', as Luther later said of it. So it was more than an incidental gift of the purchase of a textbook when Hans handed over to Martin Luther, as his education in law moved towards its intended culmination, the money to buy a copy of the *Corpus Juris*: the present was an act of symbolic conferment, the seal of a decision taken, of one man's will imposed on another's. And it was equally significant that when Luther took his own wilful decision to enter the monastery in 1505, he returned to the bookseller the weighty volume of Roman law. Already his education had opened up some of the opposed concepts at the very centre of what was to become Luther's world of thought and feeling: the law and the will; freedom versus legal restraint; German versus Latin culture and speech; reason versus impulse.[8]

The career in law that Hans Luther had pre-arranged for his son implied an essentially secular way of life, dealing with the day-to-day practical concerns of this present world, and even though his Eisenach Lindemann relations combined deep piety with such this-worldly matters as government and law, it was clear that they were operating in two separate spheres of existence when they did so. However, as his pre-university schooling advanced, matters of piety and redemption, never obscured in any late medieval European education, moved towards the front of the rows of other priorities in Luther's mind. Soon these altered priorities would induce the young man to assert his will, against his father's law. In Magdeburg between 1497 and 1498, sandwiched between preliminaries at Mansfeld and Latin-school completion in Eisenach from 1498 to 1501, Luther was exposed to the full late medieval quest for salvation by self-sanctification and indeed saw its whole programme actualised in one lastingly memorable instance.

The whole movement in late medieval spirituality known as the *devotio moderna*, the 'new devotion', was propagated by a group of Netherlands origin, the Brethren of the Common Life, an organisation with links to the school in Magdeburg which Luther attended. Founded by the Dutchman Geerd, or Gerard, Groote of Deventer (1340–84), the Brethren were identified with the outlook contained in the best-known spiritual work of their movement, 'The Imitation of Christ' by the Dutch Augustinian canon Thomas a Kempis (c. 1380–1471). The work was expressive of a practical piety that saw Christ as an exemplar for Christians' own works of meritorious holiness, earning their places in heaven by following and emulating Him in works of charity as well as in self-mortification. The extent of the impact of the 'new devotion' on Luther in his brief schooling in Magdeburg is debatable, though one particularly dramatic exposition of its principles of personal holiness and a life of penitence did make a deep and lasting impression on him, all the more profound because of the contrast between the exponent's princely social rank and the way he emptied himself to take on the condition of a slave:

> When, in my fourteenth year [1497], I went to school at Magdeburg, I saw with my own eyes a prince of Anhalt . . . who went in a friar's cowl on the highways to beg bread, and carried a sack like a donkey, so heavy that he bent under it, but his companion walked by him without a burden. . . . [H]e had so fasted, watched and mortified his flesh that he looked like a death's head, mere skin and bones; indeed he soon after died, for he could not long bear such a severe life. In short, whoever looked at him had to gasp for pity and must needs be ashamed of his own worldly position.

When Luther came to write up those impressions, in 1533, he had been teaching for years that sinners were not made acceptable in God's sight by such austerities but only through grace won in faith: his Reformation discovery. As a result of that breakthrough, he became convinced that the spectacular ascetic of Magdeburg, the Franciscan friar born Prince Wilhelm of Anhalt-Zerbst, and indeed all those who thought to win God's favour by such measures, were essentially deluded and that 'this prince might serve as an example of the grisly, shorn holiness of the world'. The Anhalt prince was deceived, for his fellow-religious 'had so stunned him that he did all the works of the cloister like any other brother . . .'. However, the discovery that the prince of Anhalt and all other pursuants of a righteousness of their own were deceived was the product of a protracted theological evolution that lay years ahead, in Luther's twenties and thirties. At the time of that little street theatre of sanctity, the whole world of religious thought that the young Luther inhabited would only have approved of and admired Prince Wilhelm as a living saint accruing merit in God's sight and as an authentic imitator of Christ, the man of sorrows and suffering servant. Perhaps there was born thereby the germ of the idea of his own imitation of that princely imitator of Christ.[9]

The impressions printed on the receptive consciousness of early teenage Luther by that powerful drama of willing self-abasement and suicide, that one-man Passion play, were confirmed by subsequent experiences during the third and final phase of his pre-university schooling, in his mother's home town, Eisenach. There the pious Lindemann family led the kind of combined religious and social life that characterised upper middle-class strata, often those closely connected with governing councils, in German cities – Nuremberg, for example – in the late fifteenth and early sixteenth centuries, where a fervent, earnest, strenuous piety, closely linked to the most arduous of the religious orders of the Catholic Church, acted as a strong bond between patrician families. A leader in that lay piety of the famously religious and priestly town of Eisenach was the municipal councillor and friend of the Lindemann family, Heinrich Schalbe, at whose home Luther boarded as a student and who fostered in his own family reverence for one of the strictest of the religious orders, the Observant Franciscans, of whose unwavering adherence to the rule of holy poverty the princely mendicant of Magdeburg was such a spectacular example. The Schalbes used some of their considerable wealth to endow an Observant Franciscan convent at the foot of Eisenach's nearby hill, the Wartburg, and Luther was a visitor to the friars, an observer of their observance. And if we sought, in a phrase, to capture the essence of the Observant ethos – whether that applied to the Franciscan rigorists, with their firm attachment to the original thirteenth-century rule of St Francis of Assisi and their refusal to modify the rule's abiding principle of total 'holy poverty', or to the other variants of Observance, in its Dominican and Augustinian forms – it was about obeying the *rules*, as if in that lay safety and perhaps salvation.

So Luther was exposed in Eisenach to influences that taught that religion was *religio*, a set of clearly understood rules, to be observed, as Observants observed their orders' rules and regulations, as their own condition for winning God's favour. Related messages were confirmed in the sermon cycles which Luther would undoubtedly have heard, courtesy of devout Schalbes and Lindemanns. Some of the themes of sermon cycles likely to be delivered to urban parochial congregations in the period of Luther's education and upbringing, as they are reconstructed by Siggins, might well have led Luther in the direction of the monastic route for which he was to opt in 1505. Common distinctions made in sermons between types of Christians, for example, conceptually separating a majority of godless goats from a minority of godly sheep, were intended to set up in the minds of young people the choice of the religious life as an elitist option, the avenue to God's favour, known as grace. Vigorous collaboration on the part of the individual in God's saving work was described as essential – God could not 'accept sinful man to grace without the help of the sinner' – though that self-help might amount to no more than contrition on the sinner's part. If that amounted, as Siggins says, to a doctrine of 'justification by contrition alone', where better than the monastery, in the monk's lifelong act of contrition, with all the means of penance and satisfaction at his disposal, to achieve those goals? As Siggins concludes, it was the kind of preaching that he heard in Eisenach that drove Luther onwards inexorably to the cloister: 'the doctrine and the spirituality that drove young Martin Luther to abandon his legal studies at Erfurt (and with them his family's ambitions for him) to seek the mercy of God in a life of devotion and penitence'. Looking ahead for a moment to the point when his decision to become a monk was fulfilled, with his priestly ordination in 1507, it was entirely appropriate that he should invite to the first Mass he celebrated a leading representative of Eisenach's devout circle, his close friend the priest Johann Braun. Always inclined both to dramatise and to compress into sudden moments his most important experiences, as if they were always akin to Paul's conversionary vision on the road to Damascus, Luther emphasised that his choice of the Observant Augustinian convent in Erfurt in 1505 was the outcome of the incident of St Anne and the storm. And indeed, his entry into the house of the Augustinians may indeed have been directly precipitated by that startling adventure, but the real trail taking him into the religious life was through phased influences going back to his mother and leading through slowly-working experiences undoubtedly culminating in his schooling years in Eisenach. The household piety he imbibed there, the austere monastic examples he witnessed, the sermons he heard all represented the gradual build-up of experiences and influences that may well have been activated in the flash-point drama of his 1505 vow.[10]

In the meantime, however, father ruled, and young Luther entered the ancient, famed University of Erfurt, founded in 1392 and one of a senior group of German universities – far more venerable, for instance, than the novice university of Wittenberg established by the Elector Frederick of Saxony and opening its doors to students when Luther was one year into his studies at Erfurt. Erfurt provided a quintessentially medieval curriculum which led from the *quadrivium* of arithmetic, astronomy, geometry and music towards what was regarded as the crown of study, the ancient Greek philosopher Aristotle (384–322 BC). In the thirteenth century at the University of Paris the leading medieval Catholic theologian Thomas Aquinas (1225–74) had helped establish Aristotelian deductive reasoning processes as the intellectual mainstay of Catholic Christianity, in the process helping to forge what came to be known as Scholasticism out of a fusion of Christian and scriptural faith and Aristotelian philosophic method. However, in the intervening centuries the European universities had tended to teach, not so much Aristotle, as commentaries *upon* the Greek thinker. In Luther's time as a student, Erfurt, under the leadership of professors Jodocus Trutvetter and

Bartholomaeus Arnoldi von Usingen, was introducing a humanist influence in restoring the prime texts of Aristotle's writings, so that the student confronted them direct rather than darkly through a glass of commentaries. In years to come, as a university teacher himself, Luther was to show the impact of this humanist respect for the raw text by making available to his own students, courtesy of the relatively new technology of printing, the Scripture sources on which he would lecture. Yet even though Erfurt incorporated humanist approaches into its syllabus, that programme was still profoundly medieval in its Scholastic inspiration. Luther was schooled at Erfurt in the methods of reasoning, and above all in verbal dialectics, honed over the centuries in the European academies. In particular, through the influence of Trutvetter, Luther became aligned in philosophy to the revisionist school within Scholasticism, the Nominalist *via moderna* ('new way') movement which tended to challenge the efficacy of human reason which Aquinas had insisted was a route to the discovery of truth. The Nominalist movement looked to the Englishman William of Occam (*c*.1270–1349) in the fourteenth century – and Luther spoke of 'my master Occam'. Melanchthon hinted that Luther struggled to familiarise himself with the Scholastic method, 'which was thorny enough', 'but which he absorbed rapidly' nevertheless. Although as a radical reforming academic he was later to disparage and reject Scholasticism, developing what became a strong animus against Aristotle and his medieval Scholastic disciples including Aquinas, Erfurt Scholasticism left a deep imprint on him, not least in his skill to be shown in the fierce debating battles in which he was to partake in the second and third decades of the sixteenth century. His eventual championing of Scripture as the sole reliable source of truth also had deep roots in Nominalism, arising from Nominalist suspicion of the efficacy of human reason.[11]

Luther's own academic progress at Erfurt was variable. At the end of his first year of studies, in his baccalaureate he was in the lower half of his class of 57. Lack of interest in aspects of his course may have accounted for this disappointing result. In a slightly confusing later reminiscence which may have conflated together in his memory his university course with his continuing studies after he had entered the monastery, he recalled, 'I read physics with great distaste . . .'. However, as he proceeded towards his MA, which he took in 1505, he emerged as a high-flier: he took his Master's degree a year earlier than expected and passed second in his class. Melanchthon summed up, '. . . he was outstanding as a youth, and the whole university admired Luther's brilliance'. However, it seems likely that, as with most students, degrees of relative enthusiasm for his subjects determined Luther's success in them. He seems to have related to his subjects in terms largely of the books and their authors he encountered, particular works and their writers encapsulating in his mind particular disciplines and intellectual approaches which he either accepted or rejected, usually with equal degrees of passion. Thus, for example, in his recollections either of his university studies or of his period of monastic apprenticeship following university, he recalled his revulsion from the commentary approach to Scripture associated with the fourteenth-century exegete Nicholas of Lyra (*c*.1270–1340): 'I *despised* Lyra' (my emphasis). He wanted, not commentary, but texts – the text of Scripture, from which he turned in his rejection of Lyra: 'Lyra I despised . . . [but] I read the Bible diligently.'

On the other hand, the texts of which he approved – indeed revered – also included the classical literary sources beloved by Renaissance humanists, though of course admiration for these went back deep into the Middle Ages. Melanchthon recorded that, on top of prescribed reading and 'on his own', as a student Luther 'read most of the collections of ancient Latin writers, Cicero, Virgil, Livy and others', and Luther himself remembered that when the time came for him to go into the monastery, he took no books with him except the pagan writers Plautus and Virgil. The impact of these pre-Christian classical sources on Luther, especially in his younger years, can be readily assessed. For instance, in the lectures on the Psalms that he was to give from 1513 onwards as a professor in the University of Wittenberg, he would invoke passages of Virgil's *Aeneid* alongside Scripture texts in order to bring out the meaning of a biblical verse, while another work by Virgil, the *Georgics*, helped him to clarify some Old Testament geography. Virgil (70–19 BC), partly because his life just preceded Christ's and partly because of the moral nobility of his work, was widely regarded in Renaissance Europe as almost a proto-Christian writer, but in his early teaching Luther was also inclined to call in other pagan classical writers such as Seneca, Scipio and Pliny to support or clarify Christian and scriptural truth. In other words, like a humanist – like Erasmus, for example, who in his literary series of parables known as *Sileni* used classical fables to uphold belief in Christ – Luther was far from setting up an antithesis between the non-Christian and the Judaeo-Christian sources of illumination to which he was exposed in his university years. He did not, as he did when opposing Lyra to Scripture, set up an either/or polarisation between the pagan 'classics' and the Bible.

Yet Luther did employ such an antithesis between texts with regard to a further source, a great compilation, the *Corpus Juris*, which in itself came to represent to his mind a whole career and way of life chosen for him, and, as it turned out, deeply repugnant to him: the law. In the course of his life he developed a detestation for the law and its practitioners – 'A successful jurist is a woeful Christian,' he was to say. True, there was a point following his Master's graduation early in 1505 when he applied himself to study law. As an MA, he was given some teaching in the Erfurt faculty of arts and on 20 May 1505 he began his postgraduate law course. As with any young student, it must have been difficult for him to reject so many relatives' voices, not just his father's, pressing in on him, so that, as Melanchthon related, 'when he had been invested with the degree of master of philosophy [sic] . . . , acting on the advice of his kinsfolk who believed that cleverness and eloquence as great as his should be brought out into the open and into public affairs, he began the study of law . . .'. Yet, as he moved towards his own acceptance of one life – that of monk – so he had to reject the other, that of lawyer, the career epitomised in the greatest of lawyers' textbooks, his copy of which, as we saw, he returned to the bookshop. The decisive rejection of one literary text in favour of another was his symbol for the choice of one life over another.[12]

Since we are on the subject of the importance of symbolic texts in Luther's development, we may also consider here the part that Scripture played in his education. Here his own narrative has been responsible for some long-establised myth-making, as, in Protestant hagiography concerning him, Luther came to be represented as a kind of Columbus of the Bible, virtually undiscovered up to that point in time. He recounted three stages of his early familiarising himself with Scripture. First he recalled that, presumably at home, 'as a boy he came across a Bible', read some of it as a story book and 'thought he would be happy if he could ever own such a book', one 'which pleased him immensely'. In Thomas Sefton Rivington's highly coloured romance woven around this vignette, the incident, illustrated in a fanciful plate, from what Luther termed his 'boyhood', is transferred to his young manhood as a student at Erfurt, aged 20 and reading in the university library, when he comes across the Bible:

> He has never before seen [a book] like it. He reads the title – it is a Bible! A rare book, at that time unknown. His interest is strongly excited; he is perfectly astonished to find in this volume anything more than those fragments of gospels and epistles which the Church has selected to be read publicly in the church every Sabbath day. . . . Soon returning to his treasure in the library, he reads and re-reads, and in his astonishment and joy returns to read again. The first rays of a new truth were then

dawning upon him. In this way God has put him in possession of his word. He has discovered the book. . . .

Though more soberly, Preserved Smith also dated Luther's discovery of the Bible to his university days, when 'One day he found a Bible in the library . . .'. Today, though, we are aware that, whether Luther's 'discovery' of the Bible is dated to his boyhood or to his young manhood, the myth of his uncovering a lost treasure concealed the truth that around a hundred Latin editions of Scripture, plus German translations, were in circulation before 1500. To a degree, Luther himself was responsible for the legend of his disinterring a forgotten treasure: 'he *came across* a Bible'. However, I suggest that the real meaning of Luther's accounts of his 'discovery' of the Bible does not lie in his uncovering of some lost text. Rather the importance of his meeting with Scripture should be seen as lying in his discovery of its personal meaning for him. For example, according to Smith the specific passage of Scripture that the boy Luther apparently stumbled upon and which enthralled him so may have acquired a particular personal resonance for him since its central character, in English Hannah, in the German Bible version Hanna, bore Luther's mother's familiar name. In the narrative in chapters 1 and 2 of the First Book of Samuel prayerful Hannah vows that if the Lord grants her a son she will in turn consecrate that son to God: 'as long as he liveth he shall be lent to the Lord'. Subsequently, the boy, Samuel, 'did minister unto the Lord before Eli the priest'. Of course it may indeed have been mere coincidence – 'by chance', as he later recalled – that young Luther's eyes lit upon this incident, of all the countless stories in the Bible, of a pious Hannah whose son was set aside for great deeds for the Lord. The episode had the central message of a vow discharged and centred on a maternal Hanna (meaning, in Hebrew, 'under grace') or Anna. The reading may well have been a personal textual encounter with Scripture in which the youthful Luther found validation of his own choice of the religious life, vowing himself to Anna.[13]

Luther's second phase of encounter with Scripture he also described as a privileged revelation: 'A little later he bought a book of gospel sermons; this also pleased him immensely because it contained more gospels than were customarily taught in the course of the year.' He went on to link the third phase of his personal discovery of Scripture with his rejection of the alternative text offered him in a kind of emblematic exchange, a symbolic trading in copies of powerfully totemic books. Having, as we saw, given up his copy of the world's law, the Roman law, when in July 1505

he entered the Augustinian cloister in Erfurt, he was given his own copy
of the Bible, God's law. However, what all these three narratives of
Luther's successive introductions to Scripture in fact mean is not that he
actually discovered the lost Bible but that he came upon the Scriptures,
appropriated them to himself, made them his own.

LUTHER THE MONK

The year 1505, when he became 22, was one of the most crucial ones in
Luther's life and its time-frame was rapid and urgent, for, from his MA
graduation in January, his law studies at Erfurt began in May and went
until the end of June when he left university for home. Perhaps, Preserved
Smith persuasively suggested, his departure from Erfurt was made in order
to get paternal agreement to give up his law course. Whatever the outcome of what seem likely to have been turbulent discussions, he was in
fact to obtain a mandate to drop his law degree. His appeal to St Anne
in the thunderstorm near Stotternheim on 2 July evoked from him the
vow, like the one that Samuel's mother Hannah made on her son's behalf,
that he would be consecrated to the Lord. Within the context of a culture
in which vows, and above all vows made to saints, had a paramount solem-
nity, Luther had to represent to himself and to his father an unanswerable
supernatural intervention in his life that took priority over other instructions, though it is not surprising that his father remained sceptical
or hostile towards the visionary encounter that was invoked in order to set
aside his own plans. At the same time, though, his decision to become a
religious should be viewed as the perfectly natural outcome of a pious
formation which, as we have seen, might have led more naturally to the
cloister than to the law courts. As he later recalled, 'The serious and austere
life they [his parents] led with me caused me to enter a monastery and
become a monk.' Melanchthon, whose biographical memoir of Luther
made no mention of the vow to Anna, but who did mention the death of
a friend (in a season of plague in Erfurt) as a trigger to Luther's monastic
entry, was also aware that such a crisis activated a longer-standing desire
for the religious life lying on a deeper level of personal aspiration: 'it
was . . . the desire for godliness, which led him into the monastic life'.
So, within just over two weeks of the vow to St Anne – Anna – on 17 July
Luther was ready to seal it by entering the Augustinian convent in Erfurt,
in preparation for taking legally and canonically binding monastic vows
which would make irrevocable the promise made in the storm to the saint.
At his pre-entry party, Luther made a statement to friends of the utter

finality of his being walled-up in the abbey: 'You see me today and never again.'

If by that Luther meant that by passing through the monastery portal, he was entering a new life, in which the old 'me' would be forsaken, that was the kind of speech convention associated with monastic entry; as he recalled later in life in his table talk, 'I was quite dead to the world . . .'. If, on the other hand, he had in mind being immured for the rest of his life in the Erfurt house, that would have been melodramatic. The order Luther chose to enter was not of the species of, say, the Carthusians, with their heroic self-exile from the world in remote fastnesses of immured contemplation. The Augustinian Eremites, organised by Pope Alexander IV in 1256 out of groups of friars and hermits in Italy, had their origins amidst those of the preaching friars in the thirteenth century and their purpose was that of the other orders of friars, engaging with the bustling world in order to preach and teach. The Erfurt house of the order had strong links with both the religious and the academic life of the city, four of the members being professors at the university at various points around the time of his entry. So, in entering the religious life Luther was not abandoning the world at large, and certainly not the university, but was about to return to study, though now in order to equip him for his order's work within society. As Melanchthon recalled, 'his entry upon that way of life . . . he believed would be more conducive to godliness and the study of the doctrine of God . . .'.

The Bible took pride of place in his new programme of study. Luther later recounted how 'the monks' of Erfurt handed to him his presentation copy of Scripture, as if it were a liturgical object, 'bound in red leather'. He went on to relate, though, that he began to absorb the actual contents of this ritual gift, transforming the book from a kind of icon into a living text with a deep personal meaning for him, knowing 'what was contained on any given page':

> There was no other study which pleased me so much at that time as Holy Writ. . . . [M]y heart used to glow when it could return to the Bible. . . . A single important statement would occupy all my thoughts for a whole day.

As on the occasion of his first reported encounter with Scripture, this later, fuller study gave him delight, and it was important to Luther to study what he loved – not law or physics but divinity, not commentaries but the actual text. However, there clearly were other subjects on his reading list

– 'other study' – and though he turned with relief from them back to intense scrutiny of Scripture, other disciplines were required, especially if he were to follow his Augustinian confrères into posts at Erfurt University.

Melanchthon described in detail the other ingredients in Luther's monastic studies. He began with the bedrock of medieval Scholasticism, the *Four Books of the Sentences* ('*Sententiae*') of Peter Lombard (*c.*1100–60). He proceeded through the classic Scholastics John Duns Scotus (*c.*1265–1308) and Thomas Aquinas and went on to the later Scholastic masters, Pierre d'Ailly (1350–1420) and William of Occam. Melanchthon also recorded that Luther was immersed in the teachings of the supposed founder of the Augustinian order, St Augustine (354–430): 'he began to read the books of Augustine . . . most often he read all Augustine's works and remembered them best of all'. Alongside his course of study, he consolidated his development as a religious. First, making canonically irrevocable the decision of the previous year, in September 1506 he moved from probationer to full religious with his acceptance of the monastic vows of poverty, chastity and obedience. These were the formal expressions of a life of self-denial in which Luther was characteristically total in his commitment. He had, after all, selected the strict Augustinian Observant religious life, and as he himself later reported, 'I was very pious in the monastery . . . I said mass and prayed and hardly saw or heard a woman as long as I was in the order. . . . I observed all our statutes very strictly. . . . I almost fasted myself to death, for again and again I went for three days without taking a drop of water or a morsel of food.' (Melanchthon was impressed by Luther's ability later in life to fast for days on end if he chose and he confirmed that his hero had been everything that a monk was expected to be, subjecting himself 'to the severest discipline, far surpassing everyone in the appointed reading, disputation, fasting and prayer'.) His monastic course also progressed towards the ordination to the priesthood, which was not mandatory for all monks but was to be expected in a religious of his excellence and promise.

Luther's reception of priest's orders, following his ordination as sub-deacon and deacon, took place in April 1507, though the celebration of his first Mass was postponed until 2 May, 'the day being chosen for the convenience of my father . . .'. Luther wrote that in an invitation he sent to Johann Braun, of Eisenach, whom he also addressed as 'father'. From one point of view, even if Braun was unable to attend, there were too many father-types crowding around Luther at his first Mass, an event of high excitement for most new priests. There was his father Hans, his monastic 'father', the Erfurt prior – and God the Father, and the conflicting demands of all these had somehow to be accommodated. The first in this trio, Hans Luther, behaved in confusing ways. He came to Erfurt from Mansfeld, with an entourage of 20 friends whose accommodation he financed, sending a demonstrative gift of money to pay for the ordination dinner and playing the part of the proud father of the new priest, whose first Mass had been delayed at his convenience. Around the time of the 25th anniversary of his ordination, in May 1532, Luther could recall those events clearly – how much his father paid for the celebration, what a commentator said about the lavish scale of generosity and so on. And it becomes perfectly clear from such recollections that, for all the paraphernalia of celebration and the showy, expensive but only apparent endorsement of his son's decision, Hans Luther was far from reconciled to Martin's defiance of his earlier career plan for him. Indeed, in his dedication of 'On Monastic Vows' to his father in 1521, he recalled that for some time before a truce that brought Hans to the ordination was made he 'had refused to be reconciled' with his son. At various points he tried to nag Martin into retracting his monastic vows of 1506: 'Again and again his father had asked him to take off his cowl . . .'. Then, at whatever juncture in the ordination festivities, Hans Luther's partially suppressed anger at being disobeyed two years previously exploded into an accusation against his son of the 'mortal' sin of disobedience of one of the ten commandments, the fourth: 'Honour thy father and thy mother'. Whatever success Luther had had in justifying his decision to his own conscience, he had clearly not been able to satisfy his own father fully on that issue. It was at another point during those tense hours that, as we saw, Hans Luther also cast grave doubt on the reality of the encounter with St Anne which Martin cited to justify his decision: was it not a mere phantom, an illusion?

Luther's recollections in the later 1530s of the timing of his father's main charge, of disobedience, are not entirely clear. The overall impression we have from later recollection in the dedication to 'On Monastic Vows' is that Hans had become at least ostensibly compliant with Martin's course and that, after a breach, the two had become reconciled – but that not far beneath the surface the older man nursed a surge of resentment that might explode if disturbed. In 1539 the sequence of events around his ordination that Luther recalled was that he celebrated his first Mass, was 'almost desperate at the altar' but then, the following day, asked his father 'why he was angry at me since everything turned out well'. In this version of the order of events, Hans Luther then threw in his son's face the allegation that in entering the monastery he had broken the fourth commandment.

This patterning of events gives rise to some difficulties, if only because what Luther recalled as the near farce of his first Mass could hardly be described as 'everything turned out well'. In another version of Luther's own chronology of the first Mass and its attendant traumas as he recalled it in 1537, first came his father's accusation of the grave sin of disobedience and then the ill-omened Mass:

> On the day on which I sang my first mass he [Hans Luther] said to me, 'Son, don't you know that you ought to honor your father? . . . *Later* [my emphasis] when I stood there during the mass and began the canon, I was so frightened that I would have fled if I hadn't been admonished by the prior. For when I read the words, 'Thee, therefore, most merciful Father,' etc. and thought I had to speak to God without a Mediator, I felt like fleeing from the world like Judas.

This sequence in fact suggests that Luther's father, whether or not he intended to do so much damage, in effect charged his son with serious sin on the brink of his celebration of Mass, when Church law required the celebrant to be in a state, not of sin against one of the commandments, but of grace. In fact, the new priest would have compounded a mortal sin in saying Mass in a state of sin. It is little wonder that, as he remembered the incident later, Luther turned in terror from an accusatory father to a judgemental God the Father whom he had to address directly in the course of the Mass, and it seems likely that he 'experienced such horrors' thanks to his father's charging him with sin on the very threshold of his saying that Mass. Then, according to Luther's recollections at least, a third father, the brisk father prior, rushed him though the remainder of the liturgy: 'I thought of running away from the altar and said to my prior, "Reverend Father, I'm afraid I must leave the altar." He shouted to me, "Go ahead, faster, faster!"'

The traumas of that day may have played some part in Luther's agony of self-accusation and guilt in the years following his ordination. What he recounted as the terror and embarrassment of his first Mass may not have initiated what was to be Luther's dark night of the soul. Even so, that Mass, when he had to address God directly in the words of the canon, '*Te igitur, clementissime Pater*', 'Thee, therefore, most merciful Father', may have been crucial in bringing him into personal unmediated contact with the God who was to be the source of his terrible anxiety, concerning what he expected to be his damnation as a sinner. We shall next examine, then, the nature of Luther's psychic plight as a monk, as well as describing his career progression and the academic work that helped him to resolve his appalling dilemmas.

We can piece together from Luther's own later conversational recollections the evidence for what he called his *Anfechtung*, his deeply disturbed mode of anxiety and acute depression:

> When I was a monk I depended on such willing and exertion, but the longer [I worked at it] the farther away I got. . . . I was very pious in the monastery, yet I was sad because I thought God was not gracious to me. . . . When I had prayed and said my mass I was very presumptuous. I didn't see the scoundrel behind it all because I didn't put my trust in God but in my own righteousness. . . . [T]he most pious monk is the worst scoundrel. He denies that Christ is the mediator and high priest and turns him into a judge.

Again, Luther reflected,

> I was a good monk and kept my rule so strictly that I could say that if ever a monk could get into heaven through monastic discipline, I was that monk. . . . And yet my conscience would not give me any certainty, but I always doubted and said, 'You didn't do that right. You weren't contrite enough. You left that out of your confession.' . . . Although I lived a blameless life as a monk, I felt that I was a sinner with an uneasy conscience before God. I also could not believe that I had pleased him with my works. Far from loving that righteous God who punished sinners, I actually hated him. . . . I was in desperation. . . . I kept my three vows devotedly day and night and yet I felt no repose in maintaining my duty so purely. . . .

Thus Luther summed up the issues that haunted and thwarted his monastic praxis, turning his quest for personal salvation into a sure prospect of eternal condemnation. The pious habits and experiences of his boyhood and adolescence inculcated in him the conviction that the route to his winning acceptance in God's sight lay in his hands, through his holiness, self-sacrifice and good deeds. That, for example, was the message that the life of the Anhalt prince taught in Magdeburg. To these perceptions, as current as wild yeast in the air of Luther's religious formation, were added the more elaborate and theoretical insights that Luther the student, both before and after entry into the monastery, encountered.

If we summarise that dominant consensus on the subject of how sinners won God's favour, it was to the following effect: men and women were desperately sinful – were literally born sinful – and deserved God's punishment. However, if they strove with might and main, with whatever resources of goodness and penitence they had in themselves, to win His kindness, He was actually committed, or even obliged, to respect and make good their efforts, to supply them with His grace and 'justify' them – make them righteous in His sight – in recognition of their overtures. And it was above all in the sacrament of penance, where sinners dredged up whatever reserves of contrition were within them, that God looked for the measure of penitence to which He would magnificently respond with golden showers of forgiving grace.

Of the range of Scholastic theologians Luther studied, the one who was closest to him, both in time, and through his own Erfurt monastic tutor, Johann Nathin, was the Nominalist theologian Gabriel Biel (c.1420–95), a member of the Brethren of the Common Life, and Nathin's teacher. It was Biel who taught that sinners could attain genuine contrition for their sins. In the sacrament of penance God would not withhold the grace of forgiveness from those who struggled, employing whatever was 'in them', to summon up repentance. However, it was in that forum of penance, which the Church taught should be an arena of peace and reconciliation, that Luther actually found the alienation of God. Essentially, his problem was that he felt he could not muster the required goodness in order to produce the indispensable meritorious impulse – called 'congruent merit' – to which God would immediately respond with amazing grace, and he sensed that he could not evoke this initiative for the very reason that he was a sinner, needing forgiveness. Perhaps his father's warning that he entered the monastery in and through a grave sin helped convince him of his personal sinfulness: he later recalled of Hans Luther's harsh little speech, 'I have scarcely heard a single word from anyone which has produced a more powerful or abiding reaction in me.' However, his studies, especially into the writings of the icon of his order, St Augustine, would have been sufficient to persuade him that a sinful condition was the human condition: *his* condition. If the school of Biel taught that people had to have a head-start of some goodness in them so as to obtain the divine response of forgiveness sought, Luther was convinced that he had none. The immediate result was a perception of penance as the theatre, not of God's forgiveness, but of His judgement. He later recalled, 'Sometimes my confessor said to me when I discussed silly sins with him, "You are a fool. God is not incensed against you, but you are incensed against God. God is not angry with you, but you are angry with God."' He also recalled his blockages over this sacrament, his all-too-frequent recourse to it, with ever-diminishing returns of peace of mind, the evident impatience and misunderstanding of confessors at his grief and scrupulosity, but the solace eventually offered by his monastic counsellor Johann von Staupitz (c.1460–1524). We can also understand his phrase 'really serious sins' to indicate a contrast with merely physical sins and to indicate the sinful state of despair, which was itself one of the six conditions of heart and mind that constituted an immensely serious 'sin against the Holy Ghost':

> I often made confession to Staupitz, not about women but about really serious sins. He said, 'I don't understand you.' This was real con-solation! Afterwards when I went to another confessor I had the same experience. In short, no confessor wanted to have anything to do with me. . . . I . . . suffered from such trials, and at the time I had nobody to console me. Then I thought, 'Nobody has this temptation except you,' and I became as dead as a corpse. Finally, when I was sad and downcast, Staupitz started to talk with me at table and asked, 'Why are you so sad?' I replied, 'Alas, what am I to do?'

The gravity of his despairing condition may be suggested in an anecdote told by the Catholic author of literary attacks on Luther, Johannes Cochlaeus (1479–1552), who had to admit that his subject, following his probation, 'fulfilled the requirements for profession in [his] order, and for four years battled strenuously for God in his study and spiritual exercises'. Then, according to Cochlaeus's narrative, at some point within the years 1506–10, with his fellow-religious finding him 'somewhat unusual', 'one day in the choir . . . he suddenly fell down, shouting: "I am not, I am not!"'

LUTHER'S RECOVERY

Depression may have arisen partly from physical causes having to do with Luther's savagely ascetic monastic regime. He imposed strenuous fasts on himself and later recalled, 'I vexed myself with fasts and prayers beyond what was common . . . if I could have got to heaven by fasting, I should have merited that twenty years ago . . . I afflicted myself almost to death . . . .' Probably with justification, he blamed his later poor health on such self-punishment, made worse by the bitter cold of his cell during the harsh

Saxon winters. However, whether or not his psychological condition was caused by physiological factors, no one is claiming that Luther was in a permanent state of dejection throughout the years within which Cochlaeus related that his crisis was made so dramatically manifest. Within that period, in 1509 he wrote Braun a letter whose breezy, friendly and out-going tone is devoid of the alleged self-preoccupation of the serious depressive: in it he included the message, 'I am well.' The letter also conveys an aura of hectic activity: 'I have succeeded in snatching this snippet of time from my very many and varied affairs to write this letter to you . . . I wanted to write to you, but I could not for lack of time and leisure. . . .' Luther had by this point secured an academic post.

For the academic year 1508–9 his superior Staupitz ordered Luther to the recently established University of Wittenberg (before his entry into the cloister he had already done some teaching as a postgraduate at Erfurt) to give a series of introductory-level lectures in philosophy on Aristotle's *Ethics*. He was also studying for his BA in biblical studies, which he achieved in March 1509. He found the going hard, as he wrote to Braun: 'the study is very severe, especially philosophy, which from the beginning I should most gladly have changed for theology . . .'. In the autumn of 1509 he achieved part of his latter wish when he was returned to his house in Erfurt to take up the post of university lecturer – *sententiarius* – on the basic textbook of Scholastic theology, the *Sententiae* of Peter Lombard (whom, long after his later repudiation of Scholasticism, he continued to admire as 'a very diligent man with a superior mind'). In the following year the tangled politics of reform and observance within the Augustinian order in Germany led to his being sent on a mission to Rome.

In 1510 the leader of the Observant wing of the order, Staupitz, obtained from Rome recognition as superior – vicar general – over all Augustinian monasteries in Saxony. Despite, or even because of, its own strictness of life, the Erfurt house joined with that in Nuremberg to defend its institutional independence in protest against Staupitz's newly achieved personal ascendancy. It was an indication of the still young Luther's prestige within the Erfurt monastery that he was chosen (though a protégé of Staupitz) as an assistant to a senior colleague to travel to Rome in the autumn and winter of 1510–11 to put the case against incorporation. The Augustinian authorities in Rome sided with Staupitz and blocked the appeal. The dispute over Staupitz's attempt to regroup the German Augustinians in a union under his leadership divided the order sharply, and Staupitz himself, despite the victory that Rome had given him, had to abandon his most ambitious plans for a unitary observance. Luther now quit the campaign against Staupitz, having carried out orders to put the case against the vicar general's scheme, and in summer 1511 moved well within Staupitz's ambit in being finally transferred to the Augustinian house in Wittenberg. There he was to take up a permanent academic post, as lecturer in sacred Scripture.

As for his Roman interlude – his only excursion out of Germany – his recorded impressions were shaped by his later alienation from Rome and the papacy and by his alignment with German nationalist anti-Italian xenophobia and the anti-papal and anti-Roman mood in Renaissance Germany on which he was to capitalise and which he was to intensify. He may have absorbed some anti-papal gossip then that he would be able to recycle for purposes of propaganda and tittle-tattle later. He would cite various authorities who 'said that Rome is the dregs of the worst people on all the earth' or who wrote, 'If you wish to live a holy life, depart from Rome; everything is permitted there except to be a virtuous man'; he also told a long-drawn-out tale of a Jew who agreed to convert to Christianity after seeing Rome, on the grounds that if God 'could endure such knavery in Rome he can easily endure all the wickedness in the world'; and he recounted the story of two critics of papal vice who were found murdered. He summed up his view of the Eternal City as 'so great and shameless is the godlessness and wickedness there that neither God nor man, neither sin nor disgrace are taken seriously'. Luther took from his Roman journey stereotypes about 'lascivious' and 'extremely jealous' Italians, along with reflections on the worldly and mercenary cynicism of Italian clerics – though he commended the excellent Italian hospitals. Alongside some tourist sightseeing, Luther also fitted a religious pilgrimage into his Roman visit, including an invocation for a deceased grandfather, and also the chance to make the exhaustive confession that had so far eluded him – 'a full confession [of my sins] from my youth' so that he 'might become pious'. He was still, of course, rooted in the then predominant religious culture of striving to achieve his own holiness, a quest centred on the sacrament of penance. Nor was it his visit to Rome that either then or in the immediate aftermath undermined his acceptance of widely accepted methods of attaining salvation through personal striving.

The visit to Rome represented something of a departure in Luther's career inasmuch as it involved temporary dissent from Staupitz's aims and policies. His transfer from Erfurt to Wittenberg was indicative of his firm political and career realignment to the vicar general's camp. The alliance was evident in May 1512 when Luther attended a convention of leading Augustinians in Cologne, where Staupitz was confirmed as vicar general – and Luther was made head of the academic division of the Erfurt house. His pathway was now clear – a disciple of and, indeed, intended eventual successor to, Staupitz. His career was taking shape as that of a leading light of his order's academic and administrative elite, involving him in continual politicking, heavy administrative burdens, teaching, research and publishing. It was not necessarily the life of prayer and personal sanctification that Luther had chosen in 1505, and he bridled at one decisive step along the route, taking his doctorate, a necessary stage on the path Staupitz had laid out for him. The collision between the two men over that issue shows how skilfully the older man handled his protégé – far more adroitly, in any case, than Hans Luther's dark moral blackmail. Staupitz, a humorist who was himself, on Luther's own evidence, no stranger to melancholy, was faced with Luther's objections to his superior's efforts apparently to overload him with work so as to distract him from his *Angst*. Staupitz talked his client round by gently mocking his gloom – and his self-dramatisation:

> Dr Staupitz said to me one day . . ., 'You should take the degree of doctor so as to have something to do.' . . . I objected that my strength was already used up, and that I could not long survive the duties of a professorship. He answered: 'Do you not know that the Lord has a great deal of business to attend to, in which he needs the assistance of clever people? If you should die, you might be his counsellor.'

The mockery was not entirely gentle but, with its allusion to Paul's words in Romans 11:34, 'who hath known the mind of the Lord? Or who hath been his counsellor?', could be read as a rebuke to Luther's self-importance.

Luther made it clear that his doctorate, which, according to him, caused resentment in university circles on account of the relative youth of its recipient, was Staupitz's idea: the latter 'drove me to it', or he took the degree 'in obedience to' the prior of Erfurt and 'our reverend vicar Staupitz'. Two further implications were contained within the conferment of the degree *'Doctor in Biblia'*, 'Doctorate in Biblical Studies', which took place on 18 or 19 October 1512. The first lay in the fact that the substantial graduation fee was provided, at Staupitz's request, by the Elector Frederick the Wise, on condition that Luther accept a permanent post at the University of Wittenberg. The payment typified the strong support given to the university by Frederick, who had set himself the task of rapidly turning what had been little more than the village of Wittenberg into the culturally embellished capital of a recently formed new dynastic state, Electoral Saxony, and who had commissioned Staupitz to recruit teaching staff, especially from his Augustinian order. As we shall see, Frederick, who insisted on a career commitment to the university from its new doctor, was to remain firmly committed to his professor in the most dangerous of times during the years ahead. The second implication of the conferment was also contained in Frederick's contract: the doctorate was automatically assumed to lead straight into the avenue of teaching in the university. In their earlier conversation in the cloister about the degree, Staupitz suggested the doctorate and Luther countered with his misgivings about the professorial chair that was assumed to go with it, for the doctorate was essentially a tertiary teaching certificate whose holder was '*doctus*', a teacher. The close identification between 'doctor' and 'professor' was evident in the reception of Luther as a colleague by the Wittenberg university senate on 22 October, within three or four days of the degree award, and Luther seems to have begun preparing his first professorial lectures thereupon.

Oberman deals with allegations sometimes made that Luther's doctorate was some kind of pay-off arranged by Staupitz for Luther's betrayal, after the trip to Rome, of the opposition led by Erfurt to his reorganisation plans. Indeed, we should never overlook how much Luther owed to the vicar general as his patron: 'Staupitz laid all the foundations', he acknowledged, and to a large extent the academic career he was to forge was one that his superior was surrendering in his favour, when Staupitz gave up his Wittenberg teaching post in order to concentrate on furthering the reform of the Augustinian order. Even so, we can confidently dismiss the idea that the first steps in Luther's new academic career were laid as a reward for his abandoning the opposition to Staupitz's designs for the Augustinian order in Germany. First, admittedly on his own evidence, if the doctorate was a reward for services rendered, it was one that the recipient did not seem to want and had had to be part flattered, part mocked into taking. Second, it is true that Luther was young for the doctorate, and in the old, staid University of Erfurt, according to him, he would have had to wait a further 20-plus years to obtain it. However, Wittenberg was a young university recruiting its faculty fast, though with an eye to the future. If he was a young doctor, so were other superstars among his contemporaries, such as Luther's later antagonist Johannes Maier von Eck, who won his doctoral cap at 20. And though he had as yet published nothing, Luther had completed all the preliminary degrees, already had plenty of teaching experience, in temporary posts at Erfurt and Wittenberg, and was regarded as a sufficient attraction to win a generous fee-waiver in order to ensure, not that the University of Wittenberg gave him its tenure, but that he gave it his. He was now a professor and was soon to begin professing.

3

FROM THE PSALMS TO
THE 95 THESES

THE DEVELOPMENT OF LUTHER'S
REFORMATION THEOLOGY, 1513–1517

In his Wittenberg university lectures from 1513 onwards Martin Luther began to assemble the theological principles on the basis of which he would eventually challenge the mighty authority of the Catholic Church. Indeed, in these lectures he was beginning to move towards the central theological principles of what was to become the Protestant Reformation. These were that our being accepted in God's sight, though sinners, is brought about not by our moral striving or even by obeying God's own law. Rather, sinners are made 'just' – 'justified' – freely by God in recognition of the atoning merits of His son Christ's death on a cross and subsequent resurrection. God transfers the merit of Christ's expiating death and resurrection to the credit of those sinful men and women He has chosen, by predestination, to save from the everlasting hellfire which they would otherwise deserve as punishment for their sins. Guilt is no longer 'imputed' to those people. They play no active part in their being redeemed from everlasting death but respond passively, in faith, to what has been done for them. Yet, as a result, though certainly not a cause, of being justified, they may proceed to become virtuous.

Luther began the lecture series in which he gradually discovered what he took to be the truth of God's salvation with lectures on the book of Psalms, known as the Psalter, probably in August 1513 and continuing perhaps until autumn 1515. He lectured for two or three hours a week, so that the depth of coverage and commentary, on a text that runs to about

70 or 80 pages in a typical modern Bible, is immense in its detail and thoroughness. He gave the series the Latin title of *Dictata super Psalterium*, 'Lectures on the Psalter'.[1]

Traditionally attributed to the Old Testament hero-king David, the Psalms were also added to after the return in 538 BC of the Jewish people from their exile in Babylon and were chanted as hymns in the course of the services in the Temple in Jerusalem. They are centred on God, expressing a passionate intensity of attitudes towards Him, swooping over a mountain range from soaring heights of ecstatic confidence in His mercy to dark ravines of anger, desolation and despair. They are, of course, Jewish prayers and Luther treated them as such: 'I understand the Psalms as referring to the Jews. . . .' Convinced of David's authorship, he saw his work of exegesis as 'the study of this illustrious prophet'. Among the up-to-date techniques available to him for his exposition was the distribution of a uniform printed Latin version of the text to his students. Though he lectured on the Latin text of the Psalms, in what was known as the 'Vulgate' version made by St Jerome (*c*.331–420), he also had access to the original Hebrew of these hymns, facilitated by the humanist linguistic scholarship of the Renaissance. Thus he was able to provide the originals of key terms and in that way to bring out the reality of the Psalms' Jewish provenance, which he also did by referring them to other parts of the Hebrew Scriptures. At the same time, though, Luther was entirely in accord with the tradition of appropriating the Psalms to the requirements, including the liturgical needs, of the Christian Church. He explained, for example, that 'the church used to read psalms before Mass. . . . To the present day some verses remain in the Introit [the entry prayer of the Mass]. And to the present day the church has the invitatory psalm in Matins [monastic morning prayer]'. More specifically, over the course of the centuries, the religious orders had made the Psalms the staple of their chanted 'office' of prayers intoned at regular intervals of the day and night. Thus, when Luther addressed the introduction of his lecture series to 'fathers and excellent men and brothers', he was speaking to an audience of fellow-monastics for whom the Psalms formed the substance of their life of prayer, so that at least the more experienced of them would have known the texts off by heart.

As well as incorporating the Psalms into its worship, the Catholic Church had also adopted them intellectually in order to establish the claim that Christ was the one prophesied in such Old Testament texts. To take the most obvious example, Psalm 21, an appeal by one who seeks refuge in God from many enemies who encircle him, was regarded as a pointer to Christ's Passion: 'They part my garments among them, and cast lots upon my vesture' (Psalm 21:18). Further, in common with all scriptural texts, the Psalms were held to have such a wealth of divine inspiration and meaning that they could be explored from four interpretative viewpoints – the so-called 'fourfold exegesis'. The first of these was the literal or historical sense and the plain meaning of the text. The second was the allegorical sense in which one topos stood for another, so that, for example, the historic holy city of Jerusalem was also an allegory for good people everywhere, whereas the evil city of Babylon allegorised evil people. The third, the tropological or moral sense, operated when, for example, Jerusalem represented virtues, while Babylon symbolised vices. The fourth interpretative level, the anagogical or prophetic sense, was regarded as the most important one of all, the main meaning or *sensus principalis*. This was the interpretation that took Old Testament passages out of their historic past tense and catapulted them forward in time towards their own fulfilment in the New Testament, specifically in Christ.

Nicholas of Lyra, the Jewish-born converted Franciscan exegete (*c*.1270–1340), had insisted, and Luther agreed, that Christ was indeed the focus of these crucial prophetic layers of meaning: as Luther stated, explicit exceptions apart, 'Every prophecy and every prophet must be understood as referring to Christ the Lord. . . .' This in turn meant in fact that the literal or historical as well as the allegorical, tropological and anagogical meanings were also centred on Christ. Thus the *literal* meaning of such an Old Testament passage as 'Why do the nations conspire . . .?' (Psalm 2:1) was to be read to point forward to the actual way that the 'Jews and Gentiles' conspired against Christ in His Passion. Further to that, those – the Jews – who could not see the centrality of Christ throughout the Scriptures, including the volume that Christians called the Old Testament, and crucially in the Psalms, were therefore blind to their real meaning. The Jews, Luther claimed in his lectures on the Psalms, 'meditate on vanities and false frenzies according to their own ideas about the Scriptures. . . . All of their things are false, as is clear from the fact that their concerns and hopes deal only with things of the flesh': the Jews were Christ's enemies. Thus, in this his first major work that has come down to us, Luther initiated the anti-Judaism that would characterise many of his writings throughout his career. However, following the line taken by St Augustine, who had claimed that the survival of Jews and Judaism testified to the superiority of Christianity, in his discourses on the Psalms Luther also argued for the preservation of the Jewish people, so that 'they might serve as an example and a memorial to all the nations': in particular, their survival and that of their religion, the Judaism of the Old Testament, bore witness to the greater revelation of Christ in the New Testament.

As his theology later developed into one of justification by faith rather than by good works, Luther came to find in the Jewish religion the quintessence of misplaced confidence that we could achieve God's favour through our own efforts, by obeying His law. How, though, did Luther stand at that relatively early stage of his intellectual career with regard to the processes by which we are made acceptable in God's sight and, in particular, to the issue of whether we or God achieve our salvation? There are conflicting answers to that question. On the one hand, in the *Dictata* Luther accepted the conventional view that God responded to the sinner's own overtures, for God had made a covenant with mankind by which He was 'bound' and 'the doctors of theology rightly say that God gives grace without fail to whoever does what lies within them (*quod in se est*)'. To set against that, though, in the Psalms lectures we will come across thinking that seems to reflect the reformer's mature teachings on justification unaided by our own efforts. Protestant commentators such as Preserved Smith and R.H. Bainton may have been eager to find early evidence of Luther's Reformation breakthrough into justification by faith, so that his own discovery of Reformation doctrine does not appear as a late event in his intellectual and spiritual life, a kind of delayed afterthought. And indeed there is indisputable evidence from within the *Dictata* that these lectures did enshrine at least some of what is called the '*initium theologiae Lutheri*', 'the beginnings of Luther's theology'. Thus the author of the Psalms, Luther claimed, did not say:

> 'I did much or earned much in deed or with the mouth or with some other member of mine.' Therefore you are to understand that he lays claim to no righteousness, he boasts of no merit, he displays no worth, but that he praises the pure and exclusive grace and free kindness of God. He finds nothing within himself on the basis of which God should answer him.

The sinner, then, has no righteousness or merit, no price to win God's forgiveness with, and 'Therefore it is true that before Him we are always in sins. . . .' Conversely, for the sinner to deny his or her sinfulness would be to make a liar of God – to say 'that he does not need God as his Saviour, and he judges God in His words and de-justifies Him and accuses Him of being a liar and false'. The Jewish people of Luther's own time were the epitome of those who 'believe that they are justified by their own righteousness' and who thereby actually 'make God unrighteous'. Yet the writer of the Psalms, though a Jew, understood the truth better than the Jews of Luther's day, and was actually 'speaking especially against the Jews' in his exaltation of guilt and self-accusation and his denial of any intrinsic worth in the human condition.

If Luther's lectures on the Psalms show the initiation of his abiding theological anti-Judaism, they also reveal another key feature of his intellectual evolution. This was his growing disparagement of the fountain-head of the medieval Scholastic intellectual tradition in which he was reared, the early Greek philosopher Aristotle. From as early as 1509–10 Luther's notes from his reading show that he was attacking the authority of Aristotle and finding it 'more than astonishing that our scholars can so brazenly claim that Aristotle does not contradict Catholic truth'. Convention, however, as yet required from the novice professor public deference to the great philosopher, and initially in the Psalms lectures Luther expressed such respect. However, as the lectures progressed, it became apparent that he held Aristotle to blame for a tradition of intellectual arrogance which he believed was inherited by the main variants of Scholasticism. That legacy meant that human minds, instead of quietly and modestly listening to God's own voice given in Scripture, used their puny reasoning powers in an over-confident way to explore the ways of God and to try to dissect 'divine matters'. And it was Aristotle who above all stood for that intellectual presumption that the Scholastics had inherited when they put study of the 'philosophy of Aristotle', along with all 'the laws and traditions of men' before 'the study of the divine Word' in the Scriptures. For there was 'more wisdom and philosophy' in one short verse of Scripture than in a major work authored by Aristotle, the *Metaphysics* – even if the philosopher had written it a thousand times over. In 1516–17 Luther was to emerge as a radical reformer of his university's curriculum, sweeping away the whole legacy of medieval Scholasticism grounded in Aristotelian confidence in the power of human reason. In February 1517, for example, he was to denounce 'that ridiculous and injurious blasphemer Aristotle. His propositions are so absurd that an ass or a stone would cry out at them . . . that Greek buffoon.' In place of Aristotle and the deductive rationalising approaches that classic Scholastics such as St Thomas Aquinas built upon his intellectual foundations, Luther put Scripture in sole place as our guide to the wisdom of God, and the whole Church should be 'captive' to it.

Scripture, though, was itself subject to interpretation. Left alone, it was potentially just 'the letter', and 'God did not put the spirit of the law into letters written on paper, in which the heretics put their trust . . .': it was the error and misfortune of the Jews that they were 'shut up . . . in the letter'. Interpretation was Luther's whole purpose in guiding his students through the Psalms, as through all his later scriptural exegeses, so that he would say of any particular passage before him, 'It means. . .'. In the first place, Scripture was best understood according to Scripture, so that 'nothing is to be expounded in Scripture, unless it be proved by and agree with the authority of either testament'. As for other expositors, Luther selected both grammatical and linguistic experts whose work could offer literary textual guidance on detailed issues of meaning, especially to clarify the original Hebrew text of the Psalms, and also thematic commentators, those whose interpretations of the religious meaning of the text Luther found congenial.

For textual clarification and the specific meaning of key words and passages Luther used such grammatical and linguistic guides as the medieval Jewish converts to Christianity Pablo de Burgos and Nicholas of Lyra, as well as his contemporary the German Christian expert on the Hebrew language, Johann Reuchlin (1455–1522). Among the thematic interpreters, Luther's omissions are as significant as his inclusions. The greatest of the Scholastics, the Catholic Aristotelian Aquinas, rated one possible allusion, though not by name. Neither Peter Lombard nor St Albert of Cologne (known as Albert the Great, 1193 or 1206–1280) nor John Duns Scotus, to take random examples of other leading classic Scholastic commentators, is cited, nor are later Scholastic teachers such as William of Occam or Gabriel Biel – although another late Scholastic, Jean Gerson (1363–1429), gets a mention and Lyra was used to illuminate the doctrine as well as the grammar of passages. However, though he was, to say the least, sparing in his deployment of traditionally revered Scholastic commentators, he was not averse to employing others we would describe as medieval. These, though, were figures of the earlier, and pre-Scholastic, Middle Ages, including the great medieval monastic founder St Bernard of Clairvaux (1090–1153) and the theologian St Anselm (1033–1109). However, Luther's quest for the ancient foundations of Christian doctrine took him above all to the Fathers of the early Church, including the theologian and Bishop St Ambrose (339–97) and the translator of the Vulgate, St Jerome: Luther used him extensively as both an interpreter and a textual translator. But of the Fathers Luther gave the palm of authority to St Augustine 'blessed Augustine', generally accepted as the founder of the religious order to which Luther belonged.

Luther cited St Augustine with reverence and with massive frequency partly because he was an Augustinian lecturing to Augustinians, men who prided themselves on deriving their vows and constitution from the great saint. However, there was more to Luther's heavy citation from Augustine than the *esprit de corps* of a religious order. The 'teacher of grace' ('*doctor gratiae*'), as Augustine was known, had emphases that were Luther's emphases and concerns that were Luther's: the pervasiveness of sin, the weakness of the human will and intellect and the utter need of sinners for God's grace. Thus Luther cited Augustine with the highest approval on such subjects as the realisation that in the face of God we 'are nothing at all' and the fact that the gospel makes it known to us that we are children of wrath, helpless without the mercy of God, 'from whom you have whatever good you have and whose mercy forgives you whatever evil you have of your own'. Luther's intellectual polarities were, then, now firmly established: Aristotle, with his confidence in human reason and human ethical capacity, *versus* Augustine with his despair at man's inherent capacity for good and his sole reliance for hope on God's mercy, evident in grace.

As well as these literary, intellectual and academic theological concerns, Luther was finding in the scriptural texts on which he was lecturing the resolution of his own personal crisis over grace and forgiveness. A key passage in which Luther's reflections brought him towards a resolution of doubts and fears came through his minute, word-by-word inspection of Psalm 85, verses 10 and 11. The lovely verses read, in the Authorised Version,

> Mercy and truth are met together.
> Righteousness and peace have kissed *each other*.
>
> Truth shall spring out of the earth;
> And righteousness shall look down from heaven.

Following Lyra, Luther glossed the passage to show that the meeting-place of mercy and truth was in Christ, the fulfilment of God's promises of clemency to men and women. Further, as well as truth and mercy, mercy and righteousness, or justice, also likewise came together in Christ for, thanks to God's mercy, Christ provided for us the righteousness we lack. Although Luther could sometimes be critical of Lyra, he gave full approval – 'a good gloss!' – to a version of his own of what Lyra had originally written about Psalm 85, verse 10: 'Christ provided righteousness for us and thus gave us peace, appeasing the things that are in heaven and the things that are on earth. For by His suffering he made satisfaction for us according to the way of righteousness. . . .' In other words, God, angered at our sins, was turned away from His wrath, instead imparting to us the righteousness that renewed peace between us and Him: 'Christ is now our Righteousness and our peace which God has given us. By it he has justified us, and so we have peace.' The awesome 'righteousness of God' which, under God's law, convicted and sentenced humanity in general and Luther in particular was resolved in the mercy of God, with the concomitant that 'the righteousness of Christ does not come from us'. Luther later recalled that he had 'hated this term "the righteousness of God", for . . . I had been taught to understand "righteousness" philosophically . . . , the formal or else the active righteousness by which God is righteousness and punishes the unrighteous'. Yet he was to discover that God's righteousness *was* His mercy, not judging, but freely forgiving, us. Such an analysis operated within a broadly Augustinian understanding of the total inadequacy of human righteousness to win God's favour. It then set out a conception of the sole sufficiency of Christ's sacrifice as the effect of God's mercy, imparting righteousness to mankind where there was none. That is why we may say that early outlines of central Reformation theological insights were already in place when Luther completed the Psalms series. Indeed, it was as he concluded his meditation on Psalm 85 that Luther drew out those implications which he was subsequently to develop further and in a direction centred on Christ. Above all, this was that 'it is faith in Christ by which we are justified and granted peace . . .'. The timing of the completion of Luther's main Reformation discovery, that we are redeemed not by our actions but by God's grace, is a subject of continuing historical controversy and we may have to accept the reformer's own word for it that all was not fully in place until as late as 1519. Even so, Luther's exegesis of the Psalms that we have been considering indicates that they do indeed represent major ingredients of the *initium theologiae Lutheri*, 'the beginnings of Luther's theology'.

The Psalms lectures also contain massive references to all the major epistles of St Paul, and over a hundred citations of Paul's cornerstone work, the Epistle to the Romans, in the first half of the *Dictata* alone. It should come as no surprise, then, that Luther next embarked on a systematic commentary on this section of the New Testament, a letter that the Apostle Paul wrote to the infant Christian Church in Rome in *c*.56. Luther began this, his second course of lecture commentaries on the Bible, in the spring of 1515 and continued the series until September 1516, commencing his talks at the customary hour of six in the morning on Mondays and Fridays. As he had done with the Psalms, so with the Epistle to the Romans he ordered for his students' use a standard copy of St Jerome's Vulgate. As a guide to the material, he utilised a text of St Paul's epistles that the French Christian humanist scholar Jacques Lefèvre d'Etaples (1455–1536) published in 1512. Then, when he was already a good way through his lectures on Romans, in March 1516 he had the great good fortune to acquire the New Testament in its original Greek that the greatest of the Christian humanists, Desiderius Erasmus (1469–1536), issued, with a Latin translation and explanatory notes, in that year. Yet as well as thus taking advantage of some of the most up-to-date developments in the Renaissance humanist linguistic scholarship of his day, in the lectures on Romans Luther also employed a highly traditional dual method of exegesis. This was carried out by means of detailed glosses, or *glossa*, short explanatory comments, as well as through longer essays of thematic commentary, known as *scholia*.

We know pretty well what Luther said in these lectures, which are so crucial to an understanding of a vital stage in his intellectual and spiritual evolution, both from a collection of his students' notebooks and from his own lecture notes. Luther kept a copy of his own notebook and it became a family heirloom, but in 1594 it was sold by the reformer's grandsons to the Margrave Joachim Friedrich of Brandenburg, who thereby became its steward in his capital, Berlin. Of this a copy was made which eventually fetched up in, of all places, the Vatican Library. Meanwhile, the Berlin original came to light in an exhibition in the Royal Library in Berlin in 1846 and eventually attracted the attention of the Luther scholar Johannes Ficker, who published an initial edition of it in 1908 and a definitive one in 1938. Thus an absolutely essential text in Luther scholarship was thereby, if somewhat fortuitously, restored to the world of learning.

For there is no doubting the importance of the Romans text to Luther or its vital value in his theological breakthrough. Luther prized Romans almost, we might think, inordinately, and in the preface he appended to it within his German-language New Testament of 1522, he described it as the kernel of the New Testament and

> the clearest of all gospels, worthy and worth that a Christian man should not only know the words by heart, but should converse with them continually, as the daily bread of the soul. It can never be too

much read nor considered, but the more it is used the more precious it becomes.

Is this, and especially its unusual description of Romans as a 'gospel' and, indeed, as a supremely clear one, to be regarded as an illustration of Luther's alleged tendency towards hyperbole? No: for Luther the Epistle to the Romans really made sense of the gospels as a series of narratives whose deeper meaning was summed up in Paul's message that sinners secured redemption by virtue of the events recounted in the gospels, those narratives of Christ's saving death and resurrection whose true significance for us Paul explained in Romans.

If Luther thus highly valued Paul's teaching in the Epistle to the Romans, so various commentators have strongly appreciated Luther's work *on* this epistle. The early twentieth-century biographer Preserved Smith, for instance, heralded appreciation of the lecture commentary on Romans as 'a great human document, priceless in its biographical interest'. Smith added that, although Luther had some years earlier 'attained his fundamental convictions' endorsed in the epistle, yet 'immense importance' must still be assigned 'to these lectures for the development and perfection of these ideas'.

Smith was certainly right to claim that Luther made his breakthrough into his essential doctrine of justification by faith in the course of his lectures on Romans because the text of the commentary tells us that this was the case. And since Smith wrote near the beginning of the twentieth century, decades of the most exacting Luther scholarship have been dedicated to attempting to date the reformer's discovery of the essence of the theology with which we associate him. In a much-discussed autobiographical fragment which he appended to the 1545 Latin edition of his complete works Luther wrote as if his discovery was made, not in the 1515–16 Romans lectures, but appreciably later – as late as 1519 when:

> I had returned to the Psalter to interpret it a second time . . . I had suddenly been possessed with an unusually ardent desire to under-stand Paul in the Epistle to the Romans, but just one phrase in chapter one – 'in the gospel the justice of God is revealed [Rom. 1:17] . . . had so far stood in my way. I hated that phrase 'justice of God'. . . . I felt that before God I was a sinner with an utterly disquieted conscience and I could not believe that He was placated by my satisfactions. I did not love, indeed I hated, that God who punished sinners. . . . Yet I

knocked persistently upon Paul in this passage, most earnestly wanting to know what St Paul intended. At last as I meditated night and day, God had mercy on me. I realised the significance of the context namely: 'In it the justice of God is revealed, *as it is written,* "*He who through faith is just shall live.*"' I began to understand that 'the justice of God' meant that justice by which the just man lives through God's gift, namely by faith. . . . Here I felt that I was altogether born again and had entered paradise itself through open gates. . . . This passage of Paul became to me a gate to heaven.

What Luther was saying there is that, as late as 1519, he was still experiencing acute difficulties – nothing short of terror – over the phrase and the reality of the 'righteousness of God' (*justitia Dei*), the perfect, unapproachable justice and justness of the Father that judged and condemned human beings such as he in all their sinfulness. However, and in that same year, he recalled, worrying away at Paul's text in Romans, he next discovered from it that the righteousness of God was in fact not His judgement that convicted but His mercy that forgave, a priceless gift of pardon that sinners receive in faith. So the problem for us is quite a tangled one of dating. For the words of Luther's 1515–16 commentary on Romans – if not that of the 1513–15 Psalms commentaries – indicates that much of the essence of the Reformation theology of justification by faith was already present in the Romans lectures, at least three years before his realisation of it dated to 1519.

What follows then is an exploration of what Luther discovered, and when he discovered it. First, lecturing in autumn 1515, on Romans 1: 8–9, he spoke of 'the faith by which you believe in Christ and also the faith that justifies'. Next, in commenting on 3:22–24 of the same epistle, Luther unfolded their meaning and in doing so brought out in concentrated form the basic lineaments of what was to become the Reformation doctrine of salvation. This was that justification comes to us solely by means of God's grace without 'good works', for the reason that our justification was won by Christ crucified, making redundant any attempt on our part to secure our justification by our own good deeds. It is, then, worth citing a key passage of Luther's Romans commentary, dating from the winter term of 1515–16, because the *basic* essence of the Reformation message is contained in it. Admittedly, subsequent and important refinements still needed to be made to Luther's full understanding of such matters as the nature of the faith that justifies and through which forgiveness is won. Indeed, these adjustments were made as Luther was constrained after 1517 to defend the fundamental positions on human and divine righteousness, justification, works, faith and Christ into which he had broken through in the Romans commentary. However, the outlines, and more than the outlines of the Luthero-Pauline theology of human acquittal of sin were evident in his commentary on Romans:

> as many as are justified, are not justified except freely, *by His*, God's *grace*, without merits or works. This grace is not given except *through the redemption which is in Christ Jesus*. By this grace He Himself [Christ] alone has redeemed those who were 'sold under sin' [made slaves to evil] . . . , making satisfaction for us and freeing us. . . . [O]ur place of propitiation is not won by our merits, but *in His*, Christ's, *blood*, that is, in His suffering, whereby He made satisfaction and merited propitiation for those who believe in Him. . . . His righteousness alone makes men righteous. . . . *He justifies*, through his grace . . . every man *who has faith . . . On what principle? On the principle of works?* No . . . *but on the principle of faith . . . a man is justified*, reckoned righteous before God, . . . *by faith, apart from works of the Law*.

Much needed to be added over the years, drawing out some of the fuller logical consequences of justification by faith, including divine pre-destination and the denial of human free will. However, it seems clear from his own notes that in those lectures of the middle of the second decade of the sixteenth century, Luther found the intellectual cornerstone of the Reformation, justification by faith. By 1516 he found it in those key texts in Romans 3:23–28 in which Paul set out as categorically as any writer could that all human beings are sinners who fall so far short of God's glory that they are made acceptable by God's grace only through the redemption won by Christ, who is our propitiation, whose righteousness alone makes men righteous. Thus there can be no credit in our good works and we are justified and made acceptable in God's sight by faith.

That still leaves the problem of reconciling Luther's dating of 1519 as the year of his release from his spiritual grief and depression as a result of his study of St Paul and our own perception that he was already teaching the basics of justification by faith in the Romans lectures. Assuming that Luther was not simply in error over the chronology, it may be that the problems of discrepant dating can be resolved partly through examining the contrasting tones of the passages in question. Thus in the lectures on the Epistle to the Romans Luther adopted the proper impersonal style of an instructor, technical and unemotional. He also dealt in broad categories of human beings: 'many . . . are justified . . . [Christ] alone has redeemed those who were "sold under sin", making satisfaction for us . . . He made satisfaction . . . for those who believe in Him. . . . His righteousness alone makes men righteous . . .' and so on. The categories are impersonal and almost abstract. In contrast, in his recollection of what happened to him in 1519, Luther wrote not only emotionally and passionately, but in a deeply personal and individual way. His words in the autobiographical fragment are not only taut and dramatic but also intensely individual. He used 'I' and 'me', the pronouns that recur 17 times in a paragraph of middle length in which he recalled the lifting of his anguish of mind. It may have been, then, that Luther did discover justification by faith twice, once in 1515–16, intellectually for his students, and again in 1519, experientially for himself.

LUTHER AND MYSTICISM

Such a deepening of interior perceptions may have been facilitated by a further instalment in Luther's self-education, his encounter with the German mystical tradition and its long-standing cultivation of the inner self. Luther approached that tradition, which exalted the deep non-rational aspects of our human nature, during a period of deep repugnance with the intellectualising methods of the Aristotelian legacy which he now decisively rejected.

Implied in Luther's understanding in the Romans lectures of how justification was won was an accelerating distancing from the Aristotelian academic legacy upheld by his own teachers, the Scholastics and Erfurt professors Jodocus Trutvetter (c.1460–1519) and Bartholomaeus Arnoldi, the latter known as Usingen (1465–1532). In the Romans lectures Luther rejected the Scholastic disciples of Aristotle, especially because of what he thought was their false position on works, faith and grace:

> [I]t is mere madness for them to say that a man of his own powers is able to love God above all things and to do the works of the law in substance . . . without grace. Fools! Theologians for swine!

Following a letter of February 1517 decrying the 'injurious blasphemer Aristotle', in May 1517 he wrote to a colleague in Erfurt to relate how in a battle of the curriculum he was waging in Wittenberg, Aristotle, the philosopher of reason, had to diminish as Augustine, the teacher of grace, increased in authority and importance. Next, just prior to issuing 97 theses of a 'Disputation against Scholastic Theology' of 4 September 1517, Luther ruthlessly launched personal attacks against his Aristotelian senior colleagues, calling upon them 'to give up their teaching, indeed stop publishing altogether. I have a full arsenal of arguments against all their teachings, which I now recognise as a waste of time.' These theses achieved the completion of the curricular revolution that Luther had steered at Wittenberg, dethroning Aristotle and his heirs, with their alleged confidence in the efficacy of ethics and good deeds – a human-centred false optimism which Luther's reading of Romans belied.

Within a couple of months, the storm over the 95 Theses would begin the process of catapulting Luther onto a European stage. Meanwhile, we need to take note of the significance of Luther's engagement with mysticism.

Germany, and in particular the Rhineland, was a centre for the flourishing of medieval Catholic mystical tradition, with its emphases on abandonment of self and on personal union of the adept with the Almighty. The great masters of the Rhineland mystical tradition, all members of the Dominican Order, were Johannes Eckhart (known as Meister Eckhart, *c.*1260–*c.*1327), Heinrich Suso (or Seuse, 1295 (1300?)–1366) and the Strassburg preacher Johann Tauler (c.1300–61). Luther felt especially drawn to the last-named, having been pointed by Staupitz in the direction of his sermons, which had been printed in 1508. Luther's approach to mysticism was Christ-centred, and Tauler seemed in particular to resonate to the so-called 'theology of the Cross' that Luther was evolving at around that time, made up of a focus on Christ's redemptive action but also on our need to share in its grief and agony. Luther was soon, in the 95 Theses of 1517, to decry the preachers of false optimism who assured their hearers that there was peace, when in point of fact there was no peace, not until the Cross had been undergone. Luther annotated Tauler's sermons along those lines: 'Thus we know that God does not act in us, unless he first destroys us by the cross and suffering'. Either late in 1515 or early in 1516, Luther came across an anonymous work in the medieval mystical tradition and proceeded to publish it in a first and incomplete version and as what was in fact his first publication. He saw in this work the strong influence of Tauler (who was in fact commended by name within the text), recommended it enthusiastically and gave it the title *Theologia Germanica* or *Theologia Deutsch*, the 'German Theology', a title that was chosen to show the vernacular simplicity of this German-language treatise. Luther returned to the 'German Theology' to publish the remainder of it in 1518. However, his link with this work, and through it to the medieval devotional and mystical tradition, took up a relatively brief period in his overall career and may even have been essentially alien to his main concerns. Within the period of his struggle with Scholasticism and its elaborate mental gymnastics, he seems to have turned to the mystical school, with their simplicity of expression and approach and their anti-intellectualism in their calls for the abnegation of pride in the mind and its achievements. He wrote of Tauler that he was ignored in the university faculties but in fact 'taught a more solid and sincere theology than is found in all the teachers of scholasticism in the universities'.

There, were, however, two reasons that Luther's link-up with mystical piety was relatively brief. The first concerned Scripture, the second the doctrine of salvation. It is significant that when Luther wrote his commendatory preface to the *German Theology*, he said that there was no better book than it – apart from Scripture and St Augustine. The message of God relayed to us through the Bible, rather than our access of the Almighty through mystical union, was to be Luther's route. He added the authority of Augustine to that of Scripture because he found in the 'teacher of grace' the theological formulae that would bring him assurance, comfort and conviction about his salvation. It can be said, then, that Luther had only passing acquaintance with the mystical tradition and was, rather, rapidly moving on to what were to be his real intellectual and spiritual preoccupations – his reliance on Scripture, and his doctrine of a redemption won independent of us, but for us, by Christ crucified.

The impressive range of Luther's responsibilities around the middle of the second decade of the sixteenth century included parochial duties, which he took up from spring 1514 onwards, and which involved him in preaching and ministering to lay people of Wittenberg. In the sermons he delivered in this role he vehemently denounced the abuses and corruption of those in high places in the state and the Church. We should, however, be wary of hearing in these early sermons Luther as the Church reformer he later became. True, he castigated the wrongdoings of Churchmen up to and including the papacy itself, but delivering such denunciations was an accepted duty of preachers as the watchdogs of the Church. Indeed Luther at that stage of his career could have been seen as one of a genera-tion of urban preachers, such as Eberlin von Günzburg (*c*.1470–1533), a popular preacher in Ulm and other cities, or the hugely influential reform-minded preacher of Strassburg, Johannes Geiler von Kayserberg (1445–1510). These were, in turn, part of a widespread culture of protest and complaint, much of it expressed in a vigorous sermon-culture, in pre-Reformation Germany.

One further intellectual interest Luther shared in the middle of that decade was in the case of Johann Reuchlin, Germany's leading Christian Hebraist, against whom a prosecution was mounted by a Jew converted to Christianity, the Dominican friar Johannes Pfefferkorn, in order to stop the study of extra-scriptural Hebrew literature. Starting up in 1510, the Reuchlin case has been widely regarded as a classic and protracted line-up between, on the one hand, liberals and humanists versus, on the other, Scholastics and conservatives, the latter led by the order that was to number among Luther's most determined foes in the years to come, the Scholastically oriented Dominicans. Luther learned Hebrew through a grammar of the language that Reuchlin had produced and in his lectures on the Psalms used Reuchlin's editions of the Hebrew texts of some of them. He certainly favoured the broadly progressive cause of humanist scholarship of which Reuchlin was the major champion in the specialist field of Hebrew studies. As we would expect, therefore, in his correspondence at the height of the Reuchlin affair, there is every sign of partisanship with 'the innocent and learned Reuchlin, our Reuchlin'. However, during that controversy there was no sign from Luther of his championing the non-scriptural Hebrew religious works, especially the Talmud and Kabbalah, whose study Reuchlin had set out to promote. At base, Luther had no real sympathy with Hebrew literature apart from Scripture. He spoke approvingly of Reuchlin probably because the latter's humanist approach denigrated Scholasticism and, no doubt, also because of who Reuchlin's foes were – conservative defenders of the ways of Scholasticism going back to the leading intellectual light of the Dominican order, the Aristotelian Aquinas.

Thus his comments on the Reuchlin case show Luther to have been aligned with the broadly humanist, as against the traditionalist and Scholastic, wings in the Church. Even so, at that point in his life he was indisputably Catholic and, indeed, firmly and passionately attached to the monastic way of life and the strict observance of his Rule, which was designed as a route to winning divine favour through a life dedicated to personal holiness and works of righteousness. This was in the devout traditions of the late medieval *devotio moderna* in which the German Augustinian Observance was born. Doubtless recognising his exemplary stature as a model of the Observance and pupil of Staupitz, in May 1516 his confrères voted him as district vicar of his order. He had eleven houses under his jurisdiction as visitor, and he showed himself to be a severe disciplinarian in pursuit of lax members who did not rise to the exacting standards of the Observance. Even so his emergent doctrine of salvation centring on the merits of Christ crucified had implications that called into question the programme of seeking God's favour by one's own good works that underlay the principles of the Observance as well as the whole programme of monasticism in general. In a letter of June 1516 he delivered the message that the peace that came from reconciliation with the Father flowed from the Cross of Christ and in the same letter he used phrases that were to be almost exactly reproduced in the conclusion to his 1517 95 Theses which were to begin the process of his alienation from monasticism and the Church:

> You say with Israel: 'Peace, peace', and there is no peace;
> Say rather with Christ, 'Cross, cross', and there is no cross.

Even more explicitly, he had written in April 1516 to the effect that either we gain God's favour through our goodness, and Christ did not need to suffer, or *vice-versa*, Christ suffered for us, removing the need for us to strive: 'For if by our own efforts we are to attain peace of conscience, why then did Christ die? Therefore thou wilt only find peace in him when thou despairest of self and thine own works.'

We may, then, establish, on the basis of the texts cited, that before the year 1516 was out Luther had already arrived at the basic intellectual and doctrinal positions from which he was to challenge 'works righteousness' as a route to salvation.

THE 95 THESES

The final months of the following year saw the end of Luther's quiet and busy life of study, prayer, administration, teaching and parish work in a German town and the beginning of his explosion onto the centre of the stage of secular and ecclesiastical politics, violent controversy and extreme danger. Even so, his denunciation of the papal indulgences hawked in Germany in 1517, which led directly to all the disputes and peril of the months and years that followed, can in fact be seen as proceeding naturally from the roles he had come to occupy up to that point in time. These were those of a university theologian – a guardian of the Church's correct doctrines – who also had pastoral responsibilities to 'the people' which required him to speak out to his ecclesiastical superiors up to the highest levels in his capacity as an accredited theological expert. As he later recalled:

> when in the year 1517 indulgences were sold . . . in these regions for
> most shameful gain – I was then a preacher, a young doctor of theology,
> so to speak – and I began to persuade the people to urge them not to
> listen to the clamours of the indulgence hawkers. . . . I certainly thought
> that in this case I should have a protector in the pope. . . .[2]

Luther was there recollecting the circumstances of the drawing up of
the 95 Theses which he delivered on 31 October 1517 and which led,
inexorably, it seems, to that whole phenomenon that we know as the
Reformation. The Theses had their origin in autumn 1517 as the agenda
for a university debate on a pressing theological issue and, as their caption
clearly indicated, this deliberation was to be primarily an academic one:
'the following theses will be publicly discussed at Wittenberg under the
chairmanship of the reverend father Martin Luther, Master of Arts and
Sacred Theology, and regularly appointed lecturer on these subjects at that
place.' It was Melanchthon who added a recollection to the effect that,
presumably in order to publicise the colloquium now being announced,
'These [Theses] he nailed up in public to the church that is near the
castle at Wittenberg on the day before the festival of All Saints in the year
1517. . . .'

Even so, the Theses were far from being the topics for an abstract and
abstruse university debate but were intended by their author to highlight
what he saw as an ecclesiastical abuse harming the laity, a wrong of which
the most senior members of the hierarchy must be made aware as a matter
of considerable urgency in order to rectify it. That was why the 95 Theses
had a double character and function, as captions for debate and also as a
letter to the episcopate – to the primate of Germany, Albrecht von
Hohenzollern (1490–1545), archbishop of Mainz – warning of a terrible
abuse of doctrine and practice within his jurisdiction and for whose suppression the Church's officialdom was responsible. Then, when the prelate
to whom they were addressed turned a deaf ear to the warning notice,
the highly adaptable 95 Theses underwent their third transformation
and became a public manifesto. This is how Luther himself recalled the
chain of events:

> I wrote two letters, one to Albrecht the archbishop of Mainz. . . .
> I begged [the prelates] to stop the shameless blasphemy of the
> quaestors [indulgence salesmen]. But the poor little brother [Luther]
> was despised. Despised, I published the *Theses*. . . .

The issue, then, could have been represented as one of abuse of practice: a variant of the financially motivated exploitation of credulity satirised so brilliantly by Erasmus as the age's leading critic of corruption in the Church. The indulgences being retailed in the German Lands by the Dominican Johann Tetzel (1465–1519) in 1517 would have made superb copy for a reform-minded satirist of the Erasmian school, for they represented a raid on the pockets of the pious sanctioned by, and indeed to the profit of, those – the archbishop of Mainz and the pope – who should have been the Church's most eager watchdogs against such crimes. As Luther himself told the tale:

> It became quite evident that Bishop Albrecht had hired this Tetzel because he was a great ranter; for he [Albrecht] was elected bishop of Mainz with the agreement that he was himself to buy . . . the pallium [woollen mantle worn by archbishops as a symbol of office] at Rome. For three bishops of Mainz . . . had recently died, one shortly after the other, so that it was perhaps difficult for the diocese to buy the pallium so often and in such quick succession, since it cost twenty-six [or] thirty thousand [gulden]. . . .
>
> Thus the bishop devised this scheme, hoping to pay the [banking firm of] the Fuggers (for they had advanced the money for the pallium) from the purse of the common man. And he sent this great fleecer of men's pockets [Tetzel] into the provinces. . . . And in addition the pope had a finger in the pie as well, because one half was to go towards the building of St Peter's Church in Rome.

There is little to add of substance to Luther's factual account, and the tone of cynical realism in which he recounted it suited the case perfectly. Hohenzollern, a nobleman of the ruling house of Brandenburg and with expensive aristocratic tastes but below the canonical age for the episcopate, had manoeuvred himself to acquire, in 1514, Germany's primatial see of Mainz, in addition to his existing holdings of the bishopric of Magdeburg and the lucrative administration of the see of Halberstadt. The arrangement was a blatant case of the grave ecclesiastical offence of pluralism and needed to be excused, by means of payment for a dispensation, by Rome in return for funds that Hohenzollern borrowed from Germany's best-known bank, the Fuggers of Augsburg. The bank had, of course, to be repaid, and the proceeds from the indulgence were the means to make that restitution, though the papacy would take 50 per cent of the proceeds, to go into the bottomless pit of expenditure on building the new basilica of St Peter's in Rome. The final element of corruption and abuse in the indulgence with which Luther took issue in autumn 1517 was in the way it was distributed: it was actually sold outright, according to a tariff of a purchaser's status, wealth and consequent ability to pay, and the 'salesman' was a disgrace, with his boast that his indulgence could cleanse the sin of rape of the Blessed Virgin Mary.

For the indulgence was about remedying offences, whether those were the ecclesiastical offence that Hohenzollern committed through his pluralism or the unimaginably serious kind of sin that Tetzel liked to depict. And in it was that issue, the doctrinal one of how sin was forgiven, that made this theologians' business, Luther's business. It rendered the matter suitable for a discussion, to be arranged, among professional theological experts. And from that point of view the abuses on the ground, up to and including Tetzel's carefully planned crudities, were far less important than the issue of principle: how were sins pardoned? As for 'abuse', Luther himself admitted that he was far from knowing the squalid, corruption-ridden details of the case at the time. This was because the secrecy of the bargain was limited to its participants – the pope, the archbishop, the banker. Luther wrote in 1541, 'I did not know at that time who would get the money', and repeated in an autobiographical fragment in 1545 that the financial irregularities 'were something I did not know at the time'. Indeed, these details only later confirmed the impression of a vice-laden institution that carried out cynical and corrupt actions, and they made good subsequent propaganda copy, but they were not the heart of the matter at the time. Luther's protest against the indulgence in 1517 went far beyond mere ecclesiastical abuse. Indeed, he had been denouncing these pardons on purely theological grounds for some time and had even risked the resentment of his patron the Elector Frederick the Wise by preaching against indulgences at the Castle in Wittenberg, where the Elector was a firm believer in indulgences and a spectacular collector of the holy relics that could accrue them. Luther had in fact preached against indulgences on three occasions in 1516, once on the very day of the month, 31 October, when he would speak out again with such vast consequences one year later.

So, if the issue was theological, then what was the theology, and, in particular, what was the applied, or pastoral, theology, of indulgences and how did it relate to, or collide with, justification by faith?

The long-term development of the concept of indulgences is inseparable from its close relatives, the sacrament of penance and the doctrine of purgatory, and this triplet of beliefs grew up together in the course of the Middle Ages. Within this conceptual cluster, sins were seen as being absolved in the sacrament of penance but 'satisfaction' still remained to be done to acquit the detritus of guilt for sin. If this satisfaction were not performed by the time of a person's death, then a period in a state or place called purgatory, a condition of intense, hellish, but only temporary pain, would be required in order to discharge that guilt. Indulgences were remissions of the guilt thus accruing to sins.

We may trace some of the key stages in the emergence of the notion of indulgences, paying special attention to the vital role of conflict with Islam, even before the end of the first millennium, in holding out papal guarantees of the payment of satisfaction as a reward for soldiering against the Muslims. By the time of the First Crusade, commencing in 1096, indulgence pardons could be applied posthumously to the credit of those who fought in such conflicts, and in the following century the benefits were extended from those who took part directly in the Crusades to those who contributed financially towards them. Indeed, what we may term the monetarisation of indulgences, which reached an outer limit with Tetzel's flagrant salesmanship in 1517, was already under way centuries earlier. The other overall trend to note was the ever-increasing extension of the applicability of indulgences, partly driven by the same kind of financial incentives that we have been tracing. In 1300, under Boniface VIII (pope 1294-1303), at the time of the initiation of the 'holy year' system of Roman jubilees (first every hundred, and eventually every 25 years) indulgences were offered to pilgrims to Rome, and a later extension delivered them to the faithful wherever they were.

Before the end of the fourteenth century, another pope, Boniface IX (pope 1389-1404), had defined indulgences as complete abrogations of guilt and penalty, and by 1476 the vital and sweeping step had been taken by Sixtus IV (pope 1471-84) of making the remissions fully applicable to the souls in purgatory, the place or state of post-mortem exoneration of guilt for sins whose existence was accepted by the Church Councils of Lyon (1274) and Florence (1439). An essential contribution was made to the theoretical underpinning of the practice by the thirteenth-century English theologian Alexander of Hales (c.1180-1245), who coined the concept of a 'treasury of merit', a quantum of virtue acquired by Christ Himself and by the saints, all of whose fruits could be applied by the pope as its custodian to make up the moral deficits of sinners. In 1343 in the bull *Unigenitus* Clement VI (pope 1342-52) proclaimed that Christ had endowed 'a treasure for the Church militant'. Alongside the acceptance of the view that indulgences were applicable to the souls in purgatory, all the pieces were in place for the kind of fully-fledged doctrinal and practical system of indulgences that Luther was to call into question in 1517 – not primarily on the grounds of financial malpractice – but on those of dubious pastoral theology.

It would be easy to attack the medieval doctrine of indulgences as a money-making racket, releasing people from the need for true repentance and offering false assurances of forgiveness in return for cash down. In point of fact, genuine penitence was essential within the long and complex process outlined, for it had to be an ingredient in the initial absolution in the sacrament of penance. At the same time, the system can be seen as operating a vast, benevolently-intentioned mutualist system of mercy in which the pope, as steward of the treasury of the merits of Christ and the saints, could be viewed as the dispenser of God's own compassion, transferring to the many the moral earnings of the few, releasing countless souls from hellish agony – surely the greatest of all 'works of mercy'.

The trouble was that the system had been allowed to develop along impersonal and formal lines, institutionalising forgiveness and taking too little account of an individual's role of contrition in achieving the final stage of absolution, satisfaction: the indulgence issued under Albrecht von Hohenzollern's endorsement in 1517 took this trend to an extreme point with the statement, 'Nor is it necessary for those who contribute to the fund for this purpose to be contrite or to confess.' What Luther was doing in the 95 Theses of 1517 was reasserting the need for contrition in every step of the way of forgiveness, including the final one. He was not the first to do so: in the middle of the previous century a fellow member of his Augustinian order had declared 'Repentance is better than indulgences'. Luther, then, could be seen as one of several voices calling for a simple return to an awareness of that need for repentance as a pre-condition of forgiveness. Therefore, we shall examine the 95 Theses – with all their mixed voices of hasty composition, satire, mockery, and even some silliness – under the overall caption of stress on the need for contrition throughout the whole process of winning God's forgiveness. They begin, as they continue to the end, on that keynote.

Their more immediate genesis was that the Dominican Tetzel, according to Luther,

> Went around with indulgences, selling grace for money as dearly or as cheaply as he could, to the best of his ability. At that time I was a preacher here in the monastery, and a fledgling doctor fervent and enthusiastic for Holy Scripture.

> Now when many people went from Wittenberg to Jütterbock
> [Jütterbog] and Zerbst [both outside the Elector's dominions] for indul-
> gences, and I did not know what the indulgences were . . . I began to
> preach very gently that one could probably do something better and
> more reliable than acquiring indulgences.

There is some mild deception, as well as some omission, in this account
from the autobiographical fragment. The ambiguous form of words, 'I
did not know what the indulgences were . . .' cannot, of course, mean,
'I did not know what indulgences were', and must therefore mean that
Luther was in ignorance about this particular indulgence, itself a slightly
implausible claim, given the extraordinary publicity surrounding and running ahead of Friar Tetzel. Even more unconvincing is Luther's depiction
of himself, a professor now of some years' standing and a senior member
of his order, as but 'a fledgling doctor'.

Omitted material, of which Luther cannot necessarily have been
fully cognisant, concerns a background of north-German princely rivalry
going back some years between the Brandenburg Hohenzollerns and the
Saxon Wettins, dynasties in rivalry for power, including the scramble for
ecclesiastical preferment, in the senior pecking-order of German princely
states. The Saxon Electors also had a long history, going back to the
fifteenth century, of keeping papal indulgences out of their territories,
or at least of demanding a hefty share of the proceeds of the sales arising
therefrom. Elector Frederick's own commitment to such an exclusion
order was intensified by his own legendary indulgence-accruing relic
collection, sedulously built up over the years from diplomatic presents
and collecting tours, and operating, in fact under papal franchise, as a
formidable indulgence dispensary, with its centrepieces a thorn from
the Crucified's crown along with one of the nails of His impaling. The
whole collection was calculated to be worth, on the right holy day, nearly
two million years of release from purgatory, and Frederick was not
about to permit a papal infringement of the assets of this papally endorsed
collection, so that Electoral Saxony, including Wittenberg, was declared
off limits to quaestor Tetzel. Thus, if Wittenbergers wished to buy the
prestigious and skilfully marketed Teztel indulgence, they would have
to leave princely territory and cross over into 'Jütterbock and Zerbst',
on the far side of the River Elbe.

We have deliberately used a language of commercial dealing for the
transactions being described here. Early sixteenth-century Germany
already possessed a sophisticated proto-capitalist commercial economy and

the distribution of the Tetzel indulgences, involving published prices, loan finance and sophisticated advertising techniques, belonged to the kind of world of marketing with which we are familiar today. To continue, then, with the retailing analogy, Luther's role in response to the indulgence was to expose the fact that, adroit advertising notwithstanding, the product itself was unsound, untrustworthy, in a word – his own – not 'reliable', but was instead deceptive, fooling people that they did not need to experience painful contrition to be forgiven, when they did.

So the 95 Theses, the fountainhead of the Reformation, is a portfolio promoting repentance. James Atkinson, indeed, helpfully subdivides the Theses into their subheadings – 1–4 on the New Testament doctrine of repentance; Theses 5–7 on the restricted scope of the Church's power to remit offences; Theses 8–29 on the pope's jurisdiction over purgatory; Theses 30–40 on the relationship between forgiveness and indulgences; Theses 41–52 on true good works versus the extravagance of the St Peter's project; Theses 53–80 on the opposition between indulgences and the gospel; the involvement of the pope, dealt with in Theses numbers 81–91; and a peroration on the theology of the Cross in the conclusion, Theses 92–5. However, over the whole 95 clauses, some are of greater significance than others. Some, indeed, seem almost flippant – for instance a discussion (Thesis 29) as to whether the souls in purgatory actually 'wish to be redeemed'. At the same time, minute consideration of the treasury of merit (56–62) and of speculations over such matters as whether the power of the pope suffices, by itself, for the remission of penalties (6) can seem legalistic. At various points, Luther's attempt to make himself the pope's spokesman against abuses for which the papacy was directly responsible – 'If the Pope knew the exactions of the preachers of Indulgences, he would rather have the basilica of St Peter reduced to ashes than built with the skin, flesh and bones of his sheep' (50) – can read unconvincingly. There is also considerable theological conservatism in the Theses, including an unquestioning acceptance of the doctrine of purgatory.

Even so, the 95 Theses caused a sensation throughout Germany when they were published. In November Luther sent copies of them to friends, and these seem to have been the origin of the printed versions that appeared in major cities before the close of the year. In Nuremberg a further breakthrough was made in turning the Theses into a public manifesto when their original Latin text was turned into a printed German version. The Nuremberg-born artist Albrecht Dürer (1471–1528) typified an enthusiastic response among large numbers of his fellow-Germans by sending Luther a set of woodcuts as a present in gratitude for the Theses.

How, though, do we really explain the positive popular response to the 95 Theses? The answer is that the Theses responded to the deep religious anxieties of many about sin and guilt, showing that forgiveness came about through genuine and individual repentance and the response that this would evoke from a merciful God when contrasted with the illusory security of indulgences. The 95 Theses formed Luther's first 'evangelical' public statement because they were based, from the very opening words in Thesis 1, on the doctrine of the Gospels, especially as revealed by the linguistic scholarship of Erasmus in his 1516 edition of the New Testament in its original Greek. In recovering the language of the original text, Erasmus's version exposed much of its basic meaning. In particular, he showed that the form in the Latin Vulgate of Christ's words in the Gospel (Matthew 3:2) *poenitentiam agere* – 'do penance' – were a mistranslation of the Greek rendition of Christ's instruction, *metanoiete* – 'transform yourselves', 'change your hearts'. Luther adopted this meaning to show in Thesis 1 that 'the whole life of the faithful should be repentance'. This opening clause then became the keynote for a thread running throughout the Theses, an insistence on repentance as a lifelong state of mind in which the penitent Christian has no presumption that his or her sins are wiped clean by any pardon conferred by anyone but God Himself. This theme recurs insistently throughout the 95 Theses. Thesis 21, for instance, states:

> Hence those preachers of Indulgences are wrong when they say that a man is absolved and saved from every penalty by the Pope's Indulgence.

Thesis 30 takes up the theme:

> No one is sure of the reality of his own contrition, much less of receiving plenary forgiveness.

Luther returned to this in Thesis 33:

> We must especially beware of those who say that the Papal pardons are that inestimable divine gift by which a man is reconciled to God.

Thus the truth of forgiveness to be won through contrition confronted the deception of indulgences:

Any Christian whatsoever who is truly repentant has, as his due, plenary remission from penalty and guilt, even without letters of indulgence.

(Thesis 36)

[Indulgences] are in truth least of all [value] comparable with the grace of God and the piety of the cross.

(Thesis 68)

Though he accorded indulgences some, minimal value, this faded into insignificance compared with 'the grace of God and the piety of the cross'. So Luther's critique of indulgences set out an alternative 'theology of the cross' according to which sinners were saved and pardoned by the expiating merits of Christ crucified, themselves sharing some of its anguish through their heartfelt contrition (whereas indulgences breathed a shallow and false peace and optimism). And so:

Away, then with those prophets who say to Christ's people, 'Peace, peace!' when there is no [true] peace.

(Thesis 92)

Christians should be exhorted to seek earnestly to to follow Christ, their head, through penalties, deaths, and hells.

(Thesis 94)

And let them thus be more confident of entering Heaven through many tribulations rather than through a false assurance of peace.

(Thesis 95)

Peace, though, was not to be Luther's lot in the months and years ahead.

4

FROM THE 95 THESES
TO THE LEIPZIG DISPUTATION,
1517–1519

THE SEQUEL TO THE 95 THESES

The 95 Theses were to springboard Martin Luther into a world of controversy and extreme peril over the next three years leading to his excommunication by the papacy in 1520 and his criminalisation in the Holy Roman Empire by the Diet of Worms in 1521. These were also the critical years in which Luther's role altered irretrievably from that of a would-be reformer of the Catholic Church to a declared foe of that institution, as it refused to heed his call to bring its beliefs and practice into line with the doctrines he had been uncovering in his lectures on the Psalms and the Epistle to the Romans.

In 1517, however, Luther was not yet the fully-fledged reformer of later years and the 95 Theses did not arise out of the doctrine of passive justification by faith alone as it was subsequently to be consolidated. Luther was aware that forgiveness came via 'the grace of God and the piety of the cross'. At the same time there was emphasis in the Theses on the responsibility of the individual to take charge of his or her being forgiven, on the sinner's struggle to be contrite. Thus the intellectual atmosphere of the 95 Theses was still suffused with insistence on the individual's indispensable repentance, to which God would respond in delivering His forgiveness: 'the whole life of the faithful should be repentance', as the first of the Theses said. In a subsequent period, and crucially in the course of a disputation in which he was engaged in Heidelberg in 1518, Luther was to make passive justification by faith the inspiration of his mounting critique of Catholicism and its ways.

For the time being, though, Luther was still emphatically a Catholic reformer, operating through the proper channels to suppress an abuse of doctrine and practice. In the period following the drawing up of the 95 Theses, we see him in the role of a kind of appellant with a grievance, bringing it to the attention of ever-widening circles of tribunals who might hear his case. He first launched his 'appeal' with his episcopal superiors, then began to take it before the bar of public opinion via the press; the papacy and its representatives soon became involved, along with his religious order, as well as academia. He also presented his case to be judged by the verdicts of the councils of the Church. He turned to his ruler, Elector Frederick (via Frederick's secretary-cum-chaplain, Georg Spalatin (1484–1545)), and then appealed to the whole ruling class of Germany, both in his pamphlet of 1520, the 'Address to the Christian Nobility of the German Nation Concerning the Reform of the Christian Estate' and in his personal appearance before the Diet and the Emperor at Worms in 1521. Finally, he was forced back on the jury of his own conscience, instructed by the word of God in the Bible.

In the very first phase Luther was appealing his case to his religious superiors in the German episcopate. On 31 October 1517 he sent the 95 Theses, possibly with an early version of what became a published 'Sermon on Indulgences and Grace' and with a deferential cover letter, to Archbishop Albrecht. In the letter he called on the prelate to withdraw from the indulgences his endorsement which Luther professed to believe was claimed 'certainly without your full awareness and consent, Most Reverend Father'. What we may term Luther's appeal to the episcopate continued to 5 November, when he sent another copy of the Theses to the diocesan responsible for his immediate area, Hieronymus Schulze, bishop of Brandenburg, who was initially sympathetic to their contents. Luther followed it up in February of the following year with a letter to Bishop Schulze which portrayed its sender as a hesitant scholar reluctantly prevailed upon by others to invite learned men to take part in a quiet discussion on an issue of the 'new and unprecedented doctrines' of indulgences. This was a matter, though, that would in the end have to remain in the care of 'holy church to determine'. Yet even while these apparently modest addresses were being made, Luther's appeal was being broadened out in a wider dimension altogether, that of public opinion, as the Theses were run off presses and made available in German and Latin versions, projecting Luther into a nation-wide literary controversy of which he was to show himself a master. He also consolidated his published output with the best-selling 'Sermon on Indulgences and Grace' of February 1518.[1]

Whether or not, as he professed in letters of March and April 1518, he was genuinely distressed at the process – 'causing me regrets . . . not pleased with [the Theses'] wide dissemination . . . forced to prepare proofs' – he was being inexorably caught up in a media campaign. Tetzel, awarded an honorary doctorate in January, marked the occasion by publishing a defence of indulgences in a set of theses ghost-written for him. These offered a critical commentary on and rebuttal of the clauses of Luther's original; they restated the need for contrition within the sacrament of penance, but they also confidently reaffirmed the function of indulgences in discharging penalties imposed on sins after they had been forgiven.

In the new year as excitement over his case mounted, Luther began preparing his 'Resolutions Concerning [or Explanation of] the Ninety-Five These'. His 'appeal' was inescapably becoming involved with the media and public opinion. In March he reported that the redoubtable disputant Johannes Maier von Eck, whom he described as a 'man of signal and talented learning and learned talent', had, in a set of observations on the 95 Theses entitled 'Obelisks', openly denounced him as a heretic – a disciple, in fact, of the early fifteenth-century Czech dissident John Hus, executed by the Church in 1415. In his own reply, 'Asterisks', Luther vilified Eck as a sterile Scholastic bereft of Scripture.

While Luther was thus extending the range and deepening the intensity of the debate over indulgences, the Church's authorities moved onto the offensive against him. In an initial response to the 95 Theses, von Hohenzollern opened what was known as an 'inhibitory', or silencing, process against the 'presumptuous' Luther. However, the Theses did raise the issue of principle of the ultimate authority that the pope in Rome claimed from Christ to issue indulgences, and so the papacy had to be involved in the matter. Thus in December 1517 the archbishop sent the incriminating Luther file, consisting of the 95 Theses, the earlier 97 Theses against Scholastic theology and other materials to Rome, where Pope Leo X (pope 1513–21) actually read the 95 Theses. It was next decided in Rome that the appropriate vehicle for controlling the protester was his own Augustinian order, whose superior, Gabriele della Volta (1468–1537), sent instructions to Staupitz to bring the errant friar to book.

THE HEIDELBERG DISPUTATION, 1518

On 11 April 1518 Luther set off from Wittenberg to begin walking the many miles to the south-west in order to attend the triennial German chapter of the Augustinian Order to be held in Heidelberg in the Rhineland Palatinate: officially he was on academic business concerned with one of his students who was due to advance at Heidelberg theological disputation theses drawn up by Luther himself. This was the first time since the outbreak of the crisis in the previous autumn that real danger stared out at him, away from the safe confines of Wittenberg, so Elector Frederick prudently arranged for various local authorities to guard him en route. One danger was that Luther had made an enemy of Tetzel's powerful Dominican order, whose members were boasting, with all-too-menacing black humour, that they would very soon have the Augustinian burned to death, the standard penalty for heresy. There was one other further possible source of danger pointed out to Luther at Heidelberg. In March, it seems, Staupitz was warning of rumours that Luther was calling for the abolition of much-loved devotions including the Rosary, the chain of prayer offered to the Virgin Mary. So it was, clearly, with some awareness of the threat that Luther's emerging doctrinal system posed to such beloved features of popular piety that a member of the Augustinian chapter in Heidelberg awoke laughter by calling out to Luther, 'If the peasants heard this [Luther's religious outlook], they'd stone you to death.'

However, there were no peasants (though there were distinguished local lay people) at the Heidelberg gathering of April–May 1518, but members of Luther's own order, sympathetic to the cause of a confrère under attack from a rival order, the Dominicans. The theological viewpoint which he presented in the Heidelberg theses certainly had its resonances with that of the reputed founder of the order, St Augustine, echoing Augustine's overall stress on human sin and its corrective, grace. The Heidelberg meeting also involved a career move for Luther when he was released from his position as district vicar, a step that may be seen as the beginning of a process of loosening his moorings with the religious life, which was to culminate in his final abandonment of the monastic habit in 1524. The lightening of his administrative load certainly freed him to become increasingly, though far from solely, preoccupied in 1518 with his public role as a disputant.

However, the Heidelberg convention's real importance for Luther lay in its allowing him to explore further the positive spirituality behind the more negative onslaught against indulgences (and, once more, against Aristotle) and to shift the ground to a discussion of grace. Theological implications arising out of justification by faith included a categorical denial of free will and a bold statement from Luther that anyone believing that he or she could acquire grace through his or her own resources actually committed sin. However, the even deeper significance of Heidelberg was that it permitted Luther, still under the influence of the medieval mystical movement that encouraged him to republish the *Theologia Deutsch* in this year, to wed himself and his protest to the theology of the Cross: 'the visible and manifest things of God seen through suffering and the cross'. Thus the closing words of the 95 Theses concerning entry to heaven, 'through many tribulations rather than through a false assurance of peace', were enfolded within this Cross-centred spirituality, which discounted indulgences as part of an illusory 'theology of glory' and of false assurances. Through grieving for sin, the truly repentant sinner, penitent throughout a lifetime, shares the sufferings of the Cross. Luther contrasted the weakness and even the folly of God (based on that idea explored in St Paul's first Epistle to the Corinthians, 1:25), who may be hidden and withdrawn but can in fact be found and recognised in the 'humility and shame of the cross', with the false human wisdom and righteousness of vainly seeking to win salvation by observing God's law. Divine grace, not human striving in attempted obedience to the law, accomplishes all: 'The law says "Do this" and it is never done. Grace says "Believe this" and it is already done.' Luther received a polite and even partly approving reception at Heidelberg for this kind of spirituality which had deep medieval roots in the Augustinian order, even though the chapter in its official proceedings could hardly give an open rebel against the Holy See any public endorsement. He made an important, and utterly dazzled, convert to his emergent cause in the person of a young Augustinian, the future religious reformer of the city of Strassburg, Martin Bützer (or Bucer, 1491–1551), who seems at that stage to have seen Luther as a kind of radical Erasmus. And, despite the earlier death-threats, instead of encountering danger, he was fêted as a celebrity in Heidelberg and received with every kindness by one of the ruling family of the Palatinate. Understandably, when Luther arrived, by 15 May, back in Wittenberg (after stopping off at the University of Erfurt where he vainly attempted peace-making with his conservative-minded tutor Trutvetter), he was encouraged and buoyed-up.

The month of May 1518 saw further progress with his defence of the 95 Theses, the 'Resolutions Concerning the 95 Theses'. He sent these to

Bishop Schulze, who delayed attending to them but eventually sent them back to Luther, with a warning not to issue them. Luther next sent these 'Resolutions' to Leo X, with a cover letter dated at the end of May complaining about the excesses of the indulgence salesmen and boldly shifting onto them the imputation of heresy which, he said, was falsely being cast at him. He aimed, he wrote, to publish this defence of the 95 Theses under papal protection in order to deflect the malice of his foes and he protested his loyalty to the holy father, whose words he would recognise as Christ's. While he thus boldly raised the level of his ongoing 'appeal', directing it to the Holy See itself, in the spring of 1518 Luther also addressed to Staupitz a cover letter to the 'Resolutions' in which he further developed his stance on the 'inner transformation of the mind' contained within the Greek New Testament noun meaning repentance, *metanoia*. This was also a 'Pauline' notion for it dispensed with works and external actions – above all *doing* penance – in favour of a state of consciousness and of being, that of deep sorrow for sin.

Whether or not we see Luther's May 1518 letter to Pope Leo as ingenuous – or even impertinent – it made no difference to the progress of a Roman anti-Luther counter-offensive. This papal campaign launched in 1518 had two instalments: one in Rome itself and the other, by a kind of transfer of jurisdiction, within Germany, at Augsburg.

Luther recalled the inception of the Roman offensive against him, in the way that 'Sylvester, the master of the sacred palace, came into the arena fulminating against me with [a] syllogism' – a philosophic formula, one in this case which underlined the absolute infallibility of the Roman Church and the heresy of casting doubt on just one of its words or actions. Indeed, once it had become evident to the papal court, the Curia, that the attempt to muzzle Luther using the structures of the Augustinian order had failed, then the Dominican theologian and student of the system of Thomas Aquinas known as 'Thomism', Sylvester Mazzolini Prierias (1456–1523), who held the office of master of the sacred palace, provided, in his 1518 'Dialogue', the doctrinal materials for a prosecution whose legal conduct was in the hands of the senior official known as the general auditor of the Curia, Girolamo Ghinucci (1480–1541). Prierias's 'Dialogue' did, indeed, as Luther recalled, take a high line on papal authority and, indeed, infallibility. On the basis of this study by Prierias, which made an accusation of heresy against anyone who denied the pope's authority to issue indulgences, Ghinucci issued a summons, which came to Luther in early August, to appear for trial in Rome within two months of receipt. Luther, taking refuge in an appeal, via Spalatin, for the Elector Frederick to intervene, riposted with a brief work, the 'Reply to Prierias', on the fallibility of the institutions of the Church and with a message of contempt for the master of the sacred palace – and for Prierias's hero Aquinas. He could perhaps afford such scorn since, protected as he was by the Elector, and, more broadly, by much of German opinion, the papal summons commanded his obedience insofar as he was willing to obey, and, of course, he was not.

PROCEEDINGS AT AUGSBURG, 1518

If Rome could not effectively conduct a direct case against Luther at a distance from Germany, the solution adopted was that of transferring it to within the German Lands, to be conducted there by another high-ranking Dominican – and Thomist theologian – the Italian Cardinal Tommaso di Vio, known as Cajetan (1468–1534), the papal legate to Germany and to its Diet meeting at Augsburg in southern Germany. It was the last such meeting to be held in the reign of the Emperor Maximilian (1459–1519), within the last months of his life. Cajetan's primary mission to Germany – an overwhelmingly unsuccessful one, in the event – was to secure from the Diet a massive cash grant in support of the campaign by Pope Leo X to raise an anti-Turkish crusade. Cajetan's secondary instructions were to bring Luther to heel.

It is worth exploring the transactions Cajetan initiated at Augsburg in a little detail since they constituted a major hiatus in Luther's career – a face-to-face confrontation with the institutional Church in the person of one of its senior official representatives and culminating in a violent breach between Luther and the Roman Church.[2] In that sense, Luther's meeting with Cardinal Cajetan in autumn 1518 was of even greater significance than the 95 Theses of the previous autumn, and deserves recognition accordingly. The talks saw Luther calling into question the received intellectual traditions of the Catholic Church, undermining the office of the pope as the Church's chief pardoner and subversively placing ecclesiastical authority in opposition to that of Scripture. Above all, the adversarial interpersonal chemistry of the meetings, the sharp collision of two strong characters, each convinced of the rightness of his own stance, helped cast Luther in the role, not now of loyal monitor to the Church, but of defiant, and perhaps insolent, rebel against it. In subsequently publishing his own account of the proceedings, the *Acta Augustana*, or 'Proceedings at Augsburg', Luther took the decision to make this rupture common media property, offering his version at the bar of public opinion in his ongoing appeal to that arbitration, through the press. And it is important to realise that this was a rift with the Church itself, for Cajetan's legatine office constituted him not as one more disputant on the side of orthodoxy but as the commissioned voice of the pope himself. Thus, late in August, Leo sent Cajetan his instructions. They were thought by some to be of unusual – if not illegal – severity, requiring the cardinal to bring Luther to Augsburg, to give him a hearing, and demand his recantation. If that were forthcoming, the legate was to reunite the penitent fully to the Church and, if it were not, he was to either send him as a prisoner to Rome or place him and his sympathisers under the ecclesiastical sanction known as the ban. At the same time, Rome's instructions to Cajetan were accompanied by a general papal call on the German ruling authorities to seize the dissident (on pain of withdrawal of spiritual services – an interdict) and by a communication from the Augustinian head, della Volta, to the regional superior of the order in southern Germany, Gerhard Hecker (or Hicker), to arrest Friar Martin and, melodramatically enough, bind him in chains as an apprehended criminal.

Rome, then, had by now, clearly, decided to treat the errant Augustinian as a malefactor needing summary treatment in order simply to silence him. Even so, there was an air of unreality about this string of orders, showing, for one thing, how ill the Curia understood Germany and its mood at that point in time. In particular, there was a weight of long-standing German nationalist resentment, voiced by a long series of diets – including this one – of Rome and its incursions in national affairs, as well as German sensitivity on the whole issue of legal due process. Against that political backdrop, the idea of simply lifting Luther at Augsburg for unimpeded transfer to Rome was bizarre. Cajetan, then, was given impossible instructions. An arrest was out of the question politically, and legally too, since Frederick the Wise, again concerned for Luther's safety, took precautions to secure in advance a safe conduct from a reluctant Emperor Maximilian, himself a determined foe of Luther.

Frederick's further constructive backstairs role was that of meeting Cajetan late in August and persuading him to tone down the action *vis-à-vis* Luther, from a punitive and disciplinary action to the 'fatherly' hearing of a petition. Then on 11 September Cajetan received revised instructions from Rome setting out an agenda for a hearing rather than a sentence (though disputation was precluded). Yet if suppression of Luther through arrest was thus out of the question, because Germans, and above all the crucially important Elector, were not prepared to let that happen, neither was the possibility of reconciliation through negotiation high. Cajetan was not endeared to Luther's contemptuous 'Reply to Prierias', or to a satirical work by Luther on excommunication procedures entitled the 'Sermon on the Ban'. In addition, the delayed appearance of Luther's 'Resolutions Concerning the 95 Theses' set out an enlarged and obdurate defence of the original position of 31 October of the previous year, counter-attacked the Tetzel anti-theses and poured fresh derision on such cherished Catholic beliefs as that of the 'keys' by which, though Christ's authority, the pope issued pardons to the living and the departed.

Thus the Augsburg conversations were not well omened for a positive outcome or for any resolution of what was becoming a crisis between Rome and much of Germany. Following one of the epic walks of his career, though with his expenses paid by the Elector, with a passport through the Electorate and letters in his support from Wittenberg University, Luther arrived in Augsburg on 7 October, to await his imperial safe conduct. He was exhausted and suffering with stomach pains which arose, no doubt, from nerves, or even from fear provoked by dire warnings offered him en route of a burning for heresy: he told himself, 'Now I must die.' Yet the situation was not quite as desperate as that. Though hot-tempered for an ambassador, the man he was to meet, Cajetan, was a scholar, an earnest reformer of clerical morals, and an early exponent, indeed, of sixteenth-century Catholic reform. A cardinal and curial insider and diplomat, he was the most elevated person Luther had ever met up to that point in time and Luther, providing for Spalatin an account of the preparations for the discussion, referred respectfully to him as 'the very reverend cardinal legate' who 'promises to treat me with all clemency'.

Even so, Luther had learned from some unattributed source that Cajetan was 'inwardly enraged at me, no matter what he may outwardly pretend': perhaps the cardinal was 'preparing some treachery'. As we have seen already, the proceedings at Augsburg were to form a key stage in Luther's alienation from the Catholic Church and we can now see that what was to be their negative outcome was partly anticipated by Luther's prior suspicion and terror of being caught unawares. This fear was, in turn, fostered by an attitude, that Luther fully shared, of German prejudice against Cajetan's nation, an anti-Italian outlook fed by German Renaissance humanists such as Conrad Celtis (1459–1508). According to some of the national-character stereotypes prevailing at that time, Germans – as long before characterised by the Roman historian Tacitus (c.55–120) in his *Germania* – were a kind of early species of noble savage, fond of drink, admittedly, rough at the edges, insufficiently civilised, perhaps easily duped, but all in all honest, brave and straightforward. Italians, on the other hand, were widely stereotyped as smooth, polished and essentially untrustworthy deceivers. Luther fully evinced a latent phobia against Italians which, as we shall see in Chapter 9, exploded into deranged anti-Italian tirades in his writing in the 1540s. The Italian Cajetan, he was convinced at Augsburg, was almost certainly 'preparing some treachery', so the prospects for the success of the talks were not helped by the latent attitude of prejudice and mistrust that Luther took to his meeting with the cardinal. Such mistrust was not at all dispelled by an intervention on the part of an Italian professional diplomat, Urban de Serralonga, who tried to intervene in the preliminaries to the talks between the cardinal and the friar. Serralonga was cynical about doctrine, realistic about money, worldly and 'suave'. In other words, for Luther 'he is an Italian and an Italian he will remain'. The Augsburg talks were to take place, then, over their three days, in an atmosphere of fundamental suspicion and prejudice on the part of one of the parties involved, so that one factor conducive to the success of all negotiations – acceptance of the integrity of one's interlocutor – was missing.

Even so, Cajetan was, after all, a cardinal of the Roman Church and therefore deserved every sign of respect. If anything, when the talks opened Luther over-reacted to this exigency by throwing himself on his face before the cardinal, initiating the detectable atmosphere of farce that increasingly characterised the Augsburg proceedings, above all on their final day. Initially, however, this flattering obeisance was well received by Cajetan, who responded by paying compliments to the professor's learning. However, if Cajetan interpreted Luther's exaggerated body language to mean intellectual surrender, he was seriously misguided. Luther took up the story in a letter he sent to Spalatin intended to update the Elector on the events taking place in Augsburg. There were three meetings in all, on 12, 13 and 14 October. Even before the interviews began, one substantive issue had already been raised in the talk with de Serralonga – the authority of St Thomas Aquinas, forming a stubborn obstacle to agreement between the German professor and the Italian emissaries: Serralonga 'cherished the opinions of Aquinas'. That issue of the status of Aquinas returned to mar the talks between Luther and Cajetan. The cardinal was a leading light in the sixteenth-century revival of the authority of Aquinas within Catholic thought, and had even altered his Christian name in honour of St Thomas. According to Luther, he simply 'trotted out and retold' only 'the teaching of St Thomas' – just as later in the interchanges he opened up a 'long-winded discourse drawn from the fairy stories of St Thomas'.

However, the issue of the authority of that principal pillar of the Dominican Scholastic tradition was related in these interchanges to the other dominant issue of authority, that of the papacy. As far as Cajetan was concerned, the pope's claims, specifically those set out in Clement VI's 1343 bull, or decretal, on the subject of indulgences and the treasury of merit, *Unigenitus* (also known as *Extravagante*) was simply incontrovertible, so that Luther had no option but to recant in face of it.

And there matters stood: Cajetan insisting on recantation, future silence from Luther on the issues and overall good behaviour; Luther refusing even a 'syllable' of retraction. On 13 October Luther, accompanied by Staupitz and members of the Elector's government, reappeared before Cajetan to read out a discussion paper affirming his essential orthodoxy and his claims to authority based on Scripture and proposing another level of appeal – one to senior northern European universities. It was on the third and final day, the 14th, of the talks that matters broke down, into a shouting-match, in fact. Luther came this time, again with representatives of his prince, to offer specific clarification of his doctrines of justification and the sacraments, as well as on the authority of the papacy and of councils, on the Church's authority and on that of Scripture.

Cajetan's exasperation was now mounting, perhaps understandably. Instead of returning, as was originally, if over-optimistically, envisaged, to a Catholic base, on the specific question of indulgences, Luther was steadily broadening out the range of discussion and debate to take in the highest questions, even those of the very nature and composition of the Church. In addition, by invoking wider university participation, the friar was implicitly calling into question the cardinal's own jurisdiction to resolve the case. Cajetan, Luther reported, now 'relied on the force of his language and shouting. . . . Eventually I began to shout too.' The written statement produced by Luther in the second meeting, on the 13th, was dismissively brushed aside by Cajetan and, in response, Luther himself abandoned all the deference he had shown to his person at the first meeting. From the start a clear added subtext of personal antagonism between these two men helped ensure the utter failure of the Augsburg talks to secure any return of Luther to the fold of the Church. The cardinal legate had been specifically forbidden by Rome to allow these sessions to be debates at all, but only acts of retraction on Luther's part. Some discussion was, clearly, always hard to avoid, and in the final session it returned to the subject of the bull *Unigenitus* – involving a technical coverage of the exact meaning of a key verb in the bull. This linguistic discussion of grammar and vocabulary had the effect of arousing once more in Luther his edgy mixture of nationalist intellectual and educational defensiveness and aggression towards suspected Italian claims to literary and cultural superiority: 'Let your Reverence not imagine we Germans are also deficient in grammar.' However, this clumsy chauvinist outburst may also have represented an attempt to break out of an impasse of fundamental divergence of views about the substantive issues. Cajetan's interpretation of the treasury of merit in *Unigenitus* was unimpeachable if one accepted the underlying assumptions about the nature of pardon which were embedded in the bull and which Cajetan upheld, while Luther had come to question them. Discussion about the incidental phrasing of *Unigenitus* was little to the point, for Cajetan, well within his Church's late medieval tradition, believed that pardons in the form of indulgences could be dispensed by the pope's transfers to sinners of moral surpluses and credits out of the treasury of merits. Luther, in contrast, had already reiterated the conviction set out in the 95 Theses to the effect that, from first to last, pardon for sins (as opposed to minor ecclesiastical disciplinary infringements) was effected only by God and involved, of absolute necessity, the sinner's constant and heartfelt individual contrition.

So in the end Luther, after the talk of taking his case around some of the leading university theology faculties, had, in effect, to reject *Unigenitus* – 'a single obscure and ambiguous decretal of a human pope' – because he repudiated its underlying assumptions. Further, he now set those assumptions at loggerheads against his now firmly established norm of truth, 'so many and such clear testimonies of divine Scripture' which gave the lie to the bull and to the presuppositions on which it rested. In doing so, Luther had already announced the position on Scripture as the sole reliable source of religious truth that he was to take at the Diet of Worms, in the spring of 1521. The Augsburg meetings moved then towards their failed and angry conclusion, with Cajetan ordering Luther out and warning him never to return to his presence, unless with a revocation in his mouth.

A further late involvement in the Augsburg discussions was that of von Staupitz, who, along with the Augustinian confrère Wenzel Link (1483–1547), had accompanied Luther to the city in order to provide moral support and who was present during the interchanges with the cardinal. Staupitz had considerable sympathy with Luther's spiritual theology, which he had indeed himself helped generate. However, he was not a natural rebel against the Church and was therefore susceptible in a conversation on the evening of the final day of the talks to what Luther called Cajetan's 'flattery' to bring about, in an oblique way, a recantation. Luther recorded that Staupitz confessed to the cardinal 'that he had urged [Luther], and was still urging [him] today, to submit humbly to the Church'. However, Staupitz also made it clear that in his view it was Cajetan's, not his own, task to extract a recantation from Luther. His other contribution, made for reasons not entirely clear – but presumably to protect his protégé from undue pressure from within the Augustinian order – was to release him from his monastic vows. Later in life, Luther professed to see this action as almost a kind of betrayal – the first in a series of 'excommunications' he underwent. It was certainly a major step in the progressive severance of Martin Luther from his monastic profession, an eventual estrangement that was inherently inevitable as a logical outcome of acceptance of justification by faith, without the entire programme and life of good deeds on which the whole edifice of monasticism rested.

Luther waited some days for a possible fourth hearing with Cardinal Cajetan and on 16 October sent a new appeal to the pope, refusing the earlier citation to Rome as being far too dangerous for him to undertake. On the following day he wrote to Cajetan a respectful letter that was clearly intended to restore some civility to the over-heated atmosphere that had arisen between the two men: 'Very Reverend Father in Christ, I come again, not personally, but in writing; deign to hear me mercifully.' Staupitz, he wrote, had set out to make the peace, and Luther had come round to realising that he had been 'too bitter and too irreverent to the name of the pope. . . . I am most sincerely sorry and ask pardon. . . .' This was as gracious an apology for intemperance as anyone might desire, but it also clothed an immovable position on the matter of substance: Luther told Cajetan in this letter that he was not in any way convinced by the Thomist arguments adduced to him, and his conscience simply could and would not allow him to recant. The case should now be referred back to the pope in Rome. However, if Luther thought that papal Rome would be too threatening for him to visit in person, he now heard from local supporters that Augsburg itself might also be dangerous for him, the cardinal's silence perhaps suggesting preparations for an arrest. So in one of the heart-stopping adventures that sprinkled that part of his life, he galloped on horseback out of a rear gate in the city walls in the middle of the night of 20–21 October, travelling in pain and exhaustion via Nuremberg. There, as in Augsburg, he was made aware of his popularity among German burghers, but was also shown the documentary evidence of the scale and danger of the Roman campaign against him. He arrived back in Wittenberg just in time to see in the first anniversary of the publication of the 95 Theses, after a year that had turned him around from appellant to heretic. His published account of the proceedings, the *Acta Augustana*, also opened up a wider offensive front by closely scrutinising, on grounds of ecclesiastical history, the papacy's claim to authority: this, Luther now insisted, was a novelty, unknown to the Church in its earlier, purer days, and likewise unaccepted by the Christian Church beyond the immediate Roman obedience.

LUTHER, GERMAN POLITICS AND ROME, 1518

In the subsequent period, Luther's case was to become caught up more and more in German imperial politics and especially the centrality of Saxony and its Elector in those political machinations. In turn, the internal manoeuvres of German politics in the closing years of the second decade of the sixteenth century were influenced by the dynastic and international situation, with which the papacy was deeply concerned.[3]

As a result of a shrewdly pursued long-term dynastic policy, the Austrian house of Habsburg had by the early sixteenth century built up an extraordinary emergent ascendancy within the European state system. The Latin motto coined to describe this policy can be roughly translated into English as 'Other royal families pursue their goals through war; you, lucky Habsburgs [*felix Austria*], are able to achieve the same results though marriage'. It was, indeed, basically as a consequence of match-making that Charles of Habsburg, the heir to the family fortune by 1518, stood on the cusp of a European hegemony greater than any seen since the days of Charlemagne in the eighth and ninth centuries – or even those of the Caesars themselves in the heyday of the Roman Empire. In the first place, through the marriage of the Holy Roman Emperor Maximilian to Mary, heiress of Charles Duke of Burgundy, their son, Philip known as the Fair, or Handsome (1494–1506), was heir to the Burgundian possessions in the Low Countries which made up what are today Belgium and Holland, at that time the economic, commercial and industrial power-house of northern Europe. A further astutely contrived dynastic marriage between Philip of Burgundy and Juana of Castile, the daughter of Ferdinand and Isabella, joint sovereigns of the major kingdoms of the Spanish peninsula, brought to the son of the Spanish–Burgundian marriage, Charles of Habsburg, born in Ghent in Flanders in 1500, the legacy of the militarily formidable and expansive Spanish realms, with a global empire in the Americas now being opened up and developed and the real possibility of a European and world empire. The deaths of his father Philip in 1506 and of his grandfather Ferdinand in 1516 realised for Charles his western inheritance, Spain, its empire, and the Netherlands.

In his last months, Maximilian schemed for his grandson also to secure all of the eastern property that fell to his due. The hereditary Austrian and Tyrolean lands from which the Habsburg dynasty had long before come belonged to Charles by indisputable right. However, Maximilian sought also the title, largely decorative yet potentially weighty in the hands of one already powerful, of Holy Roman Emperor. To this dignity, though it was elective, the Habsburgs had in the course of the fifteenth century secured, by custom and precedent, a kind of claim of right to election. Maximilian spent his last months of life attempting to fix in advance a commitment on the part of the empire's seven imperial Electors to vote his grandson into his office, once by death he had vacated it.

This steady build-up of existing and prospective Habsburg territorial and titular might inspired fear in some quarters because it threatened existing balances of power between European states. The French, for example, had every reason to be alarmed at the aggrandisement of Habsburg strength on their Rhineland, Flemish and Pyrenean borders. However, no European polity had as much cause to dread the further build-up of the Habsburg edifice as did the Holy See. As so much of the history of the Middle Ages had shown, powerful German emperors were bad news for the papacy, and Charles threatened to be a very powerful emperor indeed. In terms of political symbols, the claim of the emperor's office to be 'holy', to be exercised directly by God's right and favour, were too close for comfort to the pope's own title to possess a numinous authority. However, more practical anxieties concerned the popes' rule of an Italian state, the Papal States, forming a girdle across central Italy. Through earlier conquests which had secured his Spanish grandfather Ferdinand's claims to the kingdoms of Naples and Sicily, Charles, by the time of Ferdinand's death, was already master of much of Italy south of Rome itself. The imperial crown would further endow him with claims to the rich and extensive northern Italian duchy of Milan as an imperial feudal possession, or fief. There was thus every prospect that the papacy, ground between Habsburg millstones to north and south, would lose its freedom and independence, both politically in Italy and even spiritually in the Church, and finish as little more than a Habsburg chaplaincy.

As occupant and steward of the Holy See, Leo X had thus to do everything in his power – cultivate every ally, nourish every Habsburg foe – to head off the ultimate conferment of dynastic power and prestige on

Charles of Burgundy and Spain: the imperial title and succession. The canny Maximilian had more or less built his final electoral majority to guarantee the reversion of the imperial office to his grandson, though there were two votes unspoken for, the prince-archbishop of Trier – and the Elector Frederick the Wise. Charles of Habsburg apart, there were other young European sovereigns anxious to advertise their magnificence by strutting an imperial stage. Francis I of France was objectionable as representing what many Germans perceived to be the national enemy and Henry VIII of England must always have been a long shot. In contrast to these, as well as to the Flemish-born, French-speaking cosmopolitan Charles, Frederick, as well as being irreproachably German, was also recognised for a certain cautious good sense: 'the Wise'. His modest territorial power within Germany made him an unthreatening prospect. The Saxon Elector was the favourite – and above all the papacy's favourite – 'stop-Habsburg' candidate of the hour. Potentially, in the months surrounding Maximilian's death in January 1519, Luther faced great danger. However, the fact that Rome was cultivating and flattering his patron and protector was his life insurance policy.

Yet Rome did not renounce its vendetta against the Wittenberg professor: he was too dangerous for that. As part of the process of mopping up after the Augsburg debacle, on 25 October Cajetan produced a report on the Luther case which was then, on 9 November, incorporated into a new papal decretal. This restated the doctrine of pardons which Luther had questioned, reaffirmed the validity of *Unigenitus* and threatened Luther with excommunication if he persisted in questioning Clement VI's bull, as he had. Also following the breakdown of the Augsburg dialogue, Cajetan wrote to the Elector an abrupt letter, which was shown to Luther, requiring him to seize the friar and send him to Rome. Frederick's reply to the cardinal in December to the effect that scholars had advised him that his professor's doctrines were unacceptable only to those whose financial interests were assailed by them represented a bold and confident riposte. There was also some talk in the autumn of Luther's leaving Saxony: a sad goodbye was made to friends at the end of November and a farewell dinner was even given on 1 December. Perhaps he was to become an academic refugee, maybe, it was rumoured, to take up a post at the famous University of Paris, the Sorbonne.

Such an outcome, incidentally, would have set up more difficulties than it would have solved because, as far as Church doctrine was concerned, the University of Paris was deeply orthodox, and life there might have turned out very dangerously for an asylum-seeking Luther. However, as it happened, he would not have to pack up his books and habit and take the road for France, for he was to stay in Saxony. One other option was opened up in discussion between Luther and Spalatin early in December – to consider hiding him away in a castle somewhere in the Elector's lands – but that was an unnecessary measure to consider just at that juncture. Indeed, for the time being at least, Luther was safe in Frederick's protection and Frederick was safe in protecting him. The overall position can be said to have been that doctrinally Luther continued, ultimately, to be pursued while, politically, he was sheltered behind an Electoral shield that allowed him both to maintain and to extend his doctrinal offensive.

Frederick's resolve to harbour Luther was no doubt reinforced by a letter to him of 22 November from the teaching staff of 'your Illustrious Eminence's university school of Wittenberg'. This missive was penned at Luther's request and, indeed, was largely of his own composition. While expressing deep reverence for the Church and the papacy, the faculty in effect conceded jurisdiction in the affair to the Elector: 'he [Luther] should refer the honour of the holy Church simply and directly to your illustrious Lordship and the supreme pontiff'. The extent of Luther's genuine allegiance to the supreme pontiff was, however, revealed a few days later, on 28 November, with an appeal he launched to a general council of the Church against 'Leo badly advised and from his excommunications . . . and declarations of heresy and apostasy, which I esteem as null, nay, as iniquitous and tyrannical.' The defiant language – including a truculent allusion to the threat of excommunication made in Leo's decretal of 9 November – matched the combative substance of this formal and public appeal, which Luther both deposited with a lawyer and also placed in the hands of a printer. For he was now deliberately defying the bull of Pope Pius II (pope 1458–64) *Execrabilis* (1460) which made the very act of invoking a council in an appeal against the papacy heretical. Again, the protection that allowed him not only simply to stay alive but to remain on a mounting offensive against the papal Church in the declining months of 1518 was provided by Frederick.

Even so, a potential undermining of Luther's position *vis-à-vis* Frederick as his indispensable protector came at the very end of 1518, and not so much from Roman threats as from papal blandishments. This took place with a visit to Frederick by a relative of his, a young German nobleman in the pontifical diplomatic service, Karl von Miltitz (1490–1529). Miltitz arrived on 28 December bearing gifts, including additions to the Elector's beloved collection of indulgence-accruing relics – an attempt, perhaps, to remind Frederick of the importance of the beliefs that his protégé Luther was undermining. Other concessions included the right to nominate a cardinal – perhaps even a penitent Luther? – and the legitimising of the Elector's illegitimate progeny. However, the centrepiece was the most splendid present from the papacy's rich repertoire of trinkets and titles to beguile sovereign princes, the golden rose, ceremonially oiled and incensed, a symbol of Christ's precious blood. The Curia had arranged this gift as a bribe, offering it provisionally to Frederick in a letter to Spalatin dated 24 October and to be included in Miltitz's diplomatic bag, 'the most sacred golden rose, annually consecrated with mysterious rites'. Frederick had long coveted this decoration, which would upgrade him in the highly competitive pecking-order of German rulers – each rose award being 'sent to some powerful Christian king or prince'. The gilded flower, which was stored for safe-keeping in the Fugger bank in Augsburg, might be seen as a double bribe. First, it might be read as an earnest of good will in order to encourage Frederick to block Charles of Habsburg's candidacy in the imperial elections that were to be occasioned by Maximilian's death. More specifically, the grant of the rose, as its accompanying letter from the pope made plain, expected Frederick, not to protect, but to 'crush' Luther:

> consider how great an honour we are sending . . . and how detestable is the overbearing boldness of that only son of Satan, Friar Martin Luther. Consider also that he savours of notorious heresy, and can blacken the name and fame of the great Elector and his ancestors. . . . Let him crush the rashness of the said Luther. . . .

The Elector was certainly aware that the gift represented a *quid pro quo*: 'Miltitz may refuse to give me the golden rose unless I banish the monk and pronounce him a heretic.' However, that kind of bribe works best when minds are not made up, and Frederick's mind, slow and cautious as it was, already was resolved. The golden rose episode took place in a period when the Holy See, in the months surrounding Maximilian's death, the imperial interregnum and the new election, in June 1519, had decided to experiment with a strategy of relative pliancy and diplomacy in the Luther case. This negotiation phase was typified by the pope's even sending a conciliatory letter to Luther himself in March 1519. Miltitz – seeking to reassure everyone, promising too much, even castigating poor Tetzel as if he were to blame for the whole contretemps going back to 1517 – symbolised this stage of papal policy.

Frederick's position was obviously crucial. It was quite clear that he hankered after the sacred bauble, but not enough to comply with the papal terms on offer. He and his dynasty had for decades fought off papal intervention in the secular and religious affairs of Saxony and, as part of his state-building process, he had endowed a university of which Luther was the leading professor. True, he may not have been in sympathy with the professor's attack on the traditional mechanistic religious practices of which he remained a keen devotee, while the word he used for the man at the centre of the business – 'the monk' – indicates little personal affection or esteem. However, both his personal honour and his political credo of princely independence from Rome demanded continued support for his subject. Evidence from Luther himself suggests a final decision on the Elector's part at the beginning of December 1518, around the time when there was so much talk of Luther's departure that, as we saw, a goodbye supper was arranged. Two letters, Luther recalled, arrived for him from the castle. The first expressed surprise that Luther was still in town, but the second informed its recipient that if he had not left, he was not to. This scenario indicates that at the beginning of the month, weeks before ambassador von Miltitz's arrival, the Elector's mind was made up to defend Luther and that Frederick, golden rose or no golden rose, was not movable on that point.

Nor was Luther himself. Early in January 1519 he met Miltitz in the Saxon city of Altenburg where they came to an agreement by which each side would adopt a period of silence and accept arbitration by a bishop. Luther's report to Frederick of the interview breathed a spirit of reconciliation, until, near its conclusion, he suddenly burst into a fresh tirade against the force that he now identified as his foe:

> I fear that the Pope will allow no other judge but himself, nor can I tolerate his judgement; if the present plan fails, we shall have to go through the farce of the Pope writing a text and my writing the commentary. That would do no good.

As part of the phase of reconciliation, on 29 March 1519 Pope Leo actually offered Luther an expenses-paid trip to Rome in order to make a full confession. Yet even within this same period Luther was in fact solidifying the intellectual position that estranged him from Rome. For example, a paper Luther composed following his January discussion with Miltitz, 'An Instruction on Certain Articles', committed him to 'follow the Roman Church, obey and honour her . . .' and to make doctrinal concessions. Yet when it came to the heart of the matter, in the Instruction Luther reaffirmed a Pauline position on grace and works that would set him at loggerheads with mainstream Catholic doctrine, challenging the Catholic belief that virtuous deeds play an indispensable part in our winning God's favour:

> Of good works I have said, and still say, that no one is good nor can any one do right, unless God's grace first makes him just; wherefore no one is justified by works. . . .

Thus Luther's theology was being consolidated in 1519. In that year he published the university lectures he had delivered in 1516–17 on the Epistle to the Galatians in which St Paul had consolidated the position of works, faith, law and grace he had set out in the Letter to the Romans. In the published Galatians lectures Luther affirmed that upon the crucified Christ

> free will collapses, good works collapse, the righteousness of the Law collapses. Only faith and the invoking of God's completely free mercy remain.

Thus the rock of conviction in Luther's theological position was made clearer and harder in 1519, preparing for his next bout, that with Johannes Maier von Eck at Leipzig, in June and July of that year.

THE LEIPZIG DEBATE, JUNE–JULY 1519

The debates in which Luther was involved in the summer of 1519 had the effect of further clarifying his own ideas, sharpening his views through collision against a corrosive and critical dialectical intellect, that of Johannes Maier von Eck. His life-span pretty well overlapping with that of Luther, who, by March 1518, was referring to him as an erstwhile and lost friend, he and the Wittenberg professor resembled each other in several ways: Eck was of peasant background, a distinguished academic (chancellor of Ingolstadt University in Bavaria), a preacher, a man of vitality and hard work, a reformer and an author. However, though Eck was concerned with the reform of the Church's moral abuses, he was the most zealous guardian of undeviating Catholic orthodoxy, having even slammed Erasmus for daring to suggest that the Greek prose of the New Testament was stylistically less than perfect. In his 'Obelisks' of 1518, violently attacking one third of the 95 Theses, he had already opened the allegation that was the main feature of his indictment of Luther at Leipzig, that he was a Hussite heretic. Luther's 'Asterisks' were his reply to Eck. Then while Luther was engaged at Heidelberg in May 1518, his Wittenberg colleague Andreas Bodenstein von Carlstadt (1480–1541) took up the debate in theses on the will and on Scripture. On 29 December 1518 Eck published prior notice of a debate to be held in Leipzig between him and Carlstadt.

The new year saw some uncertainty about who would be facing whom in any such discussion. However, in 'Disputation and Defence of Brother Martin Luther against the Accusations of Dr Johann Eck', issued in May 1519, Luther wrote as if he assumed that he would be leading in the debate, with Carlstadt as a second 'who will also appear'. The thirteen articles he listed traced such already well-rehearsed topics as repentance, absolution, purgatory, free will and the treasury of merits but also touched on Church history and its role in papal claims. The 'Disputation and Defence' also gave notice of what was to be the harshly adversarial tone of the Leipzig encounter, for example when Luther lumped Eck together with Prierias and Cajetan all as 'adversaries of Christian grace'.[4]

Aware of the debating power of his redoubtable opponent, Luther prepared himself for the clash through the first half of 1519. He undertook particularly close study of Church history, canon law, the Church Fathers and the resolutions of the early councils, especially that of Nicaea (325), and rehearsed long in advance what he would say when called upon. Morally and psychologically, too, he was limbering up, now convincing himself, as he wrote to Spalatin, that Rome was the city of evil, Babylon, and the Antichrist, 'that beast' (he also reiterated his anti-Italian stereotypes: the Romans were out to get him 'by Italian subtlety . . . poison or assassination').

Rome was in fact not directly involved in this all-German, academic and princely affair, which was held, under the presidency and patronage of Duke George (1477–1539), ruler of Ducal ('Albertine') Saxony, under the reluctant auspices of the duchy's university, Leipzig. The Leipzig debates from one point of view may be seen as the belated realisation of Luther's call in the 95 Theses for a university debate on the issues he was raising. However, by the summer of 1519 when the debates opened in Leipzig, these issues had broadened out considerably to take in a whole range of matters of ecclesiastical authority and obedience.

From the time of his arrival in the city on 24 June Carlstadt had star billing on the original play bill. Before the discussions opened there were delaying procedures, including the bishop of the area's attempt, thwarted by Duke George, to scupper the whole debate. Then as a preamble there was a feast of all the colour, ceremony and theatre that Renaissance Germany did so well – Eck strutting round in priestly vestments, but also taking melodramatic over-precautions against attack; rival squadrons of armed body-guards; flags and pennants, pipes and drums; the nobility and the clergy all on parade; Mass, beautiful music and processing; splendid meals, lots of wine. Then, amidst further procedural disagreements about recording the sessions and the availability of books to the participants, the epic debates, in Latin, got under way in the duke's gorgeous Pleissenburg castle. Round 1, over a whole week, pitted Carlstadt versus Eck on grace and free will and put Eck ahead on points. On 4 July the champion of the Wittenberg cause, Luther himself, put on the gloves, described by an observer as an able contender despite his emaciation as a result of 'care and study':

> Martin is of middle height . . . in the vigour of manhood and has a clear, penetrating voice. He is learned and has the Scripture at his fingers' ends. . . . A perfect forest of words and ideas stands at his command.

The bouts began with the topic of the pope's primacy, based on the text in Matthew's Gospel in which Christ commissions Peter, held by Catholics to have been the first pope, with His own authority over the Church. The discussion with Eck then switched to more recent times, to the Council of Constance of about a century before, which had in 1415 condemned the Czech dissident John Hus for calling into question papal authority. It was, on the face of it, adroit of Eck to throw in Luther's face before a Leipzig audience of Ducal Saxony the charge that, in disputing papal power, he was in effect a Hussite: in the previous century that part of eastern Germany bordering on Bohemia had known terrorist raids by Hus's radical posthumous followers, and the University of Leipzig had itself been founded by conservative German academics at the University of Prague in flight from Hus's opposition to the Roman Church. Eck's attempt to bracket Luther with Hus, though, had two important consequences. The first was to encourage Luther to see truth in Hus's beliefs, 'taught in plain and clear words by Paul, Augustine, and even Christ himself'. The second consequence was linked, and it was significant because Luther had been drawn to the idea of a council as the antidote to the overweening claims of the Holy See. In declaring in public at Leipzig that an individual council could be in error, Luther was implying that councils in general could make mistakes about doctrine, and he followed this up with an explicit statement: 'And so councils contradict one another so that we, who build on them, ultimately no longer know where pope, council, Church, Christ, or we must stand. . . . Thus we are forced to say . . . the council has erred.' There was talk at Leipzig of a further appeal of Luther's case, to the universities, but the significance of the Leipzig debates is that they helped sideline in Luther's mind what is known as the 'conciliar' tradition of ecclesiastical constitutionalism, the late medieval school that saw in general councils the perfect antidote to all the ills of the Church. While Leipzig gave Luther a conviction of fidelity to another tradition, the medieval dissenting heritage of which Hus was a hero, the encounter with Eck further narrowed the range of Luther's tribunals by eliminating the conciliar option. More and more Luther was being driven back on his central focus on a reliable arbiter to hear and adjudicate his cause, the word of God in Scripture.

5

FROM LEIPZIG TO WORMS, 1519–1521

INTRODUCTION

The next period of Luther's life, from his disputation with Eck at Leipzig, takes in his formal severance from the papacy with his excommunication in the course of 1520 and his full emergence as a writer for a mass readership in his major writings of the same year, the so-called 'Reformation classics': 'The Address to the Christian Nobility Concerning the Reform of the Christian Estate', 'The Babylonian Captivity of the Church' and 'The Freedom of a Christian'. Having considered the contents of those works, we shall recount Luther's excommunication by the papacy in 1520 and his appearance before the German diet at Worms in 1521. One of the key features of incidents described in this chapter is Luther's dexterity in capturing what we might describe as the 'theatre' of a given occasion and his ability to exploit the propaganda value of situations presented to him.

THE SEQUEL TO LEIPZIG: LUTHER'S WRITINGS

The situation following Leipzig was summed up in the words of the disputation's chairman, Peter Mosellanus, who reported that when the debates were over 'each side claimed the victory'. Luther returned to Wittenberg and to his university duties there, resuming lectures on the Psalms which, in turn, eventually produced a published work, *Operationes in Psalmos*, a commentary on Psalms 1–21, in Latin, and intended for a scholarly readership. He complained, though, that such works were 'so little popular and do not capture many', so that he turned to the alternative of issuing 'treatises more easy to be understood'. Luther was now to emerge as a writer for what was, by sixteenth-century standards, a mass-circulation press. As an invention, the printing press had been in existence for more than half a century and had already been deployed to produce works for a large-scale readership. However, the technology's ability to function as history's first mass medium was to be fully realised in the early Reformation era. In the period 1518 to 1520 alone, German published titles rose in number from around 150 to 570 and were to reach just short of 1,000 publications by 1524. Luther and the issues he raised were responsible for his rapid escalation in output. In fact even before the Leipzig debate, in February 1519, one of those entrepreneurs who were managerially responsible for the press revolution, the Basel-based publisher Johannes Froben (c.1460–1527), wrote to tell him that his writings were circulating all around Germany and in all the major countries of western Europe.

Even so, it could be said that until well into 1520 Luther had not yet quite hit on the right level for his publications, which consisted partly of relatively brief individual fragments, including writings on economics and politics, the sacraments, prayer and good works. That said, the published writings of that period can also be seen as preparing the way for his great writings of 1520, the 'Reformation classics'. For example, his *Tesseradecas*, fourteen comforting meditations written to console Frederick the Wise during an illness that struck him in the summer of 1519, revealed him as a writer of profound spiritual guidance, in this case bringing the 'theology of the Cross' to bear on the individual's experience of pain, distress and death: 'When we feel pain, suffer, die, let us firmly believe that it is not we, or we alone, but Christ and His Church who are in pain, suffering, dying with us.' Then early in 1520 he published a work calling for debate on the possibility of the laity's receiving communion not only in the form of bread, but also that of wine, from the chalice: the Catholic Church normally reserved the chalice to the priest saying Mass. Luther also combined treatment of spiritual and sacramental issues with coverage of social issues, as can be seen in his publication in 1520 of a sermon he had delivered in the previous year on the subject of money-lending at interest. In this work his traditionally-minded refusal to accept money-lending at interest was twinned with pictorial anti-Jewish propaganda in the form of an image of an avaricious Jewish money-lender.

In another work dating from that period typified by the regular production of shorter pieces, Luther published in March 1520 a Latin version, *Confitendi Ratio* ('Method for the Sacrament of Confession'), of a

German-language manuscript on that subject he had distributed earlier. The work was then re-translated back into German, and was intended to bring comfort to ordinary people terrified by the sacrament of penance. The treatise tried to avoid the kind of extreme scrupulosity that Luther himself had known over trivial offences and recommended instead complete confidence in God's unconditional and merciful forgiveness. Another example of such practical, pastoral writing was Luther's May 1520 longer work on morality, 'Concerning Good Works', whose composition was urged on him by Spalatin. Incorporating a study of the ten commandments, this treatise was concerned with the daily lives of Christians in the world: in the home with its obligations to honour parents; in the workplace; in society at large, and the need to purify it of luxury, usury and prostitution; in the Church, and its need to accommodate the varying spiritual capacities of men and women; and in the state, and the duty to obey princes – even while the abuses of the powerful, above all those of the Roman Church, are condemned. In these ways, 'Concerning Good Works' incorporated Luther's first extended examination of issues of Christian social responsibility and can thus be viewed as an overture to two of the major compositions on that subject issued in the course of 1520, 'The Freedom of a Christian' and the 'Address to the Christian Nobility'. On the more doctrinal and spiritual fronts, 'Concerning Good Works' established that justification by faith does not dissolve the need for ethical conduct, even though it affirmed that the greatest of the commandments was centred not on works but on faith. In that respect, this work anticipated the insight that Luther was to expand in his masterpiece of 1520, 'The Freedom of a Christian'.

One of Luther's sermons, which was regularly republished in 1519–20, condemned the excesses of the carnival scenes that filled the last days before Lent. It marked Luther out as one of the many preachers of his day who spoke up for a puritanical regime of sobriety and restraint of pleasure – though he did not believe that such self-denial earned any merit in God's sight. In addition, in May 1520 Luther delivered a bitterly satirical attack, 'On the Papacy at Rome against the Famous Romanist at Leipzig', an angry denunciation of some of the more extreme claims made for the papal primacy in the Church.

THE 'ADDRESS TO THE CHRISTIAN NOBILITY'

Meanwhile, Luther's savagery with regard to the papal office now allowed him to conduct a positive evaluation of the role, and especially the religious and reformatory function, of the state, the secular authorities and the lay aristocracy. In his continuing role as an appellant presenting his case to one court of appeal after another, Luther was, in this work, published in August 1520, putting his great cause before the conglomerate loosely termed the 'estates' of the German *Reich*. These included the country's rulers, great and small, territorial and civic, from the mighty Emperor Charles, through the seven Electors (including Frederick the Wise) who voted the emperor into office every time a vacancy arose; substantial non-Electoral princes such as the Margrave of Hesse in central Germany or the Duke of Württemberg in the far south; the ruling corporations of free, imperial, and largely self-governing cities of the likes of Nuremberg and Augsburg; lesser princely states and countships and the often minuscule lands ruled by the country's independent but politically declining knights, who owed allegiance as vassals to the emperor alone: *Reichsritter* or 'imperial knights'. In 1519–20 an alliance seemed to some to be in prospect between the cause of Luther and that of the knights, a group typically marked by social and political grievances, patriotic and nationalistic, anti-clerical and anti-Roman, passionate about the need to reform the *Reich* and to halt their own progressive downgrading at the hands of the territorial princes. At the beginning of 1520 the knights seemed in some quarters to be Luther's natural constituents. Their group engagement to him was proffered by two of their number who were also their most articulate spokesmen. These were the poet, social satirist and humanist scholar Ulrich von Hutten (1488–1523) and his associate the knight Franz von Sickingen (1481–1523).

Hutten was an eloquent nationalist writer who in 1520 was writing that Luther was the champion and symbol of Germany against the 'tyranny' of Rome: his struggle and fate were those of his fellow-countrymen at large. Alongside Hutten, Sickingen promised support – military protection if necessary – from that still significant strand of German society and opinion, the imperial knights. The 'Address to the Christian Nobility' spoke some of the language of national reform and renewal that the knights used. Luther sent it for printing on 13 June and on the 23rd of the month added a dedicatory prologue addressed to a close academic friend, Nikolaus von Amsdorf (1483–1565), in which he made plain his intention to appeal from the clergy to the lay and secular estates.[1]

Given its national and patriotic inspiration, there was not much room for choice about the language for this work: it would be in the tongue which Luther was to do so much to forge into a standard national vernacular. The work came out in August 1520 with the German title, *An den christlichen Adel deutscher Nation: von des christlichen Standes Besserung*, 'Address to the Christian Nobility of the German Nation Concerning the Reform of the Christian Estate'. The title, though somewhat repetitively phrased, is effective enough in indicating the work's contents, which consisted of a programme of Christian renewal of society and was concerned with *Besserung* – making things better, reform, amendment, improvement.

The 'Address' was both exclusive and inclusive in its message: it was exclusive in denying involvement in German affairs to the alien 'Romanists', who were targets, too, of von Hutten's fierce anger, but it was inclusive of Luther's fellow Germans who made up the nation's lay estates. Among these the new Emperor, Charles V, was confidently enlisted as a fellow national. Indeed, Luther acclaimed him as the proper leader of the German people in their struggle for liberation from Rome, the herald of a new age of change, for, Luther wrote:

> God has given us a young man of noble ancestry to be our head and so has raised high hopes in many hearts.

Luther addressed himself to a national readership too in adroit allusions to his country's popular culture. For example, his self-deprecatory references to himself as a kind of meddler in people's business referred to a common German proverb: 'A monk must be in it, whatever the world is doing, even if he has to be painted in.' His proverbial reference was in fact derived from the popular urban satirical Shrovetide comedies known as *Fastnachtsspiele*, with their painted backdrops: the stereotypical figure of the monk was a frequent inclusion in the *dramatis personae*, even if he had to be 'painted in' to the backdrop.

At the same time, Luther's depiction of himself, while addressing the emperor, the estates and princes, in the role of a 'Court-fool' – 'No one needs to buy me a fool's cap nor shave me my poll' – has clear resonances to the best-selling verse satire on the world's follies, *Das Narrenschyff*, the 'Ship of Fools' (1494), by the Strassburg humanist Sebastian Brant (1457–1521). Developing the complexity of the allusion, the reference then permitted Luther to open up a short Scripture-based discourse, derived from St Paul in his First Epistle to the Corinthians (1 Corinthians 3:18), on the paradox of the foolish wisdom of divine things contrasted with the superficially wise folly of human minds. Luther involved himself in that Pauline exercise in contrast between divine wise folly and human foolish wisdom by self-mockingly alluding to his own academic qualification, ostensibly betokening wisdom but in fact revealing folly: 'since

I am not only a fool, but also sworn in as a Doctor of Holy Scripture, I am glad that I have the opportunity to fulfil my [doctor's] oath even in the guise of a fool'. This motif took Luther into a further range of well-known contemporaneous literature, that of Erasmus's satirical masterpiece, first published in 1512, the 'Praise of Folly' (*Moriae Encomium, Stultitiae Laus*). Within an extended attack on the pretensions of learning, above all that of the Scholastic variety, Erasmus showed how 'The apostles . . . confuted the heathen philosophers and the Jews . . . but they did so rather by their lives and miracles than by syllogisms; and of course they dealt with people not one of whom had wit enough to get through a single *quodlibet* [Scholastic proposition] of Scotus' – the Scholastic thinker John Duns Scotus. Thus in the opening blasts of the 'Address' Luther, the learned Scholastic doctor imaging himself as a jester, was deliberately aligning himself with the brand of anti-academicism that Erasmus voiced in the 'Praise of Folly'. The preamble to this work shows a Luther vividly aware of some of the key themes of the popular culture of his day, an undoubted contribution to his growing media success.

In its contents, the 'Address' proposed a wide-ranging programme of national reform. Luther began with an outline of the faults and griev-ances to which the 27 specific reform proposals that were to follow were offered as a cure. His chosen style echoes that of the *gravamina nationis teutonicae*, the 'grievances of the German nation', presented before one national diet after another and identifying Rome as the national foe. As Luther wrote, assuming the kind of style used in the *gravamina*, 'All classes in Christendom, particularly in Germany, are now oppressed by distress and affliction. . . .' However, whereas diets and other would-be problem-solvers had attempted political and military solutions, German history, as witnessed in the defeats by papal Rome of two of the greatest medieval emperors, Frederick I ('Barbarossa', *c*.1122–90) and Frederick II ('*Stupor Mundi*', 1194–1250), showed that the papal enemies, now identified by Luther as inspired by 'the princes of hell', were so powerful and entrenched that only recourse to divine aid would alleviate their tyrannies. Just as God's help, and it alone, was able, through Joshua, to demolish the walls of Jericho (Joshua chapter 6), so only God's succour could really aid the Germans in their life-or-death conflict to bring down the Romanists' defences.

Staying with the Joshua-reference, Luther next described three great walls with which the papalists, in their pride, defended themselves. These were, in the first place, the walls of the clergy's claim to immunity from secular state control and Rome's defiance of Church councils. The wall was to be demolished, first, by abrogating false distinctions between Christians, invalid differentiation of laity and clergy; for, according to a now-emergent Lutheran formula of the priesthood of all believers, 'our baptism . . . makes us all priests'. In this work, then, Luther made a massive contribution to scaling down the claims of the priesthood to be a special, indeed the first, estate in society, with an indelible character of ordained priesthood. A priest, for Luther, was an office-holder in the Church, exercising a ministry of service. And as he proceeded to deflate clerical pretensions, so he began to outline a theory of ministry in the Church that was intensely democratic: a 'shoemaker, a smith, a farmer', all might be 'eligible to act as priests and bishops'.

Alongside this social democratisation of the concept of religious ministry was a set of assumptions about the right of the civil authorities to control the clergy of the Church which placed Luther within the line of thought that descended from the medieval political thinkers whose writings had upheld the superiority of the state over the Church. These included the Italian Marsiglio of Padua (1275/80–c.1343), and the Englishmen William of Occam or Ockham and John Wyclif. In line with this intellectual tradition, sometimes known as 'Erastian', Luther wrote that the state was actually 'spiritual in status' and also had extensive, if not absolute, authority over all those who came within its jurisdiction.

If the arrogance of the clergy was one of the 'walls' with which the papalists defended their excessive privileges, another was the one built around the papal claim to have the sole power to interpret Scripture, along with the emergent, but not yet officially endorsed, theory of papal infallibility, all underpinned by the Church's canon law. Yet Luther showed how those claims to authority, especially that of interpreting Scripture and doctrine, were, again, exploded by the priesthood of all believers: 'each and all of us are priests, because we all have the one faith, the one gospel . . . entitled to taste or test, and to judge what is right or wrong in the faith'. Where, though, did the ultimate authority that the papalists claimed really reside in the Church? It was here that Luther opened up two possible opposing models of the location of ecclesiastical power. The priesthood of all believers might seem to pre-suppose what we might describe as a broadly 'congregational' type of democratic Church government. Then there was the role of the ruler to accommodate. As we shall see in Chapters 6 and 7, Luther's attitude to the extent of authority that rulers might exercise over the Church altered over the course of time, fluctuating in fact largely according to his own analysis of the attitude of men of power to his religious system. In 1520 his optimism about the receptivity of the political classes to his reforms was at a high point, to the extent that he was prepared to envisage secular rulers as 'priests and bishops' over the Church.

The final 'wall' that the Romanists held in place concerned councils of the Church as foci of authority within it. At around the time of Leipzig, Luther came to reject the conciliar tradition – in the form that the tradition was presented to him by Eck, revolving essentially around the late medieval Council of Constance of 1414–18. Now, though, in the 'Address', he took his readers back to the most ancient of councils, that of Jerusalem, as described in Acts 15:6, but, even more importantly, to the council of Nicaea (325), 'the most celebrated of all' and called by the Emperor Constantine (285–337): 'After him, many other emperors did the same, and these councils were the most Christian of all.' Such reflections, though, and especially Luther's celebration of the initiative that Constantine undertook at Nicaea to sort out the ecclesiastical problems of his day, suggest that Luther's preferred model for the governance of the Church was an Erastian one. It was a model in which, though all Christians had the right to call for a reforming council, the task itself was best devolved on 'the secular authorities . . . for God has given them authority over every one'.

Thus the Luther programme of reform was to be implemented by 'those who exercise authority in the state'. He was fully aware of what the abuses of the Church were – the opulence and arrogance of the papal way of life, the spreading parasitic system of cardinals, the Roman Curia and its top-heavy predatory bureaucracy. However, when it came to the cure, set out in 27 detailed reform proposals, Luther proposed putting this in the hands, not of the emperor (despite the earlier rhetoric about Charles's destiny), but of the princely and city states that made up the *Reich*. These were now appealed to in order to end the annual ecclesiastical payments to Rome known as annates, a highly visible fiscal indicator of his country's subservience to Rome.

So Luther the theologian was now turning his hand, with considerable skill and practical detailed knowledge, to the political and financial questions of Church–state relations. This involved him in well-aimed German nationalist appeals to avert 'the hurt and shame of the whole German people'. On the same nationalist grounds, Roman appointments to German benefices were denounced. A coherent legislative programme of ecclesiastical national autonomy was being assembled here which Luther linked to the historic struggles of medieval German emperors, especially Henry IV (1050–1106), for German ecclesiastical and national autonomy in opposition to Rome. Likewise, he proposed that secular matters arising in Germany should be no longer referred judicially to Rome, where, Luther claimed, corruption escalated costs, but appeals ought to be heard within Germany by its leading prelate, the archbishop of Mainz.

So Luther's programme of German national Church reform unfolds in the 'Address to the Christian Nobility'. Partly opportunistic in its appeal to the secular powers to combat the worldliness of the papacy, it was also radical in many respects, and at the same time practicable, as well as strongly reminiscent of features of the agenda of change which had been developed in Germany since the middle of the fifteenth century. It had been expressed, for example, in the reform policies put forward in the early sixteenth century by the archbishop of Mainz Berthold von Henneberg, in sermons such as those of the Strassburg preacher of moral reform Geiler von Kayserberg, and in the press in a literature of vehement denunciation of ecclesiastical abuse including such work as the mid-fifteenth-century tract known as 'The Insolence of Ecclesiastical Princes'.

In the 'Address', then, Luther was joining and reinforcing an existing German national consensus on the need for social, political and ecclesiastical renewal. However, to keep such a coalition together, with ingredients including many of the clergy and the religious orders, the knights, the humanist intelligentsia and the followers of Erasmus, required inclusiveness over the achievement of an agreed practical programme, rather than divisiveness over religious doctrine. This may explain why Luther's 27 reform proposals are largely free of distinctively 'Lutheran' religious ideas. For example, when Luther criticised pilgrimages to Rome, he did not do so on the grounds that such 'good works' were inherently erroneous because they violated the theology of justification by faith alone: 'I do not say that pilgrimages are wrong.' Rather, he wrote that in practice such expeditions were 'not exemplary, but scandalous': perhaps he had in mind his own unedifying visit to the holy city in 1510–11.

At the same time, his characteristic virulence of tone and his instinct to think and say the worst of the pope were softened somewhat in partial evasions and hesitations – 'I fear it is possible to call the pope "the man of sin"', or 'The pope seems almost the Counter-Christ'. Indeed, Luther was even prepared to concede to the pope a remnant of his powers and claims – for example, his right to act as the representative, if not of the heavenly Christ, then of the earthly one. Luther highlighted the pride and luxury of the pope's trappings of office which all made him so unlike

Christ – being carried in the portable throne known as the *sedia gestatoria*, having the unique privilege of receiving communion seated. However, his position on this was that of setting the pope himself free of all the court ceremonial that imprisoned him: 'we must help him to renounce all this' pride and pomp. At the same time, this sustained focus on external matters of reform of practical abuses helped suppress any more funda-mental and controversial assault on the papacy's underlying doctrinal and theoretical claims. Luther could not entirely restrain himself from attacking the pope in person – 'not most holy but most sinful' – but he was also inclined to lay the blame for the abuses he listed on an anonymous cast of villains termed 'Romanists'. The convention adopted here was that of the medieval and early modern literature of complaint and reform which criticised, not the sovereign, but his or her 'evil advisers' for deficiencies in good government.

In this work, then, Luther was putting forward a sweeping programme, yet one conceivably designed, not least in the relative caution of its phrasing, and its avoidance of divisive theology, to involve a mainstream of reform-minded German opinion in support of a programme of national renewal, one with many antecedents. In Brant's *Das Narrenschyff*, the focus of reform turned satirical, satirising various forms of folly in the state, Church and society, and Erasmus took up this technique in 'The Praise of Folly'. In the 'Address' Luther partly adopted that concern with exposing abuse as a species of folly: a vow to go on pilgrimage was 'foolish', as were papal jubilee years, and the pilgrim himself was merely a 'silly fellow'. Luther can be seen there as fulfilling the role he set himself at the beginning of this tract, that of the licensed jester, the fool satirising the follies of those around him.

As the author of the 'Praise of Folly', Erasmus has to be seen as the classic exponent of Catholic Church reform, devastatingly satirical but ultimately respectful of Catholic fundamentals. To what extent can Luther's 'Address' be viewed as a work of Catholic reformism, aligning Luther at that point in time with the Erasmian school? Probably because of a widespread assumption that Luther must have been at that point in his career on an unstoppable course of estrangement from Rome, much of the Catholic reformism underlying this work has been overlooked – though the historian Richard Marius noted that Luther did not call in it for the abolition of the papacy, or that of monasticism. Indeed, when we consider Luther's attitude in this work to the clergy and the religious orders we realise how much he was aligned with Catholic reformism, Erasmian style. Take, for example, the way that Erasmus's ridicule in the

'Praise of Folly' of the bewildering surplus of religious orders is echoed in Luther's call in the 'Address' that the pope should block the creation of any new ones. This, though, was also a demand that anticipated a sense among some sixteenth-century Catholic reformers that their Church already had enough monks and friars. Luther's suspicion of the profusion of orders, and his linked emphasis on the importance of a parochial ministry duly subject to bishops, anticipate similar views held by many of the delegates of the Catholic Church's Council of Trent held between 1545 and 1563 – especially those who secured the Council's official denunciation of 'wolves' belonging to the preaching orders invading the proper province of the parish clergy. Yet Luther did not set out in this work to condemn monasticism *per se* as a system based on an erroneous theology of justification by works. Rather, he took issue, as any follower of Erasmus might have done, with what he termed 'the sad condition of the monasteries' and envisaged the moral reform of the institution. He also took a protective stance towards his country's 'ancient' monastic foundations, whose incumbents should, he insisted, remain 'free to serve God'. He was careful, too, to avoid a loss of mass support as a result of any backlash of sympathy with the preaching order of friars, now under some attack from his pen but traditionally having a popular constituency: in his proposals to forbid the construction of further houses for these orders, he implored his 'dear reader', 'Do not be angry . . . I mean nothing wrong.'

Luther in this work can also be seen as exemplifying a basically reverential attitude to the central prayer of the Catholic Church, the Mass. Long before his time, Masses said for the faithful departed, especially for their release from purgatory, had become commercialised through outright payments to priests to recite them. His own call for the elimination of such abuses should be read as an exaltation of reverence for the Mass itself so as to avoid bringing it into contempt. This concern is also closely attuned to the Council of Trent's decree aiming to preserve the sanctity of the Mass, to be free from all 'avarice'.

Thus at least some of the reform proposals contained within the 'Address to the Christian Nobility' should be read as a manifesto of the pressure for Catholic reform and renewal inherited from the late medieval agenda of what was called *reformatio* and carried forward to its fulfilment in the Council of Trent. Obviously, this point should not be pressed too far. Luther's proffered olive branch to the Hussites of Bohemia could hardly be termed 'Catholic', nor could his call for the suppression of all Church festivals. Even so, the 'Address', as a manifesto of ecclesiastical reform, belongs to a period before Luther had fully become a Lutheran.

This extraordinary work is about so much more than Church reform narrowly understood. Proposals also involved reform of the universities, the elimination of canon law and most of the works of the 'blind pagan' Aristotle from their curricula and the primacy in the syllabus of Scripture rather than Scholasticism. A history essay on the relations of imperial to papal power was inserted into editions subsequent to the first, and the 'Address' rounded off with a review in sermon-style of 'temporal failings'. It condemned the alleged national vices of overeating and heavy drinking, decried early capitalist developments in banking and money-lending and denounced another supposed national moral lapse, prostitution. Towards its conclusion, the work was tinged with Luther's sense of apocalyptic – 'I verily hope the Last Day is at hand' – and also expressed its author's despair at the futility of his own moralistic admonitions: 'Preaching never makes any impression on [gluttony].'

'THE BABYLONIAN CAPTIVITY OF THE CHURCH'

Published in Latin by the Wittenberg printer Melchior Lotther on 6 October 1520, the successor to the 'Address', 'The Babylonian Captivity of the Church', would take on an entirely different character. This second major work of that year, published less than four months after the 'Address', was no longer a left-of-centre critical manifesto, broadly accepting much of the status quo and setting out to reform it extensively. Rather, it was a work of angry estrangement whose key vocabulary was not that of reform but of apocalyptic revolution and outright rejection of Rome and all its works. It is true, as we saw, that Luther's apocalyptic sense of the world's end was not absent from the 'Address'. However, in that work the apocalyptic awareness came only in its closing bars. In 'The Babylonian Captivity', in contrast, it was there from the very outset and present in the very title of this new work as its dominant chord: *De captivitate Babylonica ecclesiae praeludium Martini Lutheri* – 'Martin Luther's First Trumpet Blast against the Babylonian Captivity of the Church'.[2]

It was the inclusion of the word Babylon in the title that would have made the apocalyptic allusion of this work unmistakable to contemporaries. In the Revelation, or Apocalypse, of St John (chapter 18), the evil city of Babylon, once the place of the captivity of Israel, is transmuted into a whore, infinitely desirable and luxurious, but one with whom the godly can have no dealings, lest through her pollutions they forfeit God's favour: 'Come out of her, my people.' So 'The Babylonian Captivity' was no treatise on national reform written in German for German laymen on the 'improvement of the Christian estate'. Rather, it was a Latin work, by a Churchman, addressed in the first instance to other Churchmen throughout Christendom and signalling the author's utter rejection of the Roman Church as Babylon – and Antichrist. The specific direction at which this fundamental attack was aimed was at the seven sacramental pillars of the Catholic Church from which it claimed so much of its prestige and authority by means of channelling divine grace through them. Samson-like, Luther was now about to demolish those pillars. What, then, may account for the contrast between the 'Address to the Christian Nobility' as a late classic in the German literary tradition of complaint and reform in Church and state, and the 'Babylonian Captivity' which may be termed the first major work of the Reformation, embittered, alienated and destructive, as well as bold, decisive and unrestrained? In other words, what might explain this shift from reform to revolution? Part of the answer may be that, alongside Catholic press attacks on Luther, between the composition of the 'Address' in mid-June and the publication of 'The Babylonian Captivity' in October, news was reaching Wittenberg from July onwards that what Luther called a 'famous and ferocious' bull had been issued against him. Luther did not actually receive the bull, issued on 15 June, until 10 October – the publication day of 'The Babylonian Captivity' was the very date that Eck sent a copy of the bull entitled *Exsurge, Domine* from Leipzig to Wittenberg. Even so, 'The Babylonian Captivity' may be seen in part as Luther's defensive and aggressive response to a proposed papal attack on his very life.

The extreme gravity of Luther's message that 'the papacy was to be understood as the kingdom of Babylon' is initially belied at the start of this work by some knockabout comedy, including an introductory caption, 'The Papacy provides Grand Hunting for the Bishop of Rome': Leo X was known to be a keen huntsman, and had taken delivery in June of the first draft of the bull at his hunting lodge outside Rome. However, the tone and content of the work after the comic warm-up is profoundly serious, intensely theological and devastatingly radical, involving demolition of the 'septenary' – sevenfold – Catholic structure of the sacraments, reducing them to three, the eucharist, baptism and penance. A double dose of radicalism came when Luther, having reduced those great sources of ecclesiastical authority by more than half, began to tackle the question of the nature of the one he considered most important of them all, the eucharist or holy communion.

It was on this issue that Luther revealed the extent of his departure from the Catholic consensus of what the eucharist actually was. That consensus derived from the formula set out in the Fourth Lateran Council in 1215, was subsequently refined by the Church's most authoritative medieval theologian, Thomas Aquinas, and was restated by the Council of Constance. It was to the effect that, upon the uttering by the priest in the Mass of the words of consecration 'This is my Body' ('*Hoc est Corpus Meum*'), the substance, or internal reality, of bread and wine on the altar were utterly transformed – 'transubstantiated' – into Christ's very body and blood, all external sense appearances ('accidents') notwithstanding. Aware that his own views parted company with the orthodoxy that he had presented in 'On the Holy Sacrament' of 1519, Luther now denied this formula of such an absolute transformation of what were known as the 'elements': 'there is real bread and real wine, in which is the real flesh and blood of Christ . . .'. Denouncing the Aristotelian-derived method on which Aquinas constructed the concept of transubstantiation, he defiantly placed himself alongside the medieval heretic, the Englishman John Wyclif, who had claimed that bread and wine remained in being alongside Christ in the consecrated 'species' – a sacramental idea known as 'consubstantiation' or 'remanence' (though Luther himself totally rejected the use of such terms derived from the vocabulary of Scholasticism). Yet even while they repudiated transubstantiation, both Wyclif and Luther were in agreement that Christ was really present in the eucharist. So, we might ask, what practical difference was there between the Wyclif–Luther formula labelled 'consubstantiation' and Catholic transubstantiation – if both accepted Christ's real presence in this sacrament? An answer to that question comes from Luther's approving citation of the medieval theologian Pierre d'Ailly, who had pointed out that rather less of a miracle would be required if one believed that bread and wine remained on the altar, coexisting with Christ's body and blood, when the priest said the words of consecration. In other words, Luther, in denying transubstantiation, was radically calling into question the Catholic Church's claims as an all-powerful miracle-working agency on earth.

In this work he also dealt with the rite in which the eucharist was set, the Mass. Under that subject, a major talking-point of Luther's day concerned whether, every time a Mass was celebrated, Christ's sacrifice of Calvary was renewed. In 1510 Luther's opponent at Augsburg, Cajetan, set out the view that 'The efficacy [of the Mass] in itself is the immolation [sacrifice] of Jesus Christ,' and eventually, in 1562, the Council of Trent authorised a decree to the effect that in the Mass 'the victim is one and the same, the same now offering by the ministry of priests who then offered Himself on the cross, the manner alone of offering being different'. In 'The Babylonian Captivity' Luther abruptly dismissed as 'specious' the interpretation of the Mass as the enactment of the sacrifice of Calvary and presented the rite as essentially a subjective experience for the contrite believer, 'sad, humble, disturbed, confused, and uncertain'.

Destructive with regard to Catholic claims concerning the eucharist and the Mass, Luther turned next to one of the sacraments he insisted must be retained intact in any reformed ecclesiastical system, baptism. Alongside polemical violence against 'foul, money-grubbing and ungodly monsters of superstition' who abused this sacrament, he engaged on an extended meditative lyric on the mercy, forgiveness and grace of this sacrament which played its own part in initiating justification by faith. In the light of the emergence in the 1520s of the Anabaptists, radical Christians who set up a form of voluntary Church membership through the practice of believers', or adult, baptism, it is significant that in this work Luther took his stand on the traditional arrangement of universal membership of the Church by way of infant baptism.

Luther also turned in this work to a study of the whole sacramental arena within which the debate between him and the papal Church first began, penance, the third of the three sacraments he believed the Christian Church should retain. He now saw penitence not as an achievement towards which the sinner strives, but as being imparted, not through 'the diligence with which we have recollected and enumerated our sins, but only [through] God's fidelity and our faith'. In pastoral terms, he also valued this sacrament as 'a singular medicine for afflicted consciences'. A variant of the priesthood of all believers made it possible 'for any brother or sister to hear confession of secret sins'.

Luther's quite lengthy analyses of the eucharist, baptism and penance were followed by treatments of varying lengths of the Catholic Church's remaining four sacramental conduits of sanctifying grace. Each of these traditionally presaged entry into a new phase of an individual's life: confirmation – his or her entry into maturity as a Christian; matrimony – the married state; holy orders – the sanctified alternative to matrimony, the priesthood; and extreme unction – admittance into a further stage of life, eternal life, following death. For Luther, these 'usages' were simply not sacraments in the ways that the first three were. The criterion for a sacrament was its creation or authorisation in Scripture. The eucharist, baptism and penance Luther believed passed the test, while the other four failed.

Luther's dismissal of one of these rituals – confirmation – was relatively brusque. As for marriage, 'There is no Scriptural warrant whatsoever for regarding [it] as a sacrament.' This did not, however, impede him from a digression on some marital issues from a pastoral point of view. The priority he gave to sexual satisfaction for both partners in marriage led him to propose a drastic solution to problems arising from male impotence: the provision of a sexual partner for the wife, giving rise to the claim that he thereby sanctioned adultery.

His major conclusion regarding holy orders and the ministry can be described as both negative and positive. Negatively, ordination of priests was for Luther the source of a great clerical conspiracy to exploit the laity. Positively, though, the baptised Christian laity were 'uniformly priests'. However, in part what the statement that Christians were priests amounted to was a title of honour, like 'the saints', for example, praising the high value that should be accorded to Christians as a 'royal priesthood, and a priestly kingdom' (1 Peter 2:9). This did not mean that all Christians were actually priests, any more than they were all kings, only that they were a holy people, as priests ought to be. Ministry, though, was another matter, a matter of service and duty rather than of order and status, in discussing which the key words Luther used were 'minister', 'called', 'duty' and 'teach', rather than 'ordain', 'priest', 'sacrifice' and so on. In other words, Luther, strongly affirming the need for a special ministerial cadre in the Church, was moving towards a definition of ministry in terms of the professional competence and, indeed, qualified training of its occupants. In the Lutheran Churches whose foundation lay in the future, trained and salaried pastors were to take their own place alongside the growing ranks of those other several emergent learned professions arising in early modern Europe.

Finally Luther repudiated the scriptural status of the last of the Catholic sacraments, the anointing of those seriously ill or dying, the rite known as 'extreme unction'. Then adjusting his own schedule of approved sacraments, Luther evinced second thoughts on the status of penance, so that his own final tariff amounted to a kind of 'two-plus-one' arrangement, of baptism and the eucharist flanked by penance as a kind of reiteration of baptism. The tract drew to its close with allusions to Luther's impending excommunication, making counter-threats against Rome.

'THE FREEDOM OF A CHRISTIAN'

Given the revolutionary spirit of confrontation evident in 'The Babylonian Captivity', the third major treatise of 1520, 'The Freedom of a Christian', has been seen as generally conciliatory in tone and content. Rupp, for example, referred to it as part of an 'armistice' with the papacy, and Marius commented that its 'surface radiates conciliation and humility'. It was undertaken by Luther in the autumn of 1520 when this brief work was published, simultaneously in variant versions in Latin and German, probably before the end of October, as part of a last bid for peace engineered by von Miltitz (whom Luther met, at Elector Frederick's prompting, on 12 October). An important inclusion in this new work was an open letter, that was at least ostensibly cordial, addressed to Leo X. In this the pope was saluted as 'Leo, most blessed father', 'most excellent Leo', to whom 'Martin Luther wishes salvation in Christ Jesus our Lord': 'I freely vow that I have, to my knowledge, spoken only good and honourable words concerning you whenever I have thought of you.'[3]

If anything, Luther overstated Leo X's 'reputation and the fame of your blameless life', for, although he was untainted when compared with his notorious predecessors Alexander VI (1492–1503) and Julius II (1503–13), this pope of the Florentine family of the Medici was a cultivated and relaxed playboy, though he could be an astute political operator. However, Luther's depiction of Pope Leo as an innocent 'lamb in the midst of wolves' was in fact part of his strategy of highlighting the iniquities of the papacy as an institution by involving the person of the pope in a dramatic contrast between good and evil. In that sense, the dedicatory epistle was just as confrontational as 'The Babylonian Captivity', whose message of alienation against the papacy as an organisation it resoundingly restated: 'I have truly despised your see, the Roman Curia, which . . . neither you nor anyone else can deny is more corrupt than any Babylon or Sodom ever was . . . characterized by a completely depraved, hopeless and notorious godlessness'. The publication of this open letter in German, a language Leo did not know, underlines the fact that it was a further public statement of severance from Rome. It also provided a narrative of various steps along the way to that alienation: the bouts with Cajetan and Eck and the latter's undermining all Miltitz's attempts at peace-making.

Luther's device of divorcing the good pope from the evil papacy was not fully sustained in this work, as he began to address the pope's person in the condescending tones of a moral tutor: 'do not listen to those sirens who pretend you are no mere man'. Discounting the possibility of his own recantation, insinuating that the pope's claim to be the vicar of Christ put him in the role of Antichrist, Luther was, in the preface to Leo, giving further notice of his distancing from the Roman Church.

Even so, if the dedication still breathed much of the fire of 'The Babylonian Captivity', the work itself was of a different, and higher order. Luther displayed no false modesty of his estimate of the value of the short book that was to follow the dedication: 'it contains the whole of Christian life in a brief form'. Commentators have generally agreed with the high estimation Luther placed on this work. Fife, for example, remarked that in 'vigour of thought and natural eloquence it is among the most remarkable books of that age', and Marius described the work as 'perhaps the finest thing Luther ever wrote'. Brief as it is, it is certainly a devotional classic, comparable with great standards of that genre such as 'The Imitation of Christ' (*De Imitatione Christi*) by Thomas a Kempis or Erasmus's 'Manual of a Christian Soldier' (*Enchiridion Militis Christiani*, 1503). Though, as we have seen, the prefatory letter to Leo was adversarial, 'The Freedom of a Christian' itself is an inspiring work to read, partly because of its non-confrontational tone. In fact, based as it is largely on St Paul and centred entirely on Christ, it operates well as an eirenic treatise on the way the Christian life should be lived. It forms too a hymn of praise to its own subject, Christian liberty, grounded in justification by faith alone. What this liberty amounted to was an emancipation from the bondage of the law and works, a freedom won for us by Christ's redeeming and liberating sacrifice. A royal priesthood, true Christians have the dignity and perfect freedom of the sons of God and, having freedom, voluntarily exchange it for willing service of their neighbours, so that: 'A Christian is a perfectly free lord, subject to none,' and 'A Christian is a perfectly dutiful servant of all, subject to all.'

The message of Christian human dignity there is all the more refreshing because we often associate Luther with insistence on the worthlessness and degradation of humankind: as he wrote in 'The Freedom of a Christian' itself, 'all things in you are altogether blameworthy, sinful and damnable'. Yet he was to add that the effect of the work of Christ on us is 'the richness and glory of the Christian life', expressed in utterly willing service of our neighbours, the Christian bringing 'his body into subjection that he may the more sincerely and freely serve others'.

This great work is not without its aggressiveness, though this is, by Luther's normal standards, toned down, and quite unspecific in its general review of 'numberless mandates of popes, bishops, monasteries'. The tract also gives some notice of what was to be a relatively enlightened phase in Luther's attitude to the Jewish people, with its attack on preachers who give out the 'childish . . . nonsense' of turning 'sympathy with Christ' to 'anger against the Jews'. 'The Freedom of a Christian', finally, evolves a doctrine of free citizenship in which the Christian, 'freely and out of love', gives his or her loyalty and support to the state as the director of community efforts.

LUTHER'S EXCOMMUNICATION

This serene and elevated work, 'The Freedom of a Christian', was written by a man approaching possible martyrdom. The papal bull *Exsurge, Domine* of June was the outcome of growing impatience with Luther, felt in Rome and aroused to a considerable extent by Eck. Martin Luther was being identified primarily as the author of published printed literary works, the first leader of heresy of the new age of print, and capable of infinite harm against the peace of the Church and the primacy of the Holy See. Nevertheless, the proceedings against him, in the early months of 1520 and under Cajetan's guiding hand, were, at least initially, cautious and fair-minded, until, that is, a new investigative commission was set up by Pope Leo in which Eck's strident, aggressive voice was to be heard. The result was the 41-clause, 30-page bull *Exsurge, Domine* which was brought before four meetings of the pope's cabinet, the consistory, in the last days of May and early June and was published on 15 June followed by a burning of Luther's books in one of the great Roman piazze. Eck, and after him Archbishop Girolamo Aleander (1480–1542), were sent down to Germany to publish the bull, which gave its subject 60 days in which to submit.

The bull paid a considerable tribute to its intended victim. It did not proscribe some amorphous, headless heresy, such as that, for example, of the medieval Cathars, having no identifiable founder, but rather singled out Martin Luther as the head of something called in the Latin title a *sequacium*, literally a 'followership', or a discipleship. There were other ways of dealing with a heretic than this mode of proceeding. John Hus, for example, was condemned by a council, that of Constance, in 1415, and his fourteenth-century predecessor and mentor John Wyclif was, likewise, posthumously hereticated by the same assembly. A bull, though, was the most solemn instrument in the pope's documentary repertoire and to issue one against Luther indicated the seriousness with which the papacy under Leo X took the threat from his person. For Luther was the 'wild boar' of the bull's preamble, threatening the order of the Church's vine-yard. (The allusion was to Psalm 80:13: 'The boar out of the wood doth waste [the vineyard], and the wild beast of the field doth devour it.') This was twinned to an allusion, as we saw, to the pope's late-spring boar-hunting holiday.

This bull has sometimes been criticised for being superficial and hastily drawn up. Its order is indeed partly indiscriminate, though there is some sense of topics being grouped together, such as contrition, confession and absolution, the treasury of merit and indulgences, excommunication, papal authority, and the souls in purgatory. Without clear references to the provenance in Luther's works of statements such as 'To go to war against the Turks is to fight against God . . .', it is not always possible to authenticate them as Luther's own statements. However, any theological crudity detectable in *Exsurge, Domine* is partly beside the point because the bull was not designed to offer one more instalment in an accumulated series of doctrinal repudiations from pro-papal sources of Luther's beliefs. Instead, it delivered something so far withheld: a condemnation and a sentence. All the beliefs scheduled were described as equally heretical, and all pernicious and deceptive. So the second section of this two-part compilation was made up of the disciplinary and punitive elements. In its awareness that Luther was allowed to còntinue writing and teaching and to defy the Holy See because he was protected by important elements in Germany, Rome forbade a vast range of members of society to offer him support, or to read his writings. Then, suspended from the exercise of his priestly functions and banned from writing or teaching, Luther himself was to hear his conditional sentence: the burning of his books and the demand for recantation, ideally in Rome, within 60 days or to face final excommunication – and the penalty prescribed for heresy.

As Aleander travelled to the Low Countries in the autumn in order to promote the bull, burnings of Luther's works took place in Louvain in October, followed by similar actions in Cologne and Mainz. The docu-ment was publicly exhibited in Leipzig at the command of Duke George but was desecrated in that city, as it was in other places including Erfurt. By about 10 October it had at last found its way to Wittenberg but the conflagrations of Luther's books were to elicit from him another response, one of radical defiance, in December, in the shape of a retaliatory consignment to the flames of the papal bull as a symbolic destruction of the papacy.

As we have seen, Luther was preparing for such an offensive through 1520, and the epoch-making works of that year ensured a breach. They were followed by further manifestos: 'On the Papacy at Rome against the famous Romanist at Leipzig'; his literary offensives of October on *Exsurge, Domine* itself, 'Against the Execrable Bull of Antichrist', a savage satire published both in a Latin and a popular German edition; and 'Against the New Bull forged by Eck'. Defying the papal ban on his writing, he published in November a call for the convening of a general council. Then, with the 60 days set in the bull for his recantation concluded, on 10 December 1520 this man of gesture and drama adopted one of the boldest and most dramatic symbolic actions of his life.

Around 9 in the morning of that day, colleagues and students assembled near a church outside Wittenberg's walls, making the event one primarily concerning the university and its curriculum rather than the city or its parishes. On a bonfire already fed with volumes of canon law, of Scholastic theology and anti-Luther polemic, Luther cast the papal bull. It is indeed possible that the addition of the bull to the bonfire was Luther's own contribution, a sensational one, to the party, since the advertisement of the event drawn up the previous day in a notice by Melanchthon promised the burning only of 'impious books of papal decrees and scholastic theology'. However, Melanchthon's notice certainly did make it clear that this was a revenge destruction of the papacy's texts, since 'the enemies of the gospel . . . daily burn the evangelic books of Luther'. The burning above all represented Luther's defiance of his own excommunication and, in Melanchthon's account, was an apocalyptic moment, perhaps 'the time when the Antichrist must be revealed'.

Today, though, we may need to unpick further some of the ritual significance of this action and consider some of the ways in which it might have been understood by contemporaries. Autumn, when this conflagration took place, was a good time for lighting and enjoying bonfires, destroying the year's accumulated rubbish from farms, homes, gardens and streets. Luther's works had been set alight, as doctrinal rubbish, in German and Netherlands towns but also as an intended premonition and rehearsal of his actual burning for heresy: so much for the meaning of the authorities' casting Luther's books into the flames. His revenge had its own symbolic rhythms concerning the way that a solemn document was understood in early modern European culture as betokening the person and presence of its sender. In the case of *Exsurge, Domine*, the copy of the text which Luther obtained to destroy by fire personated Pope Leo X. The finely worked title page carried the traditional images of papal authority, the great keys, based on those claimed to have been accorded to the first pope, Peter, in Matthew's Gospel, 16:19, as well as the triple crown, or tiara, representing the pope's claims to hold sway over earth, heaven itself and purgatory. Alongside these official regalia were the pope's more personal escutcheon of his house of Medici, the five coin-like roundels widely thought to symbolise the family's role as bankers, along with the arms of their home, Florence, the Florentine version of the French fleur-de-lis. Thus, just as the setting aflame of Luther's books was intended to signal his burning as a heretic in effigy, so his counter-attack, the burning of the bull, was his burning of Leo, in all *his* error, indeed his heresy. Luther made this clear when he addressed the pope in the person of his ambassador, the bull: 'Because thou hast brought down the truth of God, he also brings thee down into this fire today.'

This part of the proceedings constituted, as Melanchthon had announced it would, a 'pious and religious spectacle' for 'pious and zealous youth', held at the sober hour of 9 a.m. on a north German late autumn morning. However, as the day proceeded, the comedic, satirical and carnivalesque potential of the episode were fully drawn out when the students took over the day for an afternoon of parade, rough music, song and a fresh burning of the bull, this time in a huge effigy, all confirming a sense of irreparable breach, since what fire destroys can never be repaired. The finality of this parting of the ways was confirmed by two further writings, one from each side. The first was Luther's 'Assertion of All the Articles Condemned by the Last Bull of Antichrist' published in Latin in December and willingly accepting beliefs such as those on free will attributed to him by his enemies. The second was the issue on 3 January 1521 of a mandate finalising the excommunication and to be definitively published as *Decet Romanum* on 6 May 1521.

LUTHER AT THE DIET OF WORMS

Martin Luther's appearance before the Emperor Charles V and the estates of the German nation at the Diet (or Reichstag) held in the Rhineland city of Worms in April 1520 has been generally regarded as the heroic apotheosis of his career and of overwhelming biographical significance. Philip Melanchthon's biography, *History of the Life and Acts of the Most Reverend Dr Martin Luther* . . . began a tradition of placing those few spring days at the centre of any account of Luther's life, devoting eleven out of 25 pages of a modern edition to the events of Worms alone. Subsequently, in Protestant Victorian texts, the high drama of the Diet of Worms provided outstanding opportunities to depict Luther's life as an adventure story of courage vindicated. Thus, Thomas Sefton Rivington's *The Story of*

Luther's Life described Luther on his way to Worms as 'the intrepid man who was on his way to offer his head to the Emperor and the Empire'. Likewise, Elizabeth Warren in *The Story of Martin Luther*, recounting Luther's 'undaunted courage', told how Luther arrived in Worms '"Strengthened with might" by the Holy Spirit of God'. For Charles Beard, in his 1896 study, *Martin Luther and the Reformation in Germany Until the Close of the Diet of Worms*, the events of the Diet were for Luther 'the crisis of his fate'. Beard in fact closed his biography with the Diet's immediate aftermath, almost as if after those stirring days in April there could not be much more of interest or importance to relate. What the nineteenth-century historian Lord Acton wrote of Luther at Worms – 'the most pregnant and momentous fact in our history . . .' – might also be applied to its place in Luther's history.[4]

Some contemporaneous sympathisers went so far as to liken Luther's trial to Jesus's coming before Caiaphas, Herod and Pilate. He himself set up such a comparison in letters in February and April in which he patterned his ordeal on Christ's: 'We see Christ suffer . . . Christ lives and I shall enter Worms. . . .' In another letter, written after the trial, he boldly applied to himself Christ's words in John 16:17, writing to a friend, 'A little while and ye shall not see me, and again a little while and ye shall see me.' Outright pastiche featured in a popular print of 1521 that drew the most explicit resemblances between Christ's trial and Luther's. More recently, James Atkinson's *The Trial of Martin Luther* (1971) joined a 'Historical Trials' series of which S.G.F Brandon's *The Trial of Jesus of Nazareth* was a core volume.

Obviously, to parallel Jesus' and Martin Luther's court appearances could provide effective supportive propaganda for the latter case. Any such parallelism, however, would break down in one key area. Gospel accounts, for example Matthew 27:14, of Jesus' own appearance before His last judge narrate His abandonment of speech and His refusal to defend Himself – 'And he answered him [Pilate] never a word. . . .' Perhaps that trope had its own model, in Isaiah 53:7, in which the passivity of the sacrificial victim is evident in his silence: '. . . as a lamb to the slaughter, and as a sheep before the shearers is dumb, so he openeth not his mouth'. However, the one thing we can say for certain about Luther in his appearance before his judges at Worms is that he was emphatically not silent and markedly not passive. Rather, the evidence we shall reconstruct indicates that, far from passive, he actively took charge and control of his own days in court.

In its role as a trial, the Worms hearing was an outcome of the papal bull, which required the German state authorities not to shelter but to take the severest action against Luther. However, as well as a product of the rift between Luther and Rome in 1520–1, the Worms appearance was also a consequence of other moves in 1520, namely what R.H. Bainton called Luther's 'appeal to Caesar'. In other words, Worms was one further step in his quest for an address at which to post his ongoing great appeal, and it meant an opportunity to deliver, as it were in person, his call on the German political authorities in the 'Address to the Christian Nobility' to take up his programme for the reform of religion, the Church and social life in Germany. Indeed, by in effect insisting, as we shall see, on the rearrangement of the Diet's agenda, Luther seems to have been determined to turn the trial into an opportunity for a national clarion call.

The opportunity to do that came with the presidency of the Diet in the person of the new emperor, Charles V, now safely elected and crowned. A new reign was opening, with a young ruler from whom so much was hoped, even with messianic expectations surrounding this new Charles: perhaps the rebirth of his mighty predecessor, another Charles, Charlemagne (742–814). This new Charles was in fact deeply conservative and, indeed, dominated by an ancestor-worshipping reverence for the traditional orthodox faith, above all that of his undeviatingly Catholic ancestors: he had, for instance, torn up his copy of the 'Address to the Christian Nobility'. That, though, did not deter him from complying with Elector Frederick's request following the imperial coronation in November 1520 that Luther be not condemned without a hearing.

The idea of a hearing being thus agreed in principle, Luther's university next suggested such an event to take place at the Diet then being scheduled, and on 28 November Charles V responded with a request that Frederick 'bring' Luther to the *Reichstag* to be 'investigated' in order to avoid 'injustice' or any breach of the law. It took nearly six months for that invitation actually to bring about Luther's appearance in Worms, and within that interval in December Charles withdrew his invitation, on the official grounds that according to *Exsurge, Domine*, any place where Luther resided was placed under interdict, which would be the unenviable fate of the host city of the national assembly. The Diet was summoned for 6 January. On 18 January Aleander, as papal legate to the Diet, lodged a protest against the transfer of the case to the secular authority (according to him, the Church had already adjudged the case and the state's only remaining duty was to carry out the sentence). The nuncio also tried to extract from the emperor a unilateral anti-Luther declaration. There were committee hearings to delve into the theology of the case and the Diet was formally opened with High Mass, on 27 January. Its proceedings were accompanied by mounting tension in the streets and inns of Worms, fed by some of the first wave of brilliant visual propaganda for Luther's cause – cartoons depicting him in alliance with heroes of reform and protest, Ulrich von Hutten, Erasmus and Hus. February 1521 saw Aleander involved in further discussion of the case, and fresh attempts to produce an edict against Luther fed violence in the hall where the Diet met. However, to move against or even discuss Luther without Luther was, surely, *Hamlet* without the prince and on 6 March the emperor renewed his invitation, this time in his own name and the Diet's.

Luther received the request, from no less a person than the imperial herald, on 26 March. A safe conduct, with guarantees covering both arrival *and* departure, as incorporated in this invitation, promised Luther the protection that would be necessary if he were to present his views unafraid. Aleander, indeed, fully grasped and regretted the probability that the safe conduct would function in such a way as to provide Luther with a sounding-board and because of it 'everyone would be led to the conclusion that he had justified his godless doctrine'. Even so, the case of Hus of just over a century before, executed at Constance in breach of an earlier imperial safe conduct, might have warned that such passports were not guaranteed life-savers. Luther himself made various observations about death as a prospect, and took up his analogy of himself with Christ by referring to those preliminary days as his Palm Sunday before his Passion week (he actually set out in Easter week). However, and despite Aleander's managing to secure an imperial edict against Luther's books, the safety pass from the emperor, a ruler distinguished by a knightly sense of honour, was backed up with a similar document from his prince, providing Luther with a sufficient measure of shelter. Thus his expedition to Worms should be regarded as more of a calculated risk rather a direct entry into the lion's den. His fortnight-long, wagon-borne, 250-mile journey once more across the German Lands, with a little entourage and with several stops, also formed a kind of preaching tour. He entered the city of the Diet with his companions on the morning of 16 April, was summoned to the assembly at four in the afternoon of the following day and had his first appearance before the emperor and the estates at six.

As we might expect of an event of which Preserved Smith rightly wrote that 'Few moments in history have been at once so dramatic and so decisive' as Luther's appearance before the emperor and the estates, there are several versions of what took place and their variant texts provide us with an excellent example of a major challenge for historians, bias in reportage. We shall observe four accounts in particular, written from various standpoints: that of Elector Frederick's secretary and intermediary with Luther, Georg Spalatin, a full, informed and pro-Luther narrative; then Philip Melanchthon's hero-worshipping account; third, the informative and hostile record made by the prosecutor, the chancellor of the archdiocese of Trier, Johann von der Ecken (d. 1524) and approved by Aleander; and, fourth, the deeply antagonistic version by the Catholic controversialist Johannes Cochlaeus. These four accounts undoubtedly exercised their authors' talents to match great events with fitting language.

An obvious art form in which to present the scene was that of the theatrical, for which the *Reichstag* hall, overcrowded with an estimated 1,500 delegates, tense with unseasonable heat, provided a fitting setting. The drama was intensified by the importance and, indeed, majesty of those present – the great world-emperor himself and mighty German princes, the nobility of the realm and the other delegates, including representatives of the splendid cities of the *Reich*. The notable absence of the piqued Aleander, though, made this a German and non-Roman affair. Within that dramatic setting, the play about to be unfolded pitted the defendant, imaged as virtually alone (though there were six Wittenberg doctors present), and as Luther *agonistes*, like the central hero who contended for the prize in the ancient Greek games. A further layer of dramatic contrast lay between the might of the assembly and the social insignificance of the main contender, a point eloquently captured by the historian Preserved Smith, who wrote of the 'son of peasants now stood before the son of Caesars', while R.H. Bainton captured 'a simple monk, a miner's son' facing the emperor. Once the proceedings got under way, Luther himself contributed to such a study in contrast by excusing his ignorance of court etiquette, being 'a man at home in the cell of a monk not the courts of kings'. The vibrancy of the drama depended on the sharpness of such contrasts, with Luther highlighting, not his professorial status, but his monastic humility and insignificance. Thus he got ready for the encounter by dramatising his own physique, taking the trouble to visit a Worms barber's shop in order to have his monastic shaven scalp – his 'tonsure' – extended.

Spalatin and Melanchthon constructed their accounts in such a way as to imply that the Luther case was the main or sole business of the Diet. Melanchthon was aware of some proceedings of the assembly before Luther's actual arrival but this in fact also concerned Luther, in the form of the edict Aleander demanded against his books, and the incident provided, in Melanchthon's eyes, an opportunity for Luther to demonstrate his courage when he insisted on proceeding to Worms despite the warning of friends along the way that he would face a hostile assembly. As far as Spalatin was concerned, the business of the Diet in effect began with Luther's entry into its meeting-place, when 'at last he stood in the presence of His Imperial Majesty, the princes, the electors, the dukes, in short, all the orders of the Empire'. (In contrast, Cochlaeus both recounted the condemnation of Luther engineered at the Diet by Aleander before his arrival and also pointed out that the *Reichstag* did have other matters on its hands – 'other matters of state' – besides the Luther issue.)

The theatrical tension of Worms was built up by various kinds of delays in the proceedings. First of all, there was the overall postponement of Luther's very arrival owing to the withdrawal and then the reissue of the imperial invitation. As we saw, he did not put in his appearance until quite late in the day following his entry into the city and even when he came to the premises he had to wait two hours before being heard. As we shall soon see, he then brilliantly initiated a further postponement in the proceedings, bringing the tension to an almost unendurable point.

First, though, came the charge against Luther – for that was what it was, rather than an open opportunity for a debate or statement. In fact, as Cochlaeus recounted, 'he was warned . . . not to speak about anything on which he was not questioned', so that his room for presenting a case was tightly circumscribed, or eliminated. When the man to whom Aleander's role as prosecutor had been transferred, Johann von der Ecken, opened the proceedings, it became clear that, in a sense, it was not Luther who was on trial at all: it was his books that were being prosecuted.

The papal bull had condemned not writings, but Luther, his followers and his opinions and had not been concerned primarily with texts. The prosecution at the Diet, in contrast, was quite clear that it was Luther's writings that were at issue. Cochlaeus, indeed, insisted that that was where the trouble started, when 'Luther published a great many books, both in Latin and in German'. (Cochlaeus gave as examples relatively minor works by Luther, except for 'The Freedom of a Christian'). The edict on which Aleander had insisted also targeted Luther's books rather than his person. Then, when the case was opened by von der Ecken at Worms, he presented Luther with a stark choice: he could recant, by disowning, not so much his opinions, but his publications. These were listed in an inventory drawn up by Aleander and included 'The Freedom of a Christian', the 'Address to the Christian Nobility', 'On the Papacy at Rome. . .' (all in German) and, in Latin, 'The Babylonian Captivity', along with his appeal for a general council and other writings. It was also important to identify these guilty texts, so that an official of the court, Dr Hieronymus Schurff, called out 'Let the books be given a name.' The prosecution's incrimination of Luther's books as the villains of the piece is also clear in an account of the charge given in the narration of the Diet compiled by von der Ecken and agreed by Aleander: 'Martin Luther, His . . . Majesty has ordered you to be called hither . . . to retract the books which you have edited and spread abroad. I refer to all the books written in either German or Latin, and the contents of the same.'

The actual point of these proceedings, though seemingly clarified by the clear alternative of Luther's either owning or disowning his writings, now began to look less clear. Evidently, these books were indisputably Luther's, bearing his name and their publishing details, in Wittenberg. He could hardly deny that and, apparently, said, though less distinctly, that he also ought to own up to other writings not appearing on the prosecution's schedule. So he was called upon 'to retract and recall them and their contents', the consequences that would follow a refusal not being at that point disclosed. This attempt to deal with mass productions in print through requiring their author to renounce them was indicative of a new uncertainty on the part of the authorities over what to do with the first media heretic. Were Luther to disown his writings, he might have been reconciled to the Church. However, although his writings might thereby have lost some of their sheen through his repudiating their contents, yet those books and tracts were at large in many multiple printed copies, and it would have been difficult, though not impossible, to destroy all copies in bonfires such as the ones ignited in university and cathedral cities in earlier months. Such difficulties were hinted at when, as recorded in the source attributable to von der Ecken and Aleander, the Emperor, in consultation with senior members of the Diet, 'expressed a wish' that 'Luther should now consider seriously to what extent he is already inevitably involved in his own errors. How difficult it is, nay impossible, to put them to rights again.' In other words, Luther might recant, but could he actually retract, his published opinions? Since the last great European heresy trial of an individual, that of Hus in 1415, the emergence of the printing press had challenged the whole nature of such actions. The prosecution at Worms tried to respond by asking an author to foreswear books which were already very much in the public domain. He might, indeed, conceivably have disowned them, yet he could hardly have denied writing them – and they were already the world's property. So the prosecution's device of focusing attention on Luther's writings caused confusion, to which Luther responded that 'he could not give an answer on the spur of the moment without time to reflect' – 'he asked most humbly that time for deliberation be given and allowed him'. The prosecution regarded that request 'for preferential treatment' as inadmissible, suggesting that Luther should have been prepared for an immediate 'yes-or-no' answer, even though, arguably, there had not been a proper 'yes/no' question. There followed an adjournment of over 20 hours, until 5 p.m. on the following day.

The recess, when Luther was compelled by Aleander's order to be unaccompanied, provided him with some opportunity to rest from a state of chronic nervous exhaustion in which he had arrived following the fatiguing journey from Wittenberg to Worms. At four in the afternoon of the following day, 18 April, the imperial herald came to collect him from his lodgings and to take him to the meeting-place. There von der Ecken addressed him in German and Latin, if not 'offensively', as Spalatin claimed, then certainly betraying considerable impatience with the delay, especially on the part of a man who was supposed to be articulate by profession. However, there was a detectable change from the interrogation of the previous day, when Luther was invited either to accept or reject his own writings in their entirety – 'all the books written in either German or Latin'. Now von der Ecken asked him if he wanted to 'disown any of them': 'Do you wish to retract any?' The altered stress may have been intended to win from Luther a renunciation of the most impassioned of the anti-papal tirades, such as 'The Babylonian Captivity of the Church'.

In his reply, which began with modest and apologetic courtesy, Luther developed a distinction between categories of his writings. There were included among them books of piety and edification which were of too much use to be abandoned, works of polemic against the papal enemy, by which writings it was his duty to stand, and works in which his violent language had been ill-judged or un-Christian. However, the last remark was the only note of concession before Luther admitted the undeniable fact of his ownership of all the categories of his works. Then, after von der Ecken had broken into Luther's speech with angry charges that he was an irresponsible egotist and a leftover of heresies going back to the early Church, demanding that he simply answer the question first put him, Luther produced his great classic of forensic eloquence, worth citing at a little length:

Since then your Serene Majesty and your lordships require a simple answer, I will give you one without horns and without teeth [Scholastic evasions], in these words. Unless I am convinced by the testimony of the Scriptures, or by evident reason, . . . I am bound by the scriptural evidence adduced by me and my conscience is captive to the Word of God. I cannot, I will not recant anything, for it is neither safe nor right to act against one's conscience.

The heroic finale 'Here I stand! I can do no other!' go back to an early version. Melanchthon included them, Cochlaeus not, but both recorded Luther's concluding invocation, 'God help me. *Amen.*'

Elevated members of the Diet next considered the debate and von der Ecken again took the floor, this time to point out that Luther was in contravention of the Council of Constance – not necessarily the most perceptive insight delivered at the Diet – and repeating the demand, which Luther had already rejected clearly enough, that he recant any of his writings. Night fell and the session broke up.

The following day the Emperor sent his personal message to the Diet. This testament fully captured the vast conceptual gulf between Luther's sense of individual integrity – unless *I* am convinced . . . *I* am bound . . . evidence adduced by *me* . . . *I* cannot, *I* will not . . . Here *I stand!* *I* can do no other! God help *me* – and Charles's sense of being bound, not by the word of God or an individual conscience but by the decisions of the past, of ancestors. In its own way, the Emperor's thoughtful statement was just as eloquent as Luther's clarion call, though manifesting a very different and, perhaps, far less 'modern' viewpoint from Luther's essential individualism. Charles took his stand on the firm Catholicism of his Burgundian, Spanish and Habsburg forebears, all of whose fidelity bound his own conscience to the Catholic Church. The safe conduct was confirmed. There were continuing attempts between 19 and 26 April to water down Luther's resistance, but on the 26th he left Worms. The Edict of Worms, construing Luther as a heretic until a terrible death sentence was carried out, was issued on 26 May, by which point Luther was firmly in protective custody. The Diet of Worms had effectively exploded the efficacy of the 'appeal to Caesar'.

Plate 1 Portrait of Martin Luther.

Lucas Cranach, the Elder (1472–1553).

Plate 2 Martin Luther, later in life.

Lucas Cranach, the Elder (1472–1553).

Plate 3 Hans Luther
(1459–1530), father of Martin
Luther.

Lucas Cranach, the Elder
(1472–1553).

Source: Sammlungen auf der
Wartburg, Eisenach, Germany.

Plate 4 Margarethe Luther
(*c.*1463–1531), mother of
Martin Luther.

Lucas Cranach, the Elder
(1472–1553).

Source: Sammlungen auf der
Wartburg, Eisenach, Germany.

Plate 5 Katharina von Bora, wife of Martin Luther.

Lucas Cranach, the Elder (1472–1553).

Source: Sammlungen auf der Wartburg, Eisenach, Germany.

Plate 6 Philip Melanchthon.

Engraving by Albrecht Dürer.

Plate 7 Erasmus of Rotterdam.
Etching by Albrecht Dürer.

6

THE DIET OF WORMS AND AFTER, 1521–1523

INTRODUCTION

In the present chapter we shall consider Luther's increasing engagement with German society and its problems in the period following the Diet of Worms in 1521. We shall review the aftermath of the Diet, focusing on Luther's voluntary protective detention between May 1521 and March 1522 in the Wartburg Castle, where he continued a campaign of extensive publishing and embarked on a translation of the New Testament. We shall go on to consider the way he coped with the radicalisation, in Wittenberg, of his own proposed religious reforms. After that we shall review his increasing involvement in politics, including a milestone in the evolution of Luther's thinking about the state, his work 'On Secular Authority' (1523). This will be followed by a study of his attitude to the Jewish people, in the work 'That Jesus Christ Was Born a Jew' (1523).

THE SEQUEL TO WORMS, MAY–DECEMBER, 1521

Attempts to seek a reconciliation between attitudes to human freedom and responsibility as fundamentally opposed as were those of Luther and Charles V foundered in the days following Luther's appearance on the *Reichstag* floor. Conversations were held involving Johann Cochlaeus in a last search for compromise but Luther found such talk 'pointless'. Given permission to depart Worms, Luther left on 26 April, intending to travel, in a wagon, with companions, back to Wittenberg via Frankfurt-am-Main. On 28 April he wrote a letter which was, ostensibly, directed at the emperor, who was addressed in it with every correct protocol, along with expressions of personal self-abasement as well as of ardent patriotism for the German fatherland. However, this letter, which never reached Charles, was really a kind of memorandum for Luther himself, recalling the stance he had adopted in the Diet: 'since I had based my books on clear and verifiable scriptural teaching, I could not yield to this request [to retract them] in any way; it was neither right nor proper to deny the Word of God and revoke my books . . . my conscience was held captive to the Word of God'. Other letters, including one to the estates who made up the Diet, were reiterations of the events that had taken place at Worms.

Charles V's statement of his own position *vis-à-vis* Luther on the day after the latter's great speech confirmed that the emperor saw himself as being bound and determined to be a Catholic ruler of his German subjects. This personal message from the emperor was followed by his summoning the Electors and other princes on 30 April to agree an edict against Luther. This in turn led to the preparation of a formal statement of the Diet, the 30-page Edict of Worms, drawn up by Aleander for Charles's signature on 6 May 1521. Just a couple of days before that fatal point Luther himself had already been taken into protective confinement at the behest of Frederick the Wise and at some distance from the city of the *Reichstag*. The Edict, shown to four of the Electors and some other delegates, was not formally issued until the 26th, the day following the *Reichstag*'s final formal session: it fully confirmed the breach. The Worms Edict was unrestrained in its denunciations of Martin Luther, whose views, the 'products and results of his depraved mind and soul', were 'dragged out of hell'. Luther was indeed – the substance of a charge that was to become a centrepiece of Cochlaeus's anti-Luther propaganda – depicted as actually demonic, 'not a man but the Devil himself in the form of a man'. The doctrines which the edict summarised taken from 'The Babylonian Captivity' were portrayed as undermining all moral order, teaching 'a loose, self-willed kind of life, without any kind of law, utterly brutish'. Held to have been impenitent at the Diet, Luther was, therefore, outlawed and all those with any obligation to the emperor were to help in his arrest and to send him on for punishment or detain him awaiting further imperial orders. His books, where his heresies were seen to be contained, were put under far-reaching censorship provisions and his followers were to be treated as severely as he was to be. Though still reaffirming the terms of the original safe conduct, the Edict condemned Luther with effect from 14 May.[1]

Following his departure from Worms and while Charles and his entourage were thus preparing this condemnation, Luther was made fully aware of his need for a refuge: as he wrote to his friend and disciple the artist Lucas Cranach (1472–1553) from Frankfurt on 28 April, 'I am going somewhere to hide, though I myself do not know where.' This indispensable hiding-place was soon to be provided by Frederick the Wise. The Elector was, pre-eminently, as the Worms edict put it, one of those who 'holds authority and administer the law' in the German Lands and was thus constitutionally committed to enforce the edict's terms. On the other hand, even before Luther's arrival at the Diet, in protesting at proceedings against his subject, Frederick had been caught up in a scuffle with another senior prince. By the time of the finalisation of the edict on 26 May, the Elector had left Worms on the 23rd, giving gout as his reason. He had, however, already made meticulous and discreet arrangements to shelter his professor.

Considering the menacing shadow cast over his life by the Worms edict, Luther's journey from Worms in late April and early May was surprisingly relaxed. From Frankfurt he proceeded to the ancient Benedictine abbey of Hersfeld, where, defying the edict's order silencing him, he stopped to preach on 1 May. By the following day he had reached the city of his maternal family and of some of his schooling, Eisenach, where, again illegally, he undertook further preaching but where he was also briefed about the arrangements for his imminent collusive kidnapping. He was now once more within the Electorate of Saxony and also deep in the land of his ancestors, including his father's birthplace, in the Möhra forest. The days, as he recounted them, have the feel of a relaxed spring tour by a distinguished man of local origin revisiting kinsfolk, old haunts and family landmarks. Then on 4 May an incident took place no less sensational for being prepared and, indeed, colluded over, in advance – an event, in its way, utterly worthy of the rich genre of folk adventure stories that were available in early sixteenth-century German popular literature. Late in the afternoon of 4 May a band of horsemen, armed with bows and led by two of Frederick the Wise's most trusted confidants, stopped Luther and the only remaining member of his earlier escort. He was lifted from his wagon and transferred to horseback. Then, in a further adventurous episode involving hours of fast riding, ostensibly so as to shake off would-be pursuers, Luther was spirited away to a Thuringian castle in the Elector's possession, the Wartburg, arriving there at 11 at night.[2]

Luther's relative seclusion in the castle meant that he was effectively removed from the acutely confrontational situation that his appearance at

Worms had exacerbated. In other words, prudently taken out of the tense equations of German politics even before the fatal edict was issued, his presence could embarrass no one. The Elector's overlord and friend Charles V, for instance, would not be put in the position of alienating German opinion by executing Luther if Frederick ensured that the heretical outlaw could not be found. At the Wartburg Luther was made comfortable, waited on by noble pages, was well-fed and treated with every courtesy. The top-security arrangements for his incognito, in an inaccessible chamber within a wing of the Wartburg, included his assumption of the cloak, beard and pseudonym – 'Junker Georg' (or 'Junker Jörg'), 'squire George' – of a knight, fittingly enough, perhaps, in the light of his recent heroic adventures.

Even for someone less highly strung than Martin Luther, the whirlwind of the previous months, especially his being placed in the fulcrum of the *Reich*, followed by his enthralling capture and subsequent hard rural rides, might have created some sense of anti-climax or even of boredom in the confines of the Elector's castle. In his table talk of later years he was to recall highly troublesome visits from the devil to his room in the castle. The acute constipation on which he reported in considerable detail in letters from the Wartburg may have been a symptom of such distress. A hunting trip left him disgusted at the cruelty of the 'worthy occupation for men with nothing to do'.

There was, however, worthy occupation for him in the Wartburg, and Luther quickly set about it. Indeed his letters out of the castle – what the Luther biographer Martin Brecht calls 'an intense and personal exchange' – read for the most part as breezy, positive and full of projects. On the day the Edict of Worms was finalised, 26 May, he wrote to Melanchthon about his riposte to an orthodox Louvain theologian, Jacobus Latomus (or Jacques Masson, *c.*1475–1544). Luther completed his work, which focused on the question of the freedom of the will, in June and it was issued in Wittenberg in September, when he also published a work, 'On Confession', disputing the pope's claim to require reception of the sacrament of penance. (All such published writings were, of course, in total defiance of the Edict of Worms.) Other works completed included expositions of Psalms and a translation of and commentary on Mary's prayer in Luke's Gospel, the Magnificat. Despite illness in July 1521, a bad month for him in the Wartburg, over the course of that summer he was at work on the 'German Postil', a series of explanatory sermons for preachers to deliver on the Advent and Christmas set of liturgical readings from Scripture. A work completed in November 1521 and ready for publication, to become a best-seller early in the following year, attacked the Catholic insistence on irreversible monastic vows, especially that of chastity: 'The Judgement of Martin Luther on Monastic Vows'. The preface of this work, dedicating it to Hans Luther, willingly conceded that his father had been right all along in his opposition to his son's taking monastic vows. Another of Luther's works from this highly productive Wartburg period, 'The Abuse of the Mass', insisted that the rite should be fully congregational. On 1 December he wrote a highly aggressive 'warning' to Albrecht von Hohenzollern who had since the previous September revivified what Luther termed the 'idol' of the exhibition of relics in Halle in Saxony in order to promote indulgences. The archbishop was also censured by Luther for suppressing the marriages of priests.

The nature and the fact of publication of such works help draw to our attention what we may term 'the myth of the Wartburg' within Luther's life. Luther himself was initially responsible for this legend, not least by writing of his place of retreat in terms of absolute exile and remoteness. In his letters from the castle he referred to it in language betokening complete isolation: 'the wilderness', 'on the mountain', 'the land of the birds'. He spoke of himself as, so to speak, at last truly an Augustinian 'eremite', the word meaning literally 'hermit'. He had, he said, 'set [his] soul on quiet studies', while years later in his table talk he recalled, 'I was far from people' – so far that at the time he referred to the castle on the hill as 'my Patmos', an allusion to the Aegean island of exile of the Apostle John according to Revelation 1:9. Patmos was in fact the term that the great biographer of Luther R.H. Bainton adopted from St John, via Luther, for his chapter on the period of his subject's apparent absence from the world.

The notion of the Wartburg as Patmos may be linked to the contemporaneous popular pictorial depiction of Luther as the evangelist John. There may even have been a further analogy with Christ, in the desert on the eve of His missions. We catch such an allusion in the bewildered words of the pro-Luther artist Albrecht Dürer whose reaction on 17 May to the news of his hero's disappearance was, 'O God, if Luther is dead who will expound to us the gospel?' The echo there is of Luke 24:27: 'he [Jesus] expounded to them all the Scriptures. . . .'

The portrayal of a complete concealment in the Wartburg went on to nourish the later Romantic portrayal built up of Luther the solitary genius. To take an example, Thomas Sefton Rivington in his heroising Victorian celebration of Luther's Protestant masculinity, *The Story of Luther's Life*, slotted the Wartburg episode into the perfection of Luther's 'apotheosis' – his culmination as hero at Worms, with no later 'blemish' to spoil the ideal:

> He was abruptly transported far from the scene where the great revolution of the sixteenth century was in course of accomplishment. . . . 'Ah', said the multitude, 'no more shall we see, no more shall we hear the noble-minded man whose voice stirred our hearts.' . . . Luther has disappeared, and is perhaps lost for ever.[3]

Rivington went further, to hint at a suggestion that Luther was so shut away in the castle that he underwent for a time a sort of death. This author had already written a hagiography of John Hus, whose execution at Constance in 1415 had perfected his martyr's crown. Though Luther came back from the Wartburg, to exhibit later a character marked by signs of 'blemish', the ten-month withdrawal in the castle was, as Dürer imagined it, a kind of mortality, when God, wrote Rivington, 'hid' Luther, or as we might say, he was 'dead to the world'. Rivington conjured up an 'unknown orator' of the time whose tale extended further the idea of a dead, and therefore Christ-like, Luther: '"The dead body of Luther . . . has been pierced with wounds."'

The reality was that in the Wartburg Luther was far from isolated and very far from dead. The place itself was not all that distant from anywhere and the hours of hectic riding on the day of Luther's arrival may even have been devised to create some illusion that the place was much more in the back-of-beyond than was in fact the case. Originally placed for defensive purposes on a pinnacle, the Wartburg was a conveniently placed hunting lodge on a wooded escarpment about a mile from the city of Eisenach, itself one of the four major towns of the Thuringian region of Germany. From it, Luther sent out a regular stream of letters and received and commented on gossip about political goings-on. Above all, as we saw, he produced a constant supply of pamphlets deeply, passionately and sometimes violently engaged with current needs and events and very promptly printed, after Luther had received proofs back and made some angry comments about the poor quality of the printers' evidently rushed work. So, the key to Luther's period in that castle that was sheltered but hardly secluded from the world, was intense contact with it, above all through controversy. Entirely typical of his two-way engagement with the world outside the walls of the hunting lodge was that violent letter of December 1521 to the archbishop of Mainz, putting him (again) on warning for exhibiting relics at Halle and for suppressing the marriage of his priests. So the Wartburg period represented no reflective sabbatical, nor entombment, but an intense continuation of Luther's highly combative period of engagement with the world of debate. As we shall soon see, he came in intimate contact with the pace of events in Wittenberg and those developments called him back to even more direct action there.

LUTHER AND THE WITTENBERG REVOLUTION

Such works as 'The Judgement of Martin Luther on Monastic Vows' and 'The Abuse of the Mass' continued in the vein of 'The Babylonian Captivity of the church' in launching a sustained, if largely theoretical, attack on the Catholic Church's actual practice and conduct of religious rites and obligations. Sooner or later, and sooner rather than later, those calls for change must issue in real and extensive alterations, in the practical expressions of a transformed Christian faith. Nor is it surprising that the theatre for that implementation, in the arena of practice, of calls for reform in the realm of theory was Wittenberg. During a first spell in the Wartburg, between May and December 1521, Luther was physically, but certainly not spiritually, absent from his adopted city, regularly writing to his lieutenants there, and above all to Philip Melanchthon, sending letters of encouragement, reproof and general intervention. As early as May 1521 he was expressing concern at the actions of student hotheads who, fired up with his gospel, were, he claimed, discrediting it by offering violence to priests. However, that was in Erfurt, where disturbances continued to bubble up into July. As far as Wittenberg was concerned, though, in the middle of the same month of July Luther was congratulating Spalatin on the fact that only good news, about university improvements, was coming to him out of the city. However, between June and July 1521 Andreas Bodenstein von Carlstadt was already setting out the academic foundations for what was to be a full implementation of a radical reformation of religious practice in the city. In the months that followed, Carlstadt, along with Luther's fellow-Augustinian, Gabriel Zwilling (c.1487–1558), were indeed translating doctrinal reformation into its necessary concomitant, practical transformations centring on the Mass, which were to involve the abandonment of traditional vestments, the partial rendering of the liturgy into German, the end of endowed Masses for the departed, erosion of the laws of fasting and abstinence, and large-scale destruction of images of Christ and the saints. From 29 September, in line with Luther's own proposals in 'The Babylonian Captivity', communion in both kinds – the wine as well as the bread – was introduced. Led by Zwilling, the city's

Augustinians were most responsive to radicalism: they began renouncing their vows and early in October gave up the Mass in its traditional form.

From early in October crowd violence fuelled by religious excitement and discord and incited by the university students had broken out, with a riot directed against members of a religious order who were following their custom of visiting Wittenberg to preach sermons and collect sums of money. Through October and November there was intense debate in the city focusing on the Mass, or eucharist – whether the chalice of wine as well as the host of bread should be given to lay people and whether private endowed Masses should continue to be celebrated. On the latter issue Luther himself stepped in with a work of November, 'The Abuse of the Mass'. In it he adopted the approach that was to characterise him consistently on this issue: change must be brought about, the Mass was not a sacrifice and private Masses should be disallowed, but reform must be gradual and must accommodate the concerns of traditionalists. Violence flared up again on 3 December when priests of the city were forcibly disturbed while they were saying Mass and the following day a Mass altar in the Franciscan friary was demolished. However, by that point, 4 December, the second day of religious rioting, Luther was secretly back in the city, following up his literary intervention with a personal visit to see for himself over the course of several days what the situation in Wittenberg was. Oddly, considering ugly bullying of priests and Franciscan friars by students on 3 and 4 December, Luther professed himself on 5 December happy with the situation in the city: perhaps he saw at that stage what he wanted to. Returning to the Wartburg on about 12 December, he sent back to Wittenberg his 'A Sincere Admonition by Martin Luther to All Christians to Guard against Insurrection and Rebellion' (published early in 1522). As we shall see, the 'Wittenberg revolution' had by no means burned itself out: indeed, fresh violence erupted in the run-up to Christmas 1521 and at that Christmas Carlstadt introduced changes to the Mass that were bound to be divisive, including the abandonment of the traditional priest's Mass vestments and the proffer of the chalice to the laity. Perhaps it would require Luther's permanent return to put an end to the turbulence in Wittenberg.

So the main challenge to Luther in the coming year, 1522, was to be that of deciding on a role to adopt: whether to stay in the Wartburg as a writer and scholar or to be actively involved in the social and religious changes taking place in his adopted city as part of the practical implementation of his own doctrines. He was torn, and, back in the Wartburg, in the sharp criticisms he made of those left in charge of affairs in the city, including Melanchthon, he was clearly showing impatience to return to Wittenberg. However, another task, a scholarly rather than a practical one, would keep him in the castle until it was complete. In a letter written soon after his entry into the Wartburg he had announced, 'I am reading the Bible in Greek and Hebrew.' Then from a week before Christmas 1521 he gave himself a timetable for the completion of a project that would require continued retreat: 'I shall be hiding here until Easter [20 April 1522] and . . . translate the New Testament into German. . . .' In the event he would have to foreshorten that schedule, returning to Wittenberg in view of a deepening crisis there and to put a brake on the pace of religious change, even though extensive change itself was to be implemented.

In the meantime Luther's months in 1522 were divided into two sectors, indicating the possible collision of his roles: action or scholarship? A first phase lay between his brief visit to Wittenberg in December 1521 and his final return there, in March 1522. Throughout those winter months he was, indeed, physically absent from the city, though anxious about its apparent descent into anarchy but was focused on the secluded scholarly task of his translation of Scripture. This was followed by a second phase following his full return in March to Wittenberg, where, with a few brief intervals, he was to spend the rest of his life.

Such peace as prevailed in the electoral capital during Luther's early December visit was indeed illusory. Between 1521 and 1522 Carlstadt seemed to have emerged as the presiding genius of religious radicalism in Wittenberg and he took the bold step, for a priest having a vow of chastity, of marrying in January. However, in the early part of 1522 he was overtaken in his role as the director of the Wittenberg revolution. Shortly after Christmas, on 27 December, a trio of inspirational 'prophets', two weavers, Thomas Drechsel, or Drechsler, and Nicholas Storch, and a student, Marcus Stübner, or Thomae, all from the town of Zwickau near Germany's border with Czech Bohemia, arrived in the city, and thereupon Wittenberg's radical reformation, already initiated by Carlstadt and Zwilling in the autumn, underwent rapid acceleration. Zwickau was an industrial textile centre close to the rich mining country of the Erzgebirge mountains and the town's sharp economic contrasts of proto-capitalist wealth and working-class debt and poverty gave the religious radicalism that was already flourishing there a militant social tinge. The particular generator of this combined social, political and religious radicalism was the Zwickau town preacher since 1520, Thomas Müntzer (c.1490–1525). A former disciple of Luther, who recommended him for a preaching position in Zwickau, Müntzer had come to see in Luther's teachings, and especially what he viewed as their spurious and over-privileged academic underpinning, a shameful compromise with the anti-Christian world of power and wealth. Until his death in the German Peasants' Revolt in 1525, leading a squadron of millenarian zealots, Thomas Müntzer was to remain Luther's radical incubus. Now his disciples, driven out, like Müntzer himself, from Zwickau by the city's authorities, arrived in Wittenberg, as if to represent, directly in Luther's headquarters, their challenge to key views of his. They rejected his insistence, set out in 'The Babylonian Captivity of the Church', on the need for infant baptism, a key sacramental cement bonding Church and society through ensuring that all members of the latter were also of the former. They relied on dreams and visions as opposed to his claim that Scripture held the key to all truth.

The grave problem with these developments for Luther was that they threatened to expedite innovations in Wittenberg which already had firm support from Carlstadt, that they built on the foundations of sweeping change laid by Zwilling and that they exposed the indecision of Luther's *locum tenens* Philip Melanchthon in resisting the prophetic revolution whose fruits were beginning to spread out into the rural areas. Continuing riot and violence were the outcome from January and on the 13th of that month Luther wrote to Melanchthon candidly to 'say that I do not approve of your irresolution' in dealing with the crisis of the prophets. Giving instructions to his ineffective lieutenant to take appropriate action 'in my place', Luther was, in one sense, calling for his own return to Wittenberg to address the anarchic situation there. That was all the more serious inasmuch as in that turbulent month of January the staunchly conservative Duke George of Ducal Saxony lodged a formal complaint in the *Reichsregiment*, the Imperial Council, decrying the events taking place in the Electorate, and Charles V's government, based in Nuremberg, issued an order to abandon all religious change in the German Lands. In the light of such pressures, measures agreed by the Wittenberg city council and Carlstadt in the *Kirchenordnung* or ecclesiastical constitution of 24 January to introduce fair poor relief with a ban on clerical begging, grants for needy schoolchildren and a health service, along with the removal of images and changes in the administration of communion by the chalice as well as the bread, were vetoed by Frederick, though supported by the Wittenberg city council. In February the extent of the dilemma of the Elector was revealed. If change went on unimpeded Frederick might even lose his principality to his cousin and arch-conservative rival, Duke George. If, on the other hand, Luther – surely the only man with the prestige sufficient to slow down change – returned openly to Wittenberg, the Edict of Worms might be triggered into operation against him and his protector, and Frederick and Luther were lost. In writing to Luther on 22 February Frederick's expressed preference was on balance for him to stay hidden, at least until the Diet scheduled to meet in Nuremberg in 1522. As for Luther himself, doubtless confirmed in his resolution by an anxious request from the Wittenberg city council that he come home, he was now all too willing to confront the radical spirits in person. Following receipt on the 28th of Frederick's letter of 22 February, the following day he set out, still disguised, to ride back to Wittenberg via Jena. In view of the radical crisis, he may have telescoped his own programme of work for the winter and spring: as late as 13 January he still intending to return to Wittenberg with his New Testament translation 'after Easter', but 'hearing wilder things' of Wittenberg, by the 17th he was planning to 'return in a short time' and now, in the event, he was coming just before Lent. As we shall see, it is possible to speculate that he rescheduled his appointments not only so as to wrest control of the Wittenberg situation from the left, perhaps before it was too late, but also to do so through the medium and spectacular impact of a cycle of sermons designed for the penitential season of Lent.

During the journey an incident took place that reveals the extent to which Luther was to acquire fabulous status in the German popular culture of his age. When on a wintry night late in February he broke his journey to stop at an inn outside Jena, still accoutred as a knight, two Swiss students on their way to study in Luther's university, one of whom, Johann Kessler, later recollected the incident in memoirs published in 1540, entered the premises. Luther, warm, genial and generous, playing, if anything, the part of an avuncular don almost suspiciously knowledgeable about the Wittenberg curriculum and staff, retained his knightly disguise. The characters in the little play that now unfolded took up their appointed parts almost as if they knew the script of such comedies:

> *Kessler* [to Luther] – Can you tell us, sir, whether Luther is now at Wittenberg, or where he may be?
> *Luther* – I have authentic information that he is not at Wittenberg, but that he will soon return.

The little interlude proceeds as Luther asks the potentially risky question, 'My boys, . . . what do they think about this Luther in Switzerland?' Then two merchants enter to join the cast, one of whom just happens to be reading Luther's sermons and expresses a desperate desire that Dr Luther (his disguise still intact) would some day hear his confession. The success of the whole *tableau vivant* depends for much of its narrative credibility on the operation of certain familiar conventions, within a culture that relied heavily on visual prompts for accepting clothes as signifiers of identity: Luther, for example, immediately knew the two students were Swiss from their clothing, and one of the young Swiss prefers to believe that their interlocutor is the famous knightly humanist Ulrich von Hutten, not Luther, because 'he certainly *looks* [my emphasis] more like a knight than a monk'. This story may also have some genre parallels with the account of the mysterious post-Resurrection appearance at Emmaus (Luke 24:13–31) of Jesus to two disciples, who, unaware of his identity, provide Him with a synopsis of His own life, death and rising again. Beyond that, the story category involving Luther here may be aligned with the motif type that we may term 'the king in disguise', making up a rich range of European folk tales involving popular or legendary rulers – King Alfred, Richard the Lionheart, Henry V, Henry VIII, James V, Ivan the Terrible, Peter the Great, and so on – all being involved in disguised encounters with subjects who are subsequently astonished when they discover the truth. The evolving Luther legend was certainly to place him, within his own lifetime, in that kind of range, partly because Germany's most famous man had disappeared into a black hole, while books in his name continued to appear, creating a story-book air of will-o'-the wisp mystery around him reflected in the scene in the inn, as recalled, with whatever embroidery, by one of its players.[4]

Luther's self-appointed role on his return to Wittenberg was that of a brakeman slowing over-rapid change. Before he assumed that task he had first to make peace with Elector Frederick, if only because for the time to come he and the constituted authorities would need to work closely to a shared purpose. He had written one fairly light-hearted letter (on 24 February) containing elaborately conceived mockery of the prince's beloved relic collection and advising the ruler to be 'wise' (his special sobriquet). A second letter, of 5 March, explained his disobedience of the Elector's stated preference that he stay in the Wartburg for the time being and did so in a language expressing some defiance: 'I am going to Wittenberg under a far higher protection than the Elector's. I have no intention of asking Your Electoral Grace for protection.' However, on 7 or 8 March, in response to a request originating with the Elector, Luther wrote in rather more conciliatory terms explaining his decision in the context of his responsibility for the spiritual welfare of his flock in Wittenberg.

THE *INVOCAVIT* SERMONS, MARCH 1522

Next, Luther was ready to deliver, from 9 to 16 March, a series of relatively short homilies, the *Invocavit* Sermons, preached one each day, in German, over eight days. It is possible that a careful choice of timing made it possible to deliver these highly appropriate Lenten addresses. The first Sunday of Lent, known as *Invocavit* and taking its name from the words of the introductory prayer of the Mass set for that day, opened up the first full week of the Lenten fast, the season of gravity, recollection, repentance and urgent awareness of the need for a new start. So Luther's sermons, carefully designed to restore his control of the religious situation in Wittenberg, were a Lenten series, and all the more effective for hinting at a well-understood contrast between the spirit of carnival and the mood of Lent. Specifically, what Luther seems to have been doing was using the liturgy and the theatre of the season in order to dispel an implied disorderly pre-Lenten carnival of radicalism and misrule and to recall the citizens to the Lenten paths of righteousness, repentance and restraint. Therefore, Luther, again showing his calculated mastery of visual symbolism, matched his own appearance to the time and season. He now very deliberately abandoned the splendours of his knight's costume, in favour of his black monastic habit, cutting off his cavalier's beard, and having his skull shaved to restore his monk's tonsure. Wordlessly, the wearing of the traditional cowl and the carefully contrived deployment of the visual drama of the speaker's body in themselves stated the message that less was to change, or less rapidly, than the radical spirits wished, but the dark gravity of the black Augustinian habit also underscored the Lenten seriousness of Luther's opening words, 'We are all held to death . . .' .

The verbal style as well as the visual aura of the *Invocavit* sermons undoubtedly enhanced their appeal and power. It was not until the following year that a version of them was printed for national consumption, for their immediate impact was not literary but that of almost intimate oral deliveries, designed for face-to-face encounters with Wittenberg people in a deeply familiar form of contemporaneous German urban collective culture, the public town sermon. An observer recalled how Luther propelled the homilies forwards with a sympathetic projection of his personality, and with what all hearers of Luther agreed was a melodious voice: 'the man is kind, gentle and cheerful. His voice is sweet and sonorous, so that I wonder at the sweet speaking of the man'. He used the informal, conversational style of the emergent genre of the Reformation town sermon and brought the deliverer to the level of his auditors: 'Take an example by me.' Despite the Lenten mode, a little light self-imaging as an ordinary townsman, just a *Kerl*, a 'bloke', with simple everyday pleasures – 'I slept, and drank beer with Melanchthon and Amsdorf . . .' – was well contrived as a crowd-pleaser.

So in their way the *Invocavit* sermons, as an oratorical triumph, stand comparison with Luther's victory at Worms, and seem to have had an almost miraculous effect in discrediting and dispersing the Wittenberg radicals. Just as various encounters with disputants following the issue of the 95 Theses had helped Luther to work out his own intellectual position, so the challenge from the left that produced the *Invocavit* homilies helped forge a definition of what was now to emerge as a Reformation. Until 1521 Luther had had to define his religious and doctrinal stance only with reference to the Catholic system he was inexorably abandoning. Now he was setting a left-of-centre reform course, steering carefully between old tradition and radical innovation. In doing so, he was die-stamping the hallmarks of what historians have come to know as the 'magisterial' (rather than the 'radical') Reformation. Its essence consisted of: partnership with the state – the 'magistrate', and hence 'magisterial'; relative gradualism in introducing change in such areas as image-breaking ('Images should be left until further notice,' he insisted); tarrying until even the least radical Christian could accept alterations; stress on Christian freedom, voluntarism and refusal to coerce except in absolute essentials; and acceptance withal of the need to introduce real transformations in religious and social life, in liturgy, doctrine, social welfare, education and so on, in the Lutheran case all in fidelity to the programme set out in the 'Reformation classics' of 1520.

A subtext of the *Invocavit* sermons was that any challenge to Luther's leadership within what he termed his 'fold' of Wittenberg mounted during his absence was to be crushed. Much of his message was in itself profoundly persuasive: 'Compel or force anyone with power I will not, for faith must be gentle and unforced.' A more ominous theme, though, was that, had he wished, he might have brought the *Reich* to a war of religion – though he did not need to, since 'the Word' acted on his behalf and carried all before it. Such claims – that Luther had the 'Word' on his side – ensured that, insofar as the radical crisis had incorporated a leadership rivalry between Luther and Carlstadt, the latter was vanquished by the *Invocavit* sermons. Through them Martin Luther decisively retrieved the support Carlstadt and the other radicals had undoubtedly secured from the populace and, for a while, the council in Wittenberg in late 1521 and early 1522. Andreas Carlstadt had now to take the consequences of a serious political defeat: he was banned from preaching, he protested at the prohibition in writing, was then called before a university disciplinary tribunal and in effect silenced. His eventual departure for a country parish, Orlamünde, where at least for a few years, as 'neighbour Andy' or 'brother Andy', he was left untroubled to live out his innocent gospel of social equality, was a necessary outcome of his defeat in the power struggle of 1521; he ended up, though, on the faculty of the University of Basel in Switzerland. As for Gabriel Zwilling, he became reconciled to Luther, who went so far as to recommend him for a preaching position. The Zwickau men could be more easily dealt with, partly because, unlike Carlstadt, they did not represent an 'insider' threat to Luther's supremacy. Luther had an interview with Storch in April in which he fairly gently ridiculed the prophets' in-house jargon of 'degrees of mobility and immobility' and the like. Radical ordinances concerning social reform along with extensive liturgical innovations passed by the council back in January were now rescinded. All this was followed in late April and early May 1522 by a kind of victory-celebration preaching tour of other Saxon towns (including Zwickau) and parishes in which Luther, still, of course, in danger from the Edict of Worms in making such a well-advertised journey, nevertheless extended the circle of his authority in his region.

LUTHER AND THE STATE: HENRY VIII

During that spring preaching tour Luther had occasion in one sermon to address the issue of obedience to the state. Taking as his support text the passage in the Acts of the Apostles, chapter 4, in which Peter evinces considerable antipathy to the 'kings of the earth . . . and the rulers', who opposed the Lord and his Christ (Acts 4:26), Luther explained that a prince who ordered a Christian subject of his to go against the gospel would forfeit any claim to that subject's obedience. Indeed, a guarded attitude of considerable suspicion of princely authorities was to characterise Luther's outlook over the following period, in which states and rulers hostile to Luther won in return his unbridled enmity. In 1522 this certainly characterised his attitude to Henry VIII of England.

Before the breach with Rome occasioned by his marital difficulties from the mid-1520s onwards, Henry was a staunchly orthodox prince who ruled an overwhelmingly Catholic realm, one in which any initial positive interest in Luther's writings in 1519 quickly gave way to official suspicion and censure. Encouraged by his leading minister, Cardinal Thomas Wolsey (c. 1474–1530), and in response to 'The Babylonian Captivity', King Henry, aided by learned subjects, produced a display of his own Catholic fidelity and learning, a defence, the *Assertio Septem Sacramentorum*, of the full range of seven sacraments of the Church. These, as we saw, Luther, in 'The Babylonian Captivity of the Church', had reduced to two or three, on the grounds that Scripture was the sole test of the authenticity of such major institutions of the Church as sacraments. Henry's work slighted Luther – 'a wolf of hell . . . limb of Satan . . . How rotten is his mind!' – and affirmed the validity of the extra-scriptural traditions and the teaching authority of the Catholic Church which proclaimed the doctrine of seven sacraments. The king's composition was published in June 1521 and won for him from Leo X the title *fidei defensor*, 'defender of the faith', desire for which had prompted Henry to write (or perhaps edit) the book in the first place. The *Assertio* appeared in June 1521 in a German translation prompted by Duke George and Luther decided to interrupt the revisions of his all-important New Testament translation so as to answer Henry. On 1 August he published what was, and was fully intended to be, a direct, insulting and personal attack on the king, 'Against Henry, King of the English', issued first in German and then republished in a Latin version. Indeed, in an age of almost universal reverence for kings as God's anointed, the most noteworthy feature of this defence of Luther's doctrines against Henry's attack was Luther's personal abuse against a monarch. But Henry had had the temerity to enter the arena as a theological opponent for Luther and was thus fair game for whatever insults came off the latter's pen. One feature of the unrestrained theological polemic of that period was the use of animal metaphors for one's enemy. In the papal bull Luther had been depicted as a 'boar', Henry had portrayed Luther as a 'wolf' and now the king himself was 'that damnable and rotten worm'. The dispute between the king and the friar rumbled on through the 1520s but in the immediate circumstances of 1522 it revealed Luther's deep distrust of most of the 'rulers of the world' – the ignorance in Henry's book, for instance, was 'not to be wondered at in a royal author'.

The broadly political campaign climaxing in March 1522 saw no let-up in Luther's literary productivity in that year. His spring preaching tour brought him once more face to face with the moral and personal problems of ordinary people, including marital issues and, probably before the end of September, he published a sermon treatise, 'The Estate of Marriage', in which he managed to break through from a preoccupation with the 'bitterness and anguish' of the married state into an appreciation of its 'real happiness . . . pleasing to God and precious in his sight'. However, his greatest literary achievement of that year was undoubtedly his production of the German New Testament. He had accomplished the translation in under three months in the Wartburg and undertook revisions of it back in Wittenberg. Printing began in July, and *Das Newe Testament Deutzsch*, 'The German New Testament', was all ready by 25 September, selling briskly at variable prices according to the quality of binding and production, and for the printers, profitably in somewhere between 3,000 and 5,000 copies. Luther received no royalties, for this or any other of his productions. A new Wittenberg edition, with corrections and some tactful amendments of some of its more combative anti-papal illustrations, came out in December.

THE NEW TESTAMENT TRANSLATION: THE 'SEPTEMBER TESTAMENT', 1522

The New Testament translation was begun, as we saw, in the Wartburg and Luther worked intensely on it in the first weeks of 1522 before his coming back to Wittenberg. He may in fact have arranged, and, indeed, expedited the translation as his major task for the winter, working full out on it, before his return to the city, so as then to be able to throw himself into the practical issues we reviewed above.

The work on the New Testament was part of a vast and partly collaborative exercise in the translation of the entire Bible into German, a task extended over the next decade, with major interruptions as a result of controversy in the mid-1520s, then further instalments. The translation of the Bible proper was completed in 1534 when it was published in around September and a final revision by the team of translators began in 1539.

In beginning the project with the New Testament, Luther was, obviously, starting at the end. This procedure could be readily justified in terms of the traditional primacy for Christians of the New Testament as the culmination and fulfilment, the 'happy ending', of the rest of the Bible. To set against that, though, was an equally traditional view that held that all of Scripture was equally the word of God – so why prioritise one section over another? One answer was to the effect that, indeed, all of Scripture was equally God's word but that some portions were, so to speak, more equally God's word than others. This claim would certainly have justified the priority Luther gave to translating first the all-important New Testament, which, for Martin Luther, contained within it the fulfilment of the promises and predictions held out in the Old. Especially from the point of view of Luther's doctrinal polarisation of law versus gospel, fear versus freedom, while the Old Testament could not be thought inferior to the New, the New Testament *was* superior to the Old Testament inasmuch as, whereas 'the Old Testament is a volume containing God's laws and commandments', 'the New Testament is a volume containing God's promised evangel . . .'.[5]

Having established the higher standing, as traditionally maintained, of the New Testament over the Old, Luther went on to draw bold distinctions of quality between sections of the New Testament itself. In this respect, it is important to realise that Luther as translator was not acting only to convert as faithfully as possible the words of one language into another. Rather, he was also working in a kind of extension of his professional role as a commentator on, interpreter of and critical evaluator of the texts before him. One important aspect of this evaluative role when it came to rendering the Scriptures into his own language was that of according varying status to the individual books that made up the whole. Traditionally, the New Testament was divided into, first, the Gospels – the three textually closely related 'synoptic' narratives of Christ's life, death and rising again assigned to Matthew, Mark and Luke, along with the more free-standing, spiritual and doctrinal Gospel of John. Next came the Epistles, or letters, and other writings of, or attributed to, Apostles such as Paul, James, Peter, John and so forth. Because they contained the actual words and deeds of Christ, the Gospels were traditionally accorded precedence, especially in their liturgical deployment. Thus when as passages of the Scriptures they were read out in instalments during the Mass, a lower-ranking minister, the sub-deacon, could deliver the Epistle, but only a deacon or the priest saying Mass could pronounce the 'holy' Gospel, whose reading was preceded by reverential introductions and a prayer to purify the lips of the reader; hearers stood to hear the gospel.

In his prefaces to the whole New Testament and to individual sections of it, boldly enough, Luther overturned this ancient precedence. He wrote, for instance, that 'the epistles of St Paul and St Peter are far in advance of the three gospels of Matthew, Mark and Luke' – though not above that of John, which Luther believed to be the best of the Gospels, recording the words, not the deeds of Christ. It was as if those more external deeds of Christ's earthly life, His miracles, for instance, were of less interest to Luther. What was of key concern to him was the message of faith in Christ's saving death and resurrection, with the meaning and interpretation that St Paul in the Epistle to the Romans and St Peter in his first Epistle placed, not on 'the works and miracles of Christ' but on drawing out the inner meaning 'of how faith in Christ conquers sin, death, and hell; and gives life, righteousness, and salvation'. So the external narratives of Christ, traditionally *the* Gospels, were not really the gospel. In the narrative Gospels, Christ 'set forth many doctrines and regulations', and we would certainly become familiar with these if we read those accounts, but if we were to know the true gospel, which was actually set out in the letters of Paul and Peter, we would find there the much more vital information that Christ conquers 'sin, death, and the devil', for us, on our behalf. Again, if we were to concentrate on the narratives of Christ's life, we might be tempted to 'imitate' His many acts of kindness and love – and perhaps even to aim to win our own merit in doing so. Luther insisted, however, that the Gospels should be overlooked as a manual of good conduct, for that would be to 'make Christ into a Moses, and the gospel is not a book of law . . .'.

Therefore, it was important to evaluate the texts of Scripture according to their own alignment with the theme of justification by faith. Thus the synoptic Gospels of Jesus themselves were secondary, containing, as they did, 'the works or the [moral] preaching', while the 'epistles of St. Paul and St. Peter are far in advance of the three gospels of Matthew, Mark, and Luke'. By the same token, a passage of the New Testament, the Epistle of James, with its teaching that faith without good works was dead, stood little chance of winning a place in Luther's list of New Testament favourites: 'an epistle of straw'. In contrast, St Paul's Epistle to the Romans was 'the most important document in the New Testament, the gospel in its purest expression', disparaging law and works, elevating grace and faith. Thus Luther's decisive qualitative ranking of the Scripture and in particular his ordering of the books of the New Testament according to a reversal of traditional scales of value, was driven by his own doctrinal determinants.

Especially considering Luther's proclamation of himself at Worms as being in effect enslaved – his conscience was 'captive' – to the word of God, in his approach to the variant texts within Scripture he was no slavish literalist. The same point about his exercise of freedom with regard to the biblical text applies not just to his ranking of the various parts of Scripture but also to the method of his actual translation, not only of the 1522 'September' New Testament but of the whole eventual translated Bible.

The freedom Luther claimed in the actual process of translating, as well as in the grading of individual books of Scripture according to their perceived doctrinal value, was deployed in his lexical and textual decisions as a translator and his choice of words. The most famous, or notorious, instance of his exercise of translator's freedom, in his case steered by doctrinal considerations, arose over his insertion into the text of St Paul's Epistle to the Romans of an 'only' (in Latin, '*sola*', in German '*allein*') between 'faith' and 'without', in the clause rendered in the English Authorised Version of Romans (3:28) as 'Therefore we conclude that a man is justified by faith without the deeds of the law', in Latin '*Arbitramur, hominem justificari ex fide absque operibus.*' Luther was aware of the allegation by Catholic adversaries that in making this intrusion into the text he was playing fast and loose with the Scripture. As the Catholic controversialist Cochlaeus was to comment, 'That man of quarrels changed many things in [the New Testament] . . . and removed many things, and added many other things. . . .' Although Cochlaeus did not mention the alteration in Romans specifically, a Catholic opponent Hieronymus Emser (1478–1527) did, as did Luther himself, when he wrote, in an open letter on translating published in 1530, that 'the papists are making a tremendous fuss, because the word *sola* is not in Paul's text . . .'. There is, first of all, some clear logical justification for the intrusion of '*sola*' in this trope, which is that the '*absque*' in '*absque operibus*', 'without the deeds of the law', might render '*sola*' necessary to hammer home the sense of the first part of the statement and that its inclusion was therefore perfectly legitimate. Second, Luther defended his insertion to Emser by citing the speech habits of the German language in which, he claimed, such an emphatic inclusion made for good writing. That was not, however, the defence that Luther stressed in the 1530 open letter on translation, but rather he defiantly stated that what he had written, in rendering the Romans verse in just that way, he had written: 'I translated the New Testament to the best of my ability and according to my conscience. . . . It is my Testament and my translation, and it shall continue to be mine.'

'It is my Testament': how did Luther proceed with the actual mechanics of translation in such a way as to personalise those Scriptures? One answer to that question has to do with the very frequency of Bible translation in German, going back, indeed, to the origins of the written form of the language. In late medieval England, the sourcing of the dissident Lollard movement from Scripture resulted in what was in effect an official ban on scriptural translations into the vernacular. In contrast, pre-Reformation Germany, in common with most of the rest of western Europe, had, as we saw in Chapter 2 above, numerous editions of biblical translations, even though these were typically renditions of the Latin Vulgate. The fact that Luther's translation was one of a number meant that it was not *the* standard or neutral form of the Scripture in German, but one version among several – 'my Testament'.

Much has rightly been made of the excellence of the entire Lutheran Bible in its great contribution to the evolution of the German language and its literature. Luther worked, with help from the Greek-language scholar Melanchthon, towards a translation of the New Testament into German using the 1519 second edition of Erasmus's version in its original Greek, first published in 1516 (for the Old Testament he was to employ an accurate Hebrew text published in Italy in 1494). His aim was to translate the whole material justly and directly into German. Indeed, he took great pride in the authentic German character of his rendition, which was aimed at ordinary fellow-countrymen and women – the housewife in the home, the children in the streets, the common man in the market-place. Lavish illustrations, some of them by the Elector's artist Lucas Cranach, patriated the text through showing biblical scenes in German landscapes and presenting rulers featured in the Bible costumed and bearded as typical German princes of Luther's day: in his version of Matthew 2:6, where the English Authorised Version has 'governor' for a ruler, Luther used the unique German word for a duke, *Herzog*. He also adopted and adapted the form of the German language that he said he himself spoke – the variant in use in the Saxon government departments, a standard dialect that was in geographical terms centrally placed between the two main variant forms of the language, the *Hochdeutsch* or 'high German' of southern Germany and the *Plattdeutsch* or 'low German' of the north of the country. Luther pointed out that this central dialect already functioned as a national *lingua franca* for regional rulers coming together in federal meetings and on that basis its use in his Bible translations also operated to provide his text with the potential for nation-wide circulation and intelligibility.

All of Luther's contributions to German language, literature and identity through the translation of Scripture are often and rightly cele-brated. For one thing, his translation gave the language whole new words as well as rich proverbs. The voice he used was elevated but intelligible, popular but not coarse. And a typical standard history of German literature exalts the way that Luther's translation 'was, above all things, a *German* Bible . . . : he gave the German people a . . . "Volksbuch" [book for the people]'. Luther himself provided an example of just such an adaptation to the needs of his fellow Germans, his sensitivity, as it were, to the 'national ear'. He said that he proposed to replace the traditional form of the angel's greeting to Mary in Luke's Gospel, 1:28. In the Latin Vulgate this salutation was rendered as '*Ave Maria, gratia plena*: in English, 'Hail Mary, full of grace', and in the received German version, '*Du vol gnaden Maria*' – 'Thou, Mary, full of grace'. Claiming that Germans did not talk in that way – that they knew all about full beer kegs, and full wallets, but not girls full of grace – Luther eventually rendered the salutation as '*Gegrüsset seist du, Holdselige* – Greetings to thee, gracious one'. However, the change (which was already anticipated in Erasmus's 1516 edition of the New Testament) was no mere idiomatic one but represented in fact a perceptible downgrading of Mary's status, from one highly favoured, full of grace, *gnädig*, to simply a beloved person. This reduction in Mary's status, albeit from the excessive levels of some forms of late medieval Marian piety, would have represented a *de*-motion of Mary, and one entirely in line with Luther's consistent stress on the *pro*-motion of Christ. The new version, albeit justified in terms of the habits of the national idiom, should be seen as representing not so much a linguistic accenting as a theological one.

That was also the case with Luther's renderings in the September Testament of other key terms. For example, reflecting his sense of the Christian community, not so much in institutional terms but as the assembly of true believers, *ecclesia*, 'Church' in the Vulgate, was altered to *Gemeinde*, 'congregation'. His replacement of the German for 'reason', *Vernunft*, instead of 'understanding' in the phrase in Philippians 4:7 about the peace of God that passes all understanding reflects another insistence of his own – his long-standing depreciation of human reason. Indeed, all are examples of earnest endeavours to produce what may well have been a German Bible, but was also doctrinally the evangelical version of the Bible, a confessional Scripture for what was to emerge as a confessional Lutheran Church.

'SECULAR AUTHORITY': LUTHER AND THE STATE

As we have seen, Luther's attitude to political authorities in the early 1520s was, on the whole, suspicious. He had, of course, to admit Frederick the Wise's constant care for him, and a typical acknowledgement came in February 1521 when he wrote of how 'Our elector acts . . . as constantly as prudently and faithfully. . . .' To set against that, he partly defied

Frederick when he returned to Wittenberg in March of the following year. Though thereafter his alignment with the Elector's interests grew more marked, Luther himself remained estranged from the greater part of the German political establishment at large, from the Emperor Charles down. At the beginning of the 1520s his natural ideological ally seemed to be Germany's restive knightly class whose most articulate spokesman was the humanist and nationalist Ulrich von Hutten, along with his fellow knight Franz von Sickingen. The summer of 1520 represented the high point of empathy between Luther and the knights as an organised political movement for national reform. While the 'Address to the Christian Nobility' articulated much of the knights' ideology of national renewal, in the dangerous summer of 1520, as the bull *Exsurge, Domine* approached him, Luther was not averse to – was even emboldened by – the offers of Sickingen and Hutten to act as his knightly protectors. On the literary front, the versatile von Hutten, soldier, poet and author, championed Luther's cause by publishing a translation of the papal bull with his own preface appealing to the 'men of Germany' to adopt Luther's cause as their own in a crusade against papal 'tyranny'. Later in the year he added his own protest 'Against the Burning of Luther's Book at Mainz'. However, Luther was never fully enlisted in the knights' movement, for the underlying reason that his cause was that of religious and doctrinal reform and Hutten's that of political change, though the latter certainly made use of religious rhetoric in order to advance his political programme. More specifically, Luther abhorred the military force that was, of necessity, involved in the promotion of the knights' cause: 'I am not willing to fight for the gospel with violence,' he wrote in January 1521. That implied violence eventually became overt late in August 1522 when Hutten's associate Franz von Sickingen, purportedly acting in support of Charles V, laid siege to the episcopal city of the elector Richard von Greiffenklau, archbishop of Trier, a prelate whom the knights considered a fitting target for their savage anti-clericalism. This so-called 'Knights' War' of 1522–3 was easily suppressed, Sickingen died of wounds in May 1523 and Hutten in August of the same year of syphilis and the cause of the imperial knights, a once formidable force in German life and politics, was extinguished. Even so, the press propaganda campaign associating Luther with von Hutten, especially the popular cartoon images – Luther and von Hutten aiming bowls against the pope, Hutten and Luther as comrades in arms, and so on – had had the undoubted effect of suggesting that Luther's political credo, like that of the knights, was largely made up of opposition and alienation, the whole spirit of his appearance at Worms.

Further circumstances of 1522 and 1523 added to the sense of Luther's estrangement from much of the German state system, the world of secular authority, *Oberkeit*. Against a dark background of increasing Turkish aggression in the east, a new Diet that was already being assembled in Nuremberg as Luther was making his way back from the Wartburg to Wittenberg met on 23 March. The new pope in succession to Leo X (d. December 1521), the reform-minded Dutchman Adrian (or Hadrian) VI (1522–3), Charles's former tutor, saw the Diet as an opportunity to destroy heresy in Germany: the pope sent the legate Francesco Chieregati to the Diet to demand the enforcement of the Worms Edict against Luther. Frederick the Wise was absent from the Nuremberg *Reichstag* and the session that opened in March certainly heard passionate denunciations against Luther from several members (though it was said that the majority of the princes' advisers were strong sympathisers). However, that first session of the 1522–3 Nuremberg *Reichstag* also revealed uncertainty or even divisions amongst the estates, and following the re-convening of the Diet to Nuremberg between 17 November 1522 and 6 March 1523, in its recess (or final act) of 18 April 1524 it resolved on the future summoning of a national ecclesiastical council in a German city to consider the religious issue, pending which the Edict of Worms was to be enforced by the various estates only 'in so far as they recognise themselves as bound to it'. Yet if this represented a truce for the Luther cause and for its champions in Electoral Saxony, such a spirit of compromise was emphatically not congenial to Duke George. His role, in the *Reich* at large, where in January 1522 he had brought formal complaints against religious change in Electoral Saxony, and as repressor of emergent 'Lutheranism' in his own lands, constituted him as one of the most active foes of heresy in Germany at that juncture. Within his principality, on 7 November and before the Nuremberg Diet had re-convened, Duke George took action to halt the distribution in his territories of the 'September' New Testament, banning its sale and purchase and requiring the surrender of all copies bought (in exchange for the original price). This was part of a then-current wave of Catholic censorship of Luther's writings that also took in the duchy of Bavaria in south Germany and the bishopric of Meissen in Saxony. Out of these circumstances issued the publication of a new tract by Luther, a work that had its origins in a pair of sermons he had preached in the autumn in Weimar in Saxony in the presence of Elector Frederick's brother, Duke John (1468–1532), who encouraged the publication. This treatise on political theory, *Von Weltlicher Uberkeyt* . . . : 'Temporal Authority: To What Extent it Should be Obeyed' was both provoked by Duke George's aggression against him and also contained some of Luther's more durable attitudes to political authority, its morality, limits and necessity. By Christmas 1522 he had written the preface to this work that was to appear in March 1523. Written in sermon style, it was a German-language work, not produced in Latin by Luther but rather addressed to the specific German context.[6]

As Höpfl points out, Luther's use of the German adjective *weltlich*, translatable by the neutral terms 'temporal' or 'secular', actually has the more loaded, indeed detectably pejorative, sense of 'worldly'. Throughout the New Testament 'world' is regularly used as the counter-attraction to spirit and has to be overcome for the latter to triumph. *Weltlich*, then, draws attention to the moral inferiority of the state to the status of the Church. That is the whole sense of 'worldly authority' and the interpretation of its exercise – which was in Luther's mind to be a restricted one – as developed in this work. 'Temporal Authority' is a booklet that sets a question in its title – 'To what extent must worldly authority be obeyed?' – and provides an answer: 'to a limited extent'.

Of course, such terms as 'authority' imply an abstract sense of the 'state' that was not active in Luther's mind. As formed by a sixteenth-century framework of assumptions that placed the state in the hands of a personal ruler, the 'prince' (compare Machiavelli's work on politics, *Il Principe*, 'The Prince', 1513), Luther thought of 'authority' as 'the authorities' – rulers. That is why he dedicated this work to a particular member of a princely dynasty, a firm 'Lutheran' and one who was soon, in 1525, to become successor to the electoral dignity of Saxony, 'the most excellent and noble prince and gracious Lord', Duke John. In fact, though, Luther also had at his disposal a more abstract term for the state, the 'sword', a traditional synonym for the state's command of force and in particular of judicial chastisement for evil-doers. But swords have to be wielded by men, and the men who exercised power in Germany were, in a studied contrast with the excellence of Duke John, seen by Luther as generally men of evil, the group of 'rulers [who] have begun to order people to hand over books and to believe and think as their rulers tell them'. Perhaps it was almost as well, though, that rulers might be supposed evil men – on the whole 'the greatest fools or the worst criminals on earth . . . God's jailers and hangmen' – for their power to exercise the sword was inseparably linked with evil since its use became essential in human society from the time that sin began to flood the earth, with the first crime, Abel's murder by Cain (Genesis 4: 1–16). So evil required the state and the state depended for its existence on evil, for government belonged essentially within the domain of wickedness, unnecessary save in a world of sin and, indeed, needless for true Christians, seeing that these 'have the Holy Spirit in their hearts, which teaches and moves them to love everyone, wrong no one, and suffer wrong gladly, even unto death'.

There were not many of those true Christians, of course, but because the state was ordained by God as a corrective for human sin and crime, true Christians were bound to serve it in such capacities as rulers, magistrates, executioners, constables and, indeed, soldiers. Once again, and as in 'The Freedom of a Christian', Luther was setting out in this work a code of Christian social behaviour; the Christian must serve his neighbour, including service to the state. Even so, 'Temporal Authority' consistently represented the state as a remedy for evil rather than a force for good. And because its competence was confined to the evil side of human nature, the state could have no jurisdiction over the spiritual aspect or over the consciences of Christian men and women, so that freedom of conscience – toleration, in another word – was mandatory and 'if someone imposes a man-made law on souls, compelling belief in what he wants to be believed, then there will probably be no word of God to justify it'. Thus out of the specific circumstances of 1522–3 and the Catholic reaction orchestrated by Duke George, Luther penned one of history's great hymns to religious toleration and freedom of belief. Yet circumstances alter cases, and as, in the course of the 1520s and '30s, Luther's practical circumstances and his relationship to radical dissidents and to the state itself changed, the clarion call for freedom set out in this work became considerably toned down, as we shall see in Chapter 7.

LUTHER AND THE JEWISH PEOPLE: 'THAT JESUS CHRIST WAS BORN A JEW'

The mounting Catholic reaction of the early 1520s took in a whispering campaign that endeavoured to indict Luther of more grievous or fundamental errors even than those so far condemned by Rome and the Diet of Worms. In the sessions of the *Reichstag* at Nuremberg, Luther was, inevitably, the main talking-point, even eclipsing the Turkish menace, and it was inevitable too that rumours, including hostile ones, about him and his beliefs would abound. Such a one, spread in January 1523, was to the effect that not only was he questioning the actual presence of Christ in the eucharist but was teaching that 'Jesus was conceived of the seed of Joseph, and that Mary was not a virgin, but had many sons after Christ'. The Emperor, involved in the suppression of a serious revolt, that of the

Communeros, in Spain, did not attend that Diet but was represented there by the regent, his brother, the markedly Catholic Archduke Ferdinand (1503–64). Ferdinand's adoption, in the form of a public accusation, of the current allegations about Luther's christology placed the claims being made about his doctrines on a new level of danger for Luther, for his reputation and for that of his friends and supporters. This was because to deny, say, the seven sacraments was heresy but to assert the merely human nature of Christ was blasphemously to undermine the very pillars of Christianity and the doctrine of the Incarnation of the Word made flesh to be our unique redeemer, alone capable, as both very God and true man, of atoning for human sin against the Godhead. As if all that were not enough, the rumour indicated that Luther was demeaning Mary – and thereby demolishing the rich and massively popular Catholic devotion to her as the virgin mother of God. Urged on by a noble supporter, Count John of Anhalt, to clear his name of such damaging charges, from probably late January 1523 Luther began work on a new tract. This was published perhaps in May as *Das Jhesus Christus eyn geborner Jude sey* – 'That Jesus Christ Was Born a Jew' – and went through an extraordinary nine editions within that year, with a Latin translation giving it access to a wider European readership.[7]

From the very start of this brief work, Luther indicated that he intended to use it as an opportunity to win conversions – selective ones – of Jews to his purified form of Christianity – 'that I might also win some Jews to the Christian faith'. His dedication of the work to a rabbi converted to Christianity and taking the name Bernard (Luther took part in his son's christening) confirmed the work's benevolence to the Jewish people and the author's hope of helping them to salvation by converting them. He dealt quite expeditiously with the task of clearing his reputation from groundless slanders concerning his spreading fundamental errors about the person of Christ and proceeded to prove to a Jewish readership the truth that Christ was the promised messiah. He also set out to make further gains in the domain of propaganda by taking the campaign into the 'papist' enemy's camp through playing a pro-Jewish card against the appalling treatment that the Jewish people had received at the hands of Catholic authorities and people – massacres and expulsions in medieval Germany and throughout western and central Europe: 'Our fools, the popes, bishops, sophists [Scholastic theologians], and monks – the crude asses' heads – have hitherto so treated the Jews that anyone who wished to be a good Christian would almost have had to become a Jew.' The work that emerged was turned around from a proposed doctrinal self-exculpation into a tract aimed at Jewish conversion by proving that the Jew Jesus, born of a virgin by the intervention of the Holy Spirit, was their true messiah and that therefore they should convert to faith in Him. As such, the ultimate genesis of this work was the pre-medieval and medieval literary type of polemical literature known as *adversus Judaeos*, literally 'against the Jews', and consisting of the assembling of arguments to prove Christianity's superiority to Judaism.

Luther's distant mentor St Augustine had advocated the voluntary conversion of Jews to the Christian religion, urging that it be brought about by kind, gentle and persuasive preaching. In the 1523 tract Luther honoured this advice and set out his purpose in the 'hope that if one deals in a kindly way with the Jews and instructs them carefully from Holy Scripture, many of them will become genuine Christians and turn again to the faith of their fathers, the prophets and patriarchs', for those Old Testament figures, in predicting and prophesying Christ, were in fact authentic Christians. Although, as we saw in Chapter 2 above, Luther's early lectures were full of denunciations of the Jewish religion as the grounds of a false works-righteousness and legalism, it was in his perceived role as a potential pro-Jewish public figure that the Jews of the south German city of Regensburg, under imminent threat of a community expulsion, appealed for his assistance in 1519, sending him a lovingly transcribed Hebrew copy of Psalm 130, known as *De profundis*: 'Out of the depths have I cried unto thee, O Lord. Lord, hear my voice. . . .'

Countering 'papistry', Luther was, on the face of it, in a favourable position to win Jewish converts and he began his conversionary strategy with high praise of the Jewish people, 'for to no nation among the Gentiles has he granted so high an honour as he has to the Jews'. There then followed a list of scriptural indicators to prove that Christ was the fulfilment of Jewish hopes: that Christ was promised in the Book of Genesis after Adam's fall; that the virgin birth proved Christ's claims to be the messiah of the Jews; that passages in Old Testament texts such as the second book of Samuel and the prophecies of Isaiah pointed to the same conclusion. It was at that point in the text, however, that Luther's intended kindliness towards the Jews dissolved into exasperation, as if he himself were aware that their acceptance of his proof-texts depended in turn on their endorsing the basically Christian message of their own Scriptures: 'It is of no help for the Jews to try to evade the issue here. . . .' To the end, it is true, Luther attempted to maintain, and reverted to, a friendly tone:

one must deal gently with them . . . and instruct them from Scripture; then some of them may come along [into Christianity] . . . we must be guided in our dealings with them not by papal law but by the law of Christian love. We must receive them cordially and permit them to trade and work with us, that they may have occasion and opportunity to associate with us, hear our Christian teaching, and witness our Christian life.

However, in this tract Luther found it hard to maintain that posture of friendship, for mounting anger kept breaking through at the Jews, who 'are such literalists', who maintained a 'futile subterfuge', 'preposterous glosses' 'worthless excuses, capricious and unwarranted evasions'; it was 'amazing that the Jews are not moved to believe in this Jesus, their own flesh and blood . . .'.

This fast-selling work of 1523 was not in fact aimed directly at a Jewish readership but rather set out a method of argument for volunteer missionaries – 'those who want to work with' Jews in order to convert them. The evident popularity of the work can have had little or nothing to do with its being purchased or read by many of Germany's shrinking Jewish community, and its underlying intention, as with its ancestors, the standard *adversus Judaeos* genre, may have been principally that of validating the Christian beliefs of the author and his sympathetic readers. Underlyingly, too, Luther himself seems even to have realised the futility of his arguments' circularity, including, as they did, convoluted chronologies to establish that, since the prophesied messiah had not come in the time since Christ, he must have come in and with Christ. Yet if Jews already accepted such premises, Luther would not have had to argue the conclusions he tried to base on them. Force might, then, have been the only way out of the closed circle in which Luther had got himself and there was an ominous sense that this was a provisional work whose contents were to be revisited: 'Here I will let the matter rest for the present, until I see what I have accomplished.'

Twenty years later, in 1543, having accomplished little or nothing in securing large-scale conversions from Judaism to Lutheranism, Luther, as we shall see, let off a vicious, indeed an hysterical, attack on the Jewish people, in particular in the work *Von den Juden und ihren Lügen* – 'On the Jews and Their Lies'. It is true that in the 1523 work Luther disparaged some of the potent and poisonous medieval folklore about Jews – the allegation that they needed Christian blood to dispel an inherited odour (and hence murdered Christian children to obtain it). However, the most virulent and enduring of all Christian myths about the Jews – 'that they crucified Jesus' – is incorporated into this work, a booklet that augured ill for Luther's evolving and ultimate attitudes to the Jewish people.

7

THE CREATION OF INSTITUTIONAL LUTHERANISM, 1525–1528

INTRODUCTION

In the present chapter we shall first of all investigate Martin Luther's involvement with the great German Peasants' Revolt of the mid-1520s, focusing on possible links between his teachings and the ideology of protest that the rebellious peasants adopted. His repudiation in 1525 of violent peasant insurgency undoubtedly facilitated accommodation between his movement and secular governments in Germany. On the more strictly religious and theological fronts, we shall examine how 'Lutheranism' was becoming more clearly defined through Luther's creation of forms of worship consistent with his doctrines and through its clear divorce from the ethical philosophy and moral reformism of Erasmus. The cleft between the latter and Luther was finalised in the mid-1520s over the issue of the freedom of the human will. In marrying in 1525 Luther set up a model for the pastorate of his rapidly emerging Church, while further institutional definition of Lutheranism came about in the late 1520s as Luther helped create a model of Church government in Electoral Saxony.

LUTHER AND THE PEASANTS

Germany between the last quarter of the fifteenth century and the first quarter of the sixteenth was a cauldron of social discontent, with the grievances of the peasants at its centre. In common with their fellows throughout Europe, German peasants had enjoyed a relative golden age of low rents and favourable tenurial terms in the conditions of population scarcity following the Black Death of the mid-fourteenth century. However, from the second half of the fifteenth century onward, as population levels began to rise again towards pre-Black Death rates, in Germany as elsewhere rural dwellers reliant on their own farming for subsistence were putting intense pressure on available cultivable soil. One consequence was the splitting and re-splitting of holdings: in the central German region known as Franconia by the early 1500s some farms were reduced to the size of an eighth or even a sixteenth of the original occupancies, leaving plots that were insufficient in each case to feed a family. In some areas of central Germany 50 per cent of households had negligible or non-existent amounts of land on which to raise crops. Bad or failed harvests, as in Franconia in 1502–3, 1505, 1515 and during the pre-Revolt years from 1517 to 1524, completed the heartbreak. Needless to say, not all peasants, or all areas, faced destitution or starvation and many peasant farmers were able to profit from the increasing demand for food, especially from the towns. Even those more fortunate ones, though, needed to be constantly on their guard against attempts by landlords – lay and clerical, nobles, monasteries, knights and corporations – to channel the profits in their own direction by taxing the proceeds of the hard work and enterprise of such peasant farmers.

For it was not simply that impersonal demographic or market forces were at work in creating an acute rural crisis in pre-Reformation Germany, but rather that the agrarian problems were exacerbated by landlords who were placed in positions to exploit the population increase and the consequent urgent peasant need for tenancies by redefining the peasants' living and working conditions once more in their own favour. One unifying trend in this general worsening of peasants' living conditions was the erosion of freedom, the reimposition of serfdom and its burdens of compulsory labour or heavy dues in money and kind, as well as restrictions on peasants' liberty of movement and opportunities to exchange landlords. In addition, new non-trespassing orders were introduced by many lords banning access to the food resources of woodlands, wastelands, common lands, streams and rivers. Yet while peasant farmers were increasingly fenced out of terrain claimed by their masters, those lords were free to hunt their way over precious growing crops.

On the financial front, quit rents, amounting to up to 10 per cent of the value of a property, were paid every time a tenancy changed or when the tenant, or the landlord, died. By the mid-1520s an average of 30 to 40 per cent of the value of all farm produce raised in Franconia was handed over in taxes, rents and dues. All over the country, rent arrears mounted to chronic levels of indebtedness and many families simply gave up the struggle, abandoned their holdings, moved into the towns or fell into vagabondage, outlawry and crime.

Germany's millions of peasants thus formed a whole social order etched with a sense of injustice and complaint. Of course, other estates in Germany felt heavy burdens of grievance, especially against the Church and its exactions, and were able to articulate them in the schedules of complaints regularly presented at diets – 'the grievances of the German nation'. For the peasants, armed revolt, locally and regionally distributed and increasingly accompanied by the listing of complaints in writing, formed their vehicle of protest. We can chart those regional revolts on a rising graph coincident with the population increase in the later fifteenth and earlier sixteenth centuries and with the consequent landlord exploitation of increasing peasant numbers: from only seven risings in the age of comparative peasant contentment with their condition, in the low population years of the whole of the first half of the fifteenth century, to eight in the century's last quarter alone and as many as eighteen in the first quarter of the sixteenth century. A key feature of this swelling of insurgency was the emergence of peasant underground movements. There were two of these. One, the *Bundschuh*, was first raised in 1493 and named after the tied working boot of the peasants, a humble, even wryly comic, image of their work and essential need for solidarity (*Bund* means bond, union). The other was the *Armer Konrad*, meaning 'Poor old Konrad', from a typical peasant first name. Leadership was provided in the early sixteenth century by the Bundschuh organiser Joss Fritz. Ideologically, a unitive thread was a haunting nostalgia for the more favourable peasant social conditions prevailing before landlords were able, typically through the use of legal devices and the introduction of new laws, to take advantage of population increase by driving down peasants' terms and conditions of life, work and tenancy.

Peasant spokesmen summed up their conservative-minded insistence on the restoration of earlier, better customs in using the simple but comprehensive slogan 'old law' to describe a golden age for the common man in the past. That slogan gradually became merged with another, to capture a sense of divine justice in society: 'God's law'. For the whole ideological atmosphere of protest preceding the German Peasant Revolt was suffused with issues of moral weight, such as freedom, justice and law, which had unavoidable religious implications. The first stirrings of the Reformation itself, its defiance and mood of disobedience, could not help but create the expectations of reform and renewal that drove other classes besides the peasant into protest and revolt. For the peasants, in particular, their entrenched anti-clericalism was undoubtedly encouraged by Luther's attacks on false priests, monks, friars and bishops. The enemies of the peasants, including the Austrian Habsburgs, the prelates and the monasteries, were also the foes of the Lutheran gospel – and the great nineteenth-century German historian Leopold von Ranke noted that the enforcement of the Edict of Worms by the imperial authorities acted as a further stimulant to organised peasant protest. Meanwhile, the enlistment of a peasant archetype, *Karsthans*, 'Jack Ploughman' in press campaigns as the folksy savant called upon to arbitrate the theologians' opinions (in favour of the Lutheran side) reversed decades of contempt from the other strata of society to give the peasant farmer a new sense of his human dignity – and rights. The eventual outcome of mounting discontent and spasms of violent localised rebellions, for example in Switzerland in 1513–15 and Württemberg in 1514, was the widespread, if not entirely pan-German, rising which broke out in summer 1524 and lasted until 1524–6. By spring 1525, indeed, great swathes of the German Lands were in the grip of armed, mobile peasant bands, and battles and sieges filled the air in provinces such as Württemberg in the south, Hesse in the centre, Thuringia in the east and Alsace in the west. That 'revolt of the common man', as one historian has termed it, also won strong support from urban workers alongside rural peasants. In Thuringia in the east Thomas Müntzer, until his death following defeat at the battle of Frankenhausen in May 1525, led a militant, millenarian sub-division of the movement, a wing whose visionary ideology contrasted with the relative conservatism of the Peasants' Revolt mainstream. That moderation, and overall preparedness to rectify the peasants' lot within a broadly unchanged social system, characterised the best known of the very large number of peasant manifestos of the period of the Peasants' Revolt. This was the document circulating in January and February 1525, drawn up in the Upper Swabian town of Memmingen and going on to provide the peasants with an agreed national platform: the 'Twelve Articles of Memmingen', printed in March 1525.

Our specific question, though, concerns the nature of Luther's involvement with, or moral responsibility for, the rising, concerning in particular any possible links between his teachings and the great rising as well as the issue of his outright repudiation of the revolt. Clearly, Luther was not responsible for peasant revolt in Germany: it preceded his birth. But was he, through his doctrines, in any way responsible for *the* Peasants' Revolt of 1524–6?

The contemporaneous accounts varied considerably in their messages on this heading. On the one hand, one printed cartoon showing the peasant rebel as 'the great Lutheran fool' obviously drew such a connection between the reformer and the rebels. However, one of the fullest contemporaneous accounts was by Cochlaeus, who knew the course of the revolt intimately, having narrowly escaped death in its opening stages. What is interesting from his account is a reluctance or inability to attach substantial direct blame to Luther for the outbreak. This apparent failure on the part of a professional polemicist to exploit a potentially glittering propaganda opportunity of blackening Luther in conservative circles as the inspiration of the most serious popular rising in German history is all the more striking inasmuch as Cochlaeus was perfectly willing to assign to Luther responsibility for the intellectual emancipation of common men and women – 'even shoemakers and women and every kind of unlearned person'. These, claimed Cochlaeus, turned the world upside-down by learning intellectual insolence out of Luther's translation of the New Testament. However, what Cochlaeus emphasised was that the 'revolutionary ideas' that the adepts of Luther's New Testament took from his writings led not to the social revolution of 1525 but to the gender equality by which the 'Lutheran women . . . proceeded to such a point of audacity that they even usurped for themselves the right and office of teaching publicly in the Church . . .'.

Then, when it came to the Peasants' Revolt itself, Cochlaeus focused his attention on Carlstadt's, not Luther's, possible blame, though even this was not entirely ascertainable, for 'the unhappy Carlstadt was held in the worst repute and was considered suspect as the author of the [1525] rebellion, the inciter of the uprisings, and the leader of the peasants'. In fact, the real villain was not even Carlstadt but Cochlaeus's 'most turbulent firebrand of war and sedition . . . the priest Thomas Müntzer, who with greater madness than Carlstadt's prepared to put Luther's words into action'. But if Müntzer was directly guilty in Cochlaeus's eyes of stirring up sedition, Luther was not, and Cochlaeus recalled that when Müntzer placed specific plans before Luther, the latter 'did not approve', and Cochlaeus proceeded to narrate in some detail Müntzer's actual revolutionary activities. Finally, Cochlaeus recalled that when Müntzer fell in the height of the rising Luther disowned him completely, as he repudiated the whole peasant cause in the work to which Cochlaeus gave a title translatable as 'Against the Robbing, Rebelling, and Murdering Peasants . . .'. Virtually all that Cochlaeus could pin down on Luther was the vaguest of charges that the peasants 'had learned whatever they unjustly attempted from Luther's books . . .'. To an accusation that imprecise, we might respond: When? How?[1]

Richard Marius found a text that he thought would have encouraged peasant rebels to believe that 'Luther was their champion' and the words cited, from Luther's 'Short Form' of the Ten Commandments and the Lord's Prayer (1520), do indeed sound astonishingly revolutionary: 'I believe that in this community of Christendom, all things are common, and all the goods of one belong to the other and that no one owns anything entirely of his own. . . .' There are, however, two problems about tracing the inspiration of the German Peasants' Revolt of 1524–6 to such a source. The first is, that if the words cited were to be given a social meaning, it might indeed have appealed to the radical millenarian minority wing of the revolt under Müntzer's leadership. However, in its apparent repudiation of private property and advocacy of community of goods, the 'Short Form' was *too* radical to speak for the mainstream moderate opinion of the German Peasants' Revolt as that was expressed in the Twelve Articles of Memmingen. The second objection to seeing the 1520 text as a social testament capable of inspiring lower-class rebellion is that it is in fact a kind of religious lyric, based on the image of the sharing Church found in the Books of Acts, 4:32. Luther's version of that ideal of the Christian Church celebrates the perfect elect community of faith in which the goods that are pooled in common ownership are 'every prayer and good work that comes to the aid of the community . . .'. To read into it a prompt from Luther to mount a peasant revolt in 1525 or at any other time represents some misreading of an essentially spiritual text.

Still within Luther's oeuvre of 1520, could the reform manifesto the 'Address to the Christian Nobility' be seen as a clarion call to peasant mobilisation? No: extensive as this work's demands for change were, it addressed them to the constituted authorities, not to the unfranchised peasants. Might we be on stronger ground, then, in finding a 'liberation theology' in Luther's great work of that year, 'The Freedom of a Christian'? It is true that phrases in this profound spiritual tract on the application to holy living of the principles of justification by faith could conceivably have been given a 'social' interpretation strong enough to inspire revolt. Thus the announcement 'A Christian is a perfectly free lord of all, subject to none . . . the freest of kings . . .' surely might be read as one of history's great ringing appeals to set mankind free – comparable, for example to similar declarations made in the course of the American and French Revolutions of the eighteenth century.

There are two major constraints on such an interpretation. The first is that Luther's true Christian who is the subject of such acclamations is not of the mass of humanity, but is that rarer creation, a real, believing Christian, on whom possession of the Word of God endows primarily spiritual gifts of 'life, truth, light, peace, righteousness, salvation, joy, liberty, wisdom, power, grace, glory, and every incalculable blessing'. Secondly, that individual is no anarchist living without restraint but, albeit most willingly, 'a perfectly dutiful servant of all, subject to all', paying his 'tribute' of obligation to society in just the way that Christ instructed the payment of the coin of tribute in Matthew 17:24–27. Conversely, there is a specific denunciation of those 'who, when they hear of this freedom of faith, immediately turn it into an occasion for the flesh and think that now all things are allowed them'. It would follow that, if a peasant, such a Christian would carry out the duties and respon-sibilities of the particular *Stand* or 'estate' to which he or she belonged, which, in the case of the peasantry, meant a life of unceasing toil.

That, for Luther, was not to say that peasants should be treated by their lords at a rate less than Christian human dignity. Thus on one occasion Luther addressed nobles at large with the warning 'the people neither can nor will endure your tyranny any longer. God will not endure it; the world is not what it once was when you drove and hunted men like wild beasts.' The same note, that lords and princes went too far and by their excesses and exploitations goaded the peasants into rebellion, was to the fore in Luther's 'Admonition to Peace: A Reply to the Twelve Articles of the Peasants in Swabia', composed in spring 1525 as a counter to the Twelve Articles, widely distributed and printed nineteen times. In the 'Admonition' Luther pointed unmistakably at the landlords' and rulers' responsibility for the build-up of protest: 'We have no one on earth to thank for this disastrous rebellion, except you princes and lords. . . . The poor people cannot bear it any longer . . . you are the cause of this wrath of God. . . .'

Freely admitting, then, that the peasants had just grievances arising out of the exactions of their lords, Luther conceded to them the rightness of some of their demands. Apart from the iniquity of death taxes, one of these – the first of the Articles of Memmingen – concerned the right of congregations to choose their pastors. It is hardly surprising that Luther supported this demand since it expressly affirmed his own proposals made in a brief work of 1523. However, Luther was at best only selectively favourable to the peasants' cause. It is true that in his self-appointed role as arbitrator in spring 1525 he handed out blame heavily, even disproportionately, to landlords and rulers: 'the princes and lords who forbid the preaching of the gospel and oppress the people unbearably deserve to have God put them down from their thrones . . . because they have sinned so greatly against both God and man. And they have no excuse.' However, Luther warned that the peasants must take up their cause 'justly and with a good conscience'. Whatever balance existed in Luther's mind at that point in time in favour of the peasants' cause would be destroyed in two sets of eventualities. The first was if the peasants translated a message of religious freedom into a demand for secular liberty, as in the denunciation of serfdom in Article 3 of the Twelve Articles. The second was if the peasants turned to violent resistance.[2]

In Luther's mind, the preaching and prestige of the Word had to have priority through that period of insurgency. Its primacy was one criterion for adjudicating the rightness or otherwise of the contending causes, those of peasants or lords. Thus, the princes who were at fault as social exploiters were in fact those 'who forbid the preaching of the gospel'. The primacy of religious considerations meant that, over two of the captions, 2 and 3, of the Twelve Articles, Luther's interest was high and positive in the proposal of electing pastors but averse to the peasants' 'physical' understanding of Christian freedom as effecting the abolition of serfdom, thus ending what Luther believed was necessary human inequality. On the other eight of the Memmingen articles, which sought moderate adjustments, in the peasants' favour, in agrarian conditions, Luther was brief and dismissive: as an 'evangelist' he was not qualified to speak on these detailed issues on which imperial law said all that was necessary to know. The peasants should simply accept the lot of the Christian as 'a martyr on earth' and cease struggling for human rights, pursuing only 'their rights as Christians'. It was the basic message of 'The Freedom of a Christian' and what we have to recognise about Luther's position on social justice through the period 1520 to 1525 is that it was underlyingly consistent in content.

This consistency lay in the fact that Luther deemed entirely inadmissible the deriving of social protest from the gospel, because, as he explained in 'Temporal Authority' in 1523, such secular matters belonged in one sphere, and spiritual things in another, so that to confound them, as for example by the peasants' calling themselves 'Christian brethren' and taking oaths on the gospels to stay united, was the worst kind of blasphemy and confusion of sacred and secular. Between April and May

1525 Luther was on a ministerial tour of Thuringia, taking in his birth-place Eisleben. Thuringia, within Electoral Saxony, was the district that contained within it the ultra-radical front of the Revolt under the spell of Thomas Müntzer. It was also within a principality in which the Elector Frederick, now terminally ill, and his brother and soon-to-be successor Duke John were showing a fatalistic defeatism in the face of a peasant insurrection. Aided by the adhesion of lower-class townsmen, the Revolt was now was at its meridian of military victory – and the depths of its brutality, as in the massacre of the inhabitants of the town of Weinsberg when peasant forces took it on 16 April. There were signs, including the interruption by bell-ringing of a sermon he tried to deliver in the town of Nordhausen, that Luther was losing whatever allegiance he had com-manded from the peasants and that he even faced danger on account of such advice as that Christians should patiently bear the burdens of this life in imitation of Christ crucified. And it was in those circumstances that on his return to Wittenberg early in May he wrote, as a supplement to a new edition of the 'Admonition to Peace' the brief, furious, revealingly unpunctuated work that came to be known as *Wider die räuberische und mörderischen Rotten der Bauern*, 'Against the Robbing and Murdering Hordes of Peasants', of about May 1525, in which, notoriously, he urged the most savage suppression of this revolt which, he claimed, caused violence:

> Therefore let everyone who can, smite, slay, and stab, secretly or openly, remembering that nothing can be more poisonous, hurtful or devilish than a rebel. It is just as when one must kill a mad dog; if you do not strike him, he will strike you, and a whole land with you.

Such sentiments, though – 'anyone who is killed fighting on the side of the rulers may be a true martyr in the eyes of God. . . . These are strange times, when a prince can win heaven with bloodshed better than other men with prayer!' – were not mere reactions to a passing situation in which the peasant rebels held the upper hand and used it to inflict death and destruction. The tide was turning against the insurgents during the month of May, when their most determined leader, Müntzer, was defeated with his army at Frankenhausen. The earlier military successes of the rebels were now dispelling the indecision of princes, who, with professional mercenaries, were moving into a front of decisive counter-offensives, eventually slaughtering perhaps 100,000 insurgents and suspected rebels across the German Lands. Was Luther to blame for the reprisals? Was it the case that in some public statements he had given moral support to the peasants and in his latest writing in his series on the 'peasant question' not only abandoned the peasants but called down their destruction upon them? In a work published in July, *Ein Sendbrief von dem harten Büchlein wider die Bauern*, 'An Open Letter on the Harsh Book against the Peasants', offered vindication of his stance but was basically unrepentant, for the 'Open Letter' contained essentially the same message of its two predecessors of 1525, the 'Admonition to Peace' and 'Against the Robbing and Murdering Hordes of Peasants'. Indeed, if anything his attack was broadened to take in not only the active rebels themselves but all who expressed sympathy for their cause and whom God 'wishes to have punished and destroyed'. The rebels were 'not worth rational argument' and:

> You have to answer people like that until the [blood] drips from their noses. The peasants would not listen; they would not let anyone tell them anything, so their ears must now be unbuttoned with musket balls till their heads jump off their shoulders.

In this colloquially written work, rich in proverbial lore, mercy for the defeated was vehemently ruled out, even for those coerced into participating in the uprisings, for an unmerciful mercy, being cruel to be ultimately kind, 'guards, bites, stabs, cuts, hews, and slays, as God has commanded . . .'. (Only in a private letter of July to Archbishop Albrecht of Mainz – one expressing surprising respect for that prince-prelate – did Luther put in a word for mercy, focusing on the case of a young man caught up in the Revolt for whose life he had been asked to intercede.)

There were other, political lessons to be learned from the breakdown of order that Luther had witnessed earlier in the year: princes and lords must now for the future ensure orderly government. His spring tour, the sights he saw and the horror stories he heard, all seem to have had a deep impact on his sense of an imminent state of nature and chaos, the war of all against all: 'No one would have been safe from another; any man might have killed another. . . . there was no order in it. . . . The devil intended to lay all Germany to utter waste. . . .' However, there was no angle-turn here in the thinking of Luther, who had all along known that the sinfulness implicit in the human condition made for indiscipline and the consequent need for order to counteract its effects. Thus he urged the necessity for authoritarian governance to curb human irregularity. Indeed, the experience of the breakdown of rule and respect for it in the Peasants'

Revolt confirmed the messages set out in Luther's 1523 work on secular governments: the state existed because men and women were debased 'and the people need to be ruled with force. God knew that full well, and so he gave the rulers not a feather duster, but a sword.'

Though Luther conferred no majesty on states in describing their policing and punitive role in such brutally utilitarian terms, his theorising in this work matched much of the establishment mood in the conservative reaction under way in post-Peasants' Revolt Germany, a mentality basically suspicious of the lower classes, morally prim and control-seeking. There were those who claimed that Luther wrote as he did in the 'harsh book' because Frederick the Wise died in 1525, that he was afraid for his future and so all of a sudden decided to ingratiate himself with the authorities. However, this was to misunderstand him and the continuous threads in his thinking about the social fabric. These were: dissociation between the gospel and the possibility of fundamental change in human society; the impossibility, because 'law' and 'gospel' belonged in entirely different spheres, of grounding the laws of the state on the principles of the gospel, as the Twelve Articles advocated; and abjuration of violence, except in the hands of divinely constituted authorities, to achieve goals.

So Luther underwent no substantive ideological conversion in the year of the Peasants' Revolt. Even so, the reinforced dour authoritarianism of his writings on politics and the social order did no harm in cultivating a firmer relationship in the years ahead with the wielders of power in Germany's princely territories and self-ruling cities. Increasing prominence was to be given to the category of 'Christian and pious rulers' – not the vindictive and thuggish knights of 1525 whom Luther denounced as little better than the rebels themselves, but responsible major rulers. The figure of the godly evangelical prince was about to emerge. So it was not a coincidence that the middle years of the 1520s began to see the first creation of confessional Lutheran princely states whose rulers were attached to Luther's doctrines and who were beginning to introduce ecclesiastical changes in their states in line with the principles he taught. Already in 1523–5 a relative of the Archbishop of Mainz, the grand master of the military order of the Teutonic Knights, Albrecht von Hohenzollern, was converting the order's estates into a new duchy, East Prussia, under Lutheran auspices. Electoral Saxony fell to the convinced Lutheran John, known as 'the Steadfast' or 'the Constant', on the death of his brother Frederick the Wise in 1525, and the years to come saw its evolution into a state with a Lutheran form of Church organisation, worship and doctrine. States such as Brandenburg-Ansbach (1524–8),

Hesse (1526–8), Braunschweig-Lüneburg (1526–7), Mecklenburg-Schwerin (initially in 1526), Anhalt-Köthen (from 1526), Mansfeld (1525–6) and Liegnitz (1527) followed into the Lutheran camp in the period covering and immediately after that of the Peasants' Revolt, the period, that is to say, when Luther's writings proved the political and social reliability of his religious doctrines to the ruling classes. The oligarchs of the great cities, led by those of Nuremberg in 1525, could also safely phase in the implementation of urban Lutheran Reformation without fearing loss of political control to radical egalitarian religious forces.

ERASMUS AND LUTHER

Just as Martin Luther in the years after 1518 was recruiting squadrons of supporters along the way – for example, the imperial knights, the humanists, progressives and reformists generally – so in the 1520s in a reverse process he was losing the attachment of various groups, albeit often collecting new allies in the process. His intellectual severance from Erasmus in the middle of the 1520s encapsulated his divorce from the Christian humanist school, with its confidence in the capacity of human reason and the effectiveness of human ethical striving.

The period between the later teens and the early twenties of the sixteenth century represented the high noon of fellow feeling between Luther and so much of what Erasmus stood for – linguistic and patristic scholarship, Scripture translation, reform of the Church. Erasmus's enemies, above all the ultra-conservative Dominicans, clinging to their Scholasticism, were Luther's foes too. In his period of most acute danger, when Luther needed his protectors, political and intellectual, Erasmus acted as his media guardian, putting a harmless gloss on Luther's teachings such as those in the 95 Theses. He placed his vast prestige at Luther's disposal, put in a good word in Luther's favour with elevated contacts including Henry VIII, Frederick the Wise and even the papacy and turned his elliptical and ironic wit to Luther's defence.

While Luther and Erasmus never met, they exchanged letters, for example one from Luther on 28 March 1519 exalting Erasmus, 'our glory and hope!' However, even before that there was an early indication of a later theological rift when Luther saw in 1516 that Erasmus's understanding of St Paul in the Greek New Testament was at odds with his own. Later, in 1520, in a period when Luther was needing Erasmus's benevolence, he could still say of the always ideologically elusive humanist scholar that he was 'an eel. Only Christ can catch him.' Erasmus's own response to Luther, in broadly supporting him, was also that of exercising the right to encourage, the right to warn, applying to Luther's alleged rashness Erasmus's own congenital caution by counselling against intemperance and violence of expression or thought. When those features broke through in 'The Babylonian Captivity of the Church', Erasmus began to draw back from his alliance with the Wittenberg professor, viewing that work as the breaker of the concord of the Church which Erasmus, seeing himself as Christendom's peacemaker, hoped to restore. A letter of Erasmus which came out in published form in August 1521 made the Dutchman's reservations plain for all to read. Meanwhile, he was himself under suspicion for his reformist views from the conservative theologians of the University of Louvain, his place of residence between the late 1510s and until 1521, and while he was not temperamentally one of nature's martyrs, there was no point in his being exposed to danger for extremist beliefs which he did not himself hold.

At the beginning of the decade there were already indications of a breach over such issues as the ability of human beings in themselves to do good, and by 1523, these had become even clearer signs, as Luther wrote dismissively of Erasmus's abilities as a theologian and of 'the pricks that Erasmus gives me now and then'. Von Hutten, now near the end of his life, had for some time been trying to force Erasmus into Luther's camp, but his *Expostulatio* of June 1523, criticising the Dutch humanist for two-facedness, drew from the latter his reply published in September, *Spongia adversus aspergines Hutteni*, 'The Sponge to Soak Up Hutten's Splatterings' which turned the attack on Luther for religious warmongering and identified his errors in the field of grace, justification and the freedom of the will. The battle lines were thus now open and Erasmus had determined what the specific areas of doctrinal conflict were to be. In choosing the issue that he did, Erasmus ensured that some of the deepest and most durable questions about our human freedom, capacity and, indeed, our very nature were raised and that decisive lines of demarcation were to be drawn between Catholic and Lutheran Christianity over the central points of our relationship with God and His righteousness and our ability to approach Him and it.

In September 1524 Desiderius Erasmus, having been encouraged to write directly against Luther by Duke George in May, launched *De Libero Arbitrio . . . collatio*, 'A Discourse on the Freedom of the Will', a delayed response, apparently composed within five days, to Luther's affirmation of predestination in his defence against his excommunication, the 'Assertion of All the Articles' of December 1520. In this new work

Erasmus acknowledged the great complexity of the issue now 'violently stirred up' by Luther as well as its hoary antiquity. The subject and stance he selected in 'On the Freedom of the Will' were, however thorny, decided by his long career as Europe's moralist. The issues surrounding the ultimate truth or falsehood of the freedom of the will were, Erasmus believed, attended by Scholastic riddles – 'hidden, not to say superfluous' abstruse questions about 'congruent' and 'condign' merit and about the extent to which God's 'contingent' foreknowledge of our deeds hemmed in human freedom of choice and action. However, in terms of practical moral results, belief in free will, along with acceptance of the consequences – credit or blame, reward or punishment in God's sight – for our own freely chosen actions provided a safe guide to people's everyday behaviour. The whole subject was convoluted and, in the end, probably unknowable, but in practical terms Erasmus believed it made more sense to accept free will than to deny it. This work, then, was a personal manifesto by the leading exponent in his day of the pietistic and moralistic traditions of the late medieval heritage of the *devotio moderna*, so lovingly nourished in Erasmus's Netherlands, in the lineage of Thomas a Kempis.

'On the Freedom of the Will' was also a deeply personal work in the sense that it arose from Erasmus's self-confessed dislike of all forms of categorical assertion – what he called his 'inner temperamental horror of fighting' – and, arguably, its effectiveness was reduced by its author's moderation and balance, especially in assembling Scripture texts both for and against free will. The issues raised in this work were central to Erasmus's practical, moral outlook. Even so, this was not the book he would normally have chosen to write, and he confessed his preference for literary rather than theological pursuits, for the 'Muses' over 'hand-to-hand fighting'. His professed 'dislike of assertion' led to an air of lethargy, amateurism and dilettantism in this work, in which Erasmus commended the attitude of the sceptics, those philosophers who tended to minimise the number of propositions that could be believed with certainty. There were many opinions on the topic of the will and its freedom, Erasmus averred, and Scripture could be obscure in the guidance it offered, though the Church, its Fathers and saints had upheld free will. In the end, though, he was inclined to come down, perhaps marginally but nevertheless decisively, on the side of the doctrine of the freedom of the will, cooperating with and aided by divine grace: he partly used an anti-Luther work by the saintly English bishop John Fisher (1469–1535).[3]

Erasmus's conviction that Scripture was obscure on these matters of the freedom of the will to choose good or evil led him on to a declaration that we should move our concerns on from these basically insoluble theoretical questions to the practical, ethical concerns of everyday Christian life and, as it were, get on with the job in hand. The task in question was that of saving our souls, using Christ as our exemplar to construct and follow His moral *philosophia Christi*. Found in the Gospels, this 'philosophy of Christ' was the composite rule-book of self-sanctification, not to be attained by following empty ceremonies, external rites and mechanical routines such as pilgrimages but by becoming genuine disciples of the mentor and role model, the 'sole archetype' of love of neighbour, Christ. Erasmus himself had produced a guide to meritorious, holy, and above all charitable, living in his best-selling *Enchiridion Militis Christiani*, the 'Christian Soldier's Manual', first published in 1503 and based on the spirit of that earlier route-map to personal holiness, a Kempis's *De Imitatione Christi*, or 'Imitation of Christ'. Such holiness and personal worth were what Erasmus intended by his citation in the text of 'On the Freedom of the Will' of the 'true religion' which should be our goal, rather than futile speculations about ultimately unknowable issues of the will versus grace. The term he used, 'true religion', should be read as a direct reference to the agenda of praiseworthy good deeds of charity towards the needy set out in the Epistle of James, 1:27, as the route to ethical merit. That was an avenue, though, that Luther disparaged in his brutal dismissal of James's Epistle as one 'of straw'.

So Luther and Erasmus were coming from fundamentally diverse directions in this debate. What Erasmus was putting forward was the view that the theoretical debate about the will was in itself unimportant. Even if the human will were unfree, it would not be expedient to publicise the fact, and the issue ought to be kept out of the ring of common discourse, lest ordinary people run away with the idea that they could safely ignore ethical Christianity since the consequences of their actions, whether good or evil, were irrelevant to their salvation or damnation, which had been predestined: as Erasmus exclaimed, 'what a window to impiety would the public avowal of such an opinion open to countless mortals'. Thus the safest assumption we could make as a working guide to how to live was that we are in fact accorded merit by God in recognition of our own free choice of living righteously. It was this ingrained assumption that we *can* earn merit that prompted Erasmus to ask:

> What merit can a man arrogate to himself if whatever, as a man, he is able to achieve by his own natural intelligence and free choice, all this he owes to the one from whom he receives these powers?

The answer that Luther would give to that question would encapsulate the whole of his theology of salvation. This was that human beings indeed have no natural capacity for merit and it is emphatically true that all the merit and grace they gain is won for them by Christ. So Erasmus adopted the cluster of beliefs that said (a) that people have freedom to choose good or evil; (b) that their fates – damnation or salvation – are not predestined; and (c) that they will be rewarded by salvation or punished by damnation for their actions, based on free choice. Luther's position was the direct opposite: men and women have no free will and their ultimate fates are decided by predestination. If that implied that God had decided to damn large numbers of people, Luther's emphasis was not on damnation but, rather, on the divine mercy through which the just were *saved* by faith, passively, lacking any capacity through free will to achieve what had to be won vicariously, on their behalf.

Melanchthon took up Erasmus's challenge, in September 1524, but the latter's view – that, since the truth of doctrine was elusive and uncertain, it was best to subordinate dogma to conduct and build an ethical system that operated on the probability that we were saved by works grounded on free will – was bound sooner or later to elicit from Luther a direct declaration of war against this combination of intellectual scepticism and practical moralism, the latter seeming to negate the need for Christ's sacrifice. In autumn and at Christmas 1524 he was preaching against free will, while around that time reading Erasmus's work on the question, with disgust. Yet despite the pressure on Luther from his supporters for him to counter Erasmus's challenge, the events, private and public, of 1525 – his marriage and his involvement in the Peasants' Revolt – held matters up, though Luther was, he said, 'hard at work' answering Erasmus in September. His riposte may have been finished in the middle of November, but did not appear until the very last day of 1525. Designed for the kind of international readership Erasmus had addressed, the work was published in Latin as *De Servo Arbitrio*, 'On the Bondage of the Will', and alongside a German translation, seven further Latin editions followed in the next year.

Many have regarded 'On the Bondage of the Will' as a Luther masterpiece, an essential addendum bringing out the further implications of the Reformation theology being developed ever since 1517. Richard Marius, however, has dissented from the 'masterpiece' consensus, seeing 'On the Bondage of the Will' as marred by its own vituperativeness. It is clear that Erasmus's work was neutral, kindly or even predominantly silent about the person of Luther to whom, he said, he had 'assumed a certain favour . . . as an investigator may towards an arraigned prisoner'. In contrast, Luther's reply was deeply confrontational towards Erasmus in person: conventional terms of respect for the senior man's reputation – 'venerable Erasmus', 'excellent Erasmus', 'a very dear brother' – carry indeed an almost audible sneering tone, as if to put into sharper and sardonic relief Luther's basic 'disgust, anger and contempt' for what Luther clearly saw as the Dutchman's glib and seductive triviality skimmed over fundamental 'ignorance' and 'puerile and indeed perverse' musings.

The underlying message was that Erasmus was a superficial, sceptical, flippant amateur and meddler whose writings on this subject had at least the merit of coaxing Luther out of his tent to express his professional theologian's correct view 'that free choice is a pure fiction'. To do so, he deployed the interpersonal abuse which was part and parcel of the long-established exchanges in Scholastic discourse, as an earnest of the sincerity and conviction of the participants. For this tract of Luther's was a work of passion on a subject over which he insisted it was essential to believe the right doctrines, regardless of whatever dire consequences Erasmus might predict for the 'peace of the world':

> Therefore, it is not irreverent, inquisitive, or superfluous, but essential, salutary and necessary for a Christian, to find out whether the will does anything or nothing in matters pertaining to eternal salvation.

However, this knowledge of the truth was not simply a matter of believing aright, important as this was, but was the precondition of our correct attitude and behaviour towards God Himself. Thus whereas Erasmus's point of departure can be said to have been humanity and human ethics, Luther's starting-point was God and the way in which His foreknowledge, that inseparable component of His divine majesty, precluded the freedom of our wills. To arrive at this position Luther resorted to a mastery of Scholastic debating technique which, for all his disparagement of Scholasticism in previous years, had never left him. A favoured topic of traditional Scholastic discourse on the will was that of 'contingency' – the possible limits placed on God's foreknowledge by our human freedom of choice, since if we were free to choose and act, God's total predictive prescience of our actions and fates would be restricted, albeit by His own consent with Himself to accept that restriction. For Luther, such a conditional and limited foreknowledge was unacceptable as a proposition concerning the Almighty, and

> Here, then, is something fundamentally necessary and salutary for a Christian, to know that God foreknows nothing contingently, but that he foresees and purposes and does all things by his immutable, eternal, and infallible will. Here is a thunderbolt by which free will is completely prostrated and shattered.

Why was God's foreknowledge uncontingent and unrestricted by any freedom of the will on our part? The short answer is that He is God, and 'the will of God is effectual and cannot be hindered, since it is the power of the divine nature itself'. There could be only one 'free will' in the universe. If man were free, God was not and, as far as human beings were concerned, apart from freedom in the secondary, mundane dealings of this life, in matters of eternal life they were slaves, their master being either God or Satan.

A striking feature certainly of the key sections of Luther's work dealing with 'God's Foreknowledge, Contingence and Necessity' is how little the supposed scripturalist Luther invoked the Bible, in contrast with Erasmus's tendency in 'On the Freedom of the Will' to pile up such citations as 'Further Old Testament Passages Implying Free Choice' and 'New Testament Texts Examined'. Of course, Luther deployed Scripture, especially the Letter to the Romans, in this work. However, in his most ratiocinative passages of 'On the Bondage of the Will' he used a kind of pure, Scholastically based rationality. His powerful, if not irresistible, argument proceeded by way of the dialectic methods of argument from premise to conclusion familiar in the Scholastic tradition in which Luther (but less so Erasmus) had been formed. It was evident in a central premise running through the work, which we might sum up in the words 'Let God be God', leading to a relentless conclusion: 'and free will vanishes'. The power and, at times, deliberate extremism of his argumentation was undoubtedly assisted by the directness of his writing, despite the fact that his work was four times the length of his opponent's. Erasmus was not at his authorial best in 'On the Freedom of the Will', not having his heart in the job, whereas Luther wrote in his response with surpassing vividness and succinctness, describing, for example, as we saw, 'the thunderbolt by which free choice is completely prostrated and shattered'. The power and rigour of Luther's logic, set out in brisk, muscular prose, also involved abuse of Erasmus in person as the ingenuous propounder of the false and dangerous optimism about man's capacity for good that he, Luther, had had to counter. Whether we like it or not, *ad hominem* venom was the unavoidable accompaniment of this tract's force and effectiveness:

> See now, my dear Erasmus, what that most moderate and peace-loving theology of yours leads to! You warn us off, and forbid us to try to understand the foreknowledge of God and the necessity laid on things and men. . . . And by this ill-advised labour of yours you teach us both to cultivate ignorance of God . . . and to despise faith.

Luther thus used the force of powerful reason and language to rebut Erasmus. But was *De Servo Arbitrio* anything more than a work of impressive rational argument, demonstrating the axiom that, if God is to be given His proper divine attributes of omnipotence and omniscience, He must control our fates? Such a position might indeed appear logically persuasive, but also cold and fatalistic, the perceptions of a remote, hidden, imponderable and immovable deity, totally unimpressed by our pleas and deeds. And yet Luther termed Erasmus's moralistic doctrines of the freedom of the will 'colder than ice itself', because they were 'devoid of Christ, devoid of the Spirit', 'relinquishing the promises of God'. So the God whose will was sovereign was not indifferent to our fortunes – far from it: His predestination was the precondition of the salvation of those He had chosen, in Christ. Grace, the Word and God's revelation of himself in Scripture were the bridges between mere deistic fatalism and Christian awareness of divine justice and mercy. The vainly optimistic confidence attributed by Erasmus to our merits attained via free will eliminated the need for the Cross of Christ. But if we trust in our own virtue we are deceived and we need to despair of our capacity to win favour, so that

> When a man has no doubt that everything depends on the will of God, then he completely despairs of himself and chooses nothing for himself, but waits for God to work; then he has come close to grace and can be saved.

Christ is the capstone:

> By the coming of Christ into the world through the gospel, whereby grace is offered and not work demanded, the opportunity is offered for all men, truly a glorious opportunity, of becoming children of God if they are willing to believe.

Following on, in a later, almost a concluding passage, based on John's Gospel, Luther argued that exaltation of free choice and its ally human morality were in denial of Christ as redeemer and of the sufficiency of His

Sacrifice. Men and women had existential free choice in the daily concerns of existence, but when it came to the only really serious issue, that of salvation, we needed Christ crucified utterly. Luther would surely have agreed with the sentiments expressed later by William Blake (1757–1827):

> If Moral Virtue was Christianity
> Christ's pretensions were all Vanity.

With all the work's antagonistic fury and its destructiveness towards human 'pretensions', the Christocentric hope contained within 'The Bondage of the Will' establishes it as a key component in Luther's Reformation corpus.

Erasmus would not have seen it in so positive a light. Luther sent him a personal copy of 'The Bondage of the Will' with a cover letter which is not extant. Erasmus's reply, dated April 1526, *has* survived and it evinces great hurt in the face of Luther's attacks, all the more deeply felt, no doubt, in view of the great humanist's earlier protection of Luther and certainly in the light of his own avoidance of excessive personal rancour in his essay on free will:

> The whole world knows your nature, according to which you have guided your pen against no one more bitterly and, what is more odious, more maliciously, than against me. . . . Wish me any curse you will except your temper. . . .

The debate continued, at least as far as Erasmus was concerned, with his publication in 1526–7 of a work in two sections, *Hyperaspistes*, or 'The Shield Carrier', a lengthy composition, broadening out the author's critique of Luther and his movement, while still, in the end, looking for olive branches. However, Luther had written more than enough on the subject in 'On the Bondage of the Will' and did not reply to Erasmus's reply. Sadly and inevitably, Luther's theological breach with the prince of the humanists partook of an angry personal rift and for ever after he spoke of Erasmus in terms of scorn.

LUTHER'S MARRIAGE

If Luther's doctrinal severance from the Erasmian school was accompanied by a personal rift with the humanist leader, a personal decision that Luther took in the same year that he turned on Erasmus – the same year when his last firm personal link to his monastic past, Staupitz, died – further confirmed his breach with Catholicism. This was his marriage to a former nun, which even the relatively mild Erasmus greeted with mockery. To the apoplectic Cochlaeus, for whom the permanence of solemn vows meant there were no such things as *ex*-monks or *ex*-nuns, this was the last straw, a deliberate defilement of holy virginity, a marriage resulting from an abduction, punishable by death in German law, an offence which took place in the holy season of Passiontide and Easter, an act of desecration: 'A nun married to a monk; a damned woman to a damned man; an infamous woman to an infamous man. . . .'[4]

The circumstances were as follow. After his return to Wittenberg from the Wartburg, Luther, with a colleague, remained in residence in the former premises of the Augustinian Eremites, all the rest of whom had left the house to enter the lay life. Luther himself, apart from his being released from his monastic vows by von Staupitz in 1518, had made no formal severance from monasticism, with its requisite vow of celibacy, and, as we saw, as late as 1522 he chose to garb himself as a monastic in order to put a brake on religious change in the Saxon capital. That said, his excommunication in 1520–1 could be said to have assumed his expulsion from the monastic order, as from the whole Catholic body. He had also, in 'The Judgement of Martin Luther on Monastic Vows' of early 1522, particularly decried the vow of permanent chastity taken by monks and nuns. In terms of his personal circumstances – occupying a house, a large one, receiving a professorial salary, albeit not a high one – and in the light of his views of marriage versus celibacy, there was no bar to Luther's choosing to wed.

His opportunity to do so arose in the case of the nun Katharina von Bora, 26 years old in 1525 and coming from a landed gentry family from near Leipzig in Ducal Saxony. In an arrangement all too common in decisions made about girls in upper-class families when family circumstances changed, her widower father, Hans von Bora, remarried, and Katharina von Bora, at the age of five, was put on a track that was designed to lead to the life of a nun. In 1515, aged sixteen, she was formally entered into a house of the contemplative Cistercian order, near Nimbschen in Ducal Saxony. No question of consent or vocation seems to have arisen and the Catholic Church had not yet, of course, delivered its ruling in the Council of Trent that entry into the religious life was to be accomplished only with the genuine assent of the would-be entrant. On the other hand, von Bora received an education in her convent, with its aristocratic membership, was literate and knew the language of the nuns' regime of prayer, Latin.

Then in the early 1520s, in the gale that arose following Luther's attack on the religious life, the gates of monasteries and convents blew open as numbers of religious – above all, perhaps, those who had been entered into those institutions involuntarily – escaped. Von Bora was one of a dozen who fled her nunnery, dangerously, because it lay in the Catholic territory of Duke George. At Easter-time 1523 a daring escape in a covered wagon was arranged by Luther and executed by a merchant who was a follower of his. In April, nine of the twelve escapers had arrived in Wittenberg. Their arrival presented Luther himself with opportunities and challenges. His work 'Why Nuns May, in All Godliness, Leave the Convents' provided the moral rationale for such emancipations and there was now a chance, never to be turned up, to deliver an anti-Catholic propaganda blow, this time in the language of melodrama, against those responsible for the enslavement of these victims: 'O tyrants! O cruel parents and kinsmen in Germany! O pope and bishops, who can curse you enough?' There was a medium-term problem of finding some financial maintenance for the women, which he set out to solve by begging money from the Electoral court. And there was the more intractable issue of what to do with unattached women, in a society that liked to have its females safely grouped under recognisable categories of subjection: the maiden to her father, the bride transferred to the authority of her husband, the nun under her enclosure and rule, and so on. The little group to which von Bora belonged thus represented a problem of uncertainty of status, which was gradually solved in most of the cases when they were re-placed with their families, married or otherwise honourably provided for. Katharina von Bora, though, her father deceased, living and working in the artist Lucas Cranach's house, remained without a fixed place and the awkward question of her status, or 'honour', was not eased by a romance with a former Wittenberg student and Luther-disciple from which the suitor withdrew. Luther's emergence as her husband-to-be represented a fairly unromantic, if perfectly solicitous, attempt to resolve those ambiguities.

Luther himself certainly shared the assumption that women needed male control, for his objection to female celibacy partook of the view that the 'female sex so very, very weak, joined by nature or rather by God to the other, perishes when cruelly separated'. That was why he acted, with utter consideration and concern, as marriage broker for the 'wretched crowd' of liberated nuns (one of whom was Johann von Staupitz's younger sister). His own initial inclination, as he wrote in a letter of November

1524, was continued bachelorhood, for although he admitted to normal sexual instincts, marriage might be thought irresponsible for one with a death sentence still hanging over his head. However, his preaching in favour of marriage in that same month, plus his publication of a letter in March commending the married state as God's intention for men and women evident in natural and powerful urges which ought not, and really could not, be denied meant that he was being compelled to apply the logic of his thinking to his own situation. He had no particular fixation on Katharina von Bora and might have chosen one of the other former nuns still un-placed, or another young woman whose name was mentioned, but von Bora partly forced the issue by refusing a spouse proposed by Luther, an older man, a parson – and opting for him instead (or perhaps his close friend Nikolaus von Amsdorf).

Amidst the high uproar of the Peasants' Revolt in spring 1525, Luther moved closer to his own nuptials, strongly encouraged by a visit to his parents and by Hans Luther's vigorous support for the decision ('encouraged by the wish of my dear father . . . I married to gratify the wishes of my father, who asked me to marry and leave him descendants'): Luther senior may well have seen in these moves the ultimate triumph of at least some of his own earlier intentions for his son, the final defeat of the monastic state he had so resented. Martin Luther was at the time of the wedding preparations far from being in love with Katharina von Bora and regarded the marriage as a testament of faith rather than a declaration of passion. Yet by the beginning of May Martin Luther's mind was made up for Katharina von Bora and in mid-June, and to avoid mounting scandalous gossip and rumour, they held a quiet but legally adequate ceremony of the exchange of vows in the former Augustinian house which they began to make their married home, as a gift from the Elector. A letter from Melanchthon, perhaps expressive of some hidden resentment, bitterly condemned the espousals. A full marriage service followed the espousals, probably using a newly designed Wittenberg order of service which stressed marriage as a Christian institution. The mandatory feast, with his parents present, and the excellent beer provided by the city of Wittenberg, was held towards the end of the month, still in the midst of the repression of the Revolt. Elector John subsequently took over responsibility for paying the professor's salary, enough for a family man.

Luther's own attitude to the wedding in letters of around that time reveals a self-deprecatory, even self-mocking, tone from which romantic passion was absent – or perhaps concealed in it: 'I was not carried away by passion, for I do not love my wife that way, but esteem her as a friend.'

While to a degree the marriage was an earnest of an ideological position, acclaiming matrimony as suited to all and sundry, the discovery of his father's enthusiasm for the match allowed Luther to represent the initiative for it as coming from that quarter – 'to gratify the wishes of my father' – rather than from any boundless romantic love he might have been expected to feel. No longer of the Romeo generation, Luther was a 42-year-old bachelor when he wed. Both he and his new wife had been formed at impressionable ages in the disciplines of the religious life, with whatever conscious or unconscious lasting effects on their characters and habits. However, the marriage quickly accrued passion and matured and blossomed in the direction of real love, while within it Luther discovered and relished his own strong sexuality. Six children were born between 1526 and 1534. Yet the Luther marriage remained perhaps throughout primarily an instance of a practical and complementary arrangement for the mutual society, help and comfort that the one ought to have of the other.

Frau Luther's high-order managerial ability equipped her to run efficiently and economically the affairs of a big household and growing family, striving successfully for a modest domestic competence, acquiring and inheriting property and correcting the effects of Luther's cavalier impracticality and over-generosity in everyday concerns. His wife acted as his doctor, while marriage and love-making helped take some of the edge off his recurrent depressed moods. Even so, for such a normally eloquent man, Luther tended on the whole to be ironic rather than lavish in his recorded appreciations of the joys of married life: there have been more effusive valentines than his statement of preference for his wife because 'other women have worse faults'. His own misogyny was fairly ingrained, and there were flashes of anger when his wife had the impertinence to interrupt his dinner table monologues: 'I must again wish that women would pray before they preach. Say the Lord's prayer before you speak.' Despite such outbursts, in both institutional and qualitative terms, Luther's married life provided a model for the norm of marriage and family existence for the Lutheran pastorate in the emergent Evangelical Churches of Germany.

THE LUTHERAN CHURCH

The second half of the decade of the 1520s saw rapid progress in the direction of the institutional emergence of a Lutheran ecclesiastical organisation, with that in Electoral Saxony providing a pattern of Churches in the Lutheran–Evangelical family elsewhere, and wherever that family extended itself, in the German Lands, and beyond into Scandinavia. The opportunity to introduce a formal Lutheran ecclesiastical regime in Electoral Saxony came with the accession there of a committed Lutheran prince, John, known as 'the Steadfast' or 'the Constant', in succession to his brother Frederick the Wise in May 1525. At the same time, the need, as well as the opportunity, to implement an orderly ecclesiastical regime in Saxony arose out of the disorder and uncertainty of spontaneous religious change introduced in the course of the decade down to 1527. One particular area in which the issues arising from abandonment of the old ways had to be confronted was over the practical consequences of the dissolution of monasticism, carried out in line with the logic of Lutheran principles of justification by faith without meritorious good works. We have seen how such changes had their marked impact on the lives of Katharina von Bora, her co-sisters and, ultimately, Luther himself. And there were other issues arising from the abolition of the religious life apart from the personal circumstances of its former adherents, issues especially concerning the disposal of often vast reserves of monastic property.

Alongside the social consequences of the breakdown of monastic life, the civil implications of liturgical change also needed to be confronted. Luther's own reforms, set out first in the *Formula Missae*, 'The Order of the Mass' of 1523 and then in the *Deutsche Messe*, or 'German Mass' of 1526, embodied sweeping changes in the theology of the Mass – it was not Christ's sacrifice, so that the central canon, which emphasised its sacrificial character, was deleted; it was essentially a eucharistic celebration in which all participated, receiving the cup as well as the bread. At the same time, much of the scenic apparatus of the service, apart from the German rendition of 1526, remained extensively unchanged, with ancient vestments and gestures retained. However, and whatever the balance between tradition and innovation in the liturgical reforms of 1523 and 1526, one thing that was needful was the standardisation of a single liturgical praxis so as to remove bewilderment on the part of the Christian people, or even to prevent the possibility of civil discord and violence over variant rites that had sprung up within the Electoral domains. Such issues as securing legally valid property transfers and preventing breaches of the peace were the appropriate points at which the state, surely, should intervene in the massive religious changes of the decade.

So, whatever the complex nuances of Luther's doctrine of the Church – his 'ecclesiology' – and whether he envisaged that institution as essentially an invisible assembly of the people of God, it was clear, first, that some working formal shape needed to be given to the ecclesiastical polity in what was by 1527 *de facto* the largely reformed entity of Electoral Saxony. Second, it was made manifest that the state – specifically, the 'prince' – must of necessity be endowed with responsibility for those practical and material issues, including the disposal of Church property, that rightly concerned the secular authority. Such close involvement of the prince in the affairs of the Church might on the face of it appear to represent an abandonment of the 'hands-off' ideas of clear separation of the spheres of Church and state set out in Luther's 1523 work 'Temporal Authority'. However, it was clear that Luther's vision of princely intervention in ecclesiastical life primarily covered the main areas of the proper responsibility of the state in human affairs. This focused on the temporal and legal rather than spiritual concerns of managing property and of keeping the peace, especially if this were endangered by religious discord. However, the prince, empowered and entrusted with this well-defined responsibility of stewardship in the practical affairs of the Church, was to be its friend, and indeed, its member: the 'godly prince'. By the later 1520s, Luther had come round to envisaging as a kind of norm of Church life and Church–state relations the situation that had actually come into being in Electoral Saxony. Beyond Saxony, too, German (and Scandinavian) rulers who were themselves Church members were increasingly to assume extensive authority and responsibility to supervise the life of the Church in those territorial principalities that were already coming to be recognised as 'Lutheran'. In this way a clear feature of what has come to be called 'confessionalisation' in early modern Germany was already becoming evident – the organisation of regional state Churches of one side or the other of the confessional divide under the guidance of princes who were themselves, at least normally, members as well as directors of those bodies.

The actual method hit upon to regularise the affairs of the Church in the Saxon Electorate was the sending out from February 1527 of teams of investigative visitors conducting a state-wide survey of the life of the Church in the principality, identifying and putting to rights what was wrong. The visitors' first reports were neither totally demoralising nor completely satisfactory, since they revealed little gross immorality, but did show up a widespread educational deficiency in which pastors were themselves unable to communicate the basics of Christian instruction, such as the Ten Commandments or the most simple prayers. However, without a clear set of guidelines, to some extent the visitors had had to devise their procedures as they went along and their findings, with

Luther's comments on them, contributed to the compilation by September 1527 of new guidance notes. Doctrinal disagreements between Luther's senior associates Melanchthon and the more radical-minded Johannes Agricola (Johann Schneider or Schnitter, 1494–1566) held up the final-isation of the paperwork for the visitors. The eventual 'Instructions for the Visitors to Parishes in Electoral Saxony', compiled in 1528 chiefly by Melanchthon, with a brief but seminal preface by Luther which the Elector requested from him in January, provided an orderly *modus operandi* for such tours of inspection. The pattern of procedure now set out for these visitors was that of the supervisory visitations of local churches which Luther in his preface was able to trace back to the New Testament. These, he claimed, were maintained by 'holy bishops' in the early centuries of the Fathers of the Church but had been allowed to decay through constant delegation to lesser officials under the later, and corrupt, papal system. The 'Instructions for the Visitors' outlined a surrogate and emergency visitatorial executive, based upon and replacing the lapsed episcopal system whose responsibilities for oversight were devolved on a temporary basis to the Elector's government. The visitors were equipped in their 'Instructions' with a coherent agenda for implementing change and amelioration, and in his preface to these Instructions Luther himself set out their conceptual underpinning.

Their key feature was princely direction. Addressing his ruler and patron with his full and solemn panoply of regional and imperial titles, Luther not only recognised his divine right to rule but also complimented his voluntary Christian assumption of the obligation to take in hand the affairs of the Church in his domains. In order to accomplish this regulation, the panel of visitors had been appointed, its membership of four named by Luther (he was an additional one, not named) reflecting close collaboration between the university and the Electoral civil service in effecting change. For all that, Luther was aware of, and perhaps embarrassed by, the way that this state system of Church reform both could be viewed, and had been interpreted by opponents such as Erasmus, as a sell-out from the principles set out in his work of 1523. Thus he explained the demarcation of responsibility according to which 'his Electoral grace is not obligated to teach and rule in spiritual affairs', but, in his capacity as a temporal ruler, was obliged so to 'order things that strife, rioting and rebellion do not arise among his subjects' – as the Emperor Constantine did when he stepped into the life of the fourth-century Church in order to prevent heresy from disrupting law and order. Thus defined, what we might term the 'Saxon model' was to be viewed as an example for 'all other German princes' to emulate. The ruler acted *vis-à-vis* the Church in line with his divinely assigned police powers, though he also functioned in a high leadership role as a Christian member of the Church. If there was any blurring of the anti-state line pursued in 1523 (issued at a time when Luther was acutely disenchanted with secular rulers), the principles of the 'Instructions for the Visitors' could be seen as returning to some of those set out in the 1520 'Address to the Christian Nobility'. And if there was a further point of difference, it was that in 1520 Luther had envisioned a coalition of princes committed to Church renewal under the direction of a godly emperor. Now, by recognising Elector John in the character of Constantine, he was in effect saluting the individual territorial ruler as an imperial sovereign in his own realm.

In terms of their actual remit, the whole agenda of the visitation could be summed up under the single word 'education', the area in which the visitors' preliminary tour revealed such deficiencies among the supposed teachers of the laity: the clergy, the intended immediate targets of the visitors' attentions. So the 'Instructions for the Visitors' comprised what was to a large extent a teaching syllabus, covering areas where the 1527 survey had revealed gaps, such as knowledge of the Commandments. In this respect 'Instructions for the Visitors', drawn up under Melanchthon's pen but constantly revealing Luther's abiding principles, should be seen as of a piece with the catechetical works Luther compiled in the spring of 1529, the Large Catechism and its own synopsis, the Small Catechism. The latter indeed represented, Luther said, an attempt to redress the

> wretched and lamentable state of affairs which I discovered lately when I acted as inspector. Merciful God, what misery I have seen, the common people knowing nothing at all of Christian doctrine . . . and unfortunately many pastors are well-nigh unskilled and incapable of teaching. . . .

The central concern in both the two catechisms and the 'Instructions' was with an intelligible Christian faith and the practical issues of the moral Christian life. That moral concern was reflected in the high placing given in the Instructions' table of contents to the teaching of the Commandments, where the visitors had reported such shortcomings. However, in a more theoretical first section, entitled 'The Doctrine', the concern was, likewise, with the moral consequences and even with the practical implications for everyday behaviour of certain readings of Luther's own theology. This difficult section of the Instructions was taken up with the doctrine of repentance, restating a need for it in the forgive-ness of sins, as if we could not be sure only of forgiveness passively won for us but had to strive by 'compunction of conscience' to achieve pardon. That was why the authors of the Instructions had admonished parish ministers 'to exhort the people diligently and frequently to repent and grieve over their sins and to fear the judgement of God'. And this was specifically in order to brush aside the opposing view, one, arguably, to be deduced from authentic Lutheran first principles – 'our former teaching' – and now adhered to by Melanchthon's doctrinal rival Agricola, that faith was all that was necessary for justification, and preceded repentance. The Instructions, aligning themselves with Melanchthon's emphases, which seem certain to have been driven by a perceived need to conserve public morals, insisted on the retention of the traditional, in other words pre-Lutheran, understanding 'of repentance, commandment, law, fear'. Unless these older emphases were conserved, people would raise pointless questions in their own minds, whereas their best recourse was to press on with the practical application of the Christian life, obeying the Ten Commandments.

The content reads indeed as if it were struggling to build a halfway house between extremes. On the one hand, there was Agricola's ultra-Lutheran emphasis on faith alone, which seemed to opponents likely, without personal repentance, to breed presumptuous over-confidence in one's justification by faith alone, and no moral exertion. On the other hand was Melanchthon's realisation of the need to preach a doctrine 'that repentance and law belong to the common faith'. The latter was a credo which, however discrepant from pristine Lutheranism's disparagement of 'the law' in favour of faith and grace, was calculated to uphold public moral order. In the end, as these paragraphs struggled to combine the claims that repentance without faith was illusory whereas faith without repentance was 'imagined', a codicil presented a compromise to the effect that while our own repentance and imparted faith were both essential, a third principle was firmly stated as a guide to conduct: 'The third element in the Christian life is the doing of good works.'

That moralism set the tone for the remainder of the 'Instructions', with a forceful advocacy of relinquishing 'sharp disputes' over whether good works are meritorious and proposing instead their performance. People were to obey the Commandments, keeping the Sabbath holy and obeying parents. The theme of obedience was then extended considerably to take in a lengthy excursus on the state, in which the Christian subject was to be admonished to have 'sincere respect for government', and avoid all the kinds of punishments so minutely recorded in Scripture for the sin of rebellion. Beyond the basic duties of paying taxes, the Christian citizen owed the state an obligation of honour, love and gratitude to government, praying for the public authorities in return for the blessings governments bestowed of peace, justice and the security of families.

All in all this represented a considerable advance in appreciation of the positive role of the state from the essential negativity of 'Of Temporal Authority' of five years before, with its acceptance of the state as little more than a necessary evil. The Peasants' Revolt was specifically instanced in commendation of the duty of paying dues. Christian freedom was not to be read as a licence for anarchy. The recently arisen radicalism of the Anabaptists was rejected in a brief excerpt on the necessity for infant baptism, and the pacifism of most of the Anabaptists was repudiated in a call to be prepared to fight the Turks (whose threat to Germany's security was once more mounting). Alongside recognition of matrimony as ordained by God, there were longer essays on the sacraments, with penance, though not in the 'papal' form, being firmly counted one of them. Instructions on the eucharist were to insist 'that this is the true body and blood of Christ, since Christ has so declared': as we shall see in the next chapter, this was the issue that was to engage Luther in his next major bout of controversy. For the meantime, though, we can appreciate the centrality of 'Instructions for the Visitors' as encapsulating a kind of applied Lutheranism conducive to the neighbourliness, docility and respectability of the Christian in society, a clear code of Lutheran civics and morality, and one in which the potential for justification by faith without the law, along with the denial of free will, to issue in individualism or the repudiation of moral responsibility was decisively averted.

8

LUTHER AND LUTHERANISM
THE QUEST FOR DEFINITION

INTRODUCTION

In the previous chapter we saw how Lutheranism acquired a sharper definition of its own identity as a 'confession' and Church in the course of the decade of the 1520s. It developed its social and political conservatism in the outcome of the Peasants' Revolt; it definitively severed its remaining links with Catholic reformism through Luther's confrontation with Erasmus; and it acquired a Church order, system of oversight and of religious education and a moral code through the institution of the visitations in 1527–8. That process of defining the new faith acquired further momentum as Luther's religious creed gained clearer shape in contradistinction with the quasi-rationalistic eucharistic theology of Huldrych Zwingli.

After justification, the nature and content of the sacrament of the eucharist, or holy communion, and above all the character of Christ's presence within it, was the second most vexed doctrinal issue of the Reformation: it produced division both between the Roman and Protestant Churches and also within the newly emergent Protestant confessions. (The new word 'Protestant' was to arise out of a protest lodged by followers of Luther at the Diet in Speyer in 1529 against a pro-Catholic majority decision.) For some, the eucharist was, and for others it represented, the body and immanence of Christ Himself within His Church, so that the exact definition of His presence in that sacrament was a matter of the utmost concern. The traditional Catholic understanding was that Christ was really, physically and miraculously present in the sacrament in the forms of bread and wine. Luther's insistence, versus Zwingli, on a traditional understanding of Christ's actual miraculous presence physically in the sacrament of the eucharist, under the appearance of bread and wine, distinguished his Church's eucharistic theology from that of the other ecclesiastical bodies engendered by the Reformation and underlined the distinctiveness of the Church or Churches that took their rise from him. That is why consideration in some detail of the eucharistic issue that set clear blue water between Luther and Zwingli will be necessary in this chapter.

In this chapter we shall also see how the Confession of Augsburg of 1530 etched out a clear doctrinal identity for Lutheranism and we shall go on to consider Luther's continuing massive literary output, including the fields of liturgy and worship, so as to establish how the Lutheran Churches received their distinctive shape, largely at their founder's hands.

LUTHER AND ZWINGLI

Huldrych Zwingli was born the son of a prosperous farmer and so into the same sort of social class as Luther – industrious, upwardly mobile 'middling sort' – in the Canton of St Gallen in Switzerland, just a few months after Luther, on new year's day 1484. Indeed, the two men developed in close parallel, Zwingli, like Luther, being groomed for advancement via education. He attended the Universities of Basel and Vienna and imbibed much of the 'new learning' of Christian humanism, becoming a passionate disciple of Erasmus, whom he met in 1515 or 1516.

The close parallels continue: Luther was ordained priest in 1507, Zwingli in the previous year. However, there the tracks diverged, for Zwingli next moved not into monasticism but into the pastoral ministry, becoming parish priest of Glarus, the capital of the Swiss canton of that name. Thence he moved in 1516 to become priest in residence of the Swiss pilgrimage centre at Einsiedeln, where his light priestly duties allowed him to deepen his Christian humanist studies, concentrating on the Fathers of the Church and continuing to study the language of the New Testament, Greek. Then, in 1519, he was appointed *Leutpriester*, or public preacher, in the Great Church in the self-governing city of Zurich, the leading metropolis of the Swiss Confederation. In this preaching appointment, Zwingli had the opportunity to develop and publicise the scriptural insights he had been acquiring during his years of study. The Zurich pulpit was to be his platform for introducing, with the full support of the city council, gradual but nonetheless extensive religious reforms into the life of Zurich over the course of the following decade.

When Zwingli was appointed to his preaching post, Luther's protest in neighbouring Germany was, of course, already well under way. Was Zwingli then or at any other time a Lutheran, and were the changes he was to introduce in Zurich in any way conditioned by the programme of the German reformer? The evidence is conflicting. On the one hand, from 1518 onwards Zwingli was acclaiming Luther as a prophet and a hero, seen in terms of biblical or classical models – 'a new Elias', a 'David', or a 'Hercules'. Not surprisingly, he helped to import Luther's writings into Switzerland; he was particularly impressed with Luther's stand in the Leipzig disputation of 1519 and in that year he called for the expulsion of an indulgence-seller from his adopted city. On the other hand, Zwingli was anxious both to draw a clear line between his teachings and the German's and to show his independence from his Wittenberg contemporary by depicting the latter as having a catalytic rather than initiating effect on his own rapidly maturing evangelical theology. Thus by 1522 Zwingli was expressing – perhaps testily – his wish not 'to be called a Lutheran, for I did not learn the teachings of Christ from Luther, but from the word of God'.

In his insistence on his doctrinal independence from Luther, Zwingli was expressing more than mere self-regard, for it was true that the two men came to a large extent from different intellectual starting-points. While Luther, as we have seen, was more than ready to use the linguistic tools shaped by the humanists in order the better to understand Scripture, Zwingli was steeped in humanism and the classics. Thus he accepted a proposition that Luther never could – the widespread conviction of Renaissance classical scholars that some of the wise and great, but pagan, philosophers and poets of ancient Greece and Rome were saved. Zwingli also remained an Erasmian reformist in some respects, even though, as a 'Protestant', he came to abjure the doctrine of free will and adopted justification by faith. Finally, where Luther rejected 'that harlot reason', Zwingli, perhaps under the influence of the modernising, metropolitan atmosphere of Zurich, inclined towards a rationalising view of Christianity in which perhaps a dawning scepticism with regard to miracles was becoming apparent.

From the spring of 1522 onwards and with the steady support of the ruling council, Zwingli introduced a whole raft of changes in Zurich in the course of the 1520s – including the suppression of the Mass, the closure of the religious houses and the purgation of the Church interiors of decorative 'idolatry' – the images of Christ and the saints inherited from the Catholic past. The reform that distanced him most clearly from Luther came with the transformation of the eucharist from the miracle of changing bread and wine into the body and blood of Christ to a simple commemorative rite. Zwingli in fact had come under the influence of a Dutch theological writer, Cornelis Hendrixzoon Hoen (d. 1524), who argued that when Christ in the Last Supper said the words 'This is my body', known as the 'words of institution', He in fact meant, 'This signifies my body.' Luther rejected that line, Zwingli accepted it. In the Zurich eucharistic service, bread and wine were no longer viewed as being miraculously converted into the actual body and blood of Christ, as both Catholic and emergent Lutheran interpretations insisted they were. Rather holy communion was a meal with a spiritual and symbolic significance, eaten in memory of the Last Supper and the subsequent saving death of the Lord: not so much 'This is my body' (Matthew 26:26; Mark 14:22; Luke 22:19) as 'This do in remembrance of me' (Luke 22:19).

Luther at first associated such opinions of the eucharist with Andreas Carlstadt, the Wittenberg academic who, as we saw in Chapter 6, had tried and failed to introduce a radical form of the Reformation into the city in 1521–2. He was notified in 1524 that Zwingli was putting a symbolic interpretation on 'This is my body'. In the second instalment of his anti-radical work 'Against the Heavenly Prophets Of Images and the Sacraments' of January 1525 Luther thundered against an interpretation of the sacrament that was essentially spiritual. Even so, by the middle of the decade, such an understanding of the sacrament was being extensively adopted in Switzerland and was spreading into the cities of neighbouring southern Germany. By January 1526 Luther was writing of Zwingli and other 'new heretics' including Carlstadt as rebellious sons, 'Absaloms' (Absalom was King David's traitorous son, in 2 Samuel 14–18) and 'scourges of the sacrament' of the eucharist. In a review of the eucharistic debate, Luther placed Zwingli as the second head of a false interpretation of the sacrament led by Carlstadt and accompanied by the reforming theologian of the city of Basel in Switzerland, Johannes Œcolampadius (Heussgen or Hüssgen, 1482–1531). This school's eucharistic doctrine Luther found to be 'childish, incompetent', 'disrupting the world' and, indeed, associated with 'the beasts of the Apocalypse'. Yet such opposing views also depressed Luther into profound self-doubt and even regret that in breaking with Rome he had opened a path that led to such errors and, as he confessed to his students, 'I have often wondered whether it would have been better to have preserved the papacy than to see such tumult.' Sermons he delivered just before Easter 1526 upholding the traditional interpretation were published in October as 'The Sacrament of the Body and Blood of Christ – Against the Fanatics'.[1]

Among the string of literary blows and counter-blows between Wittenberg and Zurich, and involving other combatants on either side, Zwingli's 'A Friendly Exposition of the Question of the Eucharist, Addressed To, Not Against, Martin Luther', of March 1527, as its title indicates, tried to pour oil on troubled water. At the same time the tract insisted that the eucharistic bread and wine were not Christ's actual body and blood, though Christ was *spiritually* present in the sacrament to believing recipients. Luther's own definitive position was set out in a work published in around early April 1527, 'That those Words of Christ, "This is my Body", Still Stand Firm Against the Ranting Spirits'. This carefully prepared book was decisive in establishing Luther's understanding of the eucharist, and on a firm foundation of a literal reading of Scripture. Christ's words 'This is my body' meant exactly what they said – and if the eucharist were not Christ's flesh, eaten for the forgiveness of sins, it would have no benefits for the believer. Attempts by Zwingli in spring 1527 to send 'friendly' olive branches simply outraged Luther with what he saw as Zwingli's patronising 'haughty spirit', while in May Zwingli wrote of the 'lies' and 'slander' contained in 'That those Words of Christ. . .'. In the course of the same year Luther was firmly placing Zwingli's writings alongside the views of the 'sacramentarians' – those who upheld only a spiritual and no physical reality of Christ in the eucharist – but was also characterising the Swiss as his 'Judas' who 'has done his worst on me'. Luther's massive 'Confession of Faith about the Last Supper of Christ' of March 1528 reiterated the scriptural grounds, as well as its defence by the ancient Fathers of the Church, of his ineradicable belief in the real presence of Christ in the eucharist, a view strongly reaffirmed in the contemporaneous 'Instructions for the Visitors to Parishes in Electoral Saxony'. A further published response by Zwingli in July 1528 confirmed the impression that by the summer of that year too much had been said and written, and far too bitterly, to make any reconciliation between the Zurich and Wittenberg positions conceivable. In particular, and as he was to show in the conference eventually, and vainly, called to settle the sacramental issue, Luther's resting of his eucharistic doctrines on a scriptural axis tended to position them in the domain of the immovable and infallible.

And yet such a reconciliation was immensely desirable, from the point of view of the progress, or even the survival, of the Reformation cause in the German Lands and the Swiss cantons. Habsburg power, backing the Catholic cause, was never to be discounted in the reign of Charles V, but in the second half of the 1520s it was at a height. Charles had decisively defeated the French at Pavia in Italy in 1525 and although King Francis I (1494–1547) refused to accept the consequences of this defeat lying down, the 'permanent' Peace of Cambrai of August 1529 freed the Emperor from pressing anxieties on his western flank. Italy and the papacy lay in Charles's grip as a result of his armies' sack of Rome in 1527. The onslaughts of the Turks on the eastern front, and their seizure of Hungary with their victory at Mohács in August 1526, if anything underscored the need for German unity through the reimposition of religious concord – and few were as insistent as Luther himself on the need to fight the Turkish national and religious enemy.

In the same year as that battle took place a compromise religious settlement reached by the first Diet of Speyer allowed each princely state and self-governing city to work out its own religious settlement, opening the door to rapid and legal Protestant growth. However, following rising inter-faith tension in Germany in 1528 in which Charles's brother and regent Ferdinand energised into militancy the Catholic side in both Germany and Switzerland, between February and April 1529 the imperial Diet met again in Speyer and produced a 'recess', or resolution, which in effect reinstated the terms of the Edict of Worms. The protest that gives us the word 'Protestant' was issued by the now recognisable body of Evangelical estates made up of six princes and fourteen cities, but it was also obvious that intra-Protestant unity would be necessary to stem the Catholic backlash. On 22 April 1529, Philip, the young Landgrave (*Landgraf*) of Hesse (known as 'the Magnanimous', 1504–67), a Lutheran convert ever since 1524 and determined since 1527 to secure Evangelical unity through positions agreed in discussions, wrote to Zwingli reporting that at the Diet the 'Papists' had aimed their propaganda against the Evangelicals 'by insisting that we, who adhere to the pure and clear Word of God, are not of one accord concerning our faith'. Supported by the Strassburg reformer Martin Bützer in a quest for Evangelical reconciliation, Philip's solution was to call Melanchthon and Luther together with the Swiss to achieve 'concord' on the sacrament. The Landgrave's grand design was in fact to create a defensive alliance of Protestant states, urban and territorial, Swiss and German, and perhaps to reach into Scandinavia, where Denmark and Sweden were then introducing Lutheranism. With those political aims in mind, Philip strove to forge a formula of concord over an agreed theology as an intellectual foundation for a political and military Protestant alliance. Luther and Melanchthon, Zwingli and Œcolampadius, with other leading reformers, were to be brought together to hammer out a unity agreement on the very sacrament of unity, the eucharist.

Luther himself had serious doubts about the proposed quest for theological accord through negotiation but on June 23, under pressure, or coercion, from Elector John to accede to Landgrave Philip's request, he consented to accept the invitation to the proposed 'friendly private discussion' planned to be held in the town of Marburg in Hesse from 29 September (in fact from 1 to 4 October). However, Luther's response was profoundly unenthusiastic, not least because he held the view that military and political alliances to defend the gospel confounded the separate spheres of the two kingdoms, the spiritual and the temporal. He was giving his assent, he wrote, in recognition of Philip's sincere intentions but he feared that this would be 'a wasted, and perhaps for us even dangerous service' which would be exploited by the 'opposition' – following what Luther confidently expected to be the failure of the talks – in order to put the blame for intransigence on the Lutherans. This negativity augured ill for the success of the planned unity talks. Luther had been writing for some time of his doctrinal foes as a kind of hydra-headed and malevolent 'spirit', and, as far as the Zwinglians and their allies were concerned, 'I know the devil well.' With no intention of giving an inch of his own eucharistic interpretation – 'I cannot give ground . . . because I am certain that they are in error' – Luther asked Philip to seek from the Swiss some prior commitment to 'soften their opinions'.

Luther also saw the forthcoming Marburg colloquy as part of the unceasing doctrinal warfare in which he had been engaged since 1517 – 'for twelve years now I have been taught my lesson soundly by such knavish play acting'. And it is true that these moves of the late 1520s show up enduring features of the mindset and make-up of the great reformer. These were: first, his utter intransigence, according to which he saw himself before and at Marburg, as he had at Worms, as simply unable, unfree, to compromise his views; next, his disregard for a human or temporal advantage when set against the primacy of religious and doctrinal truth, as he understood it; and, third, his passionate loathing and, indeed, demonisation of his theological foes: the 'turbulent spirit' of the 'sacramentarians' – those who proclaimed only a spiritual presence of Christ in the sacrament – was, he said, of the same brood of the disrupters going back beyond Carlstadt to Müntzer and even von Sickingen, 'but may Christ our Lord tread Satan under his feet'. The demonisation of opponents had certainly been evident in 'That those Words of Christ . . .', in which the figure of Satan put in about 77 appearances.

Zwingli set off for Marburg from Zurich early in September, collecting Œcolompadius along the way. He was then being joined by two other representatives of the rapidly emerging urban Protestant tradition, Martin Bützer and Caspar Hedio (1494–1552), the joint reformers of Strassburg, men positioned to help steer through a compromise position on the sacrament. Stopping to preach along the way, Luther travelled with Melanchthon and leading Lutheran urban reformers such as Andreas Osiander (1498–1552) of Nuremberg, and arrived later than the Swiss and Strassburg parties, since he was held up by the need for a safe conduct to cross over from Saxon Electoral to Hessian territory. He had already alluded to a 'dangerous service', and he did not forget, even if Landgrave Philip seemed inclined to, that he was still an outlaw. The conferees were entertained in truly princely style. Although the talks, conducted in Latin in the great hall of Marburg castle, had star billing and attracted numbers of onlookers from the learned world of theology, Philip was resolved to keep them productive and relatively confidential. To maximise their positive outcome, it was decided to avoid an initial head-on collision between Luther and Zwingli, who even the Swiss reformer's disciple and eventual successor in the Zurich ministry, Heinrich Bullinger (1504–75), admitted was as 'vehement and hot-tempered' as Luther was. Thus less confrontational conversations involving the more emollient seconds Œcolompadius (versus Luther, over six hours) and Melanchthon (versus Zwingli, three hours) were instigated.

On the second day, 2 October, beginning at 6 a.m. and with the theologically aware Landgrave in the chair, the four main disputants 'entered the area', as Zwingli put it in suitable simile, and three further debate sessions were held. Luther was the chief spokesman for his party. He insisted not on a metaphysical but on a literal acceptance of the words of institution and to this effect, in one of those famous theatrical gestures that puncuated his life, he drew in chalk on the conference table his text, the Latin words, so sacred that he also covered them over with a velvet napkin, as if it were an altar cloth in the Mass: *Hoc est corpus meum*, 'This is my body.' Whatever skill Œcolompadius went on to display in dialectic – getting Luther to agree that believers must partake of Christ spiritually – could not budge Luther from those four Latin words: they 'hold me captive . . . I stand by my verse'.

Luther thereby set an agenda for the talks revolving round those words, though the discussion also broadened to touch on the humanity and divinity of Christ. To us today it may seem extraordinary that the elevated talk in Marburg of Christ's eucharistic and celestial presence could become, as apparently it was, mired in barnyard language – that Luther could utter in pretty much the same breath both that Christ 'gives

Himself to us . . . in preaching, in baptism, in consoling our brethren, in the sacraments' and then that 'If He were to order us to eat shit I would do it.' Both Luther and Zwingli, as Bullinger implied, were tough, combative men and traded this kind of language freely. However, for some years the theologian Zwingli had acted as a practical politician, working closely with the city council of Zurich in order to introduce religious change, and he had a politician's instinct for a deal. Thus although he accused Luther of being 'prejudiced' – he had 'already made up his mind' – he also wanted reconciliation, albeit, perhaps, reconciliation of all to his viewpoint, and his leadership. Yet his insistence 'I want your friendship, not enmity' was clearly influenced by the intended purpose of the gathering. With the onset of an epidemic of a lethal fever introduced from England to the Continent in the previous year and threatening to terminate the colloquy, the chancellor of Hesse issued a reminder of that purpose: 'Your assignment was "to seek ways and means of achieving harmony".' Luther was also prepared for conciliatory speech – 'I'll keep control of myself. . . . I apologise if I have been harsh to you.' Even so, this for him was on the strict understanding that there could be no agreement except surrender on the substantive issue.

Luther added a wish that the question might have been 'resolved to our mutual satisfaction', while Zwingli was moved to tears by failure to agree and Œcolampadius evinced dark fears for God's 'poor Church' in light of the talks' breakdown when the Landgrave brought the formal part of the conference to a close on the afternoon of 4 October. Certainly what Luther called 'the hand of peace and charity' was, at least metaphorically, extended at Marburg, and, though in fact he spurned an actual hand-shake with the Swiss leader, he was temporarily won over to a proposal for intercommunion with the Swiss. Indeed, the ten signatories to the eventual Marburg agreement actually achieved consensus on fourteen out of fifteen clauses concerned with such important matters as the priesthood of all believers, clerical marriage, baptism and the role of the state *vis-à-vis* the Church. There was even some agreement on the eucharist – that it should be taken in two kinds, that the Mass was not a good work, and that the sacrament should be received in a 'spiritual partaking'.

Yet the Marburg colloquy was, in the end, a failure of the unity project as Philip of Hesse had envisaged it, and agreement of the nature of the presence of Christ in the eucharist was not secured. Indeed it is difficult to see how it could have been, for Luther was not the only adamantine presence in the Hessian town on those early autumn days. While Melanchthon, keen to achieve a rapprochement to the right, towards

Catholicism, encouraged Luther to reject a Zwinglian-style eucharistic formula that Catholics could not accept, the Swiss themselves were immovable over their spiritualising view of the eucharist and Zwingli, no less than Luther, took comfort that his side had 'fought our winning battle'. In fact, Zwingli's spiritual vision of holy communion had its own powerful scriptural warrant, in John's Gospel, 6:63, which Œcolampadius cited during the proceedings: 'It is the spirit that giveth life; the flesh profiteth nothing.' The failure of Marburg meant that from 1529, and in the face of Luther's profound unconcern, the two great streams of the early Reformation, the northern and Saxon and the southern and Swiss, were to flow in their opposing directions.

THE AUGSBURG CONFESSION

In point of fact, and the breakdown of Philip's Swiss–German unity plans notwithstanding, some measure of Protestant unity, at least in Germany, was indispensable, given the force of the Catholic recovery and in the light of Charles V's impending return to the *Reich* in 1530 after a nine-year absence following the Diet of Worms. Even while the disputants were engaged at Marburg, Elector John and his fellow Lutheran Margrave George of Brandenburg-Anspach were meeting with representatives from Lutheran cities and from Hesse to hammer out an Evangelical credo that would weld those of that confession into an anti-Catholic coalition. The urgency of the hour was that Habsburg power reached a new zenith at the turn of the 1520s and '30s. In the same month that Philip of Hesse's guest theologians quarrelled at Marburg and the German Lutheran chieftains held their own discussions, the Turks were repelled from the Habsburgs' Vienna and the threat on the Danube was lifted. In Italy the symbol of the Emperor's new and unchallenged mastery was his coronation at the hands of the pope in Bologna, early in the new year of 1530. Charles's self-confidence at a peak, he was now determined to impose his will on his German domains, to get Germans to pay for the Turkish campaigns, to allow the religious dissidents the opportunity to present their viewpoint, but then to either reconcile or crush the Lutheran party. While he was still in Italy, Charles summoned the Diet to the south-German city of Augsburg, where it was scheduled to open in April 1530 and to be chaired by the Emperor in person. Its purpose in the Emperor's eyes was to provide the taxation for the defensive crusade in the east and to restore lost religious unity to the German Lands.

Luther had returned to Wittenberg from Marburg in the previous October preaching along the way and presenting his report on proceedings in Hesse to the Elector. Anxiety over Turkish aggression contributed to a return of depression in the autumn. Then in time for the preliminaries to the Diet, Luther with Melanchthon and other colleagues was to assist with the presentation of a synopsis of the Evangelical faith. In March 1530 Luther was making preparations for a journey to do with the business of the Diet and on 3 April 1530 he set off, preaching along the way. By Good Friday in the middle of the month, in the town of Coburg in southern Saxony, the theologians met Elector John, full of optimism over the Emperor's reasonableness. However, within the same month Luther was held back at this last stop that was still within safe Saxon territory, the hilltop castle of Coburg, 'Feste Coburg', where he was lodged on the night of 23 April. And there the Electoral party left him behind and proceeded through Catholic Bavarian territory to the free city of Augsburg, where no Electoral protection could have sheltered Luther from the 1521 sentence of outlawry still hanging over his head. Indeed, it is noteworthy that the Elector and the rest of his entourage were issued with the Emperor's safe conducts to proceed to Augsburg but that no such passport was drawn up for Luther, who was thus exempted from the amnesty. So nothing had changed in his status as an outlaw since, a decade previously, he had been put in protective detention in another castle, the Wartburg. Luther was still a dangerous guest to consider accommodating and the Elector's attempt to prevail on the Luther-supporting city council of Nuremberg, nearer to Augsburg, to shelter him met with a prudent refusal.

Feste Coburg, where, in an odd echo of his months in the Wartburg, he grew a beard and dressed in lay, rather than academic, clothes, was an imposing building; it was put entirely at his disposal and he was attended with a large security staff from the Elector's court. It was, he reported to Melanchthon, 'a very pleasant place and convenient for study': he was reading Scripture and working on commentaries, including the Psalms. His 'Admonition Concerning the Sacrament of the Body and Blood of Christ' was in the form of a sermon and addressed the pastoral issue of receiving the eucharist regularly. Yet the comforts of Feste Coburg – 'I live like a lord', he told the Elector – could not conceal a palpable sense that he was being locked away there, like a loose cannon being chained to a bulwark. His own half-humorous but still evident sense of isolation was expressed in his dating of letters (as he had earlier from the Wartburg) from 'the wilderness', or otherwise 'the realm of the birds' or 'my Sinai'.

At the start of his confinement, his brooding on the Turkish threat, as well as the Catholic menace in Germany – 'the home-bred monsters of the Empire', as he described them – intensified his sense of living among the 'last woes' and the 'final assault'. Though he could receive visitors, loneliness afflicted this loving family man separated from his wife and children and renewed depression incapacitated him around mid-May, with possible symptoms of tinnitus, while his grief at the news of his father's death on 29 May laid him low for two days. The fact that he was pouring out letters, at the rate of almost one a day, from the Coburg fortress perhaps suggests a sense of frustration at enforced removal from the centre of action, itself, no doubt, a factor in lowering his spirits. For the fact was that for the months between April and 4 October, and while the *Reichstag* hammered out the most consequential issues for Germany's future, Luther was shut out of the great events taking place in the imperial city over 150 miles to the south of his abode.

There is the distinct possibility, then, that Luther was being sidelined, perhaps not altogether deliberately, by some of his own followers. At the beginning of the 1530s the German Lutheran movement had both a political programme of forging resistance, if necessary, to the Habsburg-led Catholic anti-Lutheran counter-offensive and in 1530 a religious or doctrinal strategy, associated above all with Philip Melanchthon, of finding common ground with those of the old faith. As far as the political tactics were concerned, Luther in 1530, even in the face of the new Habsburg–Catholic hegemony, seemed incapable of adjusting his teachings on resistance and self-defence in order to validate standing up for the Reformation. In the heady, revolutionary 1520s the 'word' had seemed to sweep all before it miraculously and without human agency. However, in the new conditions of the early Counter-Reformation and the Catholic and Habsburg comeback, the movement that took its name from Luther now had no alternative, if it were to survive, but to take practical political and, indeed, military means to defend itself. And this was all in clear contravention of the line that Luther had first adopted in the 1520s that no temporal methods were to be pursued either to advance or to defend the gospel. So Luther was flying in the face of his movement's increasing acceptance of the need to resist Habsburg and Catholic aggression when, in March in the run-up to Augsburg, he wrote to his Elector on the latter's role as the subject of a higher power, the Emperor's:

> According to Scripture, it is in no way proper for anyone who would be a Christian to set himself up against his government, whether it acts

justly or unjustly. Rather a Christian ought to suffer oppression and injustice by his government. For even if his Imperial Majesty were acting wrongly in this matter [of taking action against the Lutherans] and were transgressing against his duty and his oath, neither his imperial authority nor his subjects' obligation of obedience has thereby been abolished.[2]

It is true, as we shall see, that in the following year he was to modify that approach, though not too much, in the direction of devising a new theory of resistance, but he did so guardedly and without enthusiasm, as if he were now belatedly catching up with, rather than dictating, the thinking of his followers.

Yet, while the princes planned resistance, Melanchthon gambled on reconciliation, and in this respect too Luther was being sidelined. Philip Melanchthon, professor of Greek at Wittenberg and the author in 1521 of the first summary of the Evangelical faith, the *Loci Communes rerum theologicarum* ('Memoranda on Theological Issues') had been Luther's second in command throughout the 1520s. Augsburg, however, gave him his moment to take centre stage. Luther himself of course remained the deeply respected teacher of 'his' movement, but in 1530 he almost emerged as its alternative voice, if not its internal opposition, to the evident, if temporary, ascendancy of Melanchthon and his plans to bring the Catholic and Protestant Churches back together. Intended to convene on 8 April, the Augsburg *Reichstag* at which the Evangelical party was to present its case did not actually assemble until 20 June, following the Emperor's arrival (attended by 2,000 infantry whose purpose can have been only that of providing the merest glimpse of immense Habsburg military power) on the 15th of the month. The delay allowed Luther, despite sickness and depression in the spring, to draw up what Lewis Spitz has called his 'own Augsburg Confession'. Before April was out he was announcing to Melanchthon that this work was expanding in volume and power – and, significantly, that he had to restrain its vehemence. The work went to a Wittenberg printer on 12 May and by 7 June was ready for distribution in Augsburg itself, though officially banned by the city council. It was a German-language tractate whose title can be translated as 'Exhortation to All Clergy Assembled at Augsburg', an open letter, ostensibly addressed to the Catholic clergy present at Augsburg, which may be regarded as the longest of all those epistles Luther sent from Feste Coburg.

In this work Luther delivered a proud, confident and impenitent review of all that he had accomplished since 1517, thereby, conceivably, lodging a pre-emptive obstacle in the way of retreating from the steps that had been taken. As Cochlaeus wrote, 'he rehearsed at length the benefits of his teaching, by which he purged the Church of its errors and abuses. . . . And so he praised these things, and boasted over them. . . .' Indeed, the 'Exhortation' may be seen as forestalling any attempt by the Evangelical negotiators at Augsburg in any way to regret or apologise for the alterations made in the 1520s. Instead, Luther triumphed in and trumpeted those changes, claiming that they were entirely necessary and not to be reversed. They involved, he showed: the great, liberating revolution of the attack on indulgences and pardons, when clerical officialdom shamefully kept silence; delivery from the psychological terrors of the Catholic sacrament of penance and its accompanying onus of guilt and works, ignoring the satisfaction Christ had made; the drive against the sale of private Masses; abolition of the proliferation of delusive saints' cults, rosaries and pilgrimages; attacks on the promotion of good works in sermons, when, again, the official leaders of the Church had kept silence in the face of such mendacity; suppression of the casual, financially motivated use of the 'ban' of excommunication; and returning access to the eucharistic chalice to the laity. Luther also presented himself as the liberator of women from the contempt of them implied in clerical celibacy, 'for God has created women to be held in honour . . . [and] wills that they be valued and esteemed as women and that this be done gladly and with love'.

A further checklist of topics neatly summarised the way Luther had restored the doctrines of the Church: 'What law is . . . What gospel is . . . What grace is . . . What faith is . . .', and so on. The liturgical and educational achievements of the 1520s were mentioned in passing and there followed a further summary of the complex devotional routines and dramas that Luther had swept away. In thus recording and standing defiantly by his achievements as a reformer and deliverer, Luther was able once again to present himself as the heroic liberator of the early 1520s and, apart from him, he asked, 'who then stood up against innovations?' As the man appointed to make the Latin translation of the work commented, 'It is a summary of all Lutheranism. If you wish to see the whole of Luther, you ought to buy it.' Luther's whole revolutionary achievement was indeed summarised in those pages, as if the veteran guerrilla were implying that it would be inadmissible, through any deal or accommodation, to return to those Romish corruptions so graphically portrayed. Produced in advance of Melanchthon's more conciliatory Augsburg Confession, the 'Exhortation' provided Luther's alternative, opposing and bedrock view of popish abuses.

Luther's position in the year 1530 combined, then, misgivings over political and military resistance to 'the good young Emperor, . . . pious Charles . . . that noble lord, our dear Emperor Charles', along with a more resolute restatement than Philip Melanchthon's of the Lutheran doctrinal position, with no apologies, no compromise and no surrender. In other words, where Melanchthon prepared for religious compromise, and the Evangelical princely leaders were contemplating military and political resistance, Luther scorned political and military preparedness, but resisted religious concessions. Clearly annoyed at being kept in the dark by the absence of correspondence from Melanchthon in Augsburg, Luther was writing to the Lutheran delegation at the Diet to 'act manly' over religious concessions. To Melanchthon himself, on 27 June, after the Confession had been read out in a closed session of the Diet on 25 June, whether or not out of irritation with Melanchthon's failure to write to, inform or consult him, he was writing in angry terms that indicate a real breach, rebuking Melanchthon's 'greatness of your unbelief . . . vain anxiety'. On the 29th he was warning that too many surrenders had come from the Lutherans.

Was the Augsburg Confession – *Confessio* (or *Apologia*) *Augustana* – a catalogue of surrenders? Ever since its submission, it has been regarded as definitively setting out the doctrinal position of the Lutheran Churches, its main features already having been, after all, prepared by Luther with Melanchthon and other colleagues. The text that was read out in German on behalf of the Evangelical principalities and city-states at the second public 'audience' of the Diet on 25 June, in 21 substantive articles with others listing the abuses of the Roman Church, was, however, Melanchthon's and although Luther rejoiced 'mightily that I have experienced this hour, when Christ is publicly proclaimed through this glorious confession by such men in such an assembly', the document was hallmarked with Melanchthon's emphases and urgencies, and above all his Catholic-leaning ecumenism. The Confession undoubtedly preserved the keystones of the Evangelical faith. On the central issue of justification, for example, the Confession affirmed:

> Men cannot be justified before God [*coram Deo*] by their own strength, merits or works, but are justified freely [*gratis*] through Christ by faith . . . [through Christ] who made satisfaction for our sins. (clause 4)

This of course was the classic Pauline–Lutheran theology of salvation that had been announced to the world in the years since 1517. According to it, as the Confession reaffirmed, good works were the consequence, not the cause, of justification. Equally sound in terms of Lutheran dogmatics was the Confession's statement on free will: 'without the Holy Spirit [the will] has not the power to secure the righteousness of God or spiritual righteousness . . .'.

However, and while we recognise the essential Lutheran doctrinal identity of the Augsburg Confession, we must also be aware that on a spectrum of doctrinal positioning it leaned, as it were, to the centre-right and was certainly closer to Catholic, and certainly to 'evangelical', or reformist, Catholic, understandings than it was to the more far-reaching changes of belief and practice put in place by the likes of Zwingli, not to say the even more advanced radicalism of the Anabaptists. This was even true of the basic data of salvation in which the Melanchthonian observations of the fourth clause cited above were to find a remarkably close echo in the later resolutions of the Council of Trent (sixth session, January 1547):

> If anyone says that man can be justified before God by his own works, whether done by his own natural powers or through the teaching of the law, without divine grace through Jesus Christ, let him be anathema [cursed].

Of course, it is important to realise that Trent reaffirmed the necessity for works to supplement the initiating role of justifying faith. However, we should appreciate that in setting out its terms on the most pressing part of the Lutheran agenda, grace, faith and justification, the Augsburg Confession left open the door on a possible Catholic–Lutheran accord (such as eventually has come about between Catholics and Lutherans in Germany in their 'Joint Declaration' of 1999). It was likewise with such issues as the freedom of the will (clause 18) where Melanchthon's emphasis was not on pointing out where free will did *not* operate but where it *did*, and clearly indicated that with the assistance of the Spirit the will did possess the power to secure righteousness. In such matters as affirming the real presence of Christ in the eucharist (10) and private absolution (11, 12) and in licensing the retention of holy days (15) the Confession again showed its leaning towards traditional rather than radical interpretations of Church life. Indeed, it was not the Romanists but the Anabaptists, as radicals, who were expressly and recurrently singled out for vilification as sectarians from whom Melanchthon wished urgently to distance the Lutheran Churches, in no fewer than five clauses (5, 9, 12, 16, 17: the standard formula was 'Our Churches condemn the Anabaptists . . .'). At the same time, the Melanchthonian Confession stated its Catholicity, even its desire for reunion within a programme of Catholic reform:

> In [our teaching] nothing can be found differing from Scripture or from the Catholic Church, or from the Church of Rome as we understand it from its writers. We are not heretics. Our trouble is with certain abuses which have crept into the Churches without any clear authority. . . .

The last phrase in particular represented some retreat from the original Lutheran programme of doctrinal restoration, in favour of an Erasmian-style project of correction of abuses.

Melanchthon, unlike Luther, was not one of nature's bruisers, and his delicacy and refinement were, no doubt, responsible for the absence of abusive language in the Augsburg Confession. Of course, the Confession drew attention to Catholic errors, though these were partly identified as pertaining to the surface issues of the Church's inherently flexible 'by-laws', in such matters as communion in both kinds and clerical marriage, where issues were negotiable rather than essential. Verbal abuse of the papacy was absent and indeed, in the discussions surrounding the submission of the Confession, Melanchthon not only proposed the re-admission of Lutherans to the authority of bishops (in order to restrain the alleged anarchy of the Anabaptists) but actually said, 'I honour the authority of the apostolic see.' Politician and ecumenist, Melanchthon seemed instinctively aware that the Evangelical tribes could not stand alone, utterly singular and idiosyncratic, refusing to take the hand of any other Christians, whether to the 'left' or the 'right'. Out of his own relatively conservative preferences, he chose a broadly liberal-Catholic rather than radical (Anabaptist or Zwinglian) direction in which to remove the Evangelical tents. There was, then, with Augsburg, a clear rift within Lutheranism and it pitched the intractable Luther against the conciliatory Melanchthon.

That the latter could be seen as the leader of a revisionist camp is clear, for example, from the writings of the Catholic controversialist Cochlaeus. That writer branded Melanchthon a liar for claiming that Lutherans kept the Mass, when Luther in the 1520s and in 'The Babylonian Captivity of the Church' and other places had swept it away. Cochlaeus also called Melanchthon a deceiver for stating that the sacrament of penance had been retained, when Luther had, again in 'The Babylonian Captivity', repudiated it. But if 'The Babylonian Captivity' (along with the 'Address to the Christian Nobility') were to be seen as representing a fixed standard of Luther's entrenched anti-Catholicism, which Cochlaeus believed Melanchthon was attempting to deny, those works were especially outspoken on the question of the papacy – 'the kingdom of Babylon and the régime of Nimrod', as 'The Babylonian Captivity' termed it. So if Luther was to be the first rebel against Melanchthon's revisionist or neo-Catholic Lutheranism, the issue of the papacy presented as suitable an area as any to set out his intractability, or his fidelity with his own earlier and basic teachings, which Melanchthon was ostensibly making efforts to discard or soften in his crusade for Church unity.

Perhaps Luther was even issuing Melanchthon a warning of his intended outspokenness on this issue – if not his determination to sabotage reunion by decrying the Catholics' focus of unity, the papacy – when he alerted him to certain aggressive expressions that were creeping into the 'Exhortation to All Clergy' even while he was composing it. Then in a letter of 19 June he released expressions of racial, personal and sexual abuse of the pope of the day, the incompetent and more or less innocuous Clement VII (1523–34), which were sure, or even intended, to blow all reconciliation out of the water. Light years from Melanchthon's honouring 'the apostolic see', Luther portrayed the pope as 'a low Italian' and 'the son of a harlot'. That kind of abuse was more overt in 'Exhortation to All Clergy' itself, with its defence of honourable Lutheran clerical marriage in contrast with Italian and papal homosexuality: 'Roman sodomy, Italian marriage, Venetian and Turkish brides [i.e male sexual partners], and Florentine bridegrooms': the last was a clear and brutal allusion to the Florentine and illegitimate birth of Pope Clement as the son of Florence's Giuliano de'Medici. If Luther had made a conscious decision to find a topic and a language within which reunification as Melanchthon wished it was put beyond the pale, he could hardly have selected likelier themes. However, the abuse, reaching even more hysterical levels in later works such as 'The Papacy in Rome, An Institution of the Devil' (1545), should be read as no mere libellous knockabout, but rather as part of a conscious design to prevent any reintegration of Lutheranism into a Catholic stream by restating the primal certainties of 1520. Luther's Lutheranism must define itself as what it was by reference to what it was not, and most emphatically, according to its creator, it was not to be in any shape or form in communion with Rome.

AUGSBURG AND AFTER

The point that the office and symbol of the papacy was the fulcrum of division or unity between Evangelicals and Romanists was confirmed with Luther's more overt championing, in August and September 1530, of opposition to compromise. In August he wrote, 'all treaty about harmonizing our [Lutheran and Catholic] doctrines displeases me, for I know it is impossible unless the Pope will simply abolish the papacy'. Even in the unlikely event of the achievement of accord on the papal primacy, there were many other issues of unbridgeable discord, as Luther had been so careful to point out in the 'Exhortation': Masses for the dead said in private, for example, and the content of the canon of the Mass itself. So in September he wrote to Melanchthon again, 'If we yield a single one of their conditions, . . . we deny our whole doctrine and confirm theirs. . . . I would not yield an inch to those proud men. . . . I am almost bursting with anger and indignation. Pray break off all transactions at once and return hither.'

In the summer of 1530 Philip Melanchthon had been given considerable latitude in his attempt to win acceptance for Lutheranism by presenting aspects of that faith in a light and language more acceptable to traditionalists, but he was placed in the classic position of the centrist negotiator disowned by fundamentalists on his own side and also spurned by hardliners with whom he aimed to negotiate on his party's behalf. All the concessions so painfully brokered were in the end of no avail and in that sense Luther had been right to denounce them, for on 22 September, following nine full sessions of the Diet over the course of the summer, the resolution of the *Reichstag*'s Catholic majority to the effect that the Confession had been 'thoroughly refuted' was ratified by the Emperor. It was decided that Charles was to request the pope to call a council of the Catholic Church within the next half year (it took fifteen years to convene) to amend the ills of the Church, but, as the Diet's concluding recess published on 19 November made plain, in effect the Edict of Worms was renewed and the Evangelicals had no option but to surrender and, before 15 April 1531, accept the Catholic position, as set out in the document known as the *Confutatio Pontificia*. According to the resolution, ecclesiastical and monastic properties were to be restored and the Lutheran presses in the Evangelical cities and states silenced. The *Reichskammergericht*, the Imperial Chamber, was empowered to enforce the new edict, if necessary by military force.

Luther's reaction was a further tract, 'Dr Martin Luther's Warning to His Dear German People', written in October, between the first and conclusive issues of the Augsburg resolutions and appearing off the press in April 1531. The work is worth studying for the key changes it contains in Luther's political philosophy and the extent to which his evolving political thought might provide moral support for the Lutheran princely resistance movement which was prompted by the decision at Augsburg to form a defensive alliance in the town of Schmalkalden over the Christmas period of 1530. Much remained constant in Luther's political outlook, and in particular his sense of personal fealty to Charles – which had led Luther into placing him, in the 'Address to the Christian Nobility', at the head of the princes who would direct the reform of the Church – remained undiminished. A decade and more after that acclamation in 1520 Charles V for Luther was still the 'dear emperor' for whom 'our [Lutheran] people . . . have nothing but praise for his imperial virtues' of 'rare gentleness' and moderation. Luther also clung to the story that when the Evangelicals in the person of the Saxon Elector's chancellor tried to proffer to Charles a counterblast to the recess, Melanchthon's 'Apology', and Charles seemed ready to accept it, it was not he but his brother Ferdinand who blocked the submission. Luther's relating the story, whether it is a true or false one, indicates his ingenuous myopia about the reality of Charles's Catholic revanchism.

The central issue was that of resisting, passively or actively, the emperor's commands that all Germans accept and enforce the decisions of Augsburg. With the utmost caution, for the 'Warning' was hardly a revolutionary clarion call to insurgency, Luther gave approval, albeit in somewhat negative terms, to necessary defensive resistance to the emperor:

> If war breaks out – which God forbid – , I will not reprove those who defend themselves against the murderers and bloodthirsty papists, nor let anyone else rebuke them as being seditious, but I will accept their action and let it pass as self-defence.

It was in fact difficult for him to justify even this limited permissive sanction to resistance, for Luther enthused over the emperor's person and rule, at one point representing him as a fair-minded arbiter who 'stood his ground as firmly as a rock'. One way of escaping the contradiction of loyalty to and resistance towards Charles was to take refuge in an ancient convention of popular political culture concerning the way that a well-intentioned ruler's good intentions might be betrayed by those hoary traitors, 'evil counsellors'. As Luther put it:

> For whenever a prince is not half a devil and wishes to govern with mildness, the greatest rogues and villains inevitably gain a place in the government and offices and do as they like under the ruler's name. . . . Therefore no one need be astonished or alarmed if prohibitions or edicts are issued under the emperor's name which are contrary to God and justice.

Pope Clement was the arch-villain in that scenario. He also filled that role, along with Cardinal Lorenzo Campeggio (1474–1539), in a work published at approximately the same time as the 'Warning', 'Commentary on the Alleged Imperial Edict' in which Luther also took refuge in the formula of blaming underlings, in this case ill-intentioned clerics and their lay allies, for actions of which Luther could not approve:

> I have not aimed this [work] at the pious emperor or the pious lords, but on the contrary at the traitors and scoundrels (be they princes or bishops) who have appropriated the imperial name, or . . . have taken advantage of their position at court to put their malicious, desperate, capricious plan into effect.

Yet those pretences could not long be maintained. Within the text of the 'Warning' a farrago of anti-clerical, anti-papal rhetoric could hardly fend off the stark admonition to Luther's readers that 'you must refuse obedience to the *emperor*', along with 'this warning against obeying the *emperor* . . .' (my emphases). In these ways Luther's 'Warning' made an undoubted contribution to the evolution of a Lutheran resistance theory, providing Luther's own seal of approval for a civil war of religion between Catholic-and-imperial versus princely-and-Lutheran forces in the German Lands. The work also played into the hands of Cochlaeus, who was now able to portray Lutheranism as politically seditious and to clarify and redefine, on the basis of Luther's call to resistance against Charles's commands, the emerging ideological and political alliance between Catholicism and Habsburg imperialism. Cochlaeus cited with warm approval an anonymous lay-authored work (whose author was in fact John, the fervently Catholic crown prince of Ducal Saxony) that also made that alliance explicit, for Luther's 'Warning' was actually, the writer said, 'a Seduction, and an Incitement to rebellion and sedition, since in point of fact [Luther] seeks nothing else in it but to make us Germans defect from the Emperor and rebel against all legitimate powers'. Catholicism was, clearly, the religion of imperial political obedience in Germany, Lutheranism that of princely resistance.[3]

LITURGICAL AND SACRAMENTAL DEVELOPMENTS: PRAYER AND MUSIC

As the Lutheran creed was evolving its own distinctiveness in such fields as sacramental theology, doctrinal formulation, ecclesiastical government and a political theory and practice of resistance and opposition, so the Lutheran Churches were acquiring, at Luther's hand, a distinctive apparatus of their liturgy, that is, their prescribed communal and congregational prayer centred on the eucharist. In this field what immediately strikes us, especially considering the totality in almost all other respects of his rejection of the papal Church in the 1520s, 30s and 40s, is the conservatism and moderation of the liturgical regime Luther gradually built up over the course of those years. His most ardent contemporaneous literary foe, Cochlaeus, automatically, and wrongly, took for granted a depiction of him as a revolutionary in this area – one who 'vomited out to the people so much pestilence against the holy rites of the Church'. We should, indeed, not minimise Luther's real achievements in the radical alteration of the liturgy, above all in returning it to the people through the rendering of the Mass in German and the availability to the laity of the eucharistic chalice as well as the bread. However, the balance of the forms of liturgy he constructed was conservative.[4]

Luther's liturgical creativity cannot be neatly consigned to any specific period of his career as a reformer, since his work on aspects of prayer – the Mass, the other chief prayers of the Church, the mode of the administration of the sacraments, and hymns – can be traced over more than twenty years, from 1523 to 1545. Apart from devising liturgical forms to give expression to Lutheran theological principles, including the uniqueness and all-sufficiency of Christ's redeeming sacrifice on Calvary, the need to regulate public worship was given added urgency following the extensive innovations introduced by Carlstadt in Wittenberg during Luther's absence in the Wartburg in 1521–2. Luther's formative contributions included 'Concerning the Order of Public Worship' of 1523. This guide aimed to clear away recent accretions and elaborations and restore an older, purer form of the Mass. 'Concerning the Order of Public Worship' also manifested the basic caution over change that hallmarked Luther's efforts in this area. In one respect, with particular regard to the feast-days of the Church's year, Luther's insistence that 'All the festivals of the saints are to be discontinued' sounds drastically innovative – until we realise that he meant that several Catholic feasts of Mary were to be retained.

His 'An Order of Mass and Communion for the Church in Wittenberg' (also 1523) is even more unmistakable in its claim, 'Nor did I make any innovations.' This disclaimer of the will to change over matters of worship was accompanied by its own rationale that would consistently guide Luther in these matters – a pastoral concern with congregational inclusiveness: 'For I have been hesitant and fearful, partly because of the weak in faith, who cannot suddenly exchange an old and accustomed order of worship for a new and unusual one.' Though remaining in traditional Latin, with only some hymns and the sermon in German, the 'Order of Mass' did indeed lean towards change in its removal from the Mass of the canon – the central section with its treatment of the celebration as a sacrifice – and was destructive in its removal of feast-days apart from those of Jesus, and those of Mary – the Annunciation, the Visitation and the Purification – which could be seen as centring on Christ. However, this setting of the Mass respected traditions very firmly indeed, in its announcement that 'It is not now nor ever has been our intention to abolish the liturgical service of God.' Rather, Luther's quest was to find pure and ancient liturgical forms. Some of Luther's phrases most revealing of his overall liturgical strategy concern the need for continuity: 'all these [liturgical customs] have been tolerated . . . we approve and retain [existing modes of prayer] . . . prayer . . . should be retained in its accepted form . . .'. Freedom not to change also guided his thinking in the area of priests' Mass vestments, the visible signs by which a visually oriented and costume-conscious culture judged much of reality.

In 1523 Luther was already anticipating an all-German Mass: by the mid-1520s numerous variants of such a service existed in various parts of Germany and Luther was urged by supporters to produce a standard form. Opposition did arise from the vested interests of priests whose livelihoods derived from the endowed Masses that people had commissioned for souls in purgatory, a practice objectionable from the standpoint of Luther's theology. As this resistance was being overcome, the accession of the committed Lutheran John the Steadfast in Electoral Saxony in 1525 ensured the ascendancy there of an Evangelical rite. Luther issued this in 1526 as the 'German Mass and Order of Service'. With only the *Kyrie Eleison*, that is the Greek prayer 'Lord, have mercy', in anything other than the German vernacular, this form of the service obviously differed in its language from the predominant Latin of his earlier 'Order of Mass and Communion' of 1523. Its rendition in the language of the people was necessary on educational grounds, with the aim of making clear to congregations the nature of the changes, above all the excision of the canon, that had actually been brought about, and why. Again, we should not minimise the extent of real change made. In particular, the suppression of the canon created space within the order of the service into which New Testament readings and a longer sermon could be inserted. Even so, and despite the liturgical revolution of a vernacular rite, the 'German Mass', with all the clinging to tradition implied in the choice of the word 'Mass', continued along a line of respect for custom, rather than quest for innovation. And this was above all evident in the externalities of the ritual by which ordinary people might adjudge its relatively conservative or innovative nature. With its familiar vestments, bowings and kneelings, its celebrant with his back to the congregation and, at least until a further change in 1542, raising the eucharistic host above his head for worship by the congregation, the German Mass looked like the Catholic one, and certainly was to be sharply distinguished from the austere simplicity of the eucharistic services in the Churches that were to emerge in Zurich under Zwingli and in Geneva under Calvin.

As in the field of congregational and liturgical prayer, so in the arena of the sacraments, Luther's reforms were likely to tend towards the Catholic heritage. There was certainly no question in Luther's mind that the centuries-old practice of infant baptism as an avenue of automatic entry into the Church for all those born in a Christian realm would be upheld. In his 'Order of Baptism' of 1523, a German-language rite, he simply assumed that the individual being baptised was 'the child', 'the little child'. And though this form was revised and shortened in 1526, with the removal of features that might be construed as superstitious, such as the passing over of salt, the same unchanging assumption that the person christened was 'the child' remained in place.

It is also, of course, true that Luther was a revolutionary in the sacramental field. In 'The Babylonian Captivity of the Church' in 1520 he swept away the venerable sacraments of confirmation, matrimony, holy orders and extreme unction, again allowing Cochlaeus to depict him as a destructive mocker of the ancient and the holy. And it is true that those Catholic sacraments were not allowed back into the Lutheran Churches as sacraments: when the inauguration of ministers was regularised in Luther's 'The Ordination of Ministers of the Word' (1539), it involved the setting apart of preaching pastors rather than the consecration of sacrificing priests. When Luther came, in 1529, to draw up 'The Order of Service for Common Pastors', he remained true to his acceptance of matrimony as of divine institution – a 'divine estate' for all mankind and one whose creation was recorded in Genesis – but he also stuck to his refusal to accord it sacramental status. Marriage was celebrated in church, presided over by a pastor and it even had as its ideal type Christ's 'sacramental union' with the Church, but it was not a sacrament. He made no provision for a last anointing of the sick ('extreme unction').

Yet, while Luther promulgated extensive change with regard to the number of the sacraments, with regard to one of them, penance, even the radical 'Babylonian Captivity' showed considerable traditionalism. In that work he had written, 'Without doubt, confession of sins is necessary, and in accordance with the divine commandments. . . . As for secret confession as practised today, though it cannot be proved from Scripture, yet it seems a highly satisfactory practice to me. . . .' Purged of errors of understanding and of financially motivated abuses, penance was, along with baptism and the eucharist, retained as one of the 'three sacraments'.

At that point in time, it is true, Luther viewed the sacrament of penance as being administered within the lay-oriented Church that he then envisaged: 'there is no doubt in my mind that a man's secret sins are forgiven him when he makes a voluntary confession before a brother in private . . .'. The subsequent conservative drift, and, specifically, the clericalisation of the actual arrangements he was to make for the rite of penance, are evident in 'A Short Order of Confession Before the Priest for the Common Man' (1529). In this outline the imagined penitent addresses the minister – 'Reverend and dear sir' – who is asked that 'you, in God's stead, would declare unto me my sins forgiven'. The procedure closely resembles the Catholic order of lay confession to a priest, absolving sins in God's name or 'stead'. The same observation can also be made of Luther's 'How One Should Teach Common Folk to Shrive [confess] Themselves' of 1531: the penitent recites to the minister, 'Reverend and dear sir, I beseech you to hear my confession and to declare unto me the remission of sins in the name of God.'

Again we should note the real changes Luther engineered in this area. The old demand for the penitent's making amends – 'satisfaction' – as a final condition of absolution was made redundant by Christ's all-sufficing satisfaction for sins. Further, Luther cancelled any requirement of confession as a matter of ecclesiastical coercion, along the lines of the Catholic statute, set up by the Fourth Lateran Council in 1215, that all the faithful should confess annually, round about Easter time. His insistence on voluntary confession, as the need for it arose, should be seen as part of a stress on its spontaneity rather than set formal procedures. This was in turn part of Luther's emphasis on the need for genuine contrition in the penitent, though it seems slightly odd that he should prescribe a set form of words to indicate deeply felt guilt. The words that he recommended, though, in 'A Short Order of Confession. . .' evoke the contrition that was stressed in the late medieval school of Gabriel Biel which we examined in Chapter 2 above and which were summed up in the phrase '*quod in se est*', the penitent's desire for contrition to which God responds with an outflow of loving forgiveness: 'I confess before God and you [the minister] that I am a miserable sinner, guilty of every sin, of unbelief and of blasphemy.' Luther's inclusion of self-accusatory phrases in a form of sacramental penance by a private encounter between minister and penitent linked his structuring of this sacrament very closely indeed to traditional Catholic procedures and, indeed, to medieval expectations about how the sacrament of penance operated.

In the field of music and hymnody, Luther is widely regarded as a creative and poetic talent, if not genius. His awareness of the value of music in worship set him apart from the more sweeping reforms proposed by the like of Zwingli in Zurich and he explicitly rejected the tradition of St Augustine of suspicion of pleasurable liturgical music. Indeed, he loved music deeply, was a composer, a fastidious connoisseur and a good singer, played the lute, insisted on giving music a pride of place in the school timetable and required musical training and proficiency as a condition of entry into the ministry.

He was also a conservative reformer who adopted and adapted the two predominant Church-musical forms, which we may describe as choral and congregational, that were on hand in his day. As he showed in the 1523 'Order of Mass and Communion for the Church in Wittenberg', in part he aimed to take ecclesiastical music out of the hands of specialist choirs and return it to the people in intelligible words and easily manageable tunes: 'I . . . wish that we had as many songs as possible in the vernacular which the people could sing during mass . . . , for who doubts that originally all the people sang these which now only the choir sings or responds to . . .?' However, if that passage gives the impression that Luther was opposed to choral performance in church, that was not in fact the case. The complex technical requirements of the elaborate late medieval polyphonic, or contrapuntal, multi-voiced, sung liturgy did indeed make Church music a specialisation of professional, trained choirs in late medieval northern Europe. Luther himself was an admirer of the work of one of the greatest of the polyphonic composers, Josquin Des Prés (or Desprez, 1445–1521). So, he was far from seeking to dispense with the trained choirs, such as that in Torgau, the Elector's residence from 1525, where the church choir's skill won from him the exclamation, 'God Almighty has graciously blessed this city' through its fine musical provisions. Rather, he welcomed the princely patronage – even the Bavarian Catholic variety – that enriched the German choral music of his age. He also encouraged John the Steadfast to endow an Evangelical variant of choral music, citing the example of biblical kings who, he wrote, 'gave salaries to singers'. In short, in music, and in contrast with Erasmus, who was a puritan in these respects, Luther was an enthusiast for polyphony in all its complexity – 'When natural music is sharpened and polished by art, then one begins to see with amazement the great and perfect wisdom of God in his wonderful work of music, . . . like a square dance in heaven . . .' – and he sought to develop Lutheran forms of it. Indeed, the 'Booklet of Spiritual Hymns', compiled by the court chapel musician Johann Walter (or Walther, 1496–1570), published in 1524 and containing 38 pieces, 24 of them by Luther, was polyphonic music designed for choirs.

Luther also envisaged the pastor as presiding over the liturgy as an accomplished musical performer, and in the 1526 'German Mass' he directed the minister to chant in a range of complicated 'modes', or emotional tones, and registers. However, and despite his acknowledgement of the specialist musical performance arts of pastors and choirs, ultimately Luther's principles of full congregational involvement in the services of the Church impelled him to seek a genuine lay and congregational *entrée* into its music. Congregational singing was inseparable from the rendering of the liturgy in the vernacular in the 'German Mass'. The 'Booklet of Spiritual Hymns' aimed in fact to bridge the gap between professionals and amateurs, choir and congregation, by setting the former the task of leading and teaching the latter in new chorales. However, if in the 'Order of Mass and Communion for the Church in Wittenberg' he hinted that he was rediscovering congregational song from scratch, there was in fact a vigorous German legacy of congregational hymnody for him to build on.

Medieval folk hymns were composed for special occasions, including pilgrimages, and were also sung in the Mass as *Leisen* or responses. One of the several medieval German-language *Leisen* borrowed by Luther was a congregational response to the chant sung at the feast of Corpus Christi, *Lauda Sion*, rendered by Luther in 1524 as *Gott sey Gelobet* – 'Blessed be God'. Another medieval *Leise* went back as far as 1370, in a north German manuscript dialect version, which Luther rendered, perhaps as a Christmas hymn for 1523, *Gelobet seystu Jhesus Christus*, 'Praised be Thou, O Jesus Christ'. And these are merely one or two examples of Luther's highly extensive borrowing and quarrying from the thesaurus of medieval German congregational hymnody. The medieval German-language hymn, a popular version of the *Ave Maria, Maria du bist Gnaden voll*, 'Mary, thou art full of grace', lent its tune to Luther's version of Psalm 67. Note, though, at this juncture, how freely he could adapt for purposes of hymn-writing his opening of that Psalm (which in the English Authorised Version, commences 'God, be merciful unto us'). In his own translation of Scripture this starts, *Gott, sei uns gnädig*, 'God, be gracious to us' but becomes, as the first line of Luther's German hymn, *Es wollt uns Gott genedig seyn*, which may be translated as 'O That God Would Be Gracious To Us': a minor alteration, perhaps, but one showing flexibility in Luther's adaptation of the letter of Scripture itself to musical and congregational needs. The opening of Psalm 130, known as *De Profundis*, 'Out of the Depths', was to emerge in Luther's translation of the Old Testament as a literal version, *Aus der Tiefe rufe ich, Herr, zu dir*, 'Out from the depths, I call, Lord, to Thee'. However, as a hymn, Luther recast it in 1523 in the beautiful and poignant form of *Aus tieffer not schrey ich zu dyr* – 'From Trouble Deep I Cry to Thee'. The line is altered into verse, readily singable, with four syllables on either side of the division between the eight syllables midway in the line. Another Psalm, 46, which in the Authorised Version opens 'God is our refuge and strength' and in the German Lutheran Bible as *Gott ist unsere Zuversicht und Stärke* – 'God is our trust and strength' – becomes Luther's adaptation of genius, his best known musical monument, the 1529 *EIn feste burg ist unser Gott*, the musically and poetically irresistible anthem of peril overcome by trust: 'A safe stronghold is our God/A trusty shield and weapon. . . .' Again, in the New Testament prayer known as the *Nunc Dimittis* (Luke 2:29), Luther freely adapted his own translated version, *Herr, nun lässest du deinen Diener im Frieden fahren*, 'Lord, now let your servant go in peace', to the lyrical, eight-syllabled *Myt frid und freud ich far do hyn* – 'In peace and joy I now depart.' As far as hymns were concerned, then, Luther both built on long-standing popular texts and also provided non-literal variants of Scripture in order to answer to congregational and poetic needs. Indeed, quite free adaptation through the use of a poetic approach was Luther's conscious intention. He complained in 1523 that 'poets are wanting among us . . . who could compose evangelical and spiritual songs . . .' and again in the same year, to Spalatin, for whose help he was appealing 'to turn a Psalm into a hymn . . .' , he added, 'Irrespective of the exact wording, one must freely render the sense by suitable words.' As his version of the *De Profundis* shows, and despite his self-deprecating 'I myself am not sufficiently gifted to do these things as I would', Luther was fully up to the task of quite bold literary modification of literal texts.

From the early 1520s Luther was able to make use of the fast-expanding popular genre of the ballad, the mass media form of news broadcast whose commercial production was then expanding so much through the rapid exploitation of the real potentialities of print to reach a huge market for information and entertainment. From as early as 1519 Luther's message was taken up in the Low Countries, where it was to be enthusiastically propagated by fellow members of the Augustinian order. However, the devoutly Catholic Charles V exercised a far firmer hold over those hereditary Burgundian territories than he did in the German Lands proper and was determined to enforce the Edict of Worms there and to crush the first stirrings of heresy. The outcome, in July 1523, was the execution in Brussels of two young Augustinian Lutherans, Johann Esch and Heinrich Voes, who, unlike most of their confrères, refused recantation. Luther's response was the publication, in low-cost broadsheet form, of *Eyn newes lyed wyr heben an*, 'A New Song Here Shall Be Begun'. From its opening lines offering an inviting novelty, through its popular music tune, rhyme-scheme and narrative pace, the 'New Song' is pure ballad. It does not mourn but rather celebrates the horror and heroism in the case of the two martyrs, whose youth – as part of the tradition of the form – is deliberately emphasised, to the extent that Luther made them younger than by the rules of the Augustinian order they can have been. In addition, part of the journalistic and polemic point of the song was to get out the message quickly, that contrary to Catholic propaganda, defying all attempts of the 'sophists' from the highly orthodox University of Louvain to win them back, the young men had not retracted their faith:

> Two huge great fires they kindled then,
> The boys they carried to them;
>
> . . .
>
> To all with joy they yielded quite,
> With singing and God-praising.
>
> . . .
>
> The boys they stood firm as a tower,
> And mocked the sophists' trouble.

Luther had discovered a new talent, that of the street singer.

His further ability to exploit the resources of German popular song can be illustrated in the case of his lovely carol that was, probably, designed as accompaniment for a children's Christmas play, *Von himel hoch da kom ich her*, 'From Heaven High I Come to You', of 1534 or 1535: Luther took over the tune of this Christmas hymn from the song employed in a children's riddling game. He also borrowed from the sophisticated form of the *Hofweise*, the fashionable laudatory poetry of courtly love, to frame a musically complex and apocalyptically inspired hymn in honour and defence of the true Church, *Sie is mir lieb die werde Magd*, 'To Me She's Dear, the Worthy Maid', composed, possibly, in 1535. In these ways, Luther, while drawing heavily on the deep wells of the splendid German vernacular musical culture of his age, and adapting Scripture freely to the needs of congregational prayer, devised a popular religious music that inculcated key Lutheran doctrinal principles and provided the foundations for the glorious German Lutheran musical tradition in the years that were to follow him.

There was, however, one area in which Luther's hymns and devotional output parted company with tradition, and, arguably, with the aspirations of popular piety, culture and music to which, as we have seen, he was generally able to respond so adroitly. Late medieval Germany shared with the rest of Europe a rich repertoire of prayer and song in invocation and honour of the Virgin Mary. Luther by no means disparaged entirely the cult of Mary but he wanted both to cut it down to size and to restore it to its proper place – that place being not alongside but below Christ in the economy of salvation.

One instance of Luther's relative down-grading of Mary comes in the hymn just cited, *Sie ist mir lieb*. . . . The verses from the second and third stanzas of this song, adapted from those in the Revelation of St John (or Apocalypse), chapter 12, concerning the woman clothed with the sun, with the moon beneath her feet, giving birth to a man child and so frustrating the dragon, were traditionally allegorised as meaning Mary: Luther instead interpreted them as signifying the Church. Again, we have seen how Luther borrowed from the treasury of late medieval religious and popular song so as to create hymns. However, he was also capable of correcting their doctrinal emphases in order to advance popular education in Reformation theology. Thus a popular hymn to Mary whose words date from 1480 was typical of what could be seen as the excessive veneration of the Virgin in late medieval piety, since it accorded to her some of the recourses, such as saving her devotees from evil, perhaps more properly sought in the main address to God the Father, the *Pater noster* or

'Our Father'. In the 1524 *Gott der Vater won uns bey*, 'God the Father by Us Be', Luther, apparently, took over intact the melody of this canticle, but he readjusted the emphasis in the text of the 1480 version. In his textual reform the opening line replaces the earlier 'Virgin Mary with us be' and the lines proceed to displace the centrality of the Virgin in favour of that of the Father. Thus Luther used popular religious song for a didactic purpose, in this case propagating an insistence on his doctrines centred on God and Christ.

Once Mary's secondary role was thus reasserted, it was as if she could be given her proper position. Written in ballad form, *Neu freut euch, lieben Christen gmeyn*, 'Dear Christians, Let Us Now Rejoice' (1523), perhaps based on an existing folk-song, forms a remarkable experiment in conveying justification by faith simply, in vivid, first-person terms, very much like the later English Protestant hymns 'Amazing Grace' (John Newton, 1725–1807) and 'Rock of Ages' (Augustus Montague Toplady, 1740–78). In Luther's outline of how salvation is applied to the individual ('My good works they were worthless quite/A mock was all my merit'), Mary is duly honoured for her role, a crucial but essentially subordinate one, as the handmaid of the Lord:

> The Son he heard obediently,
> And by a maiden mother,
> Pure, tender – down he came to me,
> For he would be my brother.

Such an adjustment of devotional emphasis also inspired Luther's version (1533) of Mary's praise-song to the Father, the *Magnificat*. Of this Luther wrote that in it Mary 'sings with a joyous heart of the grace and blessing which the merciful God had shown to her . . .': Mary has become, like Abraham, a model of saving faith and trust.[5]

9

LUTHER'S LATER YEARS

Martin Luther's later years have not generally been regarded by his biographers as his best. Increasing narrowness and intolerance have been identified by admirers such as Gerhard Ritter, who described it as 'disappointing, almost tragic, to see how the stormy, open-hearted enthusiasm of the early years gradually changes into dogmatic rigidity'. Luther's anti-Catholic writings, and in particular his unrestrained attack on the pope and the papacy in 1545, firmly shut the door on any reconciliation with Rome. In the second section of the present chapter we shall consider his response to the bigamous marriage of a leading Lutheran prince, Philip of Hesse. His devious behaviour over that issue was described by Preserved Smith (who called the older Luther 'an embittered, almost a disappointed man') as 'a terrible scandal'. Above all, Luther's appalling anti-Jewish works of 1543 have been deplored by some of his keenest supporters among historians: Roland Bainton, in *Here I Stand*, wished that Luther had died before he wrote 'Concerning the Jews and their Lies' of that year, and the American editors of Luther's complete works in the 1971 volume of the series weighed up the pros and cons of what would have been a grave editorial decision – to delete a major item in the Luther *oeuvre*, for fear it would legitimate new waves of modern antisemitism. In this chapter, though, while not flinching from a realisation of the distasteful side of ageing Luther, we shall also evaluate his positive achievements of the 1530s and 1540s before his death in 1546, focusing on scriptural translation and continuing doctrinal creativity.

BIBLE TRANSLATION

High on the list of Luther's mature achievements was his completion of the translation of the Scriptures into German. As we saw in Chapter 6, the New Testament in German was rapidly completed for publication in September 1522. There remained the immense task of the rendition into German of the whole of the rest of the Bible, the Old Testament.

It seems clear that Luther started work on this immediately after the appearance of the New Testament, and German-language versions of individual books of the Old Testament first began appearing between summer 1523 and September/October 1524. Work was interrupted by controversy with Erasmus in the mid-1520s and in 1528 Luther reported that he was having difficulty with the prophets of the Old Testament in his bid to render them in idiomatic German. However, in the same year he was able to publish a translation of the Book of Psalms, or Psalter. His eloquent preface to it spoke of his love of those texts in which he had, back in 1513–15, found the first inkling of justification by faith. Writing of the Psalms' 'sweet and lovely fragrance', he repeated his contention that their focus was Christ, whose death and resurrection he believed the Psalter clearly prophesied. His final instalment of the Old Testament in German came off the press in March 1532, and was followed by a translation of the books known as the Apocrypha.

Luther took considerable pride in this 'German Bible . . . so good and precious that it surpasses all the Greek and Latin versions . . .'. Even so, the translation of the whole Bible, given its vast scale and the range of language skills necessary to accomplish a faithful German text based on its primary languages, Hebrew and Greek, had to be a collaborative production: Luther was in fact the editorial director of a team of linguistic experts, including Melanchthon for his scholarship in Greek. Writing in 1524, Luther reported that '*We* [my emphasis] have had so much trouble' in rendering a particular Old Testament book. The German Bible, which came out in a final revised version of 1539, was the product of such cooperative scholarship.

DOCTRINAL DEVELOPMENTS, 1531–6: THE MORAL LAW

Luther's Bible also provided a working text to proclaim a distinctive Christian theology. He showed that this was the case in a comment he made in 1540 to the effect that every individual verse of the Scripture had to agree with its overall sense, that if a single sentence would not agree with that sense it should be scrapped and even that the vowel points in Hebrew orthography (which may alter the meaning of words) should be altered in the Hebrew Old Testament if it were necessary to bend them to the overriding doctrinal meaning of the New Testament.

Luther's Bible may be seen, then, as a form of what might today be called 'an interpreter's Bible', in which doctrinal meaning is paramount. The same concern with theological meaning also underpinned Luther's continuing work as a commentator on Scripture. Thus in his published Commentary on St Paul's Epistle to the Galatians of 1531, Luther once more set out the basic principles of Evangelical theology.[1]

The Epistle to the Galatians was addressed by Paul to Christians in Asia Minor, perhaps to those in four cities to whom he had brought the gospel during his first missionary journey. The letter is datable perhaps to AD 56 and may therefore precede the Epistle to the Romans. Whether it does or not, it deals with the same sorts of questions that Romans confronted, those of law and grace, for the issue that St Paul was addressing in this letter arose out of disagreement in the earlier Church over whether converts to Christianity should qualify for entry into the Church by first becoming Jews and keeping the law of Moses requiring circumcision. This impassioned and urgent letter, personally written, rather than, as was usual with Paul, dictated, consists partly of an autobiographical account of the Apostle's conversion and his subsequent missionary work to the uncircumcised gentiles. In it Paul emphasised that it was not the law or circumcision that justified 'but faith which worketh by love' (Galatians 5:6):

> Knowing that a man is not justified by the works of the law, but by the faith of Jesus Christ, even we have believed in Jesus Christ, that we might be justified by the faith of Christ, and not by the works of the law: for by the works of the law shall no flesh be justified.
>
> (Galatians 2:16)

> But that no man is justified by the law, it is evident: for, The just shall live by faith.
>
> (Galatians 3:11)

Given the centrality of concepts set out in Galatians to Luther's whole doctrinal system, it is hardly surprising that he commented on that epistle on several occasions – in university lectures of 1516–17 which he published in 1519; in further commentaries in 1523; and in further university lectures of 1531, published as the commentary that we may now consider.

The immediate reason for the publication of this third set of lectures on Galatians may perhaps have been fear on Luther's part in the early 1530s that his bedrock Pauline doctrines were coming under threat. As we saw in Chapter 8, the Augsburg Confession of the year before the publication of the lectures on Galatians offered a formula on justification that was in some ways close to the one eventually adopted by the Catholic Church's Council of Trent: the Confession stated, 'men . . . are justified freely through Christ by faith', with the crucial Lutheran 'alone' omitted. So Luther may have had in mind an essentially defensive and anti-revisionist purpose for the publication of these lectures when he spoke of

> the greatest and nearest danger, lest Satan take from us the pure doctrine of faith, and bring into the Church again the doctrine of works and men's traditions.

At the same time, if the Commentary on Galatians was addressed to internal Lutheran doctrinal politics, it also provided Luther with fresh anti-Catholic propaganda ammunition. Those who relied on the 'active righteousness' of works (rather than the 'passive righteousness' of justification by faith) he declared 'remain the same as they were under the Pope'. However, Catholic works righteousness was also shared by 'Jews, Turks [Muslims], Papists [and] heretics' – the last meaning Anabaptists and other Reformation radicals, 'fantastical spirits and authors of sects'. Luther, then, was increasingly enunciating a view of the besieged loneliness of Lutheranism as a system that alone understood justification correctly, all the other religious systems being stuck in the righteousness of works.

At the same time, Luther had become responsible for the leadership of a Church that operated within an actual society. Doctrines known as 'antinomian', to the effect that, on account of justification by faith alone, the preaching of the gospel should overlook the demands of the moral law, led Melanchthon in particular into conflict with the Wittenberg lecturer Johannes Agricola and Luther came to believe that such ideas threatened the moral fabric of society. Galatians provided a useful kind of standpoint in any dispute about the place of the moral law, for in the epistle Paul restated that Christians, having been 'called into liberty' (4:13), were not to use freedom 'for an occasion to the flesh, but by love [to] serve one another' through 'love, joy, peace, longsuffering, gentleness, goodness, faith, meekness, temperance . . .' (4:22–23). Luther read this as meaning that the passive righteousness of grace conferred independent of the works of the law must lead on to active virtue. He emphasised the social and civic character of such virtue, for example in the callings of pastor, householder or magistrate, as well as in the subject's submitting 'through love to the magistrates and their laws . . .', and he concluded, 'When we have thus taught faith in Christ, then do we teach also good works.'

For the remainder of his life following his return to Wittenberg in 1522 Martin Luther retained his professorial academic role at the university there. His official position involved him not only in lecturing but also in other academic procedures including examinations, which also allowed him to uphold and publicise his doctrines. In September 1535, for example, two friends of Luther, Hieronymus Weller and Niklaus Medler, took their doctorates at the university and Luther composed the theses, which were printed, to be defended by the candidates in the required oral examination. These consisted of 71 propositions on faith derived from Romans 3:28 – 'We hold that a man is justified by faith apart from the works of the law' – and a further 87 on law, extrapolated out of the same text. The message seems at first sight to have been the same insistent Pauline–Lutheran emphasis on 'the faith which alone justifies us without law and works through the mercy of God shown in Christ'.[2]

At the same time, though, the opportunity of the Weller–Medler theses allowed Luther to expand extensively on the nature of the faith that justifies, since not any faith was conducive to justification. Further, the examination exercise presented a way of reconciling points of view over justification that could be summed up in apparently conflicting texts of the New Testament. Thus the New Testament Epistle of James upheld justification by faith and works, and did so especially in chapter 2, verse 17: 'faith, if it hath not works, is dead, being alone'. In his own copy of the Bible Luther wrote, 'That is false' against James, 2:24: 'You see then that by works a man is justified, and not by faith only.' So he tended to hold James's message of justification by works in contempt: 'Let us banish this epistle from the university, for it is worthless. . . . I think it was written by some Jew who had heard of the Christians but not joined them . . . a right straw epistle, for it has no evangelic matter about it.'

The outstanding problem was in matching the message in chapter 2 of the Epistle of James with that in St Paul's Epistle to the Romans and above all with the statement in the latter (3:28) 'that a man is justified by faith without the works of the law'. Leaning now in the direction of the kind of acceptance of the role of good works in justification presented in such resounding terms in the Epistle of James, in the Weller–Medler theses Luther approached closer to the mind-set of James. Faith was, after all, much more than mere acceptance of propositions, and Luther now deprecated an only 'acquired or historic faith', which, as James commented, in chapter 2, verse 19 demons also shared, along, Luther added, with 'most wicked men'. Instead, the faith that justified was a living faith that transformed and sanctified its possessors 'like the holy angels and sons of God ascending to heaven'. Being centred on Christ, this was 'a faith which not only hears the things done by the Jews and Pilate in crucifying Christ or narrated about the resurrection. But which understands the love of God the Father who wants to redeem and save you through Christ, delivered up for your sins.' And a further way of grasping the difference between 'historical' and true, living, justifying faith was that the former accepted as true a general statement – 'that the Son of God suffered and rose again' – and the latter later apprehended that statement personally, fervently – 'He did all this for me, for my sins . . .'. So justifying faith, which was so much more than acceptance of the truth of statements made, had to be a responsive faith and the response, activated by Christ Himself, issued in good works, which must follow on faith, as if to prove that it was a living, not a dead faith or merely an 'acquired' historical set of beliefs. In other words, if faith were not to be 'dead', 'good works must follow faith' – and the messages of James and Paul could now, surely, be seen to be reconciled.

So, the presentation of the 'Theses Concerning Faith and Law' in 1535 concerned more than a university examination for the award of higher degrees. Rather, involving as graduands two men who were as much Luther's disciples as his students, and attended with what Professor Spitz calls a 'stellar cast of reformers', they provided an opportunity to present a résumé of Luther's Lutheranism in the year following the submission of the Confession of Augsburg. In that sense they might be taken, alongside two other university presentations, 'The Disputation Concerning Man' of 1536 and 'The Disputation Concerning Justification' of the same year, as putting forward a moderate and, indeed, broadly catholic, view of Evangelical doctrine and moral teaching. There was no drawing back from the key propositions of the Reformation. Luther insisted, 'Our cause has triumphed and Paul's meaning stands firm; man is not justified by the works of the law, but by faith alone [Rom. 3:28].' On that point the argument between the opposing meaning of the Epistle of James and that of the Epistle to the Romans with respect to justification by faith or works could never be completely settled. However, the author of the Epistle of James certainly envisaged a sequence in which faith would precede works, the latter being the necessary outcome of the former, works making faith 'perfect'. The 'Theses Concerning Faith and Law' honoured that approach. In these Luther wrote, 'good works come from a person who has been justified beforehand by faith . . .', and added if those 'good works do not follow, it is certain that this faith in Christ does not dwell in our heart, but [only] that dead faith'.

Exactly the same point about the necessary sequence from justification by faith to its outcome in works was made in the contents of another degree examination discourse in which Luther, again, put forward the propositions to be debated, 'The Disputation Concerning Justification', of October 1536. Among these propositions is the crucial statement: 'that faith which lacks fruit [that is, good works] is not an efficacious but a feigned faith' – which was to say that faith without works is proved not in fact to be a justifying faith – not 'efficacious'.

These disputation texts of the mid-1530s, then, can be seen as restating the cardinal points of Luther's Evangelical theology, though not in any manner that would exclude the role of good deeds in the Christian life, and, as we have seen, in such a way as to find a place for 'works' in a formula that reaffirmed that justification arose from faith. In like manner, in 'The Disputation Concerning Man', of January 1536, Luther restated propositions about human nature that had a bearing on justification, including insistence on our basically sinful nature that requires our being justified by a force outside of ourselves, Christ crucified.

At the same time, though, and while reasserting Luther's earlier denial of free will, he now found a place for a celebration of human potential. It may not be quite as enthusiastic as Hamlet's hymn of praise to humanity that begins, 'What a piece of work is man! How noble in reason!' However, as with Hamlet, an emphasis on the survival beyond the Fall of Man of humanity's chief glory, reason, helps correct an impression that Luther saw the human race as being only flawed:

> Holy Scripture also makes [reason] lord over the earth. . . . That is, that it is a sun and a kind of god appointed to administer these things in this life. Nor did God after the fall of Adam take away this majesty of reason, but rather confirmed it.

Luther's old negative dismissal of 'that harlot reason', part of his pessimistic view of humanity, had, clearly, settled into a more positive view of human capacity. Luther's was nowhere as pronounced as was Erasmus's confidence in the power of the human intellect and the human will but these insights of the later 1530s helped restore some appreciation of mankind's inherent capability for wisdom and goodness.

LUTHER AND THE CHURCH: THE ANTI-PAPAL OFFENSIVE, 1538–1545

We should also be aware, in our study of the mature Luther, of a broadly ecumenical sense on his part, a quest for catholicity in the sense of seeking unitive formulae of consensual Christianity which might even override the increasingly marked credal divisions of the Churches in the age of the Reformation. Philip Melanchthon was a keen partner in such a search for an inclusive Christianity. One of its natural locations lay in the early Christian creeds, as well as in some of the most ancient prayers, all possible rallying points for those true Christians who, in Luther's doctrine of the Church, made up the real body of Christ wherever that was to be found.

In 1538 Luther published, in German, 'The Three Symbols or Creeds of the Christian Faith', focusing on those early confessions of faith, the Apostles' Creed (assembled by the fifth century), the Athanasian Creed (named after St Athanasius, c.298–373) and the hymn *Te Deum laudamus* ('We Praise Thee, O God' – early fifth century?). In these brief and simple ancient creeds and that beautiful song of praise of the Blessed Trinity of three Persons in one God, the irreducible components of core Christianity were, surely, to be discovered in what Luther called 'the common confession of the Apostles, . . . the ground for the Christian faith . . .'. Yet for Luther this essential Christianity, in all its simplicity, had to exclude Catholicism, with all its complexity and elaboration: 'so many various orders, foundations, churches, pilgrimages, brotherhoods, etc. that they cannot be counted . . .' – even though 'now the gospel comes and proclaims one common order of Christendom, which is one body in Christ'. Luther in fact held his own variant of Christianity – 'the gospel' – to represent exclusively that clear, simple, early form of the Christian faith which debarred other variants, above all papal Catholicism.[3]

Yet in the later 1530s and the early 1540s possibilities arose intermittently that the schism between the Evangelical and Catholic Churches might be reconciled in a restored catholicity, reuniting divided Christians. Powerful political momentum came from Charles V, who encouraged efforts to secure political unity in his Holy Roman Empire through the reduction of doctrinal divisiveness. From the 1520s onwards, and reflecting the fact that the Reformation movement originated in Germany and expressed German religious grievances, calls were made for a 'free Christian Council in German Lands' which would both cleanse the Church and, in doing so, restore its lost unity. In 1537 the pope of the day, Paul III (1534–49), was striving to summon to Mantua in Italy the Church council that was eventually to meet in the Italian city of Trent from 1545 onwards. Could the Lutherans attend? Could such a council act as springboard for Church unity? In fact, the prospect of taking part in the Mantua meeting inspired in Melanchthon, often regarded as, so to speak, the 'Catholic Lutheran', a recitation of Luther's own view that the unity of the true Church of Christ was not compatible with reconciliation to Rome. Melanchthon wrote: 'We embrace and defend with our whole hearts the concord of the universal church of Christ, but the name "church" must not be ascribed to the pontifical errors and tyranny.' Then, in a bitter satirical composition, a German work of 1538, 'Counsel of a Committee of Several Cardinals with Luther's Preface', Luther took full advantage of his acquisition of a copy of a frank account of February 1537, drawn up by a select commission appointed by the pope and made up of reform-minded cardinals and prelates in order to report on the corruption of the Church.[4]

What Luther did was to preface a German translation of the cardinals' report and add to it his sardonic marginal comments. The effect of the production was not only to use the Holy See's own commissioned report on itself as propaganda to blacken its reputation but also quite deliberately to close the door on reconciliation. The see of Rome was, wrote Luther, 'indeed, without God's Word and correct doctrine, etc. Nothing regarding that has to be reformed, or even considered.' So, regardless of the cardinals' candour in reporting on practical and moral abuses, calling urgently for their suppression, an unbridgeable gulf still remained between Rome and Wittenberg – as a result of the former's refusal to alter its doctrinal position in order to comply with Luther's. Meanwhile, a work of historical polemic by Luther, 'On the Councils and the Churches', of 1539, by denigrating the potential of a council to amend the state of the Catholic Church, decisively put paid to such conciliar solutions to the ecclesiastical problems of the day.

But would the situation alter if Rome did in fact rid itself of what Luther saw as its *doctrinal* abuses and saw eye to eye with Luther? Between April and July 1541 Melanchthon took part in unity talks in the south German city of Regensburg ('Ratisbon') with the Catholic cardinal (and signatory of the February 1537 select commission report), Gasparo

Contarini (1483–1542), the leading representative within his Church of the 'Catholic–Evangelical' position that accepted justification by faith. Melanchthon is often depicted as the catholic-minded Evangelical (though he had already parted company with Luther's traditional understanding of the real presence and had taken up the eucharistic theology of the reformed Churches of Switzerland and Strassburg). Facing him, Contarini is represented as the Evangelical-minded Catholic. Together they hammered out a concessionary agreement at Regensburg on justification (though they fell into disarray over the eucharist and papal primacy). Luther, however, profoundly distrusted the kind of unity Regensburg achieved over doctrinal essentials. While the Regensburg talks were being conducted, he denounced would-be mediators, Martin Bützer and Philip of Hesse, and, though he professed to believe that Melanchthon was not really a member of that conciliatory party, he wrote to him early in April 1541 putting him on warning against surrender under the 'wiles of Satan' and of 'false brethren'. The roles of Luther and Melanchthon were again what they had been at the time of the Confession of Augsburg in 1530, for while Regensburg, like Augsburg, held out political advantages for Lutheranism in exchange for flexibility over doctrine, Luther in 1541 once more set his face against a compromise agreement in favour of uncompromising adhesion to hardline truth, as he saw it.

The influence on Melanchthon of what we may term the spirit of Regensburg may be traceable in conciliatory theses that he drew up for a degree examination in February 1542. Luther's obdurate position, in contrast, was clearly set out in another series of examination propositions, again on justification, those for the licentiate examination of Heinrich Schmedenstede in July of the same year. In the way they rejected compromise, these articles may be seen as the repudiation of the mood of Regensburg. Where Regensburg, it is true, failed to find agreement on the papal primacy, Luther notched up the adversarial tone by decrying the pope as 'an instrument of the devil'. That set the tone for the stream of anti-Catholic and anti-papal vilification that Luther was to pour out in 1545.

In point of fact, a trailer to the savage anti-papal polemics of 1545 was a work of the earlier months of 1541, a satirical attack, using the conventions of the popular culture of carnival, on the die-hard anti-Lutheran prince of Braunschweig-Wolfenbüttel, Henry II: *Wider Hans Worst*, 'Against Hans Worst'. Based on a foolish figure of carnival fun found in Sebastian Brant's 1494 *Das Narrenschyff*, 'Against Hans Worst' ridiculed a major German prince as a clown. In point of fact, though, the attack on that ruler was very largely a front for vilification of the 'papists' who 'through their Harry [Heinz, Heinrich] call us heretics'. 'Against Hans Worst' also included a review of the origins and development of what Luther called the 'Lutheran rumpus', retracing Luther's own questioning of the papal system and the indulgences under Leo X.

This opening signal for anti-papal journalism was followed in March 1545 in Luther's riposte to Paul III's near-final measures to convene the council to Trent. He entitled this new work 'The Papacy in Rome, An Institution of the Devil'. He reached his sixtieth year in 1543 – not necessarily an advanced age in Luther's day, though subjectively Luther felt it was for him. His health, never good, perhaps as a result of the austerities of his monastic years, deteriorated, and broke down, for example in 1541. His consciousness of his end was underscored by the tragic death of his daughter Magdalene in September 1542. Along with this sense of his own terminus came his consciousness of the end of the world. It was perhaps because that consciousness had become so ingrained in him that he could express it in such an off-hand manner, as if it were a self-explanatory fact that hardly needed to be laboured. For example, 'if the Last Days were not close at hand, it would be no wonder if heaven and earth were to crumble because of such [papal] blasphemy', he explained in 'On the Councils and the Church' in 1539 and, in the same work, writing of the plans being made for a council, 'Before that is done we shall all be dead, and the Last Day will have long since come.' And it was within this context of apocalyptic thought that Luther was able to identify the pope and the papacy as the indispensable agents of the last days, the Antichrist, the man of sin who, according to St Paul in 2 Thessalonians 2:3–4, sits in the very temple of God,

> the head of the accursed church of all the worst scoundrels on earth, a vicar of the devil, an enemy of God, an adversary of Christ, a destroyer of Christ's churches; a teacher of lies, blasphemies, and idolatries; an arch church-thief and church-robber of the keys and all the goods of both the church and the temporal lords; a murderer of kings and inciter of all kinds of bloodshed; a brothel-keeper over all brothel-keepers and all vermin; an Antichrist, a man of sin and child of perdition [2 Thess. 2:3]; a true werewolf.[5]

In April of the same year observations made in Luther's table talk confirm how innate such convictions had become with him: 'I believe the pope is the masked and incarnate devil because he is the Antichrist.'

These were the kinds of expressions that finally put any reconciliation between Luther's and the Catholic system utterly beyond recall – though it is worth noting that, on the Catholic side, too, there were few genuine seekers after reunion, except on the Catholic Church's own terms of doctrinal surrender.

THE BIGAMY OF PHILIP OF HESSE, 1540

Part way through Luther's anti-papal offensive between the 1530s and 1540s came the crisis caused by the marital problems of a leading Lutheran prince, Philip, Landgrave of Hesse. Since his conversion in 1524, and despite leanings towards both religious radicalism and belief in toleration, Philip was a political mainstay of the Lutheran cause in Germany and, as such, arguably needed careful handling by the religious leaders of the cause. The problem was that his personal and sexual life were not in accord with Lutheran standards of fidelity within marriage.[6]

Philip's marriage was an unhappy one, made in 1523 to the daughter, Christina, of the Catholic Duke George of Ducal Saxony, and within this marriage Philip's conscience was burdened by his own regular adulteries, with prostitutes. In 1539, while recovering from syphilis, he met and fell in love with a 17-year-old noblewoman, who, as it happened, was distantly related to Luther's wife. This was Margarethe von der Saal, or von der Sale, and Philip insisted on marrying her, though remaining officially wedded to Christina. However, von der Saal's mother wanted, if not public acknowledgement of the new marriage, then at least some endorsement of its validity by the most influential Protestant theologians. Martin Bützer, a long-standing adviser to Landgrave Philip, was eventually willing not only to confer a kind of blessing on the match but, in addition, to ask Luther and Melanchthon to do so. On 9 December 1539 Bützer came to Wittenberg. He brought with him a letter from Philip in the form of a confession of sexual infidelities which, he insisted, his marriage to Christina would exonerate and sought approval from Luther and Melanchthon to add the second wife, Margarethe, to his household. However, before the Christmas of that year, by getting Landgräfin Christina's agreement to his proposed bigamy and going ahead with arrangements to marry Margarethe von der Saal, Philip was signalling that he planned to proceed with his design regardless.

If that was an argument to Melanchthon and Luther for endorsing what was rapidly becoming a *fait accompli*, the political arguments were more complex. On the one hand, Charles V had declared bigamy an offence in imperial law deserving capital punishment – a grave threat to the survival of a major defender of the Evangelical cause. On the other side, contained in the letter to the Wittenberg leaders that Bützer brought with him early in December was a veiled threat that, unless Luther and Melanchthon gave him the approval he wanted, he would secede from the Evangelical cause, in order to secure his marriage plans with approval from the papacy and the emperor.

All in all, given Philip's apparent determination to proceed anyway, and in light of his threat, blackmail or bluff, the Wittenberg chieftains seemed to have limited freedom of action in the case of the bigamy of Philip of Hesse. Most of Wittenberg's actual management of the case was in the hands of Melanchthon, who in December composed a dispensation for him and for Luther and other theologians to sign. Melanchthon also attended the bigamous marriage (Luther did not) in Hesse in March 1540. This dispensation exposed two possible, and linked, moral fault lines in the Lutheran leaders' endorsement of Hesse's actions. First, Melanchthon reaffirmed that monogamy was the law of God confirmed by Christ: 'Since the beginning of the world it has been proper for a man to have only one wife. This is an admirable law, accepted in the church, and no other law should be instituted against it.' Second, and in contravention of Philip's request for a public statement in his favour, Luther and Melanchthon strongly insisted on the secrecy and privacy of the arrangements they proposed: 'every precaution should be taken to prevent this matter from becoming public . . .'. Basically, then, Melanchthon, Luther and the other signatories were asking Hesse to keep Margarethe as a mistress – and also to keep quiet about it: a 'quiet solution'.

Luther himself did not establish direct contact with Philip over this issue until he replied in April 1540 to a cordial letter from the Landgrave following the latter's wedding, and in that letter he further urged the closest secrecy in the matter: 'we want to keep the business a secret for the sake of the example, which every one would follow. . . . Wherefore your Grace will please be secret. . . .'

Secrecy, however, came to be out of the question. First, both Philip and his new mother-in-law wanted the marriage to be as honourable as the circumstances would permit and so not to be kept in a hole in a corner. Then, outrage by the seven heirs of Philip's first marriage at the prospect of their disinheritance in the light of the new partnership was bound to cause a storm. In the event, though, the storm in fact broke out of disgust on the part of Philip's sister, the Duchess of Rochlitz, at her brother's behaviour. By late May or early June 1540, when Luther was saying at the dinner table 'Great is the scandal caused by our Hesse', news of the bigamous marriage was in the public domain. When the Landgrave's sister drew the attention of both the Saxon courts, the Electoral and the Ducal, to the issue, Luther was required by John Frederick, Elector of Saxony since the death of John the Steadfast in 1532, to explain exactly what had been going on.

Luther's quite lengthy reply to the Elector suggests some of the self-defensive embarrassment of a man caught out in secret mischief. He tried to explain that he and Melanchthon had kept the matter from the Elector since it was, he blustered, an essentially confidential matter 'of the confessional', but in fact his line during this crisis was morally ambivalent in three ways. First, he admitted to John Frederick that he and Melanchthon had, despite their better judgement, given in to Hesse's political blackmail and to his threat 'to disregard us and turn to the Emperor and pope'. Second, he was appearing to suggest that he and Melanchthon had been dispensing a marital morality custom-tailored for a prince and for princes: 'My concession was on account of the great need of his conscience – such as has happened to other great lords' (an intimation he also made in a letter of 2 June 1540 to another correspondent in which he observed, 'One must not pronounce rashly on insufficient evidence about the doing of princes.'). And, third, throughout this 'scandal' Luther was refusing to make the moral and scriptural case that might in fact have been advanced in favour of bigamy or even polygamy – such highly respectable Old Testament figures as the patriarchs Abraham and Jacob and the kings David and Solomon were non-monogamous – and the dispensation that gave Hesse his green light tended to reaffirm that monogamy was the law of God and Christ – but that the Landgrave of Hesse was exempt, and dispensed, from it.

Motives for this ambivalence were not necessarily unworthy: there was a fear that a more open statement in favour of bigamy as morally defensible, not least on scriptural grounds, would encourage mass adoption of the practice by the 'coarse peasants' and there was the chilling warning of the sexual revolution in the German city of Münster in 1535, within just five years before the Hesse marriage, when a radical Anabaptist coup had introduced polygamy into that city – on the grounds of Old Testament precedent. Openly legitimating bigamy as one acceptable ethical option, and on grounds of its biblical validation, might then have been regarded as socially irresponsible. Even so, Luther's and Melanchthon's handling of the Hesse affair reveals clumsiness in the management of an – admittedly tangled – moral case in a royal family by attempting to hush up what better judgement might have foretold was bound to leak out. If the Hesse bigamy case was not a crime for Luther and Melanchthon, it was potentially something worse, a blunder.

That case also incidentally reveals key contrasts between Luther and Melanchthon as personality types. Luther's melancholia – what he called his *tristitia*, his *Anfechtungen*, his depressions – never really left him, and in 1533, for instance, he reported that those attacks were his worst afflictions. However, it was Melanchthon, travelling to Weimar, near Erfurt, to try to resolve the Landgrave's all-too-public private affairs, whose state of mind was, of the two, the worse affected by the after-wash of the Hesse affair. He was 'consumed with grief', Luther reported, with his physical health affected, apparently, with a dangerous fever: Luther travelled to Weimar to consult with Philip of Hesse over the legal difficulties that now confronted him as a result of the bigamous wedding and to visit his ailing friend. While Melanchthon had, admittedly, been the main composer of the December 1539 'dispensation' letter to the Landgrave, Luther attributed his own immunity from excessive self-accusation to his innate resilience as 'a peasant and a tough Saxon'. In fact, part of his coping strategy with regard to the potentially damaging Hessian crisis tended to amount to a hope that all would somehow turn out for the best and that in 'a quarter of a year this tune will be played out' – perhaps through the death of Margarethe, who was in fact now a bounteously healthy 19-year-old. But Luther's response to the Hesse crisis also reveals an important aspect of his character, despite all his depressions – the remarkably resilient ability of an essentially self-confident man to admit a mistake, even a huge one: 'It is better for people to say Doctor Martinus made a fool of himself when he gave in to the landgrave. Greater men than I have made fools of themselves, and continue to do so. They say a wise man commits no small folly.'

Cochlaeus routinely reported that he 'wrote a short pamphlet against this new scandal' that made strong anti-Luther propaganda. And indeed the case showed Luther in a poorer light than the image of two decades before, with the ringing challenges at Worms. Where there had once been an impossibly brave defence of truth above all things, there was now a preference for 'a good strong lie' 'for the good and sake of the Christian Church'. Where there was once fearless defiance of powers and dominations, there were now secret deals to 'cover up' the messy sex life of a spoilt and privileged prince. Where, years before, there had been insistence that pardon for sins comes to the contrite from God alone, now there was a 'dispensation', under a kind of seal of the confessional, for a man to continue in a state of mortal sin.

From the Catholic point of view, though, the upshot of Philip of Hesse's bigamy was as much cause for rejoicing as for condemnation, for it put that powerful Lutheran prince in Charles V's hands as a public sinner and the Landgrave had in 1541 to make peace with the Emperor, thereby considerably weakening the Protestant alliance, the League of Schmalkalden, of which Philip had been the principal architect just ten years earlier.

LUTHER'S PREJUDICES: LUTHER AND THE JEWS

In the section that follows we shall proceed to explore Martin Luther's attitudes later in his life to the Jewish people. First, though, and in order fully to grasp the direction of the reformer's thinking about the Jews, we shall set it within the overall context of his generalised and stereotypical views of large categories of human beings.

Luther was a man of strongly etched presuppositions about whole groups, classes, professions, minorities and nations. We shall see that he was prejudiced against some, and in favour of other, human categories, sharing, indeed, many of the received ideas held by his contemporaries. Crucially, though, we shall see when his attitudes to nations, classes or professions were influenced by religious preconceptions, his social prejudice became intensified into religious bigotry. Thus we shall see that Luther's judaeophobia, just like his marked hostility to such groupings as peasants, lawyers, Italians and Turks, was inspired essentially by his religious convictions.[7]

We saw in Chapter 2 above that, when it suited him, Luther would claim a peasant background. However, on the whole Luther resented the peasants as an entire human category, believing that they had little to complain about: as he said, 'If the peasants only appreciated their condition, they would be in paradise where they are.' He also thought they conspired with the nobles, another group who were additionally targets for his condemnation, to drive up food prices at the expense of townsmen, of whom, of course, he was one. However, beyond simple economic indignation, there was Luther's anger, expressed in 1525 in 'Against the Robbing and Murdering Hordes of Peasants' against the insurgents' *religious* crime and error of misusing the gospel to advance a social cause – 'the pretences they made in the twelve articles [of Memmingen, 1525], under the name of the Gospel . . . they cloak this terrible and horrible sin [of rebellion] with the Gospel, call themselves "Christian brethren" . . . [and] become the greatest of all blasphemers of God and slanderers of his holy Name . . .'. He also condemned what he saw as the peasants' basically religious offence of listening to radical religious preachers: as he wrote in 1532 in his 'Open Letter about Skulking and Furtive Preachers', 'I have heard about how these infiltrators attach themselves to labourers during the harvest and preach to them in the fields while they work, and also to charcoal-burners and solitary people in the woods, and everywhere sow their seed and spread their poison. . . .'

Another social group Luther vilified were the lawyers – a 'sordid and acquisitive' profession . . . they rob their clients blind . . . [they] don't give anything to God but only to themselves . . . Lawyers' craftiness is a dangerous business . . . they seek only their own advantage and have the law in their control.' However, his strong dislike for that whole profession on more or less commonplace economic and social grounds – accusing them of deliberately protracting cases in order to increase their fees and so on – was strongly compounded by the theologically grounded distinction he drew between his own work and the whole conceptual sphere in which lawyers operated. Lawyers, he knew, traded in all that pertained to legal process – the law itself, punishment and judgement – while the concerns of theologians such as he were with God's grace, mercy and forgiveness: 'The lawyer says: "Let justice be done and the world be damned." The theologian says: "Let sin be forgiven and the world will be saved."' So, a good lawyer must by definition be a bad Christian, 'either a good-for-nothing or a know-nothing' – and he once warned his young son Martin, 'If you should become a lawyer, I'll hang you on the gallows.'

Luther's outlook on two occupational groups, peasants and lawyers, was, then, charged with doctrinal presuppositions. Luther also had a fair amount to say about nations and their collective characteristics. Patriotic German as he was, Luther was inclined to praise his fellow-nationals as 'the best nation', invincible 'with guile or with force', and unyielding 'in a just and honourable cause', 'simpler and more attached to the truth' than the other major European nations, speaking 'the most perfect [language] of all'. At the same time, Luther also frequently ridiculed and condemned his fellow-nationals, whom he thought the 'most despised of nations', regarded as beasts and barbarians by the Italians, deserving, in God's eyes, a 'beating', degenerated from the virtues that the ancient Roman writer Tacitus had found in their ancestors, incurably drunken.

However, his underlying assumption about Germans was that they had the virtues of their vices – they were unsophisticated, provincial and rough-and-ready but therefore straight as a die. Drink was their weakness, but to Luther, on the whole their national vices seemed venial. What was to be feared, though, was the prospect of an italianate German, what Luther called an 'Italo-German' (such as Albrecht, archbishop of Mainz), who, abandoning the innate simple honesty of Germans, might take up the deceitfulness, the cynicism and even the 'hellish art' of the worldly and sophisticated Italians. But what did Luther mean by 'the hellish art' of the Italians?

Italy was the only foreign country that he ever visited, and though he passed remarks about other nations – the Spanish as a potential threat to German religious freedom, the French incapable of saying what was in their hearts – his most bilious national character attributes were directed against the Italians, partly on the basis of his acquaintance with the country as a young friar on an administrative mission back in 1510–11. He thought that, like the Germans, the Italians had the vices of their virtues – but also of their very considerable abilities. They were in his eyes subtle and quick-witted, persuasive in their eloquence and their gestures. But they were also supercilious and worldly sceptics who maintained that what was important was that one should 'put on a good appearance and not believe anything'. Further, they were 'lascivious' and 'wanton' in their dancing, manifesting 'casual haughtiness', insanely jealous as husbands, over-lavish dressers, epicures whose fasts were more self-indulgent than German feasts. The Italians' worst, 'hellish', vice in his book, though, was their homosexuality, the practice which, according to Luther's mentor Paul, in Romans 1:27, became the controlling metaphor for all godlessness. Of the Italians' alleged adoption of this sexuality, Luther wrote: 'Their chastity is sodomy, as they themselves declare. Betrayed by a perverse intelligence, they do violence to natural and divine law by despotically forbidding matrimony.' 'Italian nuptials' were in fact homosexual love affairs.

Fed by the Italian Renaissance vogue for the emulation of classical culture, including the acceptance of same-gender sex among the ancient Greeks, a cliché current in early modern Europe was that Italian sex was homo-erotic. A random example comes from John Donne's allusion in *Elegy XVI: On His Mistress*, in which the poet imagines his lover in disguise as a boy on the Continent, where

> Th' indifferent [bisexual] Italian, as we pass
> His warm land, well content to think thee page,
> Will hunt thee with such lust, and hideous rage,
> As Lot's fair guests were vexed.

Donne's attitude to the possible threat of the 'hideous rage' of Italian homosexuals to his cross-dressing lover seems far from relaxed, but, even so, it is less intense than Luther's sexual italophobia, which was, in turn, derived from basic religious assumptions. The focus of Luther's hated Italian homosexuality was papal Rome, where, he alleged, the Lateran Council in 1515 'decreed it permissible . . . for each cardinal to have five boys for his Ganymedes' – male prostitutes. So the 'Italian vice' was derived from the central tenets and the principal institutions of Roman Catholicism, and Luther's attitude to what he saw as the Italians' chief sin was derived from his religious objections to Catholicism's 'doing violence to natural and divine law'. In other words, the sexual vice that Luther alleged against the Italians was more than the kind of weakness he charged against his fellow Germans, say, a fondness for the bottle. In his calendar, homosexual sex was the ultimate sexual sin and it was, he believed, ingrained among Italians. However, sexual deviance was the product of religious deviance for, as he remarked once at table, 'Every false religion is contaminated by libidinous desires,' and the sexual nature of the Italians was 'corrupted' in such a way that the divinely implanted natural 'longing' of a man for a woman was distorted and this unnatural sex took its root from their Catholic religion, in which clerical celibacy forced male sexuality into warped channels, as Luther charged in his bitterest anti-Roman work, 'The Papacy in Rome, An Institution of the Devil'. The work identified Paul III himself as the pander of Roman sodomy – 'this Sodomite Pope, founder and master of all sins', or, to alter the language to a linked charge of gender-crossing, the pope was portrayed as 'that holy virgin, St Paula III, Lady Papess'. As far as one can tell, Luther's view of Italian sexual perversion arising from Italian religious perversion was distinctive in, if not uniquely peculiar to, him.

The Italians, in Luther's imagining, were also linked up to the Turks, and in 1520 in the 'Address to the Christian Nobility', at a point in time when he seemed inclined to view the Turkish war as a papal pretext for money-raising, he exclaimed, 'If I want to fight the Turks, the worst Turks are those in Italy.' In the course of the decade that followed, the real gravity of the Turkish invasion threat to the German Lands changed Luther's light-hearted tune into a stern warning march. At the height of the Peasants' Revolt, in spring 1525, he showed how, through both the rebels and the Turks, 'God at times plagues the world with desperate men.' In the following year the crushing by Sultan Suleiman the Magnificent of the Hungarian army at Mohács, along with the killing of the Hungarian king, understandably raised panic levels. In that year in

'Whether Soldiers can be in a State of Grace', Luther provided a just-war argument in favour of the morality of national self-defence. As we saw above in Chapter 7, in the 'Instructions for the Visitors' of 1528 he and Melanchthon inserted a whole section endorsing the rightness of resisting the Turks. In the same year he fulfilled what he called his duty to 'stir up our people against the Turks'. In 1529, at the height of peril, when Vienna was under siege from the Sultan, he produced a national prayer for deliverance from the Turkish threat and in the year after that he wrote to Melanchthon that he was 'beginning to be stirred up against the Turk and Mohammed, even passionately when I see the intolerable fury of Satan waxing proud against body and soul'. When the threat from the east was once more resumed in 1539, he drew up a set of national invocations for delivery.[8]

For the Turkish threat was for Luther of an entirely different order from that of the mere violation of national frontiers, which, conceivably, might have come, for example, at some point from France. The difference was that the French might be envisaged as Germany's foe, but the Turks were God's. A national, temporal enemy, a rival Christian state, might seize German territory and, no doubt, do other fearful, material damage, but, as Luther wrote in his 'Appeal for Prayer against the Turks' of 1541, the danger from the Turks was to possessions, family and so on 'but also, what is even worse, our very soul . . .'. The reason was that 'The Turk wants to put his Muhammad in the place of [God's] dear Son, Jesus Christ, for the Turk blasphemes him and asserts that Christ is no true Son of God. . . .'

Central to his understanding of the conflict with the Turks, then, was his conviction that it was God's battle. Indeed, it had to be, because if the issue were in the merely human hands of the Habsburgs (and the pope), any successful anti-Turkish crusade on their part might turn into a 'massacre of [Lutheran?] Germany'. Thus Luther had to remain confident 'that *God* [my emphasis] will destroy the Turks'. Further, the Turkish drama was an apocalyptic one, and when the Turks' threat on the Danube was re-mounted in 1532, Luther knew that most of the pertinent scriptural prophecies had been fulfilled and that if the Turks managed to seize Rome, where the pope sat like the Antichrist in the temple of God, there was nothing left but the end of the world and the day of judgement.

A variant presented itself to that end-time scenario, and in that same year, 1532, Luther expressed his expectation that the God of battles would Himself begin to wield His terrible swift sword against the Turks – 'in a mood to fight such fellows'. He was convinced that God had been so disposed at Vienna in 1529 when He sent plague to scatter the Sultan's army, just as He had much earlier saved Israel from her enemies: 'Now God can burn them with the fire of hell. When the Turks have plundered us they will be destroyed, for God will fight against them. . . . It doesn't matter how large an army is assembled [by the Turks]. He must do it who is in heaven.' The very immensity of the Turkish military threat – 'I wonder where they got so many men – sixteen times a thousand!' – in itself meant that rescue could come only at God's hands. The recurrent Turkish crisis intensified in Luther's mind an extraordinarily optimistic messianism that God's remaining foes were about to perish at His hands, 'for the possibility also exists that the Turks, as well as the pope, will collapse. For the two kingdoms, that of the Turks and that of the pope, are the last two plagues of the wrath of God, as the Apocalypse calls them. . . .'

Though Luther's attitude to the Turks was one of apocalyptic hope, in God's victory, it was also one of immense fear, since fear for the immediate future and confidence in ultimate triumph were part and parcel of the Christian eschatological mindset. Luther was confident that God Himself – and God alone – would defeat His foes, the Turks, but in the meantime (in 1532), 'the Turks move against us with the greatest assurance, with uncommonly large forces, and with contempt for the terms of peace. They come, and this is a real coming.' In 1538 he charged that German complacency and self-indulgence 'prepare a way for the Turks to enter our land' and the immediate prospect was massacre or enslavement by the Turks (or the Spanish). Indeed, enslavement seemed such a real possibility that in the 1541 'Appeal for Prayer against the Turks' Luther offered pastoral advice to enslaved German women to submit in patience sexually to Turkish captors. In 1542, with a new Ottoman threat of invasion, he was reflecting gloomily on the inadequacy of German defences, with graphic images of terror to the effect that even were the whole *Reich* walled round with iron, besieging Turkish armies would actually be able to starve the Germans to death.[9]

Having, then, understood, that Luther's attitudes to types of human being and to whole nations was conditioned by his religious beliefs, we can better understand his view of the Jewish people, knowing also, though, that, as with his attitude to the Turks, his opinion of the Jews was created by his apocalyptic vision of the final extermination of all those who stood in God's way.

Yet when it comes to comparing his perceptions of the Jews and of the Turks, it is clear first of all that there was a close relationship between

Luther's acute perception of a Turkish menace and what we might term the objective reality of the situation. The chances of an effective alliance of Christian sovereigns, supposedly under Habsburg leadership, to withstand the recurrent threat of Islamic invasion were much reduced in the sixteenth century by the rising primacy of the interests of autonomous states and in particular by the French king Francis I's determination to score off his arch-rival Charles V by exploiting his Turkish problem, above all in allying with Suleiman in 1535. And if inter-state rivalries vitiated the prospects of an effective anti-Turkish coalition in 'Christendom', within Germany more specifically, the religious division of the country obviously reduced its ability to react as one to the common danger. Historians today tend to emphasise the limitations on the power of the Turks to strike into the heart of Europe – their operating on an Asiatic as well as a European front, their difficulties of supply in campaigning far from their bases in Asia Minor. Contemporaries, on the other hand, and markedly Luther, were impressed only by the potency of the Turkish threat. They were confirmed in their fear by the events that coincided with the years of Luther's ascendancy – on land, the capture of Belgrade in 1521, Mohács and the fall of Hungary in 1526, the 24-day siege of Vienna in 1529; by sea, the capture of Rhodes in 1522, along with constant Turkish-backed corsair activity in the Aegean and along the North African shore.

If Luther shared, and on the whole justifiably, a fear on the part of contemporaries of the Muslim Turks as a mighty force whose power the course of events, above all in the 1520s, confirmed, it is all the harder for us to comprehend a parallel fear in his mind concerning the Jewish people. For we must realise that Luther's attitude to the Jews was formed not by mere dislike, intense though that may have been, but by something stronger – an actual phobia, which may be defined as 'persistent or irrational fear or loathing'. Luther's hatred of the Jews was indeed driven by fear, which, indeed, sounds, as the dictionary says, to have been 'irrational'. For whereas the Turks in Luther's days were ruled by a superbly effective military state commanded by one of history's most brilliant generals, Sultan Suleiman, the Jews of Germany and Europe were few, defenceless and harmless. Through the sixteenth century their small communities in Europe lived under the collective psychological shock of the expulsion in 1492 from what had been for Jews during much of the medieval period a golden land, Spain, and they tended to be misled and then let down by a series of bogus messianic claimants offering visions of redemption and glory. In Germany, their long-standing presence in the rich cities of the Rhineland was sadly depleted by 1500 and their expulsion from the southern commercial centre, Regensburg, in 1519, was one further step in what was becoming in effect their cumulative expulsion from most of the Empire. Pockets of Jewish communities clung on in a few cities such as Frankfurt-am-Main in central Germany, and Prague in Bohemia.

Yet Luther feared the Jewish people. Partly this arose from his delusions over their assumed economic power, and consequent threat: in 1520, for instance, he republished a sermon on usury which included a cartoon of a wealthy Jewish money-lender rejoicing over his ill-gotten gains. However, the basis of his judaeophobia was, like his hatred of peasants, lawyers, Italians and Turks, religious, and it turned centrally on the issue of the Jews' willingness or otherwise to abandon their own religion and accept conversion. As a younger man Luther had shared the then widespread belief that, because of the 'hardness of their hearts', intrinsically the Jews could not be converted. Then, in one of the most exciting and optimistic, as well as dangerous, periods for his movement, in 1523 he produced, as we saw in Chapter 6 above, 'That Jesus Christ was Born a Jew', a work designed explicitly to make its own contribution towards the extinction of Judaism by converting the Jews, or significant numbers of Jews to Christianity.

The issue of the conversion of the Jews had featured regularly in Christian religious concerns through the Middle Ages and massacres of Jewish communities, such as those in Westminster in 1189, York in 1190 and across Iberia in 1391, had been, at least ostensibly or in part, motivated by the urge to convert the victims to the Christian faith. Yet in the late Middle Ages it came increasingly to be accepted in popular piety that Jews had murdered Christ, their heirs inheriting the guilt for that crime. Thereby the envisaged possibility of the genuine conversion of the descendants of His murderers to the faith of the descendants of His followers receded. Luther himself over the course of time came to accept as truth the myth of Jewish responsibility for what Christians recognised as the deicide of Christ. For example, in his work of 1530 'Admonition Concerning the Sacrament of the Body and Blood of the Lord', he wrote, almost casually, of the 'Jews, who crucified him, [and] were wicked', whereas in lectures on Genesis in 1539 he declared 'Thus the Jews killed Christ out of pure malice.' And while he was thus accepting the notion of Jewish guilt for Christ's death, he was also retreating from any hope of the effective conversion of the Jews, the hope that had inspired his 1523 work 'That Jesus Christ Was Born a Jew'. It seems significant, for example, that in a work of 1533 on private Masses he referred to Johann Pfefferkorn, one of the most zealous of Jewish converts to Christianity, a Dominican who had launched a prosecution of the Hebrew scholar Reuchlin as 'that poor fellow, the Jew'.

Further on in the same decade, specifically from 1537, Luther's tone towards the Jews took on an intensified ferocity. Signs of rising fury against the Jews appear in his conversation from the spring of that year. At around that time, the recognised intermediary between Germany's remaining Jews and the political, especially the imperial, authorities, the Rabbi Josel von Rosheim (1478–1554), wrote to intercede with Luther to use his good offices in order to influence Elector John Frederick to give the rabbi permission to travel safely through the lands of the Electorate (and in fact to rescind recent anti-Jewish banning orders put out by the Elector). Luther's violent reaction to Rabbi Josel's approach indicates that he now saw the Jews as a threat – 'these rascals, who injure people in body and property'. However, the principal danger that Luther feared from the Jewish community was not social or economic but religious, and the generalisation that his attitude to any group of people was shaped by his abiding religious beliefs remains as true for his outlook on the Jews as it does for any of the other categories examined above. In particular, he was convinced that the Jews were to be feared, on religious grounds, because, far from being receptive to conversion to Christianity, they were in fact withdrawing 'many Christians to their superstitions'. More specifically still, in Moravia (in the modern Czech Republic) the Jews had 'circumcised many Christians and call them by the new name of Sabbatarians'.[10]

This little-known, poorly documented Sabbatarian movement, whose existence was reported to Luther by an aristocratic correspondent, introduced observance of Saturday as the Lord's day. In that respect, it may simply be seen as one further manifestation of an important aspect of Reformation radicalism – the urge to recover the style and practices of the earliest Church, in the case of the Sabbatarians not hesitating to adopt early Christianity's origins in the Jewish religion, with its Saturday Sabbath. However, for Luther the Moravian Sabbatarian movement was, quite simply, Judaism revived and to be feared and loathed as such. Thus the first of a string of anti-Jewish works Luther wrote in later life was in fact the open letter 'Against the Sabbatarians' of 1538: as the editor of the work justly remarks, Luther 'devotes the greater part of the treatise . . . to direct attacks upon the Jews rather than upon the Sabbatarians as such'. Indeed, his rising hostility to Sabbatarianism as a threatening thinly-veiled Judaism becomes fully apparent when we realise that in remarks earlier in the decade, in 1532 and 1535, he had either been totally silent on the question of direct Jewish influence upon Sabbatarians or had put the blame for the observance of a Saturday Sabbath not on the Jews but on the members of the sect themselves, for foolishly imitating Jewish practices, just like 'apes'.[11]

Within the period between Rosheim's attempt to win Luther's support for Jewish freedom of movement and the publication of 'Against the Sabbatarians', Luther's attitudes to Jewish conversion can be seen to have hardened into a set mould of hostility born of fear. In a letter Luther sent in answer to Rosheim's petition there was an echo of the motivation of 'That Jesus Christ Was Born a Jew', in the expression of hope that treating Jews in a kindly way would induce God to bring them at last to recognise their messiah in Christ. However, that hope of conversion was eliminated in 'Against the Sabbatarians', for the work combines twinned hostile perceptions and phobias. The first was that Judaism was threateningly on the march, reviving its fortunes, in the disguised shape of radical Christian Sabbatarianism – 'the Jews are making inroads at various places throughout the country with their venom and their doctrine . . .'. The second was that, by the same token, Jews were placing their own insurmountable barriers in the way of their conversion to Christianity – 'the Jewish people have become very stubborn because of their rabbis. As a result they are difficult to win over.' The remainder of this work traced God's punishment of the Jewish people – including their loss and lack of homeland, their banishment even from Jerusalem itself – to their rejection of Christ, the messiah once sent to them, the ultimate point of their rejection of Jesus being their murder of Him. 'Against the Sabbatarians' represented no attempt to convert the Jews. Because the Jews had rejected and continued to repudiate Christ, insisting that the law of Moses would continue for ever, Luther believed that the Jews were impossible, or at best very difficult, to convert.

It is at this point that we might pick up on a further feature of Luther's growing judaeophobia: his attitude to Mary. In the later Middle Ages the figure of the Blessed Virgin Mary became redesigned as a dividing rod between the Christian and Jewish worlds. The religious art of the fourteenth and fifteenth centuries established two conventions in depictions of the Virgin, both of which were honoured into and beyond Luther's lifetime. One, rendering her gown in blue, the emblematic colour of purity, became general. The other, showing her with the light skin tone and fair hair we might describe as northern European, or even 'nordic', features, became widespread in Italian paintings and virtually mandatory in northern art, at least up to the point in time when Rembrandt, in 'The Holy Family', of 1645, had the radical audacity to depict Mary as a Jewish brunette, reading a Hebrew text at the side of Christ's cradle. The artistic conspiracy at work in this trend can be seen (along with a refusal to show Mary wearing the ear-rings associated in popular perceptions with Jewish women) as one aimed at denying the Virgin her Jewishness, imaging her as, to use an anachronism, an 'Aryan'. Beyond that, Mary was further converted into an icon of anti-Judaism especially through the practice, evident for instance in the destruction of the Jewish quarter and synagogue in Regensburg in 1519, of dedicating new churches erected on such sites to Mary herself.

Luther's reflections on Mary show the same kind of urge to 'de-judaise' her as is evident in the consensus of artists mentioned above. Of course, the Jewish identity of Jesus that Luther was keen to promote in his conversionary strategy in the 1523 'That Jesus Christ Was Born a Jew' required him to confess also that Jesus took his Jewish descent from Mary, as he showed in a sermon of the previous September on Mary's birth: to deny that Jesus was Jewish, through the Jewish Mary, would be to suppose that he was a Jew by descent from Joseph the carpenter of Nazareth, a denial of the whole doctrine of the Incarnation. However, while Luther was agreeing that Mary was Jewish – and of the princely house of David, as he owned in a sermon of 1532 – she was for him the last Jew who became the first Christian, for in a sermon on Mary's visitation to her cousin Elizabeth, delivered in the July of the year he published 'That Jesus Christ Was Born a Jew', he announced the spiritual meaning of words from Mary's prayer on that occasion, the *Magnificat*: 'Mary stands for Christianity after the synagogue, and Elizabeth stands for the people under the law in the synagogue.' Indeed, her role was to make a mockery of the long-standing messianic expectations of the Jewish people, for Christ was 'Abraham's Seed, begotten by none of his sons, as the Jews always confidently expected, but born of this one daughter of his, Mary, alone'.[12]

Thus it was in part Luther's attitude to Mary, preserving much of the Catholic cultic traditions of reverence for her from the Middle Ages, that helped trigger his late anti-Jewish works. One ingredient in the tradition was a borrowing from chivalric conventions according to which a devotee of Mary would rise in her defence against insult, as a knight would against any sleight on his mistress's honour: thus in 1523, a certain Spanish Muslim was probably not aware of how close he came to death at the point of the sword of the later Jesuit founder Ignatius Loyola for words he dared utter impugning Mary's virtue. And so it was with Luther about 20 years after Loyola's flash of holy anger when it was the defence of the Virgin that set him off on a late career of journalistic judaeophobia:

> I intend to write against the Jews once again. . . . What reason do they have to slander and insult the dear Virgin Mary as they do? They call her a stinkpot, a hag, a monstrosity. They're wretched people.

'I intend to write against the Jews once again' alludes, in fact, to the continuation of an anti-Jewish tirade that had opened with 'Against the Sabbatarians' of 1538 and which culminated in three savage attacks in works of 1543. The first of this series, 'Concerning the Jews and Their Lies', *Von den Juden und ihren Lügen*, was published, in German, early in 1543 and has been widely recognised as Luther's most violent piece of writing. Its publication was deplored at the time of its appearance by Protestant leaders, especially those in the Christian humanist tradition, and has been deeply regretted since, notably by admirers of Luther, who regard this savagely intemperate work as the most serious stain on his reputation. Many, indeed, contrast its harshness with the supposed liberalism of 'That Jesus Christ Was Born a Jew' of just two decades prior to its appearance.

In point of fact, though, these two major works of Luther on the Jewish question, separated one from another by a 20-year gap, have, in terms of content as opposed to rhetoric, more in common than we might imagine, even to the extent that the latter might be described as a natural outcome of the former. Luther finished off 'That Jesus Christ was Born a Jew' with a kind of warning: 'Here I will let the matter [of the Jews] rest for the moment until I see what I have accomplished.' In the event, achievement of the conversionary goals of the 1523 work was negligible. If anything the work's flatterings, however sincere or otherwise they were, of the Jews, alongside the general boost to Jewish morale arising from the Renaissance revival among gentiles of Hebrew studies, as well as the heavy blows delivered by Luther and the other reformers to the Jews' old oppressor the Roman Church, were more likely to have discouraged than to have encouraged conversions. Luther failed to convert Jews in any appreciable numbers and 'Concerning the Jews and Their Lies' should be seen, then, as the eventual and embittered product of his disappointment with that failure. So we are back with the issue of Jewish resistance to religious conversion as the most powerful piston driving Luther's anti-Judaism.

It is in that sense that the work of 1543 is the sequel to that of 1523, while, at the same time, being the second instalment in a four-part series of anti-Jewish writings that opened with Luther's attack on the Sabbatarians in 1538. That said, there was some uncertainty in Luther's mind between 1538 and 1542 as to whether he would in fact take up his pen again to write against the Jewish people. Concluding 'Against the Sabbatarians', he announced that he would return to the attack, subsequently changed his mind but then re-changed it. He did so when a Jewish defence of Judaism was sent him in May 1542. Polemic that he regarded as offensive was always likely to sting Luther into fury, and the violence of 'Concerning the Jews and Their Lies' should indeed be seen as a work of intense anger and brutality of expression and intention. Conversion of the Jews was now deemed 'impossible', so that, to say the least, there was no ulterior motive of evangelism to justify or necessitate a kindly tone.

In fact, the fury of Luther's voice mounts in the course of this work, indicating that anger was feeding off anger in the very course of the mad, rambling writing. It rises to a blood-curdling shriek in a third section of the work, one devoted to defending the reputation of Mary and of Christ against supposed Jewish slanders, focusing on Luther's claim that Jews alleged that Mary was no virgin, but a whore and an unmarried or adulterous mother. It was this issue, one of sexuality, that turned Luther's routine abuse of the Jewish people in this work – 'the blind Jews are truly stupid fools . . . malicious, stiff-necked people . . . boastful, arrogant rascals', and so on – into a language of sexual fixation and pathology. The work branded Israel as 'a defiled bride, yes, an incorrigible whore and an evil slut . . . a whore . . .'. So, among Luther's reversals in this work to medieval fantasies about Jews of the kind that he had mocked in 'That Jesus Christ Was Born a Jew' – that they kidnapped Christian children in order to murder them ritually, that they poisoned the wells – is a deep, brooding and sub-rational sexual fear. Luther's paranoia had finally taken up the medieval tradition of seeing the Jewish people as pollutants to be dreaded, with a dwelling on the theme of sexual impurity. Israel, he wrote, was 'a whore, [whose] garment, adornments, wreath, and jewels would better befit a sow that wallows in the mire'.

The psychopathology at work here is that not only was the pig, in the popular culture of Luther's day, a recognised emblem of filth (as for example, in Albrecht Dürer's powerful evocation of squalor in his rendition of the parable of the Prodigal Son), but in the course of the Middle Ages a myth had built up to the effect that, far from shunning pork, Jews had filthy, anal, even excremental sexual relations with pigs: the legend of the *Judensau*. (A variant in Luther's use of animal language to identify his Jewish targets as contaminants to be expelled was in his urgency 'to drive them out like mad dogs . . .'). Luther's 'Concerning the Jews and Their Lies' belongs, then, to an essentially late medieval European genre of literature, sermons and visual projections identifying Jews as frighteningly polluted and polluting.

Thus this 1543 work is *unlike* his 1523 tract on the Jews inasmuch as that latter was addressed to the improvement of the Jewish people by converting them into Christian people. 'Concerning the Jews and Their Lies' is directed instead at the protection of German gentiles, so that 'our Germans . . . might be informed' of the 'poisonous activities of the Jews'. At the conclusion of the work, Luther offered a six-point action programme against the Jews. Four of these proposals were: the destruction of the synagogues and Jewish schools; the demolition of all Jewish homes as repositories of the Jewish faith; the confiscation of prayer books and copies of the Jewish law code, the Talmud; the silencing of the rabbis. In these proposals Luther envisaged – *demanded* of the German princes, under the threat of direct vigilante action by anti-Jewish terror squads – if not the destruction of the Jewish people then certainly the elimination of the Jewish religion.[13]

The *Judensau* image inspired Luther's next 1543 work on the Jewish people, 'On Schem Hemphoras and the Lineage of Christ'. He had found a motif depicted in a piece of sculpture in a Wittenberg church showing Jews as piglets nourished by a sow and it provided him with a starting-point for a tirade which alleged that Jews accused Christ of having performed His miracles by means of unholy permutations on the Hebrew form of the divine name. The hatred that fed into the work was itself inspired by Luther's deranged fixation with what he imagined was a threat from Judaism as a religion: the sculpture featured a rabbi inspecting the pig's anus, but in Luther's obsessive condition that part of the animal's body stood for the Talmud, the great codification of Jewish religious law which guided devout Jews along their path to their goal of righteousness in God's sight. Luther feared Judaism, and did so as he saw it as the renaissance of a religious system of legal righteousness and the quest for personal holiness that defied justification by faith.

Judaism was to him all the more dangerous, all the more to be feared, insofar as it was part of the same omnipresent heresy to which Catholicism belonged. As he said in his table talk in the winter preceding the publication of the anti-Jewish tracts of 1543, Catholicism and Judaism were both 'idolatrous' and both falsely upheld 'rules and regulations' on the basis of the fond hope, '"This I will do, and that will please God."' These linked systems, failing to fade away, capable indeed of regeneration when allied with the righteousness and self-generated holiness of the Anabaptists, formed a menace that was in Luther's mind eschatological, so that he rounded off his attack on 'Jewish' Catholicism and 'Catholic' Judaism in winter 1542–3 with an apocalyptic warning that sects would proliferate until the end, which was indeed imminent. Therefore, 'Come, therefore, dear Lord! Come and strike about thee with thy day of judgement, for no improvement is any longer to be expected!' And if Judaism were a danger, the concern was, again, not with converting Jews away from it but with warding Christians away from the peril it presented from the Jewish 'devil heart that can be moved by nothing'. That day of judgement was inseparably linked with the second coming of Christ as true messiah.[14]

Since in Jewish eschatology the messiah was yet to come and in Luther's He was to come again, Luther's next and final work on the Jewish question, 'Treatise on the Last Words of David', focused on the debate about the messiah and 'the Jews' stupid conception of [him], who is to be a mortal, earthly king on earth, resident in Jerusalem'. The technique that Luther employed in this work resembled one he had used in his lectures on the Psalms of 30 years previously. Then he had deployed Jewish Old Testament texts, the Psalms, in order to denigrate the Jewish faith. Now he aimed to use the last words of their accredited author, King David (in 2 Samuel 23:1–7), to the same purpose. In 'That Jesus Christ was Born a Jew' of 1523, Luther had appealed to the Jews of his time to convert to Christianity in order thereby to revert to the faith of their fathers as a form of pre-Christianity. Now he was to deny the legitimacy of the Jews of his own day as descendants of Abraham: they were 'false and unknown Jews or Israelites . . . [who] have practised nothing but blasphemy, cursing, murder, and lies against the true Jews and Israel, that is, against the apostles and prophets'. However, if the Jews of Luther's own times were not children of Abraham, they *were* descendants of 'rabid Jews, who crucified Christ' – 'the still viler ones of today, who would fain crucify Him still more ruthlessly . . .'. Indeed, in just one page of the modern English translation text the phrase concerning Christ 'crucified by the Jews' is repeated three times over the space of seven lines, like a propaganda lie whose simple frequent repetition might ensure its credibility.[15]

Thus in these final works on the Jewish question Luther had developed a pyschotic attitude to the Jewish people, fuelled by fear and loathing. In a final chapter, in which we also review Luther's life and vast achievement, we shall further show how his savage judaeophobia was part of the range of intense animosities that filled his final years.

10

CONCLUSION

LUTHER'S LAST MONTHS

Literally to the end, Luther maintained the virulence of thought and expression against the Jews that he had poured out in his writings of 1543. In those late years, his literary output continued unabated, despite his imminent expectation of death, and his lectures at the university went on until he finished a series of commentaries on the Book of Genesis, in the month of his 62nd birthday, November 1545. In the December he travelled to Mansfeld near his birthplace Eisleben, where the local counts, two brothers, had begun a quarrel over property rights which they asked Luther to arbitrate. The same dispute required further attention from him in the January of the new year, 1546, when, late in the month, Luther set off in the direction of Eisleben. Going into February, he was making progress towards a settlement: as he reported, 'the counts of Mansfeld show wonderful good will to each other'.

Peacemaker as Luther now was, his rooted animosities still surfaced, including his old aversion to lawyers, one of whom he believed was obstructing a settlement: 'A little learning makes lawyers mad. Almost all these men seem to be ignorant of the real use of the law, base and venal pettifoggers caring not at all for peace, the state of religion about which we care now as always.' However, to the fore was still his aggression against the Jewish people. In poor health in that ill-advised winter journey, he wrote on 1 February to his wife jocularly complaining of a weakness that came upon him in travelling through a village near Eisleben that housed a Jewish community. The ailment was 'the fault of the Jews or of their God. For we had to pass through a village hard by Eisleben where many Jews live; perhaps they blew on me too hard.' Much more grimly, though, he announced what he planned as a further instalment of his anti-Jewish crusade, once the counts' business was settled: 'I must devote myself to driving out the Jews.'[1]

All that remains is to set that seemingly obsessive phobia within the context of the hatreds that haunted Luther's last years. It is true that in his article 'Teufelsdreck: Eschatology and Scatology in the "Old" Luther', H.A. Oberman warned us against continuing to accept clichés about an 'old, vile, and bitterly resigned . . . disappointed' Luther or to contrast too vividly heroic 'young Luther' with hateful 'old Luther'. The filthy language of Luther's later years, Oberman showed, can be paralleled in a vocabulary of excrement used as early as 1515 – against Satan. In his later years the violence and frequent obscenity of his speech was directed against human foes. As we saw in the previous chapter, his detestation of the resurgent Catholicism of the 1540s was expressed in a language that can shock.[2]

That was also the case with his reaction to the increasing religious radicalism of the period. Kaspar von Schwenckfeld (1489–1561) was one of the Reformation figures who sought more far-reaching religious changes than relatively conservative reformers including Luther and Zwingli envisaged. A nobleman of Silesia, an eastern, Habsburg-ruled territory, he was initially drawn both to mysticism and to Luther's Reformation but developed an understanding of Christianity and especially of the sacraments of baptism and the eucharist that emphasised their inner and spiritual rather than external character. In 1543 he sent Luther a copy of a work of his on the nature of Christ. Luther's reaction to the gift was one of monumental verbal abuse, in front of the messenger who brought the book: Schwenckfeld, he exploded, was 'a poor wretch who doesn't have talent or spirit. Like all the fanatics, he's ecstatic. He doesn't know what he's talking about.' For all her usual deference to her husband, his wife was capable of checking Luther when she felt he was getting out of hand in one way or another. On this occasion, standing by and witnessing Luther's uncontrolled display, her intervention reminded him of good manners – perhaps especially required in a reply that would be taken back to one who was, like her, of an aristocratic family: 'Ah, dear Sir, that's much too coarse!' But her interposition seems simply to have goaded Luther into further abuse and fury, telling the messenger that the sender was a 'stupid fool, who is possessed by the devil, has no understanding, and doesn't know what he's mumbling about'. If we needed any further reminder of the frightening power of Luther's rages, it is there.[3]

It is there also in some writings where we might, perhaps, expect a quieter tone. Thus a work that has been grouped by Luther's editors among his 'devotional writings', an open letter of 1545 addressed to John Frederick, Elector of Saxony, and Philip, Landgrave of Hesse, concerned moves, which were referred to Luther, to release from his imprisonment the militant Catholic Duke Henry of Braunschweig-Wolfenbüttel, the satirical target of Luther's 1541 work 'Against Hans Worst' (see Chapter 9). In 1545 Henry had been captured and deposed by the Elector and the Landgrave acting in conjunction. Even by the standards of the intensely polarised atmosphere of religious conflict in Germany in the 1540s, Luther's open letter is sharply confrontational in spirit. For example, the duke's former ally, deceased since September 1545, Albrecht archbishop of Mainz, was 'eternally damned'. As for Henry himself, he was 'completely degenerated, wild, ill-bred . . . corrupted through many years of continuous evil practices . . . angry, raving', and, although Christians must love their enemies, Luther could not 'advise that he should be set free', since his imprisonment was 'the fitting punishment of the rod, which he has deserved' – or was even a 'twofold mercy', both to his subjects and to the duke himself. Unconditional surrender and repentance were his only recourse. Versions of two Psalms giving thanks to God were appended to a later edition in gratitude for the military victory that had made the duke a prisoner. It is hardly necessary to add that this work of unforgiving vindictiveness bears nothing of any gospel messages of peace and reconciliation.[4]

Luther's hatred of Duke Henry was both intense and endemic. In 1541, when he had Henry in his sights in the satire, 'Against Hans Worst', he included him, along with the archbishop of Mainz (rhyming 'Heinz/ Mainz'), as on a par with Islam and the Turks in an unholy alliance with the papacy – 'all the devils, the Turks, Muhammad, the pope, "Mainz", "Heinz", and all evil-doers'. This bracketing of two Catholic rulers with Islam seems extraordinary, in the light of what Luther was to write in the following year in 'Comfort for Women Who Have Had Miscarriages': 'One should not despise a Christian person as if he were a Turk. . . . He is precious in God's sight . . .'. Luther's unrelenting harshness towards and contempt for Duke Henry, in particular as the epitome of Catholic counter-aggression against the Reformation, suggests that Luther did not in fact consider him and his ilk to be 'Christian persons' at all.

The intense enmity that surrounded Luther's last years and months even extended to his adopted city, Wittenberg. The place had been good to him, provided him with a refuge, a family home and a career. He had shown occasional impatience towards his parishioners there, especially over their alleged niggardliness, but in 1545 he was writing to his wife outlining what sounds to have been an impractical scheme to uproot his family from the city. His hatred was aroused by nothing more than a new fashion for revealing dress adopted by the women of Wittenberg: 'My heart has gone cold, so I do not want to be there any more' – the reason being that the local 'women and girls bare themselves behind and before . . .'. The faults of a thieving servant brought on further savagery – 'that pig-filthy knave and deceiver . . . do what you can to help the wretch befoul himself'.

And again, in the same year, Luther appended to an edition of his works a retrospective over his life written largely in terms of aggression and conflict, with a *leitmotiv* 'to rend the heavens and consume the world with a sword'. He saw himself indeed as having come not to bring peace but a sword and he tended to organise much of the narrative of his own life around a series of clashes – 'disputations', 'stormy situation', 'all that trouble', 'hatred and disgust', 'strengthened armour' and so on.[5]

Throughout his life, Luther was a man of passionate antagonisms, which also seem to have become increasingly marked in his later years and months, and in the period before his death Luther was surrounded largely by enemies, of his own making and of his own imagining. Whether we write autobiographies or not, we all construct the narratives of our lives, especially as we look back over them, for ourselves and those who are prepared to hear or read us. And it is interesting, because there were other ways in which he might have organised the conceptual shape of his life, that Luther chose to recount his largely in terms of conflict, the record of a life of collision. Yet though one part of him – perhaps the ghost of the knight of the Wartburg of 1521, 'Junker Georg' – may have rejoiced in so many jousts bravely survived, the other persona, his other self, the Catholic Christian theologian, had had a mission to bring a united Church and Christendom into a purification of religion. He had failed and that may even have been why he wanted to die at a point in his career when the fragmentation of Germany and Christendom had reached new extremes – and when he wrote in summer 1545 'I hope that my gracious lord [the Elector] will let my salary continue for the one last year of my life'. That was indeed written within the last year of his life. Perhaps he was being prescient that his great life was nearing its end, but though it is impossible to prove such a speculation, it is at least open to conjecture that the trip to Eisleben in the bleak mid-winter of 1546 may have had some of the character of a suicide mission arising out of a self-judgement for failure.

LUTHER'S DEATH

His health was appalling, for him to contemplate such a journey. For example, he wrote to Melanchthon on 1 February, 'A fainting fit overtook me on the journey and also that disease which you are wont to call palpitation of the heart. I went on foot, overtaxed my strength. . . . My age is to blame for the heart trouble and the shortness of breath.' His private life was deeply shadowed. The Luthers had four surviving children, but the death from a fever of their beloved daughter Magdalene left him with what he called a 'killing grief'.

His own death came at an inn in Eisleben, as the result of a stroke, in the early hours of 18 February 1546. Surrounded by friends and two of his sons, he spoke his last words. They brought together so much of him. There was ranting hatred, directed against 'the wretched Pope . . . the wicked Pope', and at the time sublime trust in his redeemer: 'I pray thee, dear Lord Jesus Christ, let me commend my soul to thee. . . . Father, into thy hands I commend my spirit. Thou hast redeemed me, thou true God.' Dying in his birthplace, he was returned for burial to the church in Wittenberg, where, by posting the 95 Theses, he had given birth to the Reformation.

MARTIN LUTHER: AN EVALUATION

There are three vantage points from which to adjudge Luther as success or failure and they all imply a 'conflict-model' of his life. We shall term these, first, the Catholic consensus, which Luther was himself perhaps partly to share, that he was a wrecker of Christian unity. The second view, which we may describe as the standard Protestant historiography, is that Luther was an absolutely necessary, indeed providential, force, to give the world the Reformation. The third view, which we may term the 'liberal interpretation', links this Conclusion to our Introduction in showing that, despite himself, Luther made a major contribution to the evolution of our world of freedom, centred upon dissent, variety, toleration and indeed the secularity of life.

Though Luther kept up a regular verbal stream of abuse against the papacy as an anti-Christian tyranny whose excesses justified all his offensives against it, it was when he contemplated the radical alternative that his misgivings arose and when his anti-papal language was toned down into a vocabulary closer to acceptance of the papal office and the Catholic legacy, whose rejection had unleashed religious dissent and radicalism on the Christian world. Thus, for example, in 1532 he favourably contrasted the pope, who distorted baptism yet retained it in the Church, with the Anabaptists, who, he alleged, virtually swept it away. Albeit misused, the sacraments of the Roman Church were, he maintained, 'true'; the pope held an office from which the offices of the Churches that dissented from him ultimately derived; and, even, 'those who hear [the pope] hear the true word of God'. Specifically, it was the retention of infant baptism in the papal Church that validated it. In 1533 Luther insisted that the 'church has baptised infants for a thousand years'. Though the papacy's priests were 'drowsy and drunk', God gave the sacraments through the papacy, and the long centuries of papal domination received Luther's approval for having passed on the maintenance of a valid sacramental order.[6]

Luther in those ways hinted at at least an ambivalence of view about the historical benefit or necessity of the changes he launched. If the papal Church maintained a continuity of faith and worship with the ancient Church – for example, by upholding valid sacraments for over a millennium – then was it not a sin and error to break with that Church? Luther's own self-doubts on that score may well have fed his recurrent bouts of depression, with such questionings to himself as 'Are you alone wise? What if you are mistaken, and are leading many people into error and damnation?' That self-accusation could even be read as a variant of the charge of individualist innovation made against Luther by Charles V at Worms in his personal statement to the Diet of Worms made on the morning after Luther's sensational appearance there. In the fragments of discourse cited above, Luther had intimated that the papacy had been partly right for maintaining a millennium of the orthodox administration of baptism. At Worms Charles accused Luther of being a heretical innovator for departing from the Catholic beliefs and practices maintained over a millennium: 'It is certain that a single monk must err, if his opinion is contrary to that of all Christendom. According to his opinion the whole of Christendom has been in error for a thousand years. . . .'[7]

The thousand-year dateline providing a chronology for a charge of innovation was extended by Luther's antagonist Cochlaeus by 200 years in order to frame a question about Luther's eucharistic practice: why did the Lutherans depart from 'the Church's faithful twelve-hundred-year-old' teaching concerning the eucharist? A variant on that Catholic view of Luther as the unacceptable innovator was that he did indeed have an historical pedigree but that it was the heritage of ancient errors revived: as the Edict of Worms put it, 'he has collected a lot of heresies of the very worst heretics, long since buried, into one foul cesspool, together with some new ones conjured up by himself. It was, however, this allegation that was taken up by the new school of historians brought into being by and in the Protestant Reformation, creating the image of Luther not as the reiterator of ancient heresies but rather as the liberator of long-buried truth. A Protestant historiography of the Reformation was being assembled even as the Reformation itself was under way.[8]

For the Reformation offered a debate about history as much as about doctrine. Again, it was Luther who had set this agenda, first by turning the encounter with Eck at Leipzig, which we reviewed in Chapter 4, into an argument over the history of the Church, focusing on the Council of Constance and its alleged mistreatment of Hus in 1415. The Lutheran historical industry was operating briskly well within the sixteenth century. In his funeral sermon on Luther's death in 1546 Philip Melanchthon made a major contribution to interpreting the significance of Luther within the whole of history in its character as God's plan for mankind. The best-known work of the Lutheran historian Johannes Philippson, known as Sleidanus (1506–56), whose title translates into English as 'Commentaries on the State of Religion and Public Affairs under Emperor Charles', first published in 1555, was a massive and scholarly narrative, tracing the political events of the Reformation in detail, and inspired by a vision of the working of the 'unspeakable wisdom and power of God', who 'transfers and stabilizes the Kingdoms' of the earth. Then, as we saw in Chapter 1, the emergent Protestant historiography of the Reformation was evolved in the collaborative work coordinated by Matthias Flacius Illyricus, 'The Magdeburg Centuries' which was published between 1559 and 1574 and which pointed towards a delineation of Luther's historical significance as the greatest of a series of witnesses to Christian truth, who, over the course of the centuries, had fearlessly pointed to the departures of the Roman Church from evangelical principles.

What we may term the English Protestant school of interpretation entered the field early: Luther's English disciple, the Protestant martyr Robert Barnes (1495–1540) in 'Lives of the Roman Pontiffs', 1536, a work specifically approved by Luther, traced the corruptions of the Roman Church up to the central Middle Ages, while the greatest Tudor Protestant historian, John Foxe, in his 'Commentaries', published in 1554, began the enterprise of explaining the Reformation within the entire providential drama of history.

Both Barnes and Foxe were strongly influenced by German Lutheranism, which, in the field of history, continued to develop its own approach, largely inspired by the traditions of Sleidanus and Flacius Illyricus. Completed in 1692, Veit Ludwig von Seckendorf's 'History of Lutheranism' was impartial to a degree, in the pattern of Sleidanus, but also saw Luther's Reformation as an evangelical epiphany, with the Bible translated into German and the winning over to Christ of so many Germans – even though subsequent developments added to formalisation and relative decline. Just a few years later the 'Impartial History of the Churches and the Heretics' by Gottfried Arnold, published between 1700 and 1712, leaned towards Flacius Illyricus and emphasised a pentecostal, intensely inspirational and apostolic young Luther.

If in the writings of Seckendorf and Arnold, there was a certain air of regret about a shining glorious beginning marred by subsequent institutionalisation, in an unfolding English tradition of historical writing, the Reformation was coming to be seen as a beginning and specifically as an overture to broadening human liberty. We saw in Chapter 1 how the great Scottish historian of the Reformation Gilbert Burnet celebrated Protestantism's liberating demolition of 'implicit Obedience, the priestly dominion over conscience'. More and more, and with the growing influence of Enlightenment ideals of freedom, progress and the triumph of reason, the Reformation that Luther initiated was seen as making an enormous contribution to the realisation of just those goals. Thus in the German heartland of that great religious revolution of the sixteenth century, in the years 1737–41, Johann Lorenz von Mosheim published a work whose Latin title we can translate as 'Principles of Ecclesiastical History'. Holding to a point of view above and beyond the competing 'confessions', or rival religious denominations, and relatively unconcerned with religious doctrine as such, Mosheim made a breakthrough, not in establishing that the Reformation was dogmatically 'right', but in showing that it was the necessary prelude to the broadening out of freedom and progress in Mosheim's own eighteenth century.

Kremer has shown that a leading English proponent of the rationalist Enlightenment, Joseph Priestley (1733–1804), in his *General History of the Christian Church* (1800), traced a history of human emancipation from the Reformation to its culmination in the revolution against monarchical Britain in republican, secularised America, to which country Priestley migrated in 1794. Like Mosheim, Priestley was hardly concerned with the rightness or otherwise of Reformation dogmas. Both Catholicism and Protestantism were equally misguided from the viewpoint of Priestley's adherence to Unitarian principles, seeing the godhead as single, not as a Trinity of three Persons in one God. Even so, he was convinced that the

Reformation opened the gate to Enlightenment freedom. It was not a culmination, but a beginning, from which the stream of freedom, including the severing of the unjustifiable links between Church and state, could flow.

By the time that the greatest of German historians, Leopold von Ranke (1795–1886), composed his own history of the Reformation in Germany, the influence of the Romantic movement fostered Ranke's own sharp appreciation of the vital role of the individual in history, recreating a heroic profile of Luther, as champion of defiant human courage, an unconquerable self, the master of his fate, the captain of his soul – while at the same time being, for Ranke, the supreme embodiment of his German nation. The Diet of Worms and Luther's magnificent appearance there formed the natural focus for that projection, the arena in which, wrote Ranke:

> threats alarmed him not; the universal sympathy, the warm breathings of which he felt around him, had first given him strength and courage; his feeling was . . . that had he a thousand heads he would let them all be struck off rather than recant.

Further, the political conflicts to which the Reformation gave rise issued in declarations of liberal and constitutional political principles in which Ranke's fellow-Germans were to the fore. Though Luther himself was, politically, on the side of authority, the collision from the later 1520s between Lutheran confederates and Habsburg power

> was in fact between the doctrines of passive disobedience and the right of resistance.
>
> We know how greatly these doctrines, especially in their connexion with religion, contributed to the development of political theories in Europe; it is worthy of remark that they were first brought into discussion in Germany, and at so early a period.

Though such theories, of liberty and resistance, reached their fuller development potential in 'another age and country' – by which Ranke may have meant the British kingdoms in the seventeenth century – they were born of the Reformation.[9]

One additional contribution was to make the Reformation stemming from Luther synonymous with the birth of modernity and, in alliance with an analogous movement in the fields of culture and ideas, the Renaissance, the parents of the nineteenth-century world of progress. Thus in 1896 an historian and Unitarian minister in Priestley's tradition, Charles Beard (1827–88) in his *Martin Luther and the Reformation in Germany* showed Luther as a great force for human liberation and progressive development at the dawn of the modern era: launched by 'the Saxon reformer',

> the Reformation in its wider aspects is part of the greater movement of the human mind known as the Renaissance; a rebirth, due to the revived study of classical literature and philosophy; a rebellion against mediæval systems of thought, which has issued in modern science and speculation. Without the fresh intellectual activity produced by this movement, and augmented in the fifteenth century by the invention of the art of printing, Luther might have been as ineffectual as Wiclif was. But the time was ripe for change; the seed was cast into the ground at the right moment.

Subsequently, if Lutheranism and its child Calvinism lapsed back into medieval-style dogmatic orthodoxy, yet the irreversible 'tide of free speculation has steadily risen' and 'the gradually decaying bulwarks of dogma' were 'unable to oppose any effectual resistance to it': among 'the heirs of Luther', each on his line of affiliation, was the father of evolution, Charles Darwin.[10]

So there have been several historical Luthers. They include a heavily demonised figure in Catholic historiography, lasting from Cochlaeus to a Dominican historian, Heinrich Denifle, whose 1904 work 'Luther and Lutheranism' repeated, as late as the early twentieth century, tales of serious immorality against Luther and the charge that he was driven by 'lust' to disrupt the unity of the Church. More recently, and in line with the ecumenical spirit that gained so much ground in the second half of the twentieth century, an understanding of 'Catholic Luther' features in a collection of articles, all by non-Lutheran scholars, in which the contributors see Luther as one who 'by concentrating on the uniqueness of the grace of God in Jesus Christ, deepens the perception of the Catholic faith of the whole Church'. In a study within the collection of Luther's 'Catholic Christology' the editor himself added that 'more and more [Luther] discussed justification by faith in terms of the traditional Christology of the Church'. A more recent book, Daphne Hampson's *Christian Contradictions*, provides valuable comparative insights, especially in the key area of justification. In 1999 German Catholics and Lutherans agreed on a Joint Declaration designed to make progress towards Church unity. Professor Hampson, though, points to quite deep philosophical differences between Lutheranism and Catholicism concerning basic assumptions about God and humanity.[11]

If we now have ecumenical Luther, in the nineteenth century Karl Marx's great collaborator Friedrich Engels (1820–95) first gave us a Marxist view of the Reformer, drawing him into a depiction of the revolutionary encounter of nascent capitalism against feudalism in the age of the Reformation: between, on the one hand, Müntzer, who was the authentic leader of 'the *revolutionary* party', and, on the other, the '*conservative Catholic*' camp, Luther represented the middle ground, '*moderate in the burgher manner*', the 'recognised representative of the burgher reform to preach lawful progress'. Engels also unfolded a Marxian version of Luther, who was delineated in terms of the hopes and aspirations of mid-nineteenth-century German politics, and the stirring events of recent lost revolution, that of 1848, that haunted Engels so. Engels' Luther was in fact the sixteenth-century equivalent of the nineteenth-century German middle-class liberals whose centrist reformism was overtaken by the radicalism of the genuine revolutionary working-class parties: 'From 1517 to 1525 Luther changed just as much as the present day German constitutionalists did between 1846 and 1849; and as every bourgeois party placed for a time at the head of the movement is overwhelmed by the plebeian–proletarian party standing behind it, so was Luther's.'[12]

A figure as titanic as Luther, then, will inevitably be seized upon in support of the dominant concerns of those who seek to understand him, and interpretations of such an historical personality may well reflect the issues to the fore in any writer's own period. In a highly creative period of thinking and writing under the influence of the father of modern psychiatry, Sigmund Freud (1856–1939), the American psychoanalyst Erik H. Erikson related aspects of Luther's theology to 'Freud's conceptualization of the pressure put by the superego on the ego'. In particular, Erikson drew attention to the possible impact of Luther's conflict with his father on his emerging theology: 'Martin the son, who on a personal level had suffered deeply because he could not coerce his father into approving his religiosity as genuine . . . assumes now [as a monk] on a religious level a volitional role towards filial suffering. . . .' Some have levelled a charge of psychoanalytical determinism against Erikson, alleging that he tried to explain the most profound of spiritual experiences and the most creative of theological revelations in terms of the most tenuous of psychological hypotheses. Whatever the case, there is no doubt that Erikson also understood the irreducible religious nature of Luther's crucial realisation: 'Christ . . . becomes the core of the Christian's identity.'[13]

So we are back with the obvious point that Luther has to be understood in religious terms. What has been termed a scholarly 'Luther renaissance' in the second half of the twentieth century has included work by Finnish and other Scandinavian scholars such as Uuras Saanivaara in *Luther Discovers the Gospel: New Light upon Luther's Way from Medieval Catholicism to Evangelical Faith* (1951). Some of the ongoing research has continued to address the question of *when* Luther achieved the breakthrough of realisation of justification by faith. Other work probes the exact meaning, including what is termed the anthropological meaning, of Luther's doctrines: what are the implications of such theological principles for us as human beings and our self-understanding? We might for example examine the implications and applications of a key formula associated with Luther's view of justification. The sinner, acquitted by God in recognition of Christ's sacrifice, is described as *simul justus et peccator* – 'simultaneously justified and a sinner'. But what does that *mean* in terms of his or her relationship to the Father? Does it mean that God is at the same time angry with the person as a sinful wretch but acquits him or her as a redeemed son or daughter, in recognition of Christ's sacrifice? Is the person only clothed with an external, borrowed goodness, or is it possible that the recipient of justification once *was* a sinner but *is* new-made as 'just', that he or she once was lost and now is found, was blind and now can see? Does it mean that *justitia Christi*, Christ's justness, as it were gives the sinner a transformative start whereby he or she may become inherently holy?

If those are some of the kinds of questions taken up in modern Luther research, they may indeed undoubtedly reflect our age's preoccupation with the individual self. Clearly, such endeavours as the 1999 Joint Declaration to find an agreement on justification indicate how pressing such issues may still be for significant numbers of people. At the same time, though, such questions seem increasingly to bypass our culture's relative oblivion about God, the afterlife and, indeed, the whole Christian agenda. A 'death-of-God' outlook, or at least the large-scale elimination from our world of thought of a 'personal God' who cares about our individual fates, may mean that the questions addressed in the previous paragraph will be remote from the mainstream concerns of, say, many, if not of most, modern Europeans: we may be able to understand the nature of the questions, but it is the full meaning of the answers that is largely lost on us. The concerns of a 'post-Christian' culture, at least in twenty-first century Europe, are overwhelmingly with present life, liberty and the pursuit of happiness and are in that sense broadly secular and indeed political. The political has become our religion, the polity our church. Thus we re-confront 'political' Luther – who in turn becomes 'liberal Luther', the Luther who somehow fore-fathered our modern age with its realisation of, or aspiration towards, freedom of thought and expression, respect for rights, the upholding of plurality and variety, the freedom of the media, and the whole progressive and democratic programme inherited from the Enlightenment and the American and French Revolutions. For whether he uttered the words or not, Luther's 'Here I Stand' is the initial slogan of our modernity. His own demand to be heard, above all in the medium of the press, could not forever be denied to his fellow Christians, his fellow-Germans or his fellow Europeans. His insistence, for example, in 'Temporal Authority' of 1523, that the state could not shackle the conscience of the individual must sooner or later demolish the device that brought a German civil war of religion to a close in the Peace of Augsburg of 1555 with the formula that the ruler may command the religion of his subjects. Further, Luther's insistence on recreating the ancient Church – and then stopping well short of realising it fully – set up a momentum of aspiration for apostolic perfection that would sooner or later have to be accommodated in the practical toleration of Luther's more radical spiritual and intellectual 'stepchildren'. Indeed, in dividing Germany and Christendom, Luther set up an historical logic whereby that division would eventually have to be catered for, and in no other way than through the forms of religious toleration that began to descend like a blessing on Europe, first and hesitantly in the Netherlands and Britain from the seventeenth century onwards, reaching a more confident realisation in the Enlightenment, in the French Revolution and in the nineteenth century, across Europe and the United States.

Yet Luther was of course very far from aiming to build the modern world that we aim to uphold – tolerant, as free as can be compatible with due civil order, varied, open, diverse, pluralist, and, it has to be said, to a considerable extent, in Europe at least, post-Christian. His aim was *reformatio* – to reform and restore, and to restore by reforming, the medieval *corpus Christianorum*, the body of all Christians, Christendom as an immense congregation worshipping and believing as one, the dream of Catholic renewal that had persisted for centuries and which he inherited. The creation of diversity and fragmentation, which would eventually have to be contained within structures of toleration and tolerance, was his unintended achievement and catastrophe, and he blamed himself mercilessly for bringing into being the pluralities that would, in decades or centuries ahead of him, have to be housed within pluralism. In aiming at *reformatio* and unleashing Reformation, Luther was a failure, history's most glorious case.

NOTES

1 INTRODUCTION

1 G.R. Potter, *Huldrych Zwingli*, Documents of Modern History, General Editor A.G Dickens, London: Edward Arnold, 1978, pp. 17–18; *Luther's Works*, vol. 51: *Sermons I*, ed. and trans. John W. Doberstein, Philadelphia, PA: Fortress Press, 1959, p. 62.

2 Martin Luther, *To the Christian Nobility of the German Nation Concerning the Reform of the Christian Estate*, in *Luther's Works*, vol. 44: *The Christian in Society I*, ed. James Atkinson, Philadelphia, PA: Fortress Press, 1966, p. 148; William R. Russell, 'Martin Luther's Understanding of the Pope as the Antichrist', *Archiv für Reformationsgeschichte/Archive for Reformation History* 85 (1994), 32–44; Preserved Smith, *The Life and Letters of Martin Luther*, London: John Murray, 1911, pp. 88, 65, 88, 89.

3 E. Michael Camilli, '*Six Dialogues*, 1566: Initial Responses to the *Magdeburg Centuries*', *Archiv für Reformationsgeschichte/Archive for Reformation History* 86 (1995), pp.141–52.

4 See: R.W. Scribner, 'Luther Myth: A Popular Historiography of the Reformation', in *Popular Culture and Popular Movements in Reformation Germany*, London, and Ronceverte, WV: Hambledon Press, 1987, pp. 301–22; Scribner, 'Incombustible Luther: The Image of the Reformer in Early Modern Germany', in ibid., pp. 323–53; Paul Douglas Lockhart, 'Political Language and Wartime Propaganda in Denmark, 1625–1629', *European History Quarterly* 31(1) (2001), 5–42.

5 W. Grinton Berry (ed.), *Foxe's Book of Martyrs: An Edition for the People*, London: The Religious Tract Society, n.d., pp. 158, 172, 184–5; *The Acts and Monuments of John Foxe with a Life of the Martyrologist, and Vindication of the Work by George Townsend*, 8 vols, London: Seeley, Burnside, and Seeley, 1843, vol. 2, pp. 791–6.

6 Gilbert Burnet, *The History of the Reformation of the Church of England*, London: Gibbings & Co., 1903, p. v: see also, e.g., Raymond D. Tumbleson, *Catholicism in the English Protestant Imagination: Nationalism, Religion and Literature 1600–1745*, Cambridge: Cambridge University Press, reprinted 1999, esp. ch. 3.

7 Philip Marnix, 'The Beehive of the Roman Church' (in seventeenth-century English translation), in Herbert H. Rowan (ed.), *The Low*

Countries in Early Modern Times, London, Basingstoke: Macmillan, 1972, pp. 49–50.

8 Ibid., p. 49; Damian Nussbaum, 'Laudian Foxe-Hunting? William Laud and the Status of John Foxe in the 1630s', in Robert Swanson (ed.), *The Church Retrospective: Papers Read at the 1995 Summer Meeting and the 1996 Winter Meeting of the Ecclesiastical History Society*, Studies in Church History, 33, Woodbridge, Suffolk: Boydell Press; Rochester, NY: Boydell & Brewer, 1997, pp. 329–42.

9 Tumbleson, *Catholicism in the English Protestant Imagination*, pp. 197–201: 'Maria' was Mary Tudor, with her Spanish maternity and marriage emphasised, so as to underscore the 'alien-other' threat of her Catholicism; there may also have been an allusion to the allegedly idolatrous Catholic cult of the Blessed Virgin Mary, 'Sancta Maria'; Linda Colley, *Britons Forging the Nation 1707–1837*, London: Pimlico, 1994, pp. 20–5.

10 Michael Mullett, *John Bunyan in Context*, Studies in Protestant Nonconformity, ed. Alan P.F Sell, Keele, Staffs: Keele University Press, 1996, pp. 195–6.

11 *Boswell's Life of Johnson*, intro. C.B Tinker, London: Oxford University Press, new edition, reset, 1953, reprinted 1961, pp. 426, 1055, 544, 1289, 374, 729; *The Book of Common Prayer and Administration of the Sacraments of the Church of England*: The Articles of Religion, XXXI.

12 *The Poetical Works of Wordsworth With Introductions and Notes*, ed. Thomas Hutchinson, rev. edn Ernest de Selincourt, London: Oxford University Press, 1964, pp. 432, 89, 265, 266, 329–55.

13 Cobbett, in G.G. Coulton, *Five Centuries of Religion*, 4 vols, Cambridge: Cambridge University Press, 1923–50, vol. 4, p. 714.

14 Chateaubriand, *Génie du Christianisme*, 2 vols, Paris: Ernest Flammarion, n.d., vol. 1, pp. 31–2, 44.

15 John Lingard, *The History of England from the First Invasion by the Romans to the Accession of William and Mary in 1688*, 6th edn, 10 vols, London: Charles Dolman, 1855, vol. 4, pp. 224–5.

16 Abbot Gasquet, *Parish Life in Mediæval England*, London: Methuen, 1906, ch. 7, pp. 198–9, 256, 260, 244, 238, chs 4, 5.

17 Russell Sparkes, 'Dawson and "economic man"', in Stratford Caldecott and John Morrill (eds), *Eternity in Time: Christopher Dawson and the Catholic Idea of History*, Edinburgh: T & T Clark, 1997, pp. 104–5.

18 A.G. Dickens, *The English Reformation*, London: Collins Fontana Library, 1967; J.J. Scarisbrick, *The Reformation and the English People*, Oxford: Clarendon, 1984; Christopher Haigh, *The English Reformation Revised*,

Cambridge: Cambridge University Press, 1987; Joseph Lortz, *The Reformation in Germany*, trans. Ronald Walls, 2 vols, London: Darton, Longman & Todd, New York: Herder & Herder, 1968, vol. 1, ch. 5; Michael B. Lukens, 'Lortz's View of the Reformation and the Crisis of the True Church', *Archiv für Reformationsgeschichte/Archive for Reformation History* 81 (1990), pp. 20–31; Eric W. Gritsch, 'Joseph Lortz's Luther: Appreciation and Critique', ibid., pp. 32–49.

2 MARTIN LUTHER'S BACKGROUND, UPBRINGING AND EDUCATION, 1483–1513

1 Thomas Sefton Rivington, *The Story of Luther's Life*, London: Simpkin, Marshall, Hamilton & Kent; Glasgow: Thomas D Morison, 2nd edn, n.d., pp. 6, 13, 14.

2 *Luther's Works*, vol. 54: *Table Talk*, ed. and trans. Theodore G. Tappert, Philadelphia, PA: Fortress Press, 1967, pp. 178, 458.

3 Ian D. Kingston Siggins (ed.), *Luther*, Evidence and Commentary Historical Source Books, Series Editors C.M.D. Crowder and L. Kochan, Edinburgh: Oliver & Boyd, 1972, p. 32.

4 Siggins, *Luther*, pp. 32–3; 'Luther and the Catholic Preachers of his Youth', in George Yule (ed.), *Luther: Theologian for Catholics and Protestants*, Edinburgh: T&T Clark, 1985, p. 59; Luther, *Table Talk*, p. 282.

5 *Table Talk*, pp. 72, 142, 294, 435–6, 152, 163, 180.

6 *Table Talk*, pp. 157, 235.

7 *Table Talk*, pp. 109, 234, 235, 15; Siggins, *Luther*, p. 32.

8 *Table Talk*, pp. 235, 144, 14.

9 Preserved Smith, *The Life and Letters of Martin Luther*, London: John Murray, 1911, p. 4.

10 Siggins, 'Luther and the Catholic Preachers of his Youth', ch. 4 .

11 Siggins, *Luther*, p. 33.

12 *Table Talk*, p. 14; Siggins, *Luther*, p. 33; *Luther's Works*, vol. 10: *First Lectures on the Psalms I: Psalms 1–75*, ed. Hilton C. Oswald, St Louis, MO: Concordia, 1974, pp. 159, 412, 421, 217.

13 Rivington, *The Story of Luther's Life*, pp. 23–4; Smith, *Life and Letters of Luther*, pp. 6,14. The primary sources for the remainder of this chapter are from: Siggins, *Luther*, pp. 35–40; Smith, *Life and Letters of Luther*, pp. 9–11, 20–1; Luther, *Table Talk*, pp. 13–14, 234, 156, 87, 95, 182, 15, 94–5, 208–9, 237, 296, 427, 320; Gordon Rupp, *Luther's Progress to the Diet of Worms*, London: SCM Press, 1951, p. 27.

3 FROM THE PSALMS TO THE 95 THESES: THE DEVELOPMENT OF LUTHER'S REFORMATION THEOLOGY, 1513–1517

1 Principal citations in the chapter that follow centred on the Psalms and Romans lectures and the 95 Theses are taken from: *Luther's Works*, vol. 10: *First Lectures on the Psalms I: Psalms 1–75*, ed. Hilton C. Oswald, St Louis, MO: Concordia, 1974, pp. 5, 8, 6, n. 1, 13, 327, 41–5, 3, 7, 17, 106, 272, 46, 236–7, 186, 322, 359, 462, 219, 19, 125, 64, 93, 117, 168, 222–3, and from *Luther's Works*, vol. 11: *First Lectures on the Psalms II: Psalms 76–126*, ed. Hilton C. Oswald, St Louis, MO: Concordia, 1976, pp. 39, 64, 81, 40, 327, 396, 164–171; *Luther's Works*, vol. 25: *Lectures on Romans: Glosses and Scholia*, ed. Hilton C. Oswald, St Louis, MO: Concordia, 1972, pp. 6, 31–3; and Kurt Aland (ed.), *Martin Luther's 95 Theses with the Pertinent Documents from the History of the Reformation*, St Louis, MO: Concordia, 1967, pp. 50, 46, 33–5. See also: Preserved Smith, *The Life and Letters of Martin Luther*, London: John Murray, 1911, chs 4, 5.

2 For convenient access to the 95 Theses, see E.G. Rupp and B. Drewery (eds), *Martin Luther*, London: Edward Arnold, 1970, pp. 19–25.

4 FROM THE 95 THESES TO THE LEIPZIG DISPUTATION, 1517–1519

1 For documents concerning the sequel to the appearance of the Theses, see Kurt Aland, *Martin Luther's 95 Theses With the Pertinent Documents from the History of the Reformation*, St Louis, MO, and London: Concordia, 1967, pp. 64ff. See also E.G Rupp and Benjamin Drewery (eds), *Martin Luther*, Documents of Modern History, General Editors A.G. Dickens and Alun Davies, London: Arnold, 1972, p. 26, and Ian D. Kingston Siggins, *Luther*, Evidence and Commentary Historical Source Books, Series Editors C.M.D Crowder and L. Cochan, Edinburgh: Oliver & Boyd, 1972, pp. 61ff.

2 Luther wrote up his own account of the Augsburg interviews as soon as he got back to Wittenberg, publishing it as *Acta Augustana* – 'Proceedings at Augsburg': see *Luther's Works*, vol. 31: *Career of the Reformer: I*, ed. Harold J. Grimm, Philadelphia, PA: Muhlenberg Press, 1957, pp. 255–91. For convenient accounts, see Rupp and Drewery, *Martin Luther*, pp. 30–1 and Siggins, *Luther*, pp. 68–9.

3 For material on the aftermath of Augsburg and the 'golden rose' episode, see Rupp and Drewery, *Martin Luther*, pp. 32–3; R.H. Bainton, *Here I Stand: A Life of Martin Luther*, New York: Abingdon Press, 1950,

pp.104–5; Preserved Smith, *The Life and Letters of Martin Luther*, London: John Murray, 1911, pp. 54–7; and Richard Marius, *Martin Luther: The Christian between God and Death*, Cambridge, MA, and London: Belknap Press of Harvard University Press, 1999, p. 217.

4 For sources on the Leipzig debate, see: Smith, *Life and Letters of Luther*, ch. 6; and 'The Leipzig Debate', in *Luther's Works*, vol. 31, pp. 309–25.

5 FROM LEIPZIG TO WORMS, 1519–1521

1 For a convenient edition of the 'Address', from which citations in the following pages are derived, see John Dillenberger, ed. and intro., *Martin Luther: Selections from his Writings*, Garden City, NY: Anchor Books, 1961, pp. 403–85.

2 For a convenient edition of 'The Babylonian Captivity', from which the citations which follow are taken, see Dillenberger, *Luther: Selections*, pp. 249–359.

3 For a convenient edition of 'The Freedom of a Christian', from which the citations which follow are taken, see Dillenberger, *Luther: Selections*, pp. 42–85.

4 For accounts of Luther at Worms, from which most of the citations which follow are taken, see James Atkinson, *The Trial of Martin Luther*, Historic Trials Series, General Editor J.P. Kenyon, London: Batsford, 1971, ch. 4.

6 THE DIET OF WORMS AND AFTER, 1521–1523

1 For documents covering the period following Luther's appearance at Worms, including the edict, see James Atkinson, *The Trial of Luther*, Historical Trials Series, Editor J.P. Kenyon, London: Batsford, 1971, ch. 5.

2 Detailed guidance on Luther's Wartburg period is provided in his letters, from which citations in the following section are taken: *Luther's Works*, vol. 48: *Letters I*, ed. and trans. by Gottfried G. Krodel, Philadelphia, PA: Fortress Press, 1963, pp. 210–388.

3 Thomas Sefton Rivington, *The Story of Luther's Life*, London: Simpkin, Marshall, Hamilton, Kent, n.d., pp. 340–1.

4 For the inn scene, see Preserved Smith, *The Life and Letters of Martin Luther*, London: John Murray, 1911, pp. 141–3 and E.G. Rupp and Benjamin Drewery (eds), *Martin Luther*, Documents of Modern History, General Editors A.G. Dickens and Alun Davies, London: Edward Arnold, 1970, pp. 82–6.

5 For Luther's approach, as translator, to books of the New Testament, see John Dillenberger, ed. and intro., *Martin Luther: Selections from his Writings*, Garden City, NY: Anchor Books, 1961, pp. 14–19.

6 See Harro Höpfl, ed. and trans., *Luther and Calvin on Secular Authority*, Cambridge Texts in the History of Political Thought, Series Editors Raymond Geuss *et al.*, Cambridge: Cambridge University Press, 1991, pp. vii–xvi, xxxii–xxxviii, 3–43.

7 For 'That Jesus Christ Was Born a Jew', see *Luther's Works*, vol. 45, ed. Walther I. Brandt, Philadelphia, PA: Muhlenberg Press, 1962, pp. 197–229.

7 THE CREATION OF INSTITUTIONAL LUTHERANISM, 1525–1528

1 For Cochlaeus's analyses, see Elizabeth Vandiver, Ralph Keen and Thomas D. Frazel, trans and eds, *Luther's Lives: Two Contemporary Accounts of Martin Luther*, Manchester and New York: Manchester University Press, 2002, pp. 106–7, 154ff.

2 For key documents on Luther and the peasants, see *Luther's Works*, vol. 46: *The Christian in Society, III*, ed. Robert C. Schultz, Philadelphia, PA: Fortress Press, 1967, pp. 5–85.

3 For key documents on Luther's debate with Erasmus, see E. Gordon Rupp *et al.*, eds and trans, *Luther and Erasmus: Free Will and Salvation*, The Library of Christian Classics, General Editors John Baillie *et al.*, vol. 17, London: SCM Press, 1969, *passim*.

4 For Cochlaeus's reaction, see Vandiver *et al.*, *Luther's Lives*, pp. 129–30; for key documents on Luther's marriage, see Preserved Smith, *The Life and Letters of Martin Luther*, London: John Murray, 1911, ch. 15.

8 LUTHER AND LUTHERANISM: THE QUEST FOR DEFINITION

1 For documents illustrative of Luther's involvement in eucharistic disputes in the 1520s, see: Preserved Smith, *The Life and Letters of Martin Luther*, London: John Murray, 1911, ch. 21; Ian D. Kingston Siggins, *Luther*, Evidence and Commentary Historical Source Books, Series Editors C.M.D. Crowder and L. Cochan, Edinburgh: Oliver & Boyd, 1972, pp. 111–16, 132–5; E.G. Rupp and Benjamin Drewery, *Martin Luther*, Documents of Modern History, General Editors A.G. Dickens and Alun Davies, London: Edward Arnold, 1970, pp.132–7; and a reconstruction of the Marburg Colloquy in William G. Naphy, ed. and trans. *Documents*

on the Continental Reformation, Macmillan Documents in History, General Editor Jeremy Black, Basingstoke and London: Macmillan, 1996, pp. 94–100.

2 For Augsburg see: *Luther's Works*, vol. 47: *The Christian in Society IV*, ed. Franklin Sherman, Philadelphia, PA: Fortress Press, 1971, Intro., p. 6; for Luther's letters from Feste Coburg, see Smith, *Life and Letters of Luther*, ch. 22; for the 'Exhortation', see *Luther's Works*, vol. 34: *Career of the Reformer IV*, ed. Lewis W. Spitz, Philadelphia, PA: Muhlenberg, 1960, pp. 5–61; for a summary version of the Confession of Augsburg, see Rupp and Drewery, *Martin Luther*, pp. 144–8.

3 For Luther's 'Warning' see *Luther's Works*, vol. 47, pp. 5–55; for the 'Commentary on the Alleged Imperial Edict', *Luther's Works*, vol. 34, pp. 65–104; for Cochlaeus's propaganda on Luther in 1531, see Elizabeth Vandiver, Ralph Keen and Thomas D. Frazel, trans and eds, *Luther's Lives: Two Contemporary Accounts of Martin Luther*, Manchester and New York: Manchester University Press, 2002, pp. 258–72.

4 For Luther's work in the fields of liturgy and music, see *Luther's Works*, vol. 53: *Liturgy and Hymns*, ed. Ulrich S. Liupold, Philadelphia, PA: Fortress Press, 1965, pp. 24–5, 240–1, 233, 221–4, 243–5, 247–8, 211–16, 289–91, 292–4; for scriptural passages in Luther's translation: *Die Bibel oder die ganze Heilige Schrift des Alten und Neuen Testaments nach der deutschen Uebersetzung Dr. Martin Luthers*, Cologne: Britische und Ausländische Bibelgesellschaft, 1881, pp. 520, 551, 512, 61.

5 For Luther's work on Marian prayer, see *Luther's Works*, vol. 53: *Liturgy and Hymns*, pp. 294, 268, 220, 176–7.

9 LUTHER'S LATER YEARS

1 For Luther's Commentary on Galatians, using the 1575 English 'Middleton' version, see John Dillenberger, *Martin Luther: Selections From His Writings*, Garden City, NY: Doubleday Anchor Books, 1961, pp. 99–165.

2 For the 'Theses Concerning Faith and Law' ('The Weller–Medler Theses'), see *Luther's Works*, vol. 34: *Career of the Reformer, IV*, ed. Lewis W. Spitz, Philadelphia, PA: Muhlenberg Press, 1960, pp. 107–32; see also 'The Disputation Concerning Man' and 'The Disputation Concerning Justification', in ibid., pp. 135–44, 147–96 (noting p. 176).

3 For 'The Three Symbols', see *Luther's Works*, vol. 34, pp. 199–229.

4 For the 'Counsel of a Committee of Cardinals', see *Luther's Works*, vol. 34, pp. 233–67.

5 For 'Against the Roman Papacy . . . ', see *Luther's Works*, vol. 41: *Church and Ministry, III*, ed. Eric W. Gritsch, Philadelphia, PA: Fortress Press, 1966, pp. 259–376 and esp. 357–8.

6 For sources on the bigamy of Philip of Hesse, see Preserved Smith, *The Life and Letters of Martin Luther*, London, John Murray, 1911, ch. 34; *Luther's Works*, vol. 54: *Table Talk*, ed. and trans. Theodore G. Tappert, Philadelphia, PA: Fortress Press, 1967, pp. 379–82, 387–9; H.G. Haile, *Luther: A Biography*, London: Sheldon Press, 1981, pp. 273–7.

7 For Luther's observations on the Germans, various other nations, especially Italians, and social classes and professions, see especially *Table Talk*, *passim*, and for prejudice against Italians, Haile, *Luther*, p. 21; for the peasants' proclivity to religious radicalism (in 'Open Letter about Skulking and Furtive Preachers'), Ian D. Kingston Siggins, *Luther*, Evidence and Commentary Historical Source Books, eds C.M.D. Crowder *et al.*, Edinburgh: Oliver & Boyd, 1972, pp. 116–17; and for the excerpt from 'Against the Robbing and Murdering Hordes . . . ', E.G. Rupp and Benjamin Drewery (eds), *Martin Luther*, Documents of Modern History, General Editors A.G. Dickens and Alun Davies, London: Edward Arnold, 1970, p. 122.

8 For examples of Luther's thinking about the Turks, see Smith, *Life and Letters of Luther*, pp. 82, 161, 226–7, 248; *Table Talk*, pp. 28, 46, 149, 419–20 and *passim*; and *Luther's Works*, vol. 43: *Devotional Writings*, ed. Gustav K. Wiencke, Philadelphia, PA: Fortress Press, pp. 215–41.

9 For Luther's further observations on the Turkish peril, see, for example, *Table Talk*, pp. 148, 269.

10 *Table Talk*, p. 239.

11 'Against the Sabbatarians: Letter to a Good Friend', in *Luther's Works*, vol. 47: *The Christian in Society, IV*, ed. Franklin Sherman, Philadelphia, PA: Fortress Press, 1971, pp. 59–98.

12 For Luther on Mary, see Susan C. Karant-Nunn and Merry E. Wiesner-Hanks, *Luther on Women: A Sourcebook*, Cambridge: Cambridge University Press, 2003, ch. 3.

13 For 'The Jews and Their Lies', see *Luther's Works*, vol. 47: *The Christian in Society, IV*, pp. 123–306.

14 *Table Talk*, pp. 436–7.

15 For the 'Treatise on the Last Words of David', see *Luther's Works*, vol. 15, St Louis, MO: Concordia Publishing, 1972, pp. 265–352.

10 CONCLUSION

1 Preserved Smith, *The Life and Letters of Martin Luther*, London: John Murray, 1911, pp. 418–20.

2 H.A. Oberman, 'Teufelsdreck: Eschatology and Scatology in the "Old" Luther', *Sixteenth-century Journal* 19 (1988), pp. 435–50.

3 *Luther's Works*, vol. 54: *Table Talk*, ed. and trans. Theodore G. Tappert, Philadelphia, PA: Fortress Press, 1967, pp. 469–70.

4 'To the Elector of Saxony and the Landgrave of Hesse Concerning the Imprisonment of the Duke of Braunschweig', in *Luther's Works*, vol. 43: *Devotional Writings, II*, ed. Gustav K. Wiencke, trans. Frederick C. Ahrens, Philadelphia, PA: Fortress Press, 1968, pp. 253–88.

5 'Appeal for Prayer Against the Turks', in *Devotional Writings, II*, pp. 215–41; 'Comfort for Women', in *Devotional Writings, II*, p. 248; Ian D. Kingston Siggins (ed.), *Luther*, Evidence and Commentary Historical Source Books, Series Editors C.M.D. Crowder *et al.*, Edinburgh: Oliver & Boyd, 1972, pp. 174–5; E.G. Rupp and Benjamin Drewery, *Martin Luther*, Documents of Modern History, General Editors A.G. Dickens *et al.*, London: Edward Arnold, 1970, pp. 173–9.

6 *Table Talk*, pp. 48, 113.

7 James Atkinson, *The Trial of Luther*, Historical Trials Series, Editor J.P. Kenyon, London: Batsford, 1971, p. 178.

8 Atkinson, *The Trial of Luther*, p. 182; and, for the following, A.G. Dickens, *The German Nation and Martin Luther*, London: Fontana/Collins, 1974, ch. 10; and Ulrich Michael Kremer, 'Martin Luther in the Perspective of Historiography', in Peter Newman Brooks (ed.), *Seven-Headed Luther: Essays in Commemoration of a Quincentenary 1483–1983*, Oxford: Clarendon, 1983, ch. 10.

9 Leopold von Ranke, *History of the Reformation in Germany* (alias 'German History in the Era of the Reformation', 1839–47), ed. R.A. Johnson, trans. Sarah Austin, London: George Routledge, 1905, pp. 240, 572–3.

10 Charles Beard, *Martin Luther and the Reformation in Germany: Until the Close of the Diet of Worms*, ed. J. Frederick Smith, London: Philip Green, 1896, pp. 3, 449.

11 George Yule (ed.), *Luther: Theologian for Catholics and Protestants*, Edinburgh: T&T Clark, 1985, Preface and p. 87; Daphne Hampson, *Christian Contradictions: The Structures of Lutheran and Catholic Thought*, Cambridge: Cambridge University Press, 2001, esp. ch. 5.

12 Friedrich Engels, 'The Marxist Interpretation of Luther' (excerpted from

Engels' *The Peasant War in Germany*, 1850), in H.G. Koenigsberge (ed.), *Luther: A Profile*, World Profiles, General Editor Aïda DiPace Donald, London and Basingstoke: Macmillan, 1973, pp. 97–105.

13 Erik H. Erikson, 'The Search for Identity' (excerpted from Erikson's *Young Man Luther*, 1958), in Koenigsberger, *Luther*, pp. 106–24; see also Roger A. Johnson (ed.), *Psychohistory and Religion: The Case of Young Man Luther*, Philadelphia, PA: Fortress Press, 1977.

Given the immense quantity of scholarship and literature on Luther, the bibliography that follows is highly selective.

For my own principal primary sources, I have relied heavily on the American edition, *Luther's Works*, published in 55 volumes between 1955 and 1986 by Concordia of St Louis, MO, and Fortress Press, of Philadelphia, PA, and having as general editors Jaroslav Pelikan (vols 1–30) and Helmut T. Lehmann (vols 31–55). For a useful digest of some of Luther's key writings, see: John Dillenberger (ed. and intro.), *Martin Luther: Selections from His Writings* (Doubleday Anchor Books, 1961). Students can make ready use of comprehensive and convenient selections of documents on Luther in Ian D. Kingston Siggins's well-chosen compilation, *Luther* (Oliver & Boyd, 1972), and the wide-ranging collection, edited by E.G. Rupp and Benjamin Drewery, *Martin Luther* (Edward Arnold, 1972); see also William G. Naphy (ed. and trans.), *Documents of the Continental Reformation* (Macmillan, 1996), especially chapter 2, and Susan C. Karant-Nunn and Merry E. Wiesner-Hanks (eds and trans), *Luther on Women: A Sourcebook* (Cambridge University Press, 2003).

For a general overview of the Reformation and its ideas, Euan Cameron's *The European Reformation* (Clarendon Press, 1991) can hardly be bettered. See also: Alister E. McGrath, *Reformation Thought: An Introduction* (2nd edn, Blackwell, 1997) and Bernard M.G. Reardon, *Religious Thought in the Reformation* (Longman, 1981). The collection edited by C. Scott Dixon, *The German Reformation: The Essential Readings* (Blackwell, 1999) brings together, with an introduction, eight key articles on aspects of religious change in sixteenth-century Germany. In the ground-breaking *The German Nation and Martin Luther* (Fontana/Collins, 1974), A.G. Dickens succinctly explored Luther's impact within the context of German religion, culture, politics and ideology in the sixteenth century.

Hard as it is to select from the vast list of lives of Luther, James Atkinson's *Martin Luther and the Birth of Protestantism* (Marshall Morgan & Scott, revised edn 1982) offers a lively, sympathetic and comprehensive survey. E.G. Schwiebert, in *Luther and His Times: The Reformation from a New Perspective* (Concordia, 1950) provides both volume and surpassing interest, though is relatively light on the years after 1530. Both weight and depth on the period down to Worms are provided by Robert Herndon Fife, in *The*

Revolt of Martin Luther, first published by Columbia University Press in 1957. *Shaping and Defining the Reformation 1521–1532*, Martin Brecht's second volume of his great biography, provides in-depth guidance for the important years following the crucial Diet (trans. James L. Schaaf, Fortress Press, 1994).

R.H. Bainton's *Here I Stand: A Life of Martin Luther* (Abingdon Press, 1950) has been a standby for a good number of years, as has Gerhard Ritter's inspirational *Luther: His Life and Work* (trans. John Riches, Collins, 1963), as well as Heinrich Boehmer's account of the years down to Luther's stay in the Wartburg, *Martin Luther's Road to Reformation* (trans. John W. Doberstein and Theodore G. Tappert, Meridian Books, 1957).

Published by the SPCK Sheldon Press, in 1981, H.G. Haile's *Luther: A Biography* delivers a highly readable life. The opportunity of the five-hundredth anniversary of Luther's birth elicited the fascinating thirteen-essay collection edited by Peter Newman Brooks, *Seven-Headed Luther: Essays in Commemoration of a Quincentenary 1483–1983* (Clarendon Press, 1983). Exploring visual images of Luther enabled R.W. Scribner to open for readers the rich resources of German popular culture that carried forward the Reformation: *For the Sake of Simple Folk: Popular Propaganda for the German Reformation* (Clarendon Press, 1994).

In *Luther: Man between God and the Devil* (trans. Eileen Walliser-Schwarzbart, Yale University Press, 1989), Heiko A. Oberman explored the issues of sin and evil in Luther's thought and theology. Subsequently, Richard Marius adapted Oberman's title to argue convincingly that it was the prospect of death that haunted Luther: *Martin Luther: The Christian between God and Death* (Harvard University Press, 1999).

A condensed introduction to Luther's religious thought is Karl Holl's essay, *What Did Luther Understand by Religion?* (trans. Fred W. Meuser and Walter R. Wietzke, Fortress Press, 1977). A clear summary is provided by Heinrich Bornkamm in *Luther's World of Thought* (trans. Martin H. Bertram, Concordia, 1965). Particular aspects of Luther's thought and doctrine are ably examined in: Alister E. McGrath, *Luther's Theology of the Cross* (Blackwell, 1985); B.A. Gerrish, *Grace and Reason: A Study of the Theology of Luther* (Clarendon Press, 1962); Ian D. Kingston Siggins, *Martin Luther's Doctrine of Christ* (Yale University Press, 1970); and Thomas M. McDonough, OP, *The Law and the Gospel in Luther: A Study of Martin Luther's Confessional Writings*.

INDEX